UNDER ATTACK

To Greg
For daring me to disturb the universe

To Klaus, Marilyn and Thomas
For supporting me all the way and in every way

Under Attack
Challenges to the Rules Governing the International Use of Force

BELINDA HELMKE
University of Sydney, Australia

ASHGATE

Published by
Ashgate Publishing Limited
Wey Court East
Union Road
Farnham
Surrey, GU9 7PT
England

Ashgate Publishing Company
Suite 420
101 Cherry Street
Burlington
VT 05401-4405
USA

www.ashgate.com

British Library Cataloguing in Publication Data
Helmke, Belinda.
Under attack : challenges to the rules governing the international use of force.
1. Intervention (International law) 2. Aggression (International law)
I. Title
341.6'2-dc22

Library of Congress Cataloging-in-Publication Data
Helmke, Belinda.
Under attack : challenges to the rules governing the international use of force / by Belinda Helmke.
p. cm.
Includes bibliographical references and index.
ISBN 978-0-7546-7989-9 (hardback) -- ISBN 978-0-7546-9971-2 (e-book)
1. Intervention (International law) 2. War (International law) 3. Security, International.
I. Title.

JZ6368.H45 2010
341.6--dc22

2010004859

ISBN 9780754679899 (hbk)
ISBN 9780754699712 (ebk)

Mixed Sources
Product group from well-managed forests and other controlled sources
www.fsc.org Cert no. SGS-COC-2482
© 1996 Forest Stewardship Council
FSC

Printed and bound in Great Britain by
TJ International Ltd, Padstow, Cornwall

Contents

Foreword by Richard Falk *vii*
Acknowledgements *xiii*
List of Abbreviations *xv*

Introduction: Plan of Attack 1

PART I GREAT DECISION OR GREAT ILLUSION: INTERNATIONAL LAW AND THE USE OF FORCE

1 Outlawing the Mob: International Law and the Use of Force Prior to 1918 13

2 Renouncing Luxury: International Law and the Use of Force in the Interwar Years 31

3 Where there's a Will: International Law and the Use of Force During the Cold War 41

4 The State of Play: Developments in the Contemporary International System 57

PART II FOR THE GOOD OF HUMANITY: THE USE OF FORCE FOR HUMANITARIAN REASONS

5 The Snail and the Slug: The Protection of Nationals Abroad 77

6 From Dawn to Dusk: Humanitarian Intervention 95

7 The Uninvited Guest: Intervention in Failed States 125

PART III FOR THE GOOD OF THE STATE: THE USE OF FORCE FOR INDIVIDUAL AND COLLECTIVE SELF-DEFENSE

8 Bolt from the Blue: The Pre-emptive Use of Force 149

9 The Remains of the Reign: The Use of Force to Counter Terrorism 167

10 The (Un)Usual Suspects: The Use of Force against Rogue States 197

Conclusion: The Road (Not) Taken 215

Bibliography *227*
Index *281*

Foreword

The ending of World War II was accompanied by three momentous occurrences that have left a lasting legal imprint on world order: the atomic attacks on Japanese cities, the Nazi Holocaust, and a consensus among the victors that a third world war must be avoided. This imprint exhibited the geopolitical truism that international legal norms and institutions are shaped by the winners in any major war. In practice, this meant no effective repudiation of nuclear weaponry. Instead, a poor substitute has resulted: a non-proliferation regime for nuclear weaponry, thereby shifting attention away from the countries that have possessed the weaponry to those that have aspirations to acquire it. In contrast, genocide (the main crime of the losers) has been criminalized in a treaty that enjoys universal adherence, and aggressive war (also the crime of the losers), was criminalized at Nuremberg and Tokyo when in 1945 the surviving wartime leaders of Germany and Japan were prosecuted, convicted, and punished.

At the same time, the United Nations was established, embodying the victors' vision of a constitutional framework for world order taking the form of the UN Charter. Again the outcome of the recently concluded war was prominently reflected: the defeated countries were even initially excluded from membership, and the victors were rewarded with a permanent seat on the Security Council, as well as given a veto power that conferred, in its effect, an exemption from the obligations of international law. The Charter also embodied a compromise between the Westphalian ideal of unrestricted territorial sovereignty for member states and the core undertaking of the UN "to save succeeding generations from the scourge of war." In effect, the compromise was expressed by way of an unconditional prohibition on the use of force in international relations (Article 2(4)) unless employed in self-defense against a prior armed attack (Article 51), with the final assessment of the claim to be determined by the Security Council (Article 39) and by denying the UN any right to intervene in the internal affairs of sovereign states (Article 2(7)) unless international peace and security were seriously at stake. In effect, two kinds of conciliation were fused: geopolitical freedom of action for the dominant states with the rule of law for the community of states; collective responsibility for the management of global security with continuing deference to national sovereignty.

More or less, with deviations in practice, this conception of a global legal order persisted unchallenged and unchanged during the several decades of the Cold War. To be sure the main antagonists, the United States and the Soviet Union, used non-defensive and interventionary force on several occasions, but always tried to reconcile their behavior within this accepted legal framework, claiming in most circumstances that force had been previously authorized by some multilateral institution, usually of a regional character, or that the state in question had invited the intervention, thereby giving its consent. Since the UN Security Council was paralyzed by the use of the veto, departures from the legal regime established in 1945 were never definitively censured, although condemned in the *métier* of political propaganda. At the same time, there was a rather strong consensus, despite the Cold War, that opposed lending legitimacy to outright cases of aggression across international borders. The UN did condemn all the main instances: the attack by North Korea on South Korea in 1950, the Suez Operation of France, the United Kingdom, and Israel in 1956, the Turkish attack and occupation of Cyprus in 1974, and the Indonesian attack on East Timor in 1975. In a real sense, the prohibition on aggressive force across established international boundaries was consistently supported in the latter half of the 20th century. This support was undoubtedly reinforced by the nuclear standoff between the two superpowers that made the risks of World War III appear unbearable, and shifted the terrain of violent conflict to the internal war zones of the global south that accompanied or followed decolonization struggles.

With the ending of the Cold War, both geopolitically due to the collapse of the Soviet Union and ideologically as a result of all important countries opting for participation in the world economy in accord with a neo-liberal version of capitalism, it appeared as if the legal regime that was nominally in existence since 1945 could now be much more fully implemented. Such expectations seemed partially realized by the Security Council agreement to oppose with overwhelming collective force Iraq's conquest and annexation of Kuwait in 1991, which led to a response within the United Nations, proclaimed at the time by the American president, George H. W. Bush, as the birth of a 'new world order.' But unanticipated concerns soon arose: the rise of human rights generated pressures to engage in humanitarian intervention, and with the Cold War over, there was less reluctance, in part, due to the disappearance of escalation risks. Also, it became evident that certain governments could not provide domestic security or prevent the use of their territory by terrorists or pirates, and could not begin to meet the basic material needs of their populations. Such state were labeled 'failed states' or 'outlaw states,' and deprived of their status as sovereign states. A doctrine of 'responsible sovereignty' came gradually to displace notions of unconditional sovereignty. Further, there arose the related contention that certain states posed dangers beyond their borders, either because seeking nuclear weaponry or by being disruptive of economic globalization. These states were called 'rogue states' by the main geopolitical manager of world order and treated as a threat to regional and global security. The cumulative effect of these developments was to encourage the imposition of sanctions and even threaten or embark upon military intervention according to justifications with little basis in post-World War II international law.

But what really unhinged the stability of world order were the 9/11 attacks on the United States by a non-state actor with extremist objectives and tactical skills that exposed the vulnerabilities of modern industrial societies. The global legal order was designed to address conflict among states and to some lesser extent, conflict within states. It was not conceptually or psychologically equipped to deal with a conflict between non-territorial global actors: either the *Al Qaeda* hidden transnational network or the American planetary presence based on over 700 overseas military bases and navies in every ocean. The neo-conservative response to 9/11 during the presidency of George W. Bush was administratively preoccupied with this tension between adherence to law and responding to a new kind of adversary. In clumsy and regressive ways the Bush response was both alienating and dysfunctional, validating torture and repudiating the relevance of legal restraints on war making whether derived from the Geneva Conventions or the United Nations. Guantanamo, Abu Ghraib, and the 2003 non-defensive invasion and subsequent occupation of Iraq were illustrative.

With the election of Barack Obama as American president there came the promise of a new more law-oriented, less unilateralist approach, and clearly the bestowal of the 2009 Nobel Peace Prize can be best understood as anticipating and affirming such a policy shift. And yet the Nobel acceptance speech by President Obama revealed that the global crisis of authority that surfaced after 9/11 would not be easily overcome. Despite some eloquent language it was clear that in essential respects that Obama's view of post-9/11 security imperatives was disturbingly similar to that of the Bush presidency. Obama did attempt to substitute the vague directives of the just war doctrine for the UN Charter framework with respect to assessing the rightness of recourse to war, and spoke favorably about adhering to 'standards' rather than to the rule of law, but in the end such moves were sophisticated evasions of the much stricter limitations on the use of force set forth in the Charter and international law. In reminding his Oslo audience of the transnational extremist threat, of evil forces at play, and of the unacceptability of non-action in the face of severe denials of human rights, Obama was basically rejecting the relevance of the old legal regime of restraint as being incapable of offering appropriate guidance to uphold 21st century security. Obama did pay homage to the idealistic orientations of Martin Luther King and Gandhi, but mainly to express his judgment that however inspiring their examples and outlook, their nonviolent views were not responsive to current threats by truly evil adversaries. He compared *Al Qaeda* to the Nazis, insisting that neither challenge could be addressed via diplomacy and negotiation, leaving war as the only option.

It is against this background that Belinda Helmke's fine book should be read and appreciated. What Helmke does with admirable scholarly clarity and depth it to look systematically at the practice of states with respect to the use of international force in the period since the end of the Cold War. She carefully considers the basic question as to whether these new patterns of practice can be regarded as having had a lawmaking effect, becoming what international law specialists, identify as 'customary international law.' Helmke concludes that these departures from prior notions of the sanctity of territorial sovereignty or of the prohibitions upon aggressive force have remained controversial, and have not yet morphed into a new framework of global legal order. As suggested above, Obama's Nobel speech drawing on the just war tradition is a tacit acknowledgement of the persuasiveness of Helmke's analysis suggesting that international law governing the use of force is in disarray. To understand this tension between state practice and legal norms in this manner means that we are condemned to live in a world order no longer underpinned by an agreed set of legal guidelines. It also means the absence of authoritative constraints on the behavior of the more powerful states and also the degraded character of previously respected guidelines relied upon to shape the responses of the UN and regional actors when faced with appeals to engage in peacekeeping operations or urged to address humanitarian crises.

What Belinda Helmke achieves is an illuminating contrast between the authoritative legal regime established after World War II and the relative degree of incoherence that has emerged since the end of the Cold War. She also makes the important argument that this incoherence reflects disagreements among states about whether the governance of force in the 21st century needs to be modified to take account of the emergence of non-state actors as participants in strategic conflict. Many persons have been disappointed by the renewed American emphasis on counterinsurgency warfare in Afghanistan, thereby seeming to ignore the broad historical trend toward respecting the outcome of struggles for self-determination in the ex-colonial world, as well as refusing to recognize that in the last 70 years foreign military intervention has only in rare instances triumphed over national resistance movements, and then only at the greatest cost to the target society and to the intervenor. Helmke's inquiry allows us to think more clearly about the importance of shaping a new coherence based on law, justice, and human rights given these changing patterns of conflict in the world, as well as the rise of non-state actors and transnational networks. Her work also helps us to rethink the role of the United Nations and regional actors in relation to international peace and security, given both the reality of disruptive uses of force by transnational non-state actors and the widespread belief in UN circles that unconditional claims of sovereignty must give way to 'the responsibility to protect' if crimes against humanity or other forms of humanitarian catastrophe are taking place within a state.

Helmke has produced a vital text that is impressively responsive to the originality of this evolving global setting. As such, it provides an important grounding for any serious effort to (re)establish an agreed global architecture relating to the use of force, whether in its defensive modes or under the auspices of a UN mandate. It will not restore confidence in world order to abandon the lawmaking effort by taking regressive refuge in a revived just war doctrine, which is little more than a slightly disguised insistence that dominant states, the geopolitical actors, are reclaiming their former discretion to use international force whenever it in their interest to do so. If this nihilistic tendency is being accurately depicted, it suggests an abandonment of the major effort of the prior century to confine authority to use force as narrowly as possible so as to minimize the incidence of war and to enable the identification of wrongful claims of self-defense. I read Helmke as seeking to surmount the prevailing incoherence through a renewed effort to establish *legally* accountable guidelines that are reinforced by *political* resolve and *institutional* mechanisms dedicated to achieving compliance and implementation by all relevant political actors. The restoration of a global legal regime for the use of force whose validity is widely accepted by political actors will not be easy to accomplish, but without such a normative recovery, world order will be enfeebled by contradictory regressive views that virtually ensure a dangerous new era of power politics. In the course of his Nobel speech President Obama, despite seeking to occupy the high moral ground, disclosed his adherence to *realpolitik:* "I – like any head of state – reserve the right to act unilaterally if necessary to defend my nation." Of course, it is not helpful to romanticize the old consensual regime. It never really provided much more than an agreed discourse and provided leading states with a set of instruments with which to vindicate the outcome of a major war. Despite the hopes of legalists, this regime was never able to constrain the behavior of major actors determined to make war or to protect the victims of aggression.

To fulfill the needs of a globalizing planet the peoples of the world need and deserve not only a new agreed discourse on international force, but also patterns of principled implementation that apply to strong and weak alike. Helmke has identified this momentous challenge with precision and insight, now it is up to her, but also the rest of us, to do our best to conceptualize and promote a response that restores public and governmental confidence that the rule of law can provide a viable alternative to violent geopolitics, making it again relevant and worthwhile to dedicate our energies to the strengthening of law norms in war/peace contexts.

Richard Falk 2010

Acknowledgements

This book is the result of four years of intense research and a journey which was as enjoyable and unforgettable as it was exhausting. This project and the subsequent manuscript could have not been completed without the support of a number of people. In different ways they all contributed to this book.

I would like to begin by thanking the team at Ashgate for putting the final touches to this book. My particular gratitude goes to my Commissioning Editor, Kirstin Howgate and Senior Editor, Pam Bertram for their effort and efficiency. Both Richard Falk and Simon Chesterman provided me with invaluable feedback and enabled me to refine the manuscript. I owe Richard, who has assumed a mentor-like role for me, my particular gratitude. He generously agreed to write the foreword to this book. Richard's work has always been an inspiration to me and his modesty regarding his achievements has been striking.

Jake Lynch facilitated my appointment to the Centre for Peace and Conflict Studies (CPACS) at the University of Sydney. The Centre's promotion of interdisciplinary research and teaching on the causes of conflict and the conditions that affect conflict resolution and peace is a concern close to my heart. I would therefore like to thank Jake for allowing me to be a part of CPACS.

The Vienna-based Society for South-East Asian Studies (SEAS) has given me a further intellectual home in Europe. It has been a great pleasure to work with the SEAS team in organizing annual conferences and publishing our peer-reviewed journal.

I had the great privilege of sharing my road towards this book with three fellow researchers and good friends, Ann El Khoury, Raphael Veit and David Santoro. I was not only able to share the burden of thesis writing with them but also our passion for international relations and international law. Ann in particular showed me that there is a greater purpose to undertaking such research. I have always admired her outspokenness and effort in promoting peace issues.

The work on a book project inevitably leads to the neglect of friends and family. I would therefore like to thank the following people for their support and understanding: Iris Dinkloh, Sonja Kahl, Angelika Heinrich, Christina Kuhn, Bianca, Marc, Leonie and Pauline Scharenberg, Jude and Michael Thomas, Bonny Maddah, Gail Burke, Carol-Ann and Terry McLean, Tyler and Serena Rivett, Peter and Colleen Dunn, Michael and Roz Dunn, Gloria Dunn, and Herta Helmke.

My former colleagues and good friends Marijana Wright, Alfred Gerstl and Virginia Small always had words of encouragement for me. I would like to say thanks for all the laughter and lunches we shared. They made my work thoroughly enjoyable.

Furthermore, I am particularly thankful to Nicole Henderson. She sacrificed many hours to edit this book and her encouragement, as a friend and editor, has been fantastic.

My brother Thomas and my parents Marilyn and Klaus supported me all the way and in every way throughout this book project. I would like to thank them for allowing me to 'overeducate' myself.

Last but not least I would like to thank Greg Pemberton – brilliant writer and incomparable friend. He challenged me to push my boundaries and he dared me to disturb the universe in so many ways. Greg always believed in my ability to complete this project, even in the occasional moments when I myself did not. Without him this book would have never been completed and for that I will always be grateful.

Belinda Helmke, 2010

List of Abbreviations

ANO	Abu Nidal Organization
ANZUS	Australia, New Zealand and United States
AU	African Union
BPC	British Phosphate Commission
CENTO	Central Treaty Organization
DGICCP	Declaration on the Granting of Independence to Colonial Countries and Peoples
DID	Department for International Development
DPRK	Democratic People's Republic of Korea
DRV	Democratic Republic of Vietnam
ECOWAS	Economic Community of West African States
ERP	European Recovery Plan
EU	European Union
FASC	Foreign Affairs Select Committee
ICBM	Intercontinental Ballistic Missiles
ICC	International Criminal Court
ICCPR	International Covenant on Civil and Political Rights
ICERD	International Convention for the Elimination of all Forms of Racial Discrimination
ICESCR	International Covenant on Economic, Social and Cultural Rights
ICISS	International Commission on Intervention and State Sovereignty
ICJ	International Court of Justice
ICTY	International Criminal Tribunal for the former Yugoslavia
IDIP	*Institut de Droit International Penal*
IGAS	Intergovernmental Authority on Development
IICK	International Commission on Kosovo
ILC	International Law Commission
INTERFET	International Force East Timor
IUAR	International Union of American Republics
IWA	International Workingmen's Association
MIPT	Memorial Institute for the Prevention of Terrorism
NATO	North Atlantic Treaty Organization
NMD	National Missile Defense
NSS	National Security Strategy
OAS	Organization of American States
OAU	Organization for African Unity
OECS	Organization of Eastern Caribbean States

OIC	Organization of the Islamic Conference
PCIJ	Permanent Court of International Justice
PFLP	Popular Front for the Liberation of Palestine
PLO	Palestine Liberation Organization
PRIO	Peace Research Institute, Oslo
PWG	Policy Working Group
SADC	Southern African Development Community
SEATO	South East Asia Treaty Organization
SIPRI	Stockholm International Peace Research Institute
UCDP	Uppsala Conflict Data Program
UDHR	Universal Declaration of Human Rights
UNGA	United Nations General Assembly
UNOC	United Nations Operation in The Congo
UNSC	United Nations Security Council
UNTAG	United Nations Transition Assistance Group
UNTC	United Nations Trusteeship Council
WMD	Weapons of mass destruction

Introduction: Plan of Attack

> Out of these troubled times a new world order can emerge: a new era – freer from the threat of terror, stronger in the pursuit of justice, and more secure in the quest for peace … Today that new world is struggling to be born, a world quite different from the one we've known. A world where the rule of law supplants the rule of the jungle.
>
> George H.W. Bush (1990: 91)

George H.W. Bush, like many others, hailed the end of the Cold War as coinciding with the arrival of a new world order in which the established rules of state conduct would be obeyed. This book argues that, in fact, state practice since the end of the Cold War has demonstrated that there is a challenge to the long established legal regime on the international use of force.

Simon Chesterman, Professor of Law at New York University, claims that the Persian Gulf War (1991) and the Iraq War (2003) book-ended "the post-Cold War flirtation with a 'new world order'" (2004: 112). The Iraq War unquestionably had a severe impact on the notion of collective security, the use of force outside the established limitations of self-defense following an armed attack, and on United Nations' (UN) authorized military action. Richard Falk (2003), American academic and UN Special Rapporteur on the situation of human rights in the Palestinian territories, even argues that the actions of the George W. Bush administration not only damaged world order but also led to the "abandonment of legal restraints on the use of international force, the heart and soul of the UN Charter". This is a strong judgment which this book will evaluate.

The use of force against Iraq, rather than marking a monumental historical turning point, was the latest, albeit crucial, step in a development within the international system which has taken place since the end of the Cold War. Rather than being an overnight event, the challenge to international law has occurred since 1990. Only in a few instances, including states' use of the concept of rogue states and pre-emption to justify their use of force, has the challenge been obvious. Generally speaking, the challenges have been more covert in nature. It is these 'subtle' challenges which have posed the most substantial threat to the established rules for the international use of force.

Prior to the establishment of the League of Nations (1919) and later the Kellogg-Briand Pact (1928) the use of force was conducted predominantly along moral guiding principles. An international legal regime prohibiting and criminalizing the use of force did not exist before the 20th century. International law, during the two world wars, subsequently moved the justifications for the use of force from political and moral to legal grounds. Yet, the significant rules established were supported by states more in theory than in practice. Nothing exemplified the disregard for the legal regime more than the commencement of the Second World War.

During the Cold War period, if not beforehand, state practice did not constitute a substantial challenge to the established norms of international law. Instead, states justified their use of force within the existing framework of individual and collective self-defense including a form of collective security. Since the end of the Cold War, the challenge of state practice to the long-established legal regime on the international use of force has occurred in the form of six additional justifications for intervention split evenly into two groups: under intervention for humanitarian reasons, the protection of nationals abroad, humanitarian intervention and intervention in failed states; under self-defense, pre-emption, counter-terrorism and rogue states. Bush is the recent state leader most associated with an expanded view of the right of self-defense. Britain's Tony Blair is the one most associated with an expanded view of the right of humanitarian intervention.

The 'Bush Doctrine', as echoed in the *National Security Strategy (NSS)* 2002, includes the promotion of the pre-emptive use of force against rogue states and those supporting terrorism. It further announces the United States' (US) determination to undertake military intervention alone if necessary. Although often interpreted as advocating unilateralism, US military interventions in recent years, while not necessarily UN-authorized, have been collective in nature, usually in the form of *ad hoc* coalitions: a small consolation perhaps for those concerned particularly with the format of military intervention in the contemporary international system.

In light of the Kosovo Crisis, Blair (1999a) announced his 'Doctrine of the International Community', a policy better known as 'liberal interventionism'. Blair promoted the intervention of states in the domestic affairs of others based on humanitarian reasons: a policy reiterated in 2004. Unlike Bush, Blair advocated the UN as the 'central pillar' of this new interventionist policy, stressing the need to find ways to enable the effective operation of the Security Council. Yet, the use of force outside of the UN framework was not entirely ruled out as the United Kingdom's (UK) participation in both the North Atlantic Treaty Organization-led (NATO) Kosovo and US-led Iraq intervention showed.

These leaders have not stated they are acting illegally or even 'illegitimately' on occasions but have instead argued that the established rules on the use of force are out of date. Consequently, they have at times employed moral justifications which, they imply, override out-dated legal rules. State leaders such as Bill Clinton (1999), Tony Blair (2001b) and John Howard (2004), in a speech given to the House of Representatives, have even invoked some of the religious terminology of the long-defunct Catholic framework for the use of force, that is 'just war'.

What may have been seen as mere rhetorical flourishes for public consumption, terms employed by Bush (2001a) such as 'evildoer' and 'crusade', acquire a new significance in this light. There is almost a sense in which the Islamic term *jihad* is being countered by its Christian twin.

State Practice, International Law and the Use of Force

British lawyer and politician W. Vernon Harcourt stated during the 19th century that "it must be admitted that in the case of intervention, as that of revolution, its essence is illegality, and its justification is its success" (1863: 41). Indeed, for a state's use of force to be 'successful', regarding its acceptance by the international community, it arguably needs a sound legal basis. State practice, however, does not always coincide with the rules for the international use of force even if they are agreed upon. The core question regarding state practice is consequently whether it constitutes a violation of international law or the establishment of new rules.

State practice as evidence of customary international law is considered a source of international law under Article 38(1) of the Statue of the International Court of Justice (ICJ). This is distinct from the three other sources, namely international conventions, the general principles of law as recognized by civilized nations, as well as judicial decisions and teachings of the most highly qualified publicists. All of these sources have shaped modern international law since its emergence in the 17th century.

Not every act of state practice, however, leads to the creation of a custom under international law. According to the ICJ in the *Asylum Case*, to constitute custom the rule must be "in accordance with a constant and uniform usage practiced by the states in question" (1950b: 14).

The *North Sea Continental Shelf Case* similarly argued that state practice had to be "both extensive and virtually uniform in the sense of the provision invoked, and should moreover have occurred in such a way as to show a general recognition that a rule of law or legal obligation is involved" (1969: 43).[1]

The reference here is to the concept of *opinio juris*: the belief that action taken was done so on the basis that it is a legal obligation. This is a very subjective issue. States are aware that the use of economic, political and strategic justifications will not invest any degree of legality in their practice. Consequently, governments will strive to justify their use of force on a legal basis, arguing that action was taken in the belief it constitutes *opinio juris*.

The ICJ in the *Nicaragua v. United States of America* case argued that "in order to deduce the existence of customary rules, the Court deems it sufficient that the conduct of states should, in general, be consistent with such rules, and that instances of state conduct inconsistent with a given rule should generally have

1 The ICJ (1969: 4) furthermore states "for, in order to achieve this result [*opinio juris*], two conditions must be fulfilled. Not only must the acts concerned amount to a settled practice, but they must also be such, or be carried out in such a way, as to be evidence of a belief that this practice is rendered obligatory by the existence of a rule of law requiring it. The need for such a belief, i.e., the existence of a subjective element, is implicit in the very notion of the *opinio juris sive necessitatis*. The States concerned must therefore feel that they are conforming to what amounts to a legal obligation. The frequency, or even habitual character of the acts is not in itself enough".

been treated as breaches of that rule, not as indications of the recognition of a new rule" (1986: 9).

Malcolm N. Shaw, British lawyer and Professor of International Law at the University of Leicester, consequently argues that for state practice to create a legally binding custom, it does not only have to constitute *opinio juris* but there is also a need for it to be viewed as constituting legally obligatory action by other states. It is furthermore reliant on what Shaw (1991: 65–6) describes as the strength of already existing legal regulations. Only if the existing rules are viewed as lacking in effectiveness or appropriateness, especially by major powers, is there a substantial chance of state practice challenging them, and possibly even leading to the establishment of new rules.

States, particularly in the post-Cold War era, also often claim that their use of force is, if not legal, then at least legitimate. International law is ideally viewed as an objective and normative force, meaning action can only be either legal or illegal. Governments, organizations and commentators alike agree, however, that legality, as argued by UN University academics Vesselin Popovski and Nicholas Turner, "is not the only criteria for determining acceptable state behavior" (2008: 1).

The concept of legitimacy, invoked particularly for humanitarian, political and moral reasons, also plays a crucial role in justifying the use of force. When legal rules alone cannot justify an action that is perceived as morally right by the intervening state, as was the case with Kosovo in 1999, legitimacy "can introduce constructive flexibility in international law" (Popovski and Turner 2008: 1). This also means that there is a real potential for abuse when justifications based on the concept of legitimacy (and therefore moral perceptions) rather than on legal rules are used for intervention. The use of force against Iraq in 2003 is one such example. The fact that legitimacy is "fluid and changing, and depends on perceptions and outcomes" (Popovski and Turner 2008: 3) can consequently be both a beneficial and detrimental challenge to international law and world order. This is something which will be analysed more closely in Part II and III.

This book will examine whether, as stated in the Statue of the ICJ, "international custom, as evidence of general practice accepted as law", has been created by states' challenge to the long-established legal regime regulating the international use of force. It will focus on both the actions of states and their justifications, thereby assessing the extent of this challenge. The book is concerned with the use of force generally understood as armed force, primarily in the form of an intervention in the territorial integrity and sometimes, but not necessarily, the political independence of another state.

The terms 'war', 'use of force' and 'intervention' are largely used interchangeably in literature on the subject of the current development within the international system. War is the concept which has informed the legal term 'armed attack'. Yet, there can be more types of the use of force which would not conventionally be seen as war. This becomes crucial if states have the right of self-defense against uses of force which are not part of war.

The term 'use of force', by contrast and with regard to the international system, seems to refer to any forceful employment of military power by a state. Not only is it the term used (but not defined) in the UN Charter, it is also a phrase whose scale is not defined. Today the term refers mostly to the use of force in instances of intervention. The term intervention, in its broadest sense, describes the general interference in another state which can include both forceful and non-forceful means such as political pressure or economic sanctions (Detter 2000: 70). The focus of this book is the military aspect of such intervention, described by German-born jurist Lassa Oppenheim as "the dictatorial interference by a state or group of states in the affairs of another state for the purposes of maintaining or altering the actual conditions therein" (1912: 188). American Taylor B. Seybolt's contemporary definition is very similar and labels intervention as "the use of foreign troops for the purpose of affecting the outcome or consequences of an armed conflict in another country to which at least one primary belligerent does not give its consent" (2000: 22). For this reason, this book does not include peacekeeping as a form of intervention.

The focus of this book is the examination of whether there is a challenge posed by states' use of force in the post-Cold War era to the long-established legal regime. It focuses on the most prominent instances of such use of force over the last two decades, as well as occurrences during the pre-1945 and Cold War era. It cannot examine every instance of intervention not only due to restrictions in space but also because not all instances of the use of force challenge the rules in a substantial way. The selection of case studies consequently focuses on controversial and key instances which were viewed as posing a strong challenge to established international law regulating the use of force. Naturally, most of these incidents were undertaken by major powers with both the military and economic capacity to use force and whose actions are more likely to be seen as a change and not a violation of international law.

In addition, it is important to stress that the emphasis is on military enforcement action rather than peacekeeping. Peacekeeping has been a prominent feature of the post-Cold War era, particularly with regard to deployments in instances of civil war, humanitarian crisis and failed states. Such action, however, is bound by the strict organizing principles of consent, impartiality and limited force, as first expressed in the organizing principles of the United Nations Emergency Force I (1956–1967) on the Sinai peninsula. While peacekeeping operations involve military personnel, such troops have no enforcement powers and are limited to using force only for self-defense purposes. In recent years this has been expanded to the protection of civilians if the situation warrants. Overall, however, the gravity and extent of force used cannot be compared to military enforcement action by states which do not have to adhere to these three core operational principles.

States' intervention in civil wars is a further core area which will not be covered by this book. Internal wars have been the major form of armed conflict since 1945 and, according to former UN Secretary-General Kofi Annan, "have violated, not so much borders, as people" (2000b: 43).

There are two core reasons why civil war is not allocated a separate chapter with regard to states' use of force: first, civil war tends to be connected with humanitarian intervention and failed states, the two areas which will be examined in Part II of this book; second, peacekeeping operations, rather than military enforcement action, have mainly been deployed in instances of civil war.

Filling the Void

The literature regarding states' international use of force is vast. Armed conflict in general remains one of the most popular fields in academic publishing. The Library of Congress alone holds more than 10,000 secondary publications on the topic. Despite this, observers such as Margaret G. Hermann and Charles W. Kegley, have argued that "given the prominent place military intervention occupies in the discourse and actions of democratic states in the contemporary international arena, there is a pressing need for more research in the current time period" (2001: 244).

This book makes a new contribution to the field of international relations in general and the study of international law, and armed conflict in particular, in two core ways: first, it links information from varying disciplines, most notably international relations and international law to form a comprehensive picture of state practice and the challenges it poses to the legal rules for the use of force; second, it organizes the information in such a way to identify two core groups of contemporary justifications used by states: humanitarian reasons and self-defense, both with their sub-categories.

The existing literature displays a gap in examining all six additional justifications used by states for intervention in an equally balanced and comprehensive manner. This book aims to fill this opening in the literature by furthering understanding of how state practice since the end of the Cold War has challenged the long established rules of international law. While some justifications occur more frequently than others in state practice, this book argues that the application of all six warrants an examination. Only taken together can they explain the extent of the challenge to the existing legal regime.

It is important to point out that the six categories of justifications as such are not new but have, instead, been used by states to validate their use of force since the 19th century. Explaining how these justifications have developed over the years is one of the core concerns of this book. Only by looking at the development of the justifications can we discover how their current use by states challenges the contemporary rules governing the international use of force. In order to understand the present we must examine the past.

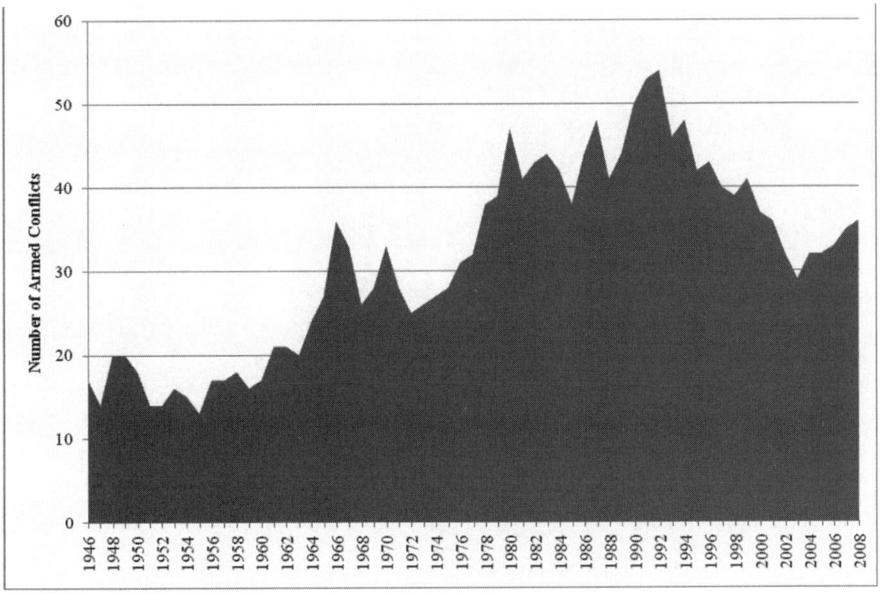

Figure I.1 Incidents of armed conflict 1946–2008
Source: UCDP/PRIO Armed Conflict Dataset v.4-2009, 1946–2008

Armed Conflict

Prior to examining state practice with regard to the international use of force, the trend and developments regarding the nature of armed conflict warrant a brief examination. Armed conflict remains a major concern in the international system with almost 2,000 recorded incidents since the end of the Second World War. A tripling of the number of states in the international system since 1945 and the largely violent process of decolonization, brought with them an increase in the number of conflicts. An annual all time high of 54 armed conflicts was recorded in 1992, as illustrated in Figure I.1. In the immediate aftermath of the Cold War, competing groups fought over the power vacuums left by the end of superpower rivalry, and a number of multiethnic states, such as Yugoslavia and the Soviet Union, disintegrated. The number of armed conflicts began to increase again from 2004 onwards, implying that warfare remains an area in which continuing research is necessary.

The regional distribution of armed conflicts, as seen in Figure I.2, demonstrates that conflicts since 1946 have been concentrated foremost in Asia and Africa. During the Cold War period, indirect and direct involvement of superpowers caused escalation in the intensity of pre-existing conflicts. With the end of the decolonization process in the mid-1970s and ultimately the Cold War, one might have expected the escalation to decline. The reasons for the continuing prevalence

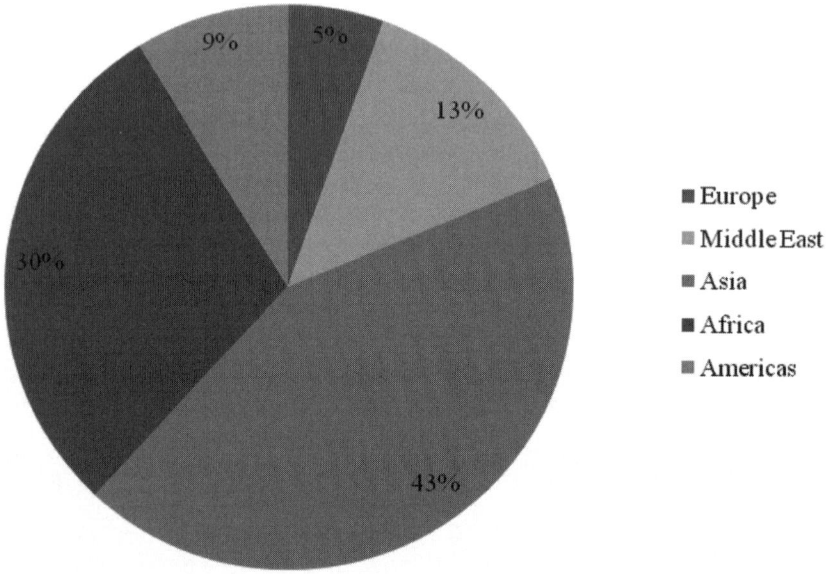

Figure I.2 Regional distribution of armed conflict 1946–2008
Source: UCDP/PRIO Armed Conflict Dataset v.4-2009, 1946–2008

of Asia and Africa as the hotspots for armed conflict are manifold. Violent tensions in recently established, disparate states, with weak governments are just some of the explanations. Closer attention will be paid to these issues in Part II and III of this book.

At the turn of the millennium Annan observed that "wars since the 1990s have been mainly internal [and] have violated, not so much borders, as people" (2000b: 43).

Indeed, internal armed conflicts have dominated the international system over the past six decades. Since the end of the Cold War almost 90 per cent of armed conflicts have taken place within states, occasionally involving outside interference by third parties (UCDP/PRIO 2009). The demise of the bipolar global order, decade-long accumulation of civil conflicts, ethnic tension, poverty, and weakness of government have all led to increased internal strife. Such hostilities have posed a major threat not only to the respective states but often also to international peace and security on the whole. Due to growing interdependence between states, internal wars have often come to be of regional or even global concern, regularly leading to foreign military interventions. This includes the use of force for humanitarian reasons, in instances of failed states and to counter terrorism, as will be discussed in subsequent chapters.

The examination of armed conflicts suggests interesting implications for the international rules covering the use of force. Those rules, as we will see, were developed with the notion that the prevalent form of armed conflict was state versus state. Classical interstate war, however, due to stricter legal regulations of the use of force, has been of decreasing importance since the end of the Second World War. Perhaps, like the mythical story of the guns of Singapore, the rules are pointing in the wrong direction.

Structure

In order to establish what actually is state practice and what have been and currently are the rules of international law regulating the use of force by states, this book will examine a mix of primary and secondary sources. Combined, the existing challenges to the international legal regime regulating the use of force can then be determined.

The book is composed of three parts: the first consists of four chapters, the second and third part has three chapters each. Part I examines the legal regime of the international use of force from its origin in the 17th century up to the post-Cold War era. The four chapters deal respectively with the period prior to 1918, the inter-war era, the Cold War years and the post-Cold War period. This first part focuses particularly on the development of three key concepts, namely sovereignty, the rules governing the use of force and international institutions including law. It aims to show how these concepts shaped the rules and the environment in which states resorted to force. Instead of coinciding, it appears that there has always been an uneasy relationship between the established rules and state practice.

In order to determine whether there has been a challenge to the long-established legal regime in the contemporary international system, it is crucial to compare state practice in different periods. Consequently, when examining the six additional justifications offered by states since 1990 in their use of force, there will also be an examination of this practice in two additional periods: first, the pre-1945 era; second, the Cold War era. Analyzing state practice across these three time periods enables the determination of whether there is a genuine challenge of some scale in existence.

Part II studies the first three additional justifications used by states for military intervention: first, the protection of a state's own nationals abroad; second, the protection of foreign nationals, also better known as humanitarian intervention; third, intervention in so-called failed states which are characterized by political instability, internal conflict and economic hardship. Rather than marking a phenomenon of the post-Cold War era, intervention for (alleged) humanitarian purposes has a long tradition. Yet, legal grounds for such interventions have often been difficult to find, meaning there has been a resort to moral justifications and 'just war' terminology.

Part III focuses on the remaining three types of justification used by states for the international use of force: first, the pre-emptive use of force against imminent or future threats; second, the use of force to counter terrorism in instances in which it is both harbored and sponsored by states; third, the use of force against so-called rogue states which are seen to violate what are perceived as standards of acceptable international behavior. As self-defense, together with the authorization of force by the Security Council, remains the only exception to states' legal use of force in the international system, these 'expanded' notions or interpretations have been controversial.

In the post-Cold War era, intervention based on the six additional justifications is clearly linked to a softened interpretation of sovereignty which makes the right to non-interference conditional rather than absolute. The contemporary format of the use of force shows that there has been a gradual development towards collective action as the ultimate arbitrator of legitimacy regarding the use of force. Unilateral intervention rarely occurs. Instead, states focus on intervening, if not through the UN, then at least multilaterally in form of regional organizations and *ad hoc* coalitions. Collective action is viewed as encompassing greater legitimacy. Just war theory, while replaced by international law from the 17th century onwards, has achieved a certain comeback since 1990. It has been controversially argued that such moral justifications override out-dated legal rules.

At the core of this book is consequently the question of how state practice since 1990, in form of the six additional justifications, has challenged the long-established legal regime on the international use of force. Are we merely witnessing a temporary and insignificant challenge to international law or are the rules genuinely under attack?

Part I

Great Decision or Great Illusion: International Law and The Use of Force

The examination of the current challenge to the long-established legal regime on the international use of force must begin with a study of the rules themselves. Some writers and government officials, among them Bush (2003a) and Howard, have recently argued that international law in its current form is outdated and does not address contemporary threats.

It is important to stress, however, that there has always been an uneasy dynamic in the relationship between the established international rules and state practice. In theory, of course, the two should coincide. In reality, when inevitable differences emerge the question is raised whether the state practice is a violation or an indication of a potential change in international law. This problem, while of particular concern today, has surfaced throughout the history of international law on the use of force.

Part I aims to examine four distinct periods of international law, focusing in particular on the development of three key concepts, namely sovereignty, the rules governing the use of force and international institutions.

The first period pre-1919, was marked largely by an absence of international regulations on the use of force. This meant a conflict between state practice and the non-existent rules for the use of force could not exist. The second period, the inter-war years between 1919 and 1939, witnessed the first serious constraints on a state's ability to use force internationally. During this time, state practice unashamedly challenged the new rules, culminating ultimately in Germany's invasion of Poland. The third period, the Cold War era, was characterized by state practice not constituting a substantial challenge to the established norms of international law. Instead, states justified their use of force within the existent framework of individual and collective self-defense, including a form of collective security in Korea.

The fourth chapter summarizes the core post-Cold War developments, as evident in state practice. The focus is on the concept of sovereignty, the format of the use of force, as well as just war theory. What becomes evident is that the post-Cold War has witnessed a substantial softening of the notion of sovereignty. Today such a right to non-interference is strongly linked to governments' need to fulfill certain responsibilities, most notably the protection of human rights. While the doctrine of intervention has consequently been expanded, it has been done so on the *proviso* that the use of force is undertaken collectively. Multilateral action, though not necessarily through the UN, is viewed as a crucial legitimizing factor for the use of force in the contemporary international system. Finally, some states have resorted to just war theory with its quasi-legal basis to justify their use of force. This discourse has controversially been used to expand the ground for the use of force beyond the legal one of self-defense to moral reasons.

Chapter 1

Outlawing the Mob: International Law and the Use of Force Prior to 1918

> Das Recht muss nie der Politik, wohl aber die Politik jederzeit dem Recht angepasst werden.[1]
>
> Immanuel Kant (1797: 312)

Immanuel Kant, like Dutch jurist Hugo Grotius, lamented the habitual use of force by states. In his famous 1795 essay, *Perpetual Peace,* Kant tried to draw up a workable program for the future in order to secure peace in Europe's new emerging international system of sovereign states. His aim was to liberate humankind, once and for all, from the brutality which accompanies the use of force (Kant 1957). This was quintessentially the major theme of the Enlightenment on the issue of violence, political or otherwise. Violence was an irrational and even immoral part of the primitive past preserved by monarchies and aristocrats. Violence in all dimensions of human existence could and should be eliminated.

Kant's theory had one important flaw which, in the eyes of many, rendered its realization impossible: he based such an achievement on the rationality of humankind. There were other Enlightenment figures, including another Prussian, Carl von Clausewitz, who, within forty years, advised the world that violence was an integral part of political behavior (2007: 28). The contemporary international system has not contradicted those who doubted the realization of an age of perpetual peace. The possibility of an international system free from the use of force, seems as unlikely today as it has at any stage of the history of humankind. The world, in the dramatic words of Scotland's Mary Campbell Smith, translator of an early 20th century edition of *Perpetual Peace*, has had "no golden age, no peaceful beginning" (1903: 3–4).

Kant had envisaged that the creation of a league of the new republican states replacing the old monarchies would deliver peace. This did not prove so. Only one republic, briefly, made it constitutionally illegal to undertake aggressive war: France in 1791. Since this time, efforts with regard to achieving a more peaceful global order have centered on developing a regime of international laws to restrain the international use of force by restricting the rules for its deployment. This occurred most notably due to the development of three key concepts, namely sovereignty, the rules governing the use of force, and international institutions.

---

1 "The law never has to be adjusted to politics but politics always have to be adjusted to the law".

This chapter will examine these developments regarding the regulation of states' international use of force. State action in this sphere was initially influenced by the just war doctrine, a religious notion of the regulation of state behavior. St. Augustine of Hippo, writing in the 3rd–4th century, and St. Thomas Aquinas, writing in the 13th century, bookend this phase when Christian societies sought a legal basis to justify what Christian theology seemed to condemn: war. Subsequently, with the secularization of the modern era, there was a move towards natural law and the paradoxical notion of sovereignty which included both aspects of intervention and non-intervention. Niccolò Machiavelli pronounced the 'just war' era dead in 1505 when, quoting early 1st century Roman historian Titus Livius (1854: 242), he wrote that "a necessary war is a just war and where there is hope only in arms, those arms are holy" (2003: 83). Rather than restricting states' use of force with a new secular just war doctrine, the period prior to 1918 saw two core occurrences: first, the minor limitation of state violence in war; second, the establishment of prior arbitration as a preferable alternative to the use of force.

The Prized Possession

With the emergence of the secular concept of sovereignty during the 17th and 18th century, Swiss jurist Emerich de Vattel (1964: 154) vocalized the then commonly held belief that sovereignty was the most prized possession of a state. Today, this observation no longer holds the same significance. Even though the concept of sovereignty has been, according to British historian Ivor Wilks, the "cornerstone of political theory ever since" (1955: 342) and remains one of the core prerequisites for order and stability in the international system, its interpretation has changed greatly. The majority of contemporary observers agree with the judgment of Canadian-born Professor of International Relations from Columbia University, James T. Shotwell, that "absolute, unqualified, and unchecked sovereignty is a conception of anarchy" (1944: 202) and thereby no longer possible to uphold in an interdependent world.

French philosopher Jean Bodin, who is credited with the first significant theory of the concept, viewed sovereignty as the principle of absolute and unlimited power, once God's superior authority was relegated to the religious world only; its essence being the authority to make law (Bodin 1955).

Bodin largely saw the existence of a sovereign as constituting a state. Other philosophers refined the concept.

Although personally favoring monarchies, Thomas Hobbes (1996) argued along the same lines as Bodin, agreeing sovereignty arose from the consent of the people, and introduced the abstract notion of the state as the unit holding sovereignty. Johannes Althusius (1965) and Jean-Jacques Rousseau (1997) agreed. Their belief was recently echoed by the Commission of Global Governance which said that "sovereignty ultimately derives from the people [and] is a power to be exercised by, for and on behalf of the people of a state" (1995: 69). This is a concept originally voiced by Abraham Lincoln in 1863 and commonly present in contemporary interpretations of the concept of sovereignty.

Another familiar contemporary concept, humanitarian intervention, is reflected in John Locke's belief that only a government which protects the rights of its citizens gains the right to political sovereignty. This was a significant move away from understanding sovereignty as absolute or unconditional, towards the belief that it should only be respected if certain prerequisites have been fulfilled.

Generally speaking, the importance attached to the concept of sovereignty became most prominent with the Peace of Westphalia which, signed in 1648, ended the Thirty Years' War. The peace treaties are seen, not only as being synonymous with the rise of the modern state system and the nation state in 17th century Europe but also establishing two core principles of sovereignty: *rex est imperator in regno suo* and *cuius regio, eius religio*. These constitute the two sides of the concept of sovereignty, namely internal and external. The former means there is only one central authority within the state – depending on the form of government (monarchy, republic, etc.) this authority may lie in a different branch of the government. The latter is concerned with the state's role in the international political system, notably its right to independence and freedom from interference. The mutual respect of both was one of Kant's requirements for a functional peaceful global order. Peace meant non-intervention.

The concept of the external sovereignty of states has been of growing importance since the emergence of the modern international political system and the establishment of one of the first permanent international institutions, the League of Nations, in 1920. The reason for this is that, with the introduction of the League and its successor the United Nations, aspects of member states' sovereignty were in fact, if not in law, surrendered. Some people recognized that, in order to establish a secure and peaceful global order, state sovereignty could not be absolute. India's J. P. Anand concluded that these steps were the "most serious and important inroads into the traditional concept of sovereignty" (Martinez 1996: 66). Kant's prescription of absolute non-intervention was under challenge.

Although the restrictions put in place were numerous, including those over territory, as well as over individuals and property, the one on which this book concentrates is the restriction of the right to use force internationally.

Surrendering sovereignty, however, was something members of the League were reluctant to do, probably the key reason why the institution failed.

Reverting to the use of force was still, under Article 12 of the Covenant, permitted if, for example, a state adhered to a three month period of delay. It was not until the Kellogg-Briand Pact of 1928 that 65 signatory states bound themselves to renouncing the use of force as an instrument of national policy. This stopped short of banning force. The UN continued with this aspect and, according to its Charter (Article 2, 4), the use of force is considered impermissible, with the exception of individual and collective self-defense or collective force sanctioned by the UN Security Council as provided for under Article 51 and Chapter VII respectively.

Hence the state, which was seen previously as the only authority for the legitimate use of violence, greatly surrendered its legal power to use force (Weber 1926).

Some have argued that states have benefited from the numerous instances in which states have voluntarily placed limits on their sovereignty. The Permanent Court of International Justice (PCIJ) in the *S.S. Wimbledon* case rightly described a state's "right of entering into international engagements as an attribute of state sovereignty" (1923: 25) rather than an unwelcome burden.

The European Union (EU), according to British academic and lawyer Elihu Lauterpacht, shows "the manner in which states can accept major limitations upon their freedom of action without at the same time losing their national sovereignty" (1997: 147). The ability to sign treaties and conduct relations with other states is, together with a permanent population, a defined territory and a government, a measure of a state "as a person of international law" as understood in Article 1 of the 1933 Montevideo Convention on the Rights and Duties of States.

Recently, the President of the Council of Foreign Relations Richard N. Haass (2003), has built on these issues by declaring that state sovereignty is associated with four core characteristics: first, the holding of supreme authority and the monopoly over the legitimate use of force; second, the regulation of movements across its borders; third, the ability to make foreign policy decisions; and fourth, recognition by other governments, thereby giving a state the right to non-intervention.

The change in the interpretation of sovereignty has, inadvertently, had an impact on the rules governing the conduct between states. Originally titled with the French term *droit de gens* (law of nations) and later the English term 'international law', these are the essential rules regulating the international use of force.

Playing by the Rules

Kant in 1797 argued that the law never had to be adjusted to politics but politics always had to be adjusted to the law. This reflects a very idealistic view on how international law and politics interact.

In contrast, Professor of Public International Law at the University of Edinburgh Stephen C. Neff, has recently argued that "the world at large ... has done far more to mould international law than vice versa" (2003: 56). His argument is that economic, political and religious forces can never be controlled or subjugated and that international law makes no exception to this. Despite regular attempts by states to interpret international law in ways which favor their beliefs and the action they have taken, just as in municipal law, international law nevertheless remains a powerful force in the international system. States have to shape their policy and certainly their justifications for action to take account of international law. The volume, breadth and acknowledgement of international law by states clearly attest to its significance as a factor in state policy. The obvious respect states show towards concepts of diplomatic immunity, commercial air navigation and international communication, just to mention a few areas, confirms this.

State practice over the last fifty years shows that states using force or resorting to war always refer to international law. This alone attests to the importance which states attach to international law as a mechanism for regulating international relations, as well as securing international peace and security. Cambridge University's Martin Dixon, nevertheless, claims that international law today fails one of its major purposes, that is, the "regulation of an ordered community where the weak are protected from arbitrary action from the strong" (2005: 1). The recent challenges which state practice has posed to the established rules for the international use of force indeed suggest that despite the existence of international law, militarily weaker states are not protected from the use of force by stronger states. This, however, has always been the case.

As will be shown in the subsequent parts of this chapter, the supreme legal power of states to use force has been diminished over time. This is due to a new understanding of sovereignty as no longer being absolute, as well as the constriction of the grounds for the legal use of force. Both are signs that states have recognized that, in order to guarantee a more peaceful and secure global order, there have to be rules to which they all abide. International law represents these rules.

Establishing exactly what are the rules is more complex than a state's written constitutional law. The four sources of international law, as established in Article 38 of the Statue of the ICJ, namely international conventions, international custom as evident in state practice, the general principles of law as recognized by civilized nations, and judicial decisions and teachings of the most highly qualified publicists, have shaped modern international law since its emergence in the 17th century. These disparate sources can create a disparate mix. Above this complexity of sources is the change in the 'rules' over time.

Wilhelm G. Grewe (1984), German Professor of Law and later diplomat, classified the development of international law into different periods. He distinguishes between the French (1648–1815), English (1815–1919), and American eras (post-1919). Grewe last updated his book *Epochen der Völkerrechtsgeschichte* in 2000 and, while he did not classify the post-Cold War era as a new period, for clarification purposes this will be done in this book. In order to show the challenge of recent state practice to the rules governing the international use of force, it is necessary to examine the development of international law more generally.

A State of War, A Vision of Peace

The term 'international law' as understood and used today is a relatively recent one; first used in English by philosopher Jeremy Bentham in 1780. In *An Introduction to the Principles of Morals and Legislation,* Bentham describes international law as "principles of legislation in matters betwixt nation and nation" (1823: x). This is not to say that legal principles of one sort or another between states did not exist prior to this. The existence of legal agreements in form of general practice and specific treaties, for example, can be traced back 4000 years and to the regions of Mesopotamia, Egypt, Greek city states and the Roman empire. The latter created the *ius gentium* (rights of people) to regulate the relationship between Romans and non-Romans.

As 'international law' developed, however, the term *ius gentium* acquired a dual meaning, referring both to law between and among nations. Spanish philosophers Francisco de Vitoria and Francisco Suarez in the 16th and 17th century subsequently clarified and subdivided the concept of *ius gentium* into two areas: first, the term *ius inter gentes* which referred to law between nations and is reflective of contemporary international law; second, the concept of *ius intra gentes*, today's so-called civil law. Hugo Grotius, the acclaimed founder of modern international law, later refined the concept even further by introducing the phrase *ius inter civitates* (law between civilized nations).

When scholarly language departed from Latin, the French term *droit de gens* began to replace *ius gentium* and related phrases such as *ius inter gentes*. Bentham's English phrase 'international law' has since gathered wide usage beyond the English-speaking world as English replaced Latin and superseded French and Esperanto as the international language. *Ius gentium* was usually coupled with the concept of *ius naturale*, the law of nature. Hugo Grotius described natural law as "the dictate of right reason, shewing the moral turpitude, or moral necessity, of any act from its agreement or disagreement with a rational nature, and consequently that such an act is either forbidden or commanded by God" (2001: 9). His mixture of human rationality ('right reason') with religion ('commanded by God') illustrates the half-way stage international law had reached towards secularization at that time.

Modern international law was, however, not the only approach with regard to the regulation of the international use of force at the time – the older religious framework survived. As Grotius' words attest, the religious law approached the legal use of force through just war doctrine. Robert Tucker, Emeritus Professor of American Foreign Policy at the John Hopkins University, writes that this doctrine seemed to reflect an inherent trait of human beings, especially when it comes to the use of force, namely the "eternal human need to justify action" (1978: 1). Unlike Kant's later doctrine of perpetual peace, just war doctrine, writes American philosopher Michael Walzer (2002), "*liefert keine Apologie für irgendeinen bestimmten Krieg, aber sie ist auch keine Absage an den Krieg als solchen*".[2]

Some of these modern writers do not acknowledge that the doctrine of just war is explicitly connected to a specific time which began and came to an end.

In different times and places in the past there have been varying notions of limiting the resort to the use of force, even as early as the writings of Aristotle, Plato and Cicero. With the rise of Christianity as a state religion under Roman emperor Constantine, the peaceful characteristics of Christianity appeared untenable to a

2 "Although not giving an apology for a specific war, it is also not a rejection of war as such".

state which not only had to defend itself but may also seek expansion in the name of Christianity. St. Augustine of Hippo, who is widely credited with giving birth to the just war doctrine in the 4th century, used, amongst other things, biblical texts to justify the use of force.

St. Augustine set up criteria according to which the resort to force could be made 'just' even for a religion claiming to be peace-loving. Just war theory was reaffirmed under St. Thomas Aquinas in the 13th century even as the religious era was closing. Aquinas (1947), writing in the context of the crusades, drew heavily on Augustine's ideas and stated three criteria of just war, namely legitimate authority, right intention and just cause.

Although the just war doctrine is largely associated with Christianity, it is important to point out that similar concepts can also be found, in varying forms, in other religions such as Judaism, Buddhism, Hinduism and especially Islam.

The 7th century concept of *jihad*, so talked about today, echoes in some respects Christianity's just war doctrine. By the 16th and 17th century, writers such as de Vitoria (1917) and Suarez (1944) started to move away from accepting religious differences as a just cause for the use of force. Thus began the process of secularization which was carried on by the likes of Grotius, Locke, Emerich de Vattel and German philosopher Samuel von Pufendorf.

This is what makes the parallel doctrine of *jihad* seem so exotic today. Yet, arguably, *jihad*'s sibling, the just war doctrine, is making a comeback as we will see below.

The natural law approach remained the dominant one until the late 16th and early 17th century when Italian jurist Alberico Gentili published *De Jure Belli* (1598) and Grotius *De Jure Belli ac Pacis* (1625). While Grotius' work is widely seen as the first major book on the subject of modern international law, it was Gentili who began to step away from a strictly natural law approach to the law between nations, and towards a more secular attitude. Grotius then took this secular approach a step further by also affirming Suarez' belief that states could create laws amongst themselves, an act known as positive law or 'man-made' law. While some observers, such as von Pufendorf, continued to stress the dominance of natural law, positive law gained more influence from the 17th century onwards. Most debates and works on international law from that period on combined the natural and positive law approaches, as reflected in the works of de Vattel (1805).

Grotius' work, as Oppenheim observed, "conquered the world and became the basis of all following development" (1912: 17) regarding modern international law and particularly its relationship with, and influence on, the use of force by states. Grotius lamented the frequent recourse to war and inquired into its lawfulness, yet he never totally condemned the use of force as a means for pursuing a state's interest (2001: 23). He did distinguish between attack and defense with regard to the use of force and established three justifiable causes for the use of force by a state, namely defense, indemnity and punishment (2001: 62). He opposed the use of force for financial advantages and called for war to be formally declared.

Grotius's writings alone, however, were not enough to establish and develop modern international law. The Peace of Westphalia in 1648 put into practice the theory as present in the writings of Grotius, Gentili and others. The Peace of Westphalia was seen as marking the emergence of the modern state and, with it, as giving rise to the concept of international law as understood today. The treaties of Westphalia furthermore established the modern concept of both internal and external state sovereignty, declaring states the only relevant actors within the international system and stating their right to independence and non-interference. Yet, paradoxically, this meant they retained a right to intervene as central to sovereignty.

This doctrine of non-intervention was, indeed, the main aspect of this era and saw its culmination in Kant. He proposed ways of permanently ending the use of force in the international system. Kant saw the natural state of things as one of war but added that reason "absolutely condemns war as a means of determining the right" (1983: 116). In his preliminary articles for perpetual peace amongst nations, Kant called for the respect for the principles of sovereignty and non-intervention, as well as disarmament. In order to fulfill the dream of perpetual peace Kant (1983: 111–12), similar to the French writer Abbé de Saint-Pierre's 1713 proposal of an international federation of states and court, suggested the establishment of a league of peace. His concept of sovereignty meant non-intervention.

During the 18th century, following the industrial revolution, which led to greater economic and political interdependence between states, war was increasingly viewed as an instrument that governments should not be able to deploy at their every whim. This became particularly clear in the French Republican Constitution of 1791, established during the French Revolution. The Constitution stated in Chapter 3 On The Exercise of the Legislative Power (Article 2) that if it were found by the legislative that war were "a culpable aggression of the part of the ministers, or of any other agent of the executive power, the perpetrator of the aggression shall be prosecuted criminally". However, this was domestic law: there was no corresponding doctrine in international law.

The Road to Codification

In the mid-19th century the first substantial shift in the area of international law and the use of force by states was witnessed. The years until the commencement of the First World War saw the establishment of five core factors: first, the promotion of arbitration; second the start of the progressive codification of international law including the use of force by states; third the establishment of a doctrine of self-defense; fourth the creation of international humanitarian law and, fifth, the foundation of the world's first regional organization, unlike a military alliance, to intervene collectively rather than unilaterally on the basis of order and justice not state interest.

The main trigger for this shift in international war law can be found in the Revolutionary and Napoleonic Wars of 1792–1815, with its more than three million casualties. 'Inspired' by this substantial loss of life, a number of peace societies emerged, most notably the Quaker-established Society for the Promotion of Permanent and Universal Peace. These societies opposed war and promoted arbitration and international law as an alternative to the use of force. As a consequence of these movements, the first World Peace Congress took place in London in 1843. The conference recommended the establishment of a council of states, as well as embracing arbitration and disarmament as ways of limiting the use of force in the international system. The planned bi-annual congresses did not, however, continue as regularly as envisaged.

This was a policy direction by non-state actors. Yet, there were signs states were moving in the same direction. The treaty of 1815 between Russia, Austria-Hungary, Prussia and the UK against Napoleon spoke repeatedly in legalistic language of the justice of combining to uphold the peace treaty of 1814 and the Congress of Vienna, and to ensure the 'security', 'tranquility', 'order' and 'general peace' of Europe 'against all violation' and "under the protection of which the rights, the freedom and the independence of nations have been established and secured". Those who supported Napoleon's challenge to the above would be brought to 'justice'. The basis of the first modern notions of 'self-defense', 'war crimes', 'international peace and security' and 'collective security' are clearly detectable.

Yet, in advancing a doctrine of intervention to suppress further revolutionary republican outbreaks in Europe and Latin America, the so-called Concert of Europe and especially the Holy Alliance (Russia, Prussia and Austria-Hungary) propounded a path which could undermine the development of the legal doctrine of non-intervention which was, in its earliest stages, not dissimilar to today's new doctrine of 'liberal interventionism'. Similarly, Britain and France respectively, exhibited an almost converse doctrine of intervention in support of self-determination in Greece and Belgium. Even today's Christian-Muslim antagonism was present, expressed in the actions against the Ottoman Empire and Egypt.

In the Southern hemisphere, President Simòn Bolìvar's proposal for a league of American states at the 1826 Congress of Panama, contained a concept of a mutual defense pact between his Gran Colombia (today's Colombia, Panama, Ecuador and Venezuela), Peru, Mexico and the United Provinces of Central America. In the end only Gran Colombia ratified the notably titled Treaty of Union, League, and Perpetual Confederation. The dream soon broke up over civil and national conflicts. Yet, this also marked the path not only towards the Organization of American States (OAS) but also to both the League of Nations and the UN.

The further development of the formal international rules governing the use of force by states was just one part of these substantial developments in the international system. The causes were long-term but the increasingly larger wars of the 1850s, 60s and 70s were immediate triggers. There were significant new initiatives in four respects: international law, academic institutions, international non-governmental organizations and international agreements for cooperation between states.

In international law, the Paris Declaration of 1856 abolished privateering, thus banning war-like actions by non-state actors if not states themselves. The US Republic was the first state to outlaw mercenaries in 1794 and by the Second World War nearly two thirds of states had followed suit (Burmester 1978). The Geneva Convention of 1864 created an unprecedented legal protection of the wounded on the battlefield. The Lieber Code (Instructions for the Government of the US Army in the Field) was passed by the US Congress the previous year. The St. Petersburg Declaration of 1868 renounced the use of explosives projectiles under 400g in weight in times of war. The Brussels Declaration of 1874 on the laws and customs of war was never ratified but formed a basis for the Hague Conference of 1899. The Brussels Declaration had been initiated by the Russian Czar, advised by Friedrich Fromhold Martens, an ethnic-Estonian Russian diplomat and lawyer, who contributed its main proposals.

In academic institutions, two early developments were the publication of Henry Wheaton's *Elements of International Law* in 1836 and William Oke Mannings' *Commentaries on the Law of Nations* three years later. The 1848 Revolutions and Crimean, Italian Independence and American Civil wars provided much stimulus for new thinking on international law. In 1854 Lord Robert Phillimore published *Commentaries on International Law* and in 1860 Montague Bernard, just appointed the first Chichele Professor of International Law and Diplomacy at Oxford University, published *Principles of Non-intervention.* English law scholar John Westlake published in 1858 his *Treatise on Private International Law,* followed by Terenzio Mamiani della Rovere's *Rights of Nations* and, the same year, Theodore Dwight Woolsey's *Introduction to the Study of International Law.* Henry Wager Halleck in 1861 published *Rules Regulating the Intercourse of States in War and Peace*, the same year as Travis Twisser's *The Law of Nations considered as Independent Political Communities*. In 1863 Carlos Cavlo published *International Law of Europe and America in Theory and Practice*. James Lorimer took the University of Edinburgh Chair in Public Law and Law of Nations in 1862 and William Vernon Harcourt was appointed the first Whewell Chair of International Law at Cambridge in 1869. Europe's first academic journal of international law, *Revue de droit international et de législation comparée*, started circulating the year prior.

The wars of German unification provided further stimulus, especially the Franco-Prussian war of 1871–72. August Wilhelm Heffter's, *Le Droit International Public de L'Europe* followed in 1873. The same year F.F. Martens was appointed Professor of International Law at St Petersburg, publishing his *International Law of Civilised Nations*, a decade later, a year before Lorimer's *The Institutes of the Law of Nations*. The year 1880 was a bumper one, with Sheldon Amos, of the University College London, publishing his significantly entitled *Political and Legal Remedies for War*, the first edition of Hall's *Treatise on International Law* being released, and the publication of I. Camazza-Amari's *Traite De Droit International en Temps de Paix*.

The output continued with P. Pradier-Fodere's *Traite de Droit International Europeen et Americain* in 1885 and T.J. Lawrence's *Principles of International Law* in 1897. France's Antoine Pillet *Principes de droit international prive* appeared in 1903, the same year as the new English edition of *Perpetual Peace*, with Lassa Oppenheim's *International Law: A Treatise* following in 1905. That year, the American Society of International Law was established and started the first academic journal of international law in English. The symbolism is obvious in that Emeric Cruce's *The New Cyneas* was republished in 1909, reviving his call for an international council for discussion of conflicts in order to avoid war.

The 19th century also witnessed the establishment of the first permanent international non-governmental organizations. The International Committee of the International Red Cross and the American Red Cross were created in 1863 and 1881 respectively, following the Battle of Solferino and the American Civil War. In quick succession after the Franco-Prussian War, the International Penal and Penitentiary Commission and Brussels' International Law Association were established in 1872. The following year the *Institut de Droit International Penal (IDIP)* was founded at Gent. In 1880 at Oxford the *IDIP* adopted the *The Manual of Laws and Customs of War*. The International Union of Penal Law and the Inter-Parliamentary Union were established in 1889.

States also began to see the virtues of international co-operation, especially in policy areas more distant from sensitive questions of sovereignty, such as the use of force. States agreed to establish the Telegraphic Union in 1865, the Universal Postal Union in 1874, the International Meteorological Organization in 1878 and the Convention for the Protection of Submarine Cables in 1884. The limits on such cooperation were reflected in the reluctance of states to take up the 1874 proposal by Gustav Moynier for the establishment of an international criminal court, as well as Bluntschli's new concept of war crimes for which the Geneva Convention had laid the basis (Pemberton 2008). The Concert of Europe, by no means permanent let alone widely international, but one foundation for the future League of Nations, reached the height of its power in the 1878 Congress of Berlin. The Spanish-American War of 1898 relegated the Congress to history in opening a new, more truly international era. At the first International Conference of American states in 1889–90, 18 states founded the International Union of American Republics (IUAR), with a permanent secretariat, making it the world's oldest regional organization. This attested to the growing trend towards international cooperation and collective defense albeit on a regional basis.

Promoting Peace

The continuing primacy of state sovereignty was reflected in the fact that the promotion of arbitration, before the recourse to war, was the cornerstone of the development of international law in the area of the use of force during the 19th and early 20th century and not the proscription of war. Writing in 1892, America's

Eleanor L. Lord noted the increase in the application of arbitration in the settlement of disputes by states from the 1850s onwards. Lord stated that arbitration was more popular due to the improvement of international law and diplomacy, as well as “the growth of democratic ideas leading to the participation of the people in questions of peace and war” (1892: 49). T.J. Lawrence (1895: 464–72), Professor of International Law at the Royal Naval War College, Greenwich, also discussed the prevention of war through arbitration in an optimistic manner. Kant would have approved.

The First Hague Conference on the Pacific Settlement of International Disputes in 1899 established the Permanent Court of Arbitration, thereby giving states a stable point of contact for the mediation of disputes. The Hague Conference was matched by the establishment of the Central American Court of Justice in 1907, as well as a number of bilateral arbitration agreements between states. Most notable were the 1903 Agreement [between the United Kingdom and France] providing for the Settlement by Arbitration of Certain Classes of Questions which may arise between the Two Governments, the Arbitration Convention between the United Kingdom and the United States of America in 1908, and the establishment of the Treaties for the Advancement of Peace by the United States in 1913–14. Known as the Bryan Treaties, the latter agreements promised the use of arbitration before resort to force in instances of disputes. By the beginning of the First World War, the principle of arbitration as a means to settle disputes had gained widespread acceptance but states had stopped well short of restricting their right to go to war.

To Intervene or Not to Intervene

The first major attempt to codify international law with regard to the resort to force by states was the Declaration of Paris in 1856 which had concentrated on maritime law in time of war. At the first IUAR conference in 1890, members agreed not to recognize territorial acquisitions made through the use of force.

The Hague Conferences of 1899 and 1907 were seen as setting in concrete the codification of the laws of war. Article 1 of the First Hague Conference stated as its aim “obviating, as far as possible, recourse to force in the relations between states ... to use their best efforts to insure the pacific settlement of international differences”. The use of force for the recovery of contract debts was prohibited and rules on humanitarian law and arbitration established: the first time that such detailed regulations on the use of force and behavior in war had been incorporated into international law since the Geneva Convention of 1864. Writers of the time, such as American delegate Frederick W. Holls (1900), viewed the conferences as bringing impressive results. Despite this and the belief that conflicts would become fewer and less intense, Lord viewed the outlawing of war as being something not possible at that time.

With regard to the codification of the international law of war, there was a further focus on the issue of intervention. As we have seen, the Holy Alliance agreed on a principle of military intervention to suppress all democratic and national efforts within states in order to uphold the European political order, in particular the monarchical system of governments. Membership was restricted to some of the core European powers, most notably Austria, Russia and Prussia which, as reflected in the Holy Alliance Treaty of 1815, saw themselves "all as members of one and the same Christian nation". This suppression of democratic and republican ambitions occurred within the German Federation, Italy, Greece and Spain. The Monroe Doctrine of 1823 can, in many ways, be seen as a reaction by the US to these policies. US President James Monroe in his Annual Message to Congress argued that "the American continents ... are henceforth not to be considered as subjects for future colonization by any European power" (1823: 13–14): a doctrine of non-intervention to counter a new doctrine of intervention which did not develop into a principle of international law. The pre-emption doctrine of 2003, as will be discussed later, may prove as stillborn a challenge to orthodox international law.

The question of the permissibility of the international use of force remained then, as it does today, a core concern. Military intervention was largely, as University of Pennsylvania International Law Professor William E. Lingelbach put it, an integral and essential part of international law and "an act of police for enforcing recognized rights, and the only means, apart from war, for enforcing the rules of international law" (1900: 32). Yet, how was this right of intervention reconciled with a doctrine of non-intervention also at the core of modern sovereignty?

As we will see in greater detail, a doctrine of intervention soon (1880) to be termed 'humanitarian', was already in development, commonly justified by fusing modern secular humanitarian notions with older notions of Christian superiority. The story is complex but there is much in the early development of modern international law where 'foreign', 'uncivilized' and even non-Christian (all three are sometimes used as synonyms) elements were not accorded the same legal rights as their counterparts. In the 19th century German jurist and diplomat Georg Friedrich de Martens wrote "vis-à-vis non civilized nations ... intervention by the civilized powers is in principle legitimate when the Christian populace of those countries is exposed to persecutions and massacres" (Fonteyne 1974: 219). Interventions by various European powers against the Ottoman Empire ostensibly for the protection of Christians occurred over Greece (1827–30), Syria (1860–61), Crete (1866), Bosnia, Herzegovina and Bulgaria (1876–8) and Macedonia (1903–08, 1912–13). Even among the Christian European world, the concept was entertained as legal. Protests against Russian behavior were not followed by intervention for obvious military reasons. The US and European powers protested about policies in Peru and the US used humanitarian grounds as part of the basis for its intervention in Cuba.

According to Oppenheim, dealing with the issue in great detail in his *magnum opus* of 1905–06, interventions were permissible for the sake of self-preservation, if they served the interests of a balance of power (only, however, in the absence of an international organization of states), and on humanitarian grounds (1912: 55).

American Amos Hershey expanded the permissibility of intervention to include those cases undertaken for the purpose of "preventing or terminating illegal and unjustifiable intervention in the affairs of a fellow-member of international society" (1898: 58). This was the case, for example, when in 1895, Russia, France and Germany forced Japan, through intervention, to return territory in Southern Manchuria which it had earlier forcefully annexed from China. The collective nature of this counter intervention arguably gave it greater legitimacy: perhaps a foretaste of post-1920 collective security.

With reference to US actions in Cuba in 1898, E.J. Phelps, diplomat and Professor of Law at Yale, stated that intervention by force of arms would be a 'crime'. He conceded only 'necessary self-defense' as a justifiable forcible intervention, though adding, that the "sole and rare exception ... where to prevent unjustifiable slaughter and outrage in another country it becomes absolutely necessary" (Editorial 1898).

In 1913, American Professor of Law at Yale, Edwin Borchard wrote "where a state under exceptional circumstances disregards certain rights of its own citizens, over whom it presumably has absolute sovereignty, the other states of the family of nations are authorized by international law to intervene on grounds of humanity" (1913: 507). French compatriot, Antoine Rougier, published an often quoted article on the subject in 1910.

States and, in particular, writers on the international use of force, increasingly believed that the doctrine of absolute sovereignty had become obsolete. This was best reflected in the issue of humanitarian intervention: a doctrine arising from the modern notion of universal human rights, dating from even before the American and French Revolutions which it inspired. The original assumption was, like Kant, that republican constitutions would ensure respect for human rights: at least for their own citizens. What about people outside these republics? If rights were universal, did not the republican states have a duty to all humanity despite the principle of local sovereignty?

English lawyer William Edward Hall, despite being described by American Ellery C. Stowell as a "severe ... critic of humanitarian intervention" (1921: 126), was the first legal writer to propose a systematic approach. Hall (1884: 262) acknowledged that the use of force against tyrannical conduct of government gave outside states the moral, if not yet the legal, right to intervene. Lingelbach (1900: 25), however, opposed intervention in the internal affairs of other states and was critical of humanitarian intervention. Oppenheim (1905) was also cautious about the topic, hoping that over time intervention, taken on a collective or multilateral basis, would be recognized. Overall, state sovereignty remained paramount.

From Excuse to Doctrine

The third major feature in the development of international law in the time leading up to the First World War, was the establishment of the doctrine of self-defense which previously did not need to be legally formulated as an explicit right while states retained an unlimited right to self-help.

In 1837 the *Caroline*, a ship owned by US nationals, was allegedly providing assistance to Canadian rebels fighting the UK. The ship was set on fire in US waters by British troops and several Americans killed in, what the British authorities claimed to be, an act of self-defense. In the correspondence between the US Secretary of State, Daniel Webster, and the British Ambassador at Washington, Henry Fox, regarding the arrest and imprisonment of a Mr. McLeod for the destruction of the *Caroline*, Webster stated that in order for the use of force to be considered self-defense "it will be for the government to show a necessity of self-defense, instant, overwhelming, leaving no choice of means, and no moment for deliberation" (1857: 1129). Little did Webster know that these requisites would remain recognized by states up to the current time, thereby turning into customary international law which informs the interpretation of the more explicit provisions of the UN Charter. *Caroline* would also resurface as part of the US justification for the intervention in Iraq in 2003 (Bush 2003b, Government of the United States of America 2002).

The *Caroline* incident, according to British jurist and later ICJ judge R.Y. Jennings, changed "self-defense ... from a political excuse to a legal doctrine" (1938: 82). Hersch Lauterpacht stressed the dangers inherent in such a doctrine of self-defense, stating that only an outside authority, not states themselves, could assess whether a situation warranted genuine self-defense or not (1952: 159). He consequently promoted a system of collective self-defense as a "proper expression of the ultimate identity of interest of the international community in the preservation of peace" (1952: 156): thereby laying the legal foundations for the concept of collective security as a preferable alternative to self-help in the form of self-defense. No accepted legal doctrine of self-defense arose before the First World War. The emphasis, as we have seen, was placed on prior arbitration as an alternative to restricting war. There was a second alternative or complementary path which received more attention than self-defense: humanitarian law in war.

The Necessity of Humanity

The establishment of international humanitarian law had an important impact on the regulation of the use of force by states as it recognized the inhuman conditions to which military personnel were subject in time of war. The foundation of the International Committee of the Red Cross in 1863 and the First Geneva Convention of 1864 were aimed at protecting the military victims of armed conflict. States increasingly recognized that there was a need to "conciliate the necessities of war with the laws of humanity", as stated in the Declaration of St. Petersburg in 1868. The pronouncement further prohibited the use of certain weapons and agreed to limit the use of force to weaken, rather than annihilate, the enemy. Yet, states did not seem interested in Swiss jurist Gustave Moynier's more radical proposal for an international criminal court to try those accused of violating the new international law of Geneva and St. Petersburg (Pemberton 2008). The ban on certain weapons and technology in war was reinforced by the Hague Conferences on the Pacific Settlement of International Disputes in 1899 and 1907. In 1908, Germany's Alex Meyer made the first study of anticipated laws of aerial warfare in *Die Erschließung des Luftraums und ihre rechtlichen Folgen* [The legal consequences of 'opening up' air space]. This path of limiting force in war may be seen as either a supplement or an alternative to limiting the recourse to force.

The Zero-Sum Game

Britain's 1933 Nobel Peace Prize recipient Norman Angell, in his ground-breaking publication *The Great Illusion*, said that the use of force was a decreasing factor in human affairs and that cooperation was being viewed as more important than ever (1911: 144). Similar to Angell, Oppenheim also previously believed that the "independence of every state finds its limitation in the independence of every other state" (1919: 77–8). Angell did not believe that war was economically profitable, given the growing interdependence in the area of trade, which in his eyes had led to the formation of an international bond or union. This is a view later shared by another leading British liberal G. Lowes Dickinson (1917). The fact that many did see the international use of force as psychologically and economically profitable is what Angell views as "the great illusion".

The lead-up to and beginning of the First World War gave further stimulus to the infant concept of collective security against threats which we have seen embryonically in the Concert of Europe, Holy Alliance and the intervention against Japan. English liberal J.A. Hobson formulated the idea that states would have to cede their right to use force to an international organization, as well as binding themselves to "make concerted war at the behest of this new international authority" (1915: 81). The dissolution of the *IDIP* at the outbreak of war in 1914 symbolized the halt in pre-war momentum towards a more comprehensive structure of international law including against war.

Summary

There had been major developments in international law prior to 1914 yet these had mainly addressed the need to restrain violence in war rather than restrain war itself. Hall rightly observed that international law, while forced to accept war, at least did determine "the maximum of violence which can be regarded as necessary at a given time" (1884: 62). This was a succinct and accurate if regrettably resigned, statement of the position.

In 1914 the rules for the use of force which were in existence failed to stop a conflict which turned out to be the first global war witnessed by the international system. The European powers allowed the assassination of Austrian archduke Franz Ferdinand to develop into the bloodiest conflict to that date. Very soon after the outbreak of the war, the belligerent governments began mounting a case for which state was responsible for-indeed guilty of-starting the war. Such a burden of guilt required a legal framework which clearly pronounced some types of war illegal.

The All-Russian Congress in 1917, committed to disengaging post-Czarist Russia from the war, declared aggressive war a crime against humankind (Ferencz 1972: 491). Few in the West would take the pronouncement of a revolutionary government seriously. Many moderate liberals in Europe, however, like Dickinson, Hobson and Australian-born Oxford Professor, Gilbert Murray, now shared a similar, if not as extreme, perspective. Dickinson declared the same year that "war is insanity" (1917: 116). Yet, war on any basis was not yet illegal. Samuel P. Orth, Yale's Professor of Political Science, accurately stated "international thinking [international consent] has not yet come to the point of outlawing war, as municipal law has outlawed the mob" (1916: 340). In the aftermath of the outbreak of the war, many leading figures, liberal and conservative alike, now worked assiduously to move international law and policy in that direction.

By 1917, British lawyer Alexander Pierce Higgins, editor of Hall's *A Treatise on International Law*, wrote that international law may have "often been quietly ignored or brutally disregarded [but] no state could venture to declare itself independent of it" (1917: xviii). International law had achieved this importance by limiting state violence in war, as well as establishing arbitration as precedent to the use of force. The religious notion of just war theory had been replaced with the secular concept of international law. As a consequence of this shift, and the establishment of the concept of sovereignty, there existed, however, a paradox between the doctrine of intervention and non-intervention. This intensified in the post-First World War period.

Chapter 2
Renouncing Luxury: International Law and the Use of Force in the Interwar Years

La guerre d'aggression est un crime![1]

Vespasian V. Pella (1925: 3)

The First World War demonstrated that even though international law regarding the use of force had changed, most notably through the growing acceptance of arbitration as a prior step to war, it failed to stop the outbreak of such a catastrophe. The post-1919 era, consequently, saw more substantial moves towards the further restraint on the use of force in the international system and the development of a security framework other than self-help. The years until the Second World War were defined by three core developments: first, the placement of growing limitations on the use of force through numerous non-intervention and war renunciation treaties; second, the recognition that wars of aggression, as yet undefined, constituted an international crime; third, the establishment of the first permanent international (as opposed to regional) organization entrusted with the securing of peace.

Treating War, Preserving Peace

The League of Nations Covenant, in its preamble, bound its members to the acceptance of an obligation not to resort to war. This was a significant step but by no means did it outlaw war totally. States' obligations, as reflected in Article 12, were largely limited to presenting their disputes for arbitration and adhering to a three-month period of delay before resorting to force, including further restrictions on the resort to war as inherent in Articles 13(4) and 15(6).

The rule for such a 'cooling-off' period was similar to that of the Bryan Treaties of 1912 and was viewed, as time developed, as largely ineffective. Britain's J.L. Brierly, however, defended this approach, stating that "if nations are resolved on war in such a case, no scheme for preserving peace, however theoretically perfect, will hold them back" (1928: 214). Others disagreed.

After the Second World War many more liberals and conservatives, in the American sense, had come to believe in the necessity of the prohibition of war and the enforcement of international rules on both sides of the Atlantic. In England,

1 "War of aggression is a crime".

Dickinson now suggested the establishment of an international force for the protection of peace and security while acknowledging the difficulties in realizing such an aim. He insisted, however, that collective security arrangements, in form of a league of nations, was a realistic and workable project. Dickinson, Hobson and Murray opposed war generally speaking, with Murray declaring it "a luxury which modern civilization cannot afford" (1929: 36). Yet, all three acknowledged that the use of force in some instances, for example for the reestablishment of peace in Europe, could be necessary (Murray 1914). At the University of Chicago, where he was in charge of the massive multi-authored and multi-disciplinary *Study of War*, Professor of International Law, Quincy Wright (1924: 766), believed that an increasing demand for the elimination of war in the international system could be witnessed. In Europe similar views were held by the German turned-Swiss Professor of Law Ottfried Nippold (1923).

This steady shift in academic legal opinion was reflected in state practice. Under the Locarno treaties of 1925, Germany, France and Belgium renounced the use of war against each other. Aside from the establishment of the League of Nations, the most important treaty of the decades between the two world wars was the Pact of Paris, also known as the Kellogg-Briand Pact, of 1928. The treaty, consisting of only three articles, was signed by 63 states. Article 1 stated that the contracting parties "condemn recourse to war for the solution of international controversies, and renounce it, as an instrument of national policy". While it was the first time that war had been so clearly condemned, the Pact did not totally outlaw war. Instead, it permitted the use of force in instances of self-defense, for the purpose of enforcing international obligations or sanctions and, at least theoretically, against states which were not contracting parties to the pact. The term 'war' was not defined, something states would use as a legal loophole to resort to the use of force without declaring their actions to be war.

The growing acceptance of the ideas in the Pact were reflected in the Stimson Doctrine of 1932. In response to the Italian attack on Abyssinia (1930) and the Japanese annexation of Manchuria (1931), the US announced that it would not accept any treaties, agreements or actions inconsistent with the Kellogg-Briand Pact. The forceful acquisition of territory and the possible establishment of a new state following from it, were therefore not recognized. The renunciation of war as an instrument of policy implicitly created a category of illegitimate war. Yet, since the fading of the religious based just war doctrine, there was no such clearly defined category in modern international law. A war of aggression was obviously the new illegitimate category of war.

Crimes and Misdemeanors

The Treaty of Versailles established the concept of war as an act of aggression in the mainstream of the international system in a way in which the all-Russian declaration of peace, stating aggression was a crime against mankind, did not

(Ferencz 1972: 491). Under Article 231 of the Treaty, Germany accepted sole responsibility for the war, described as an act of aggression. Germany's Kaiser Wilhelm I was accused of being a war criminal, a term which had now a strong legitimacy since Swiss jurist Johann Kaspar Bluntschli first coined it in the 1870s, not least of all for waging an aggressive war and violating treaty obligations relating to Belgian neutrality. Reinforcing this development was the Treaty of Sèvres (1920) between the allies and the Ottoman Empire which, according to Pemberton (2008) identified a category of international crime, distinct from war crimes – crimes against humanity. The Belgian minister and Professor of International Law, Edouard Deschamps, recommended, in 1920, a High Court of International Justice, along the lines of the 1907 Hague Conference proposal, to deal with crimes constituting a breach of international public order, including the crime of waging war.

The legacy of Versailles was reflected in both Article 1 of the Draft Treaty of Mutual Assistance (1923) and Article 2 of the abortive Geneva Protocol (1924) which declared wars of aggression to be an international crime although neither became effective. Symbolizing the refreshed determination of governments to cooperate in restricting international crimes including war crimes, the *UIDP* was revived in Paris in March 1924. Romania's Vespasian Pella was in attendance and, having completed his legal studies in Paris, was busy finishing his major work *La Criminalité collective des États et le droit penal de l'avenir,* which opens with the blunt exclamation that "war of aggression is a crime" (1925: 3). The Inter Parliamentary Union in 1924 at Berne, following the lead of the League of Nations, recommended a draft penal code for nations. Pella was *rapporteur* at the subsequent Washington conference in October 1925 attended by representatives of 41 governments. He published his contribution to the conference shortly after as *La guerre d'aggression et la constitution d'un droit répressif de nations*.

Driving this reinvigorated push for the restriction of the recourse to war was not just moral repugnance to the horrific consequences of the First World War. Political self-interest, as always, played a role. Pella's Romania was a key anti-revisionist state. It had benefited enormously in territorial terms from the post-war settlement (Treaty of Trianon). Yugoslavia, Bulgaria, Czechoslovakia, Poland, even France, as well as the three Baltic states all had an interest in maintaining the post-war *status quo*. As armed force was the only likely way that the *status quo* would be disturbed, it was in their interest to develop a strong international legal regime against the use of such armed force, including not only by states but also by non-state actors such as terrorists (Pemberton 2008). The Soviet Union, which had suffered one post-war attempt already at the 'revision' of its revolution, shared the desire for a strong anti-aggression regime.

Despite ever-widening agreement that war of aggression was illegal, a major problem remained that no definition of aggression existed, making it difficult to establish a universal condemnation of such an act. Attempts to achieve a more detailed condemnation of war of aggression continued. The Protocol for the Pacific Settlement of International Disputes of 1924, a resolution by the

League of Nations Assembly, stated in Article 10 that "every state which resorts to war in violation of the undertakings contained in the Covenant or in the present Protocol is an aggressor". This included a refusal to submit disputes to the procedure of pacific settlement. In 1927 the League Assembly furthermore passed a resolution, submitted by anti-revisionist Poland, condemning all wars of aggression as international crimes (Cecil 1933). The following year the Pan-American Conference adopted a resolution which stated that "war of aggression constitutes a crime against the human species [and] all aggression is illicit and as such is declared prohibited" (Scott 1928: 357).

By the start of the next decade, the international *status quo* was coming under increased pressure. As well as Italian actions in Abyssinia and Japanese in Manchuria, war broke out between Bolivia and Paraguay over the Grand Chaco region in 1932. In 1933 both the London Convention on the Definition of Aggression and the Convention for the Definition of Aggression (between the Soviet Union and its neighbors) took place. The latter was more specific and declared an aggressor to be a state which was the first to commit any of the following actions: a declaration of war; invasion by armed force; attack on territory, vessels and aircrafts; naval blockade; and provision of support to armed bands formed in its territory. The latter is an early expression of today's state-sponsored terrorism.

Wright now picked up the baton from Pella to lead the academic legal debate, describing an aggressor in 1935 as "a state which is under an obligation not to resort to force, which is employing force against another state, and which refuses to accept an armistice proposed in accordance with a procedure which it has accepted to implement its no-force obligation (and such an aggressor) may be subjected to preventative, deterrent or remedial measures by other states bound by that obligation" (1935: 395).

The international community, however, seemed no closer to a universal definition of aggression despite the fact that in 1935 a Committee of Experts at the League of Nations had drafted a definition of terrorism in which Pella played a leading role. Significantly, the League's Committee on the Codification of International Law did not incorporate war crimes including war of aggression within its terms of reference probably because it felt, wrongly, it could secure agreement on non-state violence but probably correctly not on war (Pemberton 2008).

The desire by some for a clear and accepted definition of aggression became more urgent later in the decade. In 1936, Germany committed the first forcible act of revision when it marched into and re-militarized the Rhineland. The Spanish Civil War erupted the same year. Japan escalated its conflict with China to open war in 1937. The following year Germany absorbed Austria, the Sudetenland and, finally, all Czechoslovakia. These ominous developments inspired English writer Leonard Woolf, husband of Virginia, to observe that, for such aggressive or revisionist states, "the prevention of war is no longer considered important" (1933: 7).

The ultimately unsuccessful attempt at defining aggression inevitably raised the separate but distinct question of which wars were legal. Dijon's Professor of Law Georges Scelle, a former student of Antoine Pillet, expressed an extreme anti-war view, equating every resort to international violence with war and every war with aggression. Thus, every act of war was illegal (1936: 377–79). Here Scelle virtually echoes Kant's implicit doctrine of absolute non-intervention.

The importance attached to the issue of non-intervention following the experiences of the First World War, was well reflected in Article 10 of the League Covenant in which Members agreed to "undertake and preserve as against external aggression the territorial integrity and existing political independence" of the signatories. Britain's Polish-born Professor of Law, Hersch Lauterpacht, reflected this dominant view of the time by stating that "there is, in international law, no right [and no corresponding duty] more absolute, more rigid and more formal than freedom from external interference" (1927: 156–57). The principle of absolute state sovereignty remained, based primarily on the belief that sovereignty followed from the right to independence. As intervention violated this independence, it was presumed illegal (Mosler 1937: 31). Of course, this did not raise, let alone solve, the perennial dilemma of whether a state can intervene to stop another's prior intervention.

The further push to establish formally this principle of non-intervention took place in 1936 when European governments agreed in principle with regard to non-interference in the Spanish Civil War. The volunteers of the International Brigade showed that a part of the Left still believed in armed intervention even if liberals and conservatives did not. The Pan-American Conference's Additional Protocol Relative to Non-Intervention furthermore stated in Article 1 that "the high contracting parties declare inadmissible the intervention of any one of them, directly or indirectly, and for whatever reason, in the internal or external affairs of any other of the parties". Nevertheless, many states found ways of supporting sides in the conflict. Of course, Latin American states, which had won their independence from Spain and Portugal, like the new European states, and non-colonized Asia, jealously valued their sovereignty and were strongly for non-intervention.

Legal authorities, such as Australia's former League official and later Professor of Law, J.G. Starke, a staunch non-interventionist of Russian parentage, deplored states in Spain "virtually declar[ing] open season for breaches of the law" (1947: 62). The liberal University of Bonn's Professor of Law, Herman Mosler, in his daring book, argued against interventionist doctrines but criticized the contemporary literature for elevating the principle of non-intervention to the status of a dogma whose basis was no longer being questioned (1937: 10).

Despite the theoretical dominance of non-interventionism, states continued to intervene – Italy in Abyssinia, Germany in the Sudetenland and Japan in Manchuria. Ironically, as is shown below, all justified their intervention in varying terms as defense of what would soon become known as human rights. Liberals rightly rejected such pretences.

The position of non-intervention had considerable popular and political support at this time due to the strong pacifist sentiment in many parts of the world, ranging from liberal across to conservative ranks. Lord Robert Cecil was a conservative politician educated at the liberal University College London. After working for the Red Cross during the Great War, from 1916 he advocated proposals for the avoidance of war including through a mechanism not unlike the eventual League (1933: 266). An Esperantist, he was President of Britain's League of Nations Union 1921 to 1945 and published *The Way to Peace* in 1928.

Liberals agreed with Cecil's views. Francis Anderson, the retired Scottish-born Professor of Philosophy at the University of Sydney remained deeply active in the League of Nations Union whose values he shared. Anderson observed that the attitude towards the use of force had changed with the international system "beginning to see war as it is [as] ... a crime against humanity" (1935: 7).

Others had views more located in the middle-ground: some wars were justified. Joachim von Elbe was a liberal of a very different stripe to Anderson. He was a German diplomat and lawyer of partly Jewish background, educated in liberal Hamburg, which denied him public office and lead to his departure to the US in 1934. He argued that the use of force by states was illegal unless undertaken for just causes (1939: 688). Yet, in order to establish in which instances the resort to force was legal, aggression had to be defined, a view supported by numerous other writers such as Pella, Britain's (soon to be Australian-based) Julius Stone and Lithuanian lawyer and diplomat Lazare Kopelmanas (1937: 244).

Wright (1925) went further, stating that it was not only aggression but self-defense which required definition. Like Stowell before him, Brierly took a robust view on the legitimate use of force. He certainly believed some wars to be just: notably in self-defense, adding that it constituted "the clearest of legal justifications for intervention" (1928: 157). No authority seriously questioned whether a state had a right to self-defense under customary international law. Wright's views were reflected in the US government's correspondence associated with the Kellog-Briand Pact which made explicit references to the right of self-defense (Atherton 1928). Yet self-defense like aggression remained undefined through to the war.

A definition of self-defence would not even be addressed comprehensively with the UN Charter and would only be partly achieved with the Nicaragua judgment of 1986. The lack of effort in defining self-defense at this time was probably because most authorities preferred the development of collective security rather than self-helping self-defense as the path to international peace and security.

Paying the Price

The decades after 1919 witnessed a move towards breaking the dominance of the principle of absolute state sovereignty, as states had to adhere to certain rules by being members of the League and other treaties. The right to intervention was furthermore reflected in the Peace Treaty of Versailles which allowed the victorious states of the First World War to, for example, occupy German territory and control the country's economy temporarily. The League of Nations Covenant in Article 10, 16 and 17 permitted intervention of the organization, particularly with regard to sanctions, in both the affairs of members and non-signatories. The Soviet Union and Nazi-Germany, too, established what they believed to be their rights to intervene. Grewe states that this clash of different perceptions meant that the principle of non-intervention, which continued to be formally upheld and confirmed, became more complicated than ever before in practice (1984: 70).

Liberals, similar to Kant, had believed that the empowering of public opinion by enfranchisement and institutional mobilization through peace societies and bodies like the Union for Democratic Control, would prevent democratic states going to war. After the war, some came to believe non-intervention could only be guaranteed ultimately by the threat or act of intervention or, to put it more accurately, counter-intervention. As Brierly realistically put it, the international system could "no longer rely on moral influences to secure the observance of law, which must henceforth be enforced" (1924: 125). Such a right to counter-intervention was, as we have seen, reflected in the Peace Treaty of Versailles' provisions on Germany.

While seeking to close one door to intervention, the League was opening others. The League was the first international organization to make it its purpose to "promote international co-operation and to achieve international peace and security". The organization thereby established the concept of collective security through an international body, as opposed to alliances. In Article 16, the Covenant established this collective approach by stating that "should any Member of the League resort to war in disregard of its covenants under Articles 12, 13 or 15, it shall *ipso facto* be deemed to have committed an act of war against all other Members of the League".

There was, in the Covenant, an implicit assumption that such counter-interventions would carry more legitimacy if collective. Hall wrote in 1880: "Interventions, whether armed or diplomatic ... would have had to justify themselves, when not authorized by the whole body of civilized states accustomed to act together for a common purpose" (1884: 266). Borchard wrote "the other states of the family of nations are authorized by international law to intervene" (1913: 507) in special circumstances. Other authorities such as Mosler (1937: 68–9), argued that it made no legal difference whether a state intervened individually or collectively, even though the latter may be given an unequally larger political and moral weighting.

Leaving this issue aside, critics such as Cecil (1929: 278) and Scelle stressed that even if there was a clearly defined law, the validity of its justification had to be determined by an authority other than the respective state, and that international society had to "wholly remove from international law the possibility of taking justice into one's own hands" (Scelle 1936: 377–79). This endorsement of intervention, being not only collective but also under the auspices of an international organization, was a powerful argument which would echo in 2003 when the US asserted the right of intervention in Iraq on its, not the Security Council's, interpretation that Iraq's non-compliance with Security Council resolutions justified armed intervention.

Whatever the merits of any of the arguments above, as is widely known, the theory of collective security was not so easily put into practice. Following the above mentioned invasions of Italy, Japan and Germany, it became clear that, as Stone pointed out, "the League's collective measures ... lack[ed] the universality for real effectiveness" (1936: 144). Keeton and Schwarzenberger agreed (1939: 144).

If collective security had failed, arguably so did the older scheme of self-help which was unable to prevent the use of force and war in the international system (Wright 1936: 100). The problem was, in Anderson's eyes, "the refusal of all the leading nations to pay the price for international security, the price being collective responsibility for the maintenance of world peace" (1935: 15). Grewe points out that the resignation of Japan and Germany from the League in 1933 announced a new international dynamic which could no longer be controlled by the mechanism inherent in the League (1984: 682). After, as Stone reminisced, "the heat of war and the warmth of post-war idealism" (1959: 176) were over it became clear that regulations set up by the League of Nations were insufficient to stop both minor and major conflicts between states.

While the League Covenant codified international law in the area of the use of force between states in a way never seen before, including the establishment of a Permanent Court of Justice, it was not able to prevent the outbreak of the Second World War in 1939. The international system had learnt a painful lesson about the teething troubles of its newly established machinery and rules: a system which declared wars of aggression a crime, had established an international organization entrusted with collective security and had a growing amount of treaties limiting the use of force, was nevertheless not able to prevent the largest international war to date.

If the system of counter-intervention through collective security remained controversial and still-born, the concept of intervention on other grounds, notably, humanitarian intervention, was even more debated and debilitated. As seen above, the principle of near absolute state sovereignty remained, based primarily on the belief that sovereignty followed from the right to independence. As intervention violated this independence, it was presumed illegal, especially if it was not in response to a prior intervention. Yet this absolutist view was on a collision path with the increasing importance given to international humanitarian law (Mosler 1937: 31).

As we have seen, the phrase 'humanitarian intervention' is at least as old as Hall's first edition in 1880. The concept and practice is even older. No issue bore more marks of the legacy of the religious concept of just war than humanitarian intervention. Most, though not all, purported instances before the Great War were based on religious grounds of protecting Christian minorities from Muslims (the Ottoman Empire), the last pre-First World War instance only ending in Macedonia in 1913.

At the end of the Great War, the Treaty of Sévres condemned Turkey for its treatment of its own subjects during the war. The peace treaties and the League Covenant reflected a heightened international humanitarian concern through treaty obligations on some states to protect their minorities' rights and implied something similar to the government of mandates. There were many calls for the US to help Turkey's subjects by taking Armenia as a mandate. Concerns were also raised about the treatment of Christians in the Ukraine. Yet, the more radical doctrine of legitimating forcible intervention to uphold human rights was mentioned nowhere in the Covenant or treaties.

The first person to discuss the legal aspects of humanitarian intervention in any great depth was Stowell. He had resigned from Columbia University in 1918 amid public controversy over his press articles advocating the justice of the allied war against Germany. At the war's start, he spoke of a 'duty to humanity' (1914: SM2). He insisted on international co-operation by states in the enforcement of international obligations and explained he was "for war and not a pacifist or of the anti-militaristic type" (Editorial 1918).

In *Intervention in International Law* in 1921 he went into further detail, studying and supporting humanitarian intervention: in instances of slavery/slave trade, for the protection of native people, in favor of self-determination, in violations of the laws of war, in instances of suppression and persecution, as well as for the protection of people against abusive treatment.

There was a strong tradition of the opposite view with Calvo, Heffter, Phillimore, Woosley, Fiore and Bello amongst its proponents. Lawrence had argued that accepting such a doctrine would be devastating for the international system (1895: 121). He reportedly said it "is destitute of technical legality, but it may be morally right and even praiseworthy to a high degree" (Editorial 1898).

Tony Blair has said much the same. Dickinson, so concerned over peace, staunchly opposed any interventions including humanitarian, arguing that "never has any nation intervened in any country genuinely and solely in the joint interest of the native inhabitants and of civilization as a whole" (1917: 101). Despite the growing news of Nazi atrocities against Jewish German citizens, the isolated calls for action by people such as the League's minority spokesman, a Jewish Englishman, Norman Bentwich, in 1933 were ignored.

So, the international system had not developed a practical framework for humanitarian intervention. Self-defense remained undefined. Terrorism was defined but its enclosing convention remained unratified by all but one. Some progress had been made with defining aggression. The 1939 Draft Convention on Rights and Duties of States in Cases of Aggression in Article 1 (c) stays in a more general realm by defining aggression as "a resort to armed force by a state when such resort has been duly determined, by a means which that state is bound to accept, to constitute a violation of an obligation." But the job was far from over even as the war clouds loomed. Schwarzenberger, of the University College London, reflected the sentiment of many at the time when he stated, in his appropriately titled 'Power Politics', that "the disintegration of the international society has reached its culmination point" (1941: 28). Schwarzenberger, like German-born realist Hans Morgenthau (1948), was fast losing his faith in the ability of international law to provide peace, security and justice.

Summary

Grewe (1984) claims that while rules renunciating, legalizing and countering the use of force were established and there was progress in the normative aspects of international law, state practice largely showed a backward move in the period between 1919 and 1945. This seems overly harsh. The era between the two World Wars made an important contribution, least of all because it helped to set into gear a shift in the use of force away from something determined by political objectives and towards something regulated by legal principles. Lauterpacht argued that states were "better protected by the recognition of the reign of law administered through the agency of international tribunals than by formally safeguarding, through the usual reservations, the ultimate right to have recourse to force" (1966: 177).

Chapter 3
Where there's a Will: International Law and the Use of Force During the Cold War

> Until the world achieves some form of international government in which a collective will takes precedence over the individual will of the sovereign state, the ultimate function of international law, which is the elimination of force for the solution of human conflicts, will not be fulfilled.
>
> Philip C. Jessup (1959: 2)

The significance of the UN Charter of 1945 as a milestone in the development of international law is debated. Grewe believes that the break made in 1919 with regard to the development of international law was more distinctive and incisive than either 1648 or 1815. He does not see 1945 as having the same historical significance as 1919. He claims that, as opposed to previous eras of international law, the two sections of the post-classical period (that is 1919–1944, and post-1945) merge to form a consistent and cohesive overall picture (1984: 679). In his view, the end of the First World War saw the establishment of the *nachklassische Völkerrecht*, the post-classical international law. This post-classical international law was merely given new traits through the shift in power balances and the change in the structure of the international system caused by the Second World War. Grewe's assessment invites a closer examination of the changes of 1945.

Surrendering to Security

The foundational doctrine of almost absolute non-intervention remained essentially unchallenged by the Charter. In some senses it was strengthened. The legal use of force by states was now even more restricted, although in one respect (collective security) it was extended. There was no reflection in the Charter of the pre-war debate over humanitarian intervention, despite a dozen explicit references to 'human rights' in contrast to the silence of the Covenant. This greater emphasis on restriction of force superseded the previous period's emphasis on arbitration. This unambiguous restriction also superseded the previous era's focus on the explicit renunciation of recourse to war by states, although the Kellogg-Briand Pact, seemingly dormant in terms of state policy, continues to inform international understanding governing the use of force: including in Article 2(4) of the Charter, the *Nürnberg* Tribunal and citations by courts and authorities to this day.

The Charter placed less emphasis on the restriction of the use of force in war than on the avoidance of war altogether. The security framework envisaged both continued, and added to, the League of Nations concept. The partial surrender by states of their right to war, restricted to self-defense rather than an overall renunciation of war, was to be compensated by a more explicit system of collective security: though quite deliberately that discredited phrase appears nowhere in the Charter.

The pre-1945 concern, which authority was to decide whether there had been an illegal use of force, was addressed explicitly. The Security Council had the authority to authorize the use of force and even acts of purported self-defense had to be reported to the Council. The provision for a military staff committee in the new organization to coordinate armed Security Council action was an unambiguous statement that this time the international community was serious. Although the committee has met every fortnight for the past 63 years, it remains little more than a paper tiger, having taken no concrete action since it came into existence.

The Charter added an extra dimension to the League's two-pronged security framework: global collective security and restriction of force to self-defense. The Charter provided for a new type of international institution: regional organizations which would act as a complementary or alternate body to the UN as potential vehicles for the enforcement of such collective action. The expanded concept of self-defense including 'collective self-defense' reinforced the importance of this innovation.

The pre-1945 era's focus on the term 'aggression' as the singular form of illegal force survived in that it was invoked in the military tribunals. The UN decided in 1947 to establish a commission to define the term. There did not seem to be a matching concern to define self-defense for which some authorities had called for before 1945. The necessity of such a clarification was now more essential because of the expanded notion of 'collective self-defense', mentioned above, which had the potential to reopen the door closing on the state's right to use force.

When self-defense is mentioned in the Charter; aggression is not connected to it. Indeed, the meaning and consequences of 'aggression' in the Charter were complicated by the explicit use in it of two new terms 'threat or use of force' (Article 2,4) and 'armed attack' (Article 51). The relationship between these two terms, 'use of force' and 'aggression', and their relationship with 'self-defense' was left unexpressed. In short, were all acts of 'aggression' and all illegal 'threats or uses of force' equal to 'armed attack', thereby invoking the right of self-defense? Quincy Wright thought so. Did the relationship operate in exactly the same way in the case of 'collective self-defense'? Such questions would not be explicitly addressed until 1986 in the ICJ.

In summary, many developments commenced in the years between the First and Second World War, found their continuation after 1945. The conflict of 1939–1945 had been an enormous setback for those who believed that the use of force by states could be restrained. Yet, there was still enough idealism and, at the same time, realism, left to recognize that the path embarked upon in 1919 had to be pursued. This belief is best reflected in Shotwell's *The Great Decision,* in which he stated that "no greater mistake could be made than to conclude from this tragic page of history ... that international law is no longer important or valid. On the contrary, it must be strengthened and reformed as the safeguard for these stable relations between nations" (1944: 227). The obvious liberalism of the Canadian legal authority contrasts with the direction taken by many states and authorities, like Morgenthau and Schwarzenberger, within a few years of the heady days of San Francisco in 1945.

Very quickly after 1945, the Cold War rivalry of the US and the Soviet Union stalled many of these developments. The numerous armed conflicts of decolonization, separate but connected to the Cold War, also greatly complicated matters. In the following pages the uneven progress of the developments outlined above are examined in detail in three key categories: firstly, the rules of international security put in place in 1945; secondly, the structures developed to enforce those rules; thirdly, the legal definition of the crucial terms involved.

The Rules of San Francisco

The UN Charter explicitly endorsed the standing doctrine of non-intervention for the UN itself as well as states. Article 2(4) states "all Members shall refrain in their international relations from the threat or use of force against the territorial integrity or political independence of any state, or in any other manner inconsistent with the Purposes of the United Nations." Article 2(7) added: "nothing contained in the present Charter shall authorize the United Nations to intervene in matters which are essentially within the domestic jurisdiction of any state." There was, however, a 'get-out' clause for the UN if not for states. Article 2(7) concluded "but this principle [non-intervention] shall not prejudice the application of enforcement measures under Chapter Vll." As shown below, collective UN action could thereby breach the non-interventionist principle in the sense that Hall had endorsed in 1880. The threat or use of armed force by states, with two exceptions, was now clearly illegal.

States, even, perhaps especially, new ones, by their words if not always their actions seemed heartily to endorse the principle of non-intervention. This was subsequently incorporated into a number of declarations, including the principles of the Bandung Conference (1955), the Charter of the Organization for African Unity (OUA) (1963), the General Assembly's Declaration on the Inadmissibility of Intervention in the Domestic Affairs of States and the Protection of their Independence and Sovereignty (1965), the Charter of the OAS (1967), and the Helsinki Final Act (1975).

As states who had just escaped European colonization, often by armed struggle against counter-interventions, their disposition is understandable.

Furthermore, the prohibition of the threat and use of force, as reflected in Article 2(4) was accepted by authorities as *jus cogens* (ICJ 1986).

Jus cogens, as defined by Article 53 of the Vienna Convention on the Law of Treaties (1969), is a "peremptory norm of general international law [which] is accepted and recognized by the international community of states as a whole as a norm from which no derogation is permitted".

These laws are understood to be so fundamental for the functioning of global order that states are automatically seen to be bound to them, regardless of the treaties and organizations to which they are a party. In addition to the prohibition of the threat and the use of force, *jus cogens* norms include most prominently legal equality of states with regard to international law, meaning they are subject to the same rights and duties, as well as the prohibition of acts of genocide.

Any military intervention or recourse to force under the Charter could now only be justified on the basis of individual or collective self-defense, or Security Council-authorized collective action. Article 51 proclaims that "nothing in the present Charter shall impair the inherent right of individual or collective self-defense if an armed attack occurs against a Member of the United Nations, until the Security Council has taken measures necessary to maintain international peace and security." So the right to self-defense under customary international law was preserved. Some authorities, such as a Czech-born and Austrian-raised American lawyer and professor Hans Kelsen, argued that a states' only legal right to use force, should also be considered *jus cogens* (1920: 69).

Self-defense was given an added legal dimension in the Charter. Reportedly at the insistence of the US, driven by the mutual defense aspects of the Union of American Republics (later OAS), the concept was broadened to include 'collective self-defense.' This thereby gave states the right to use force against another state or states even though the former had not directly suffered an armed attack. In short, they could come to the armed support of a third state, which was the subject of armed attack, though not in the same sense as a military alliance. Some feared this would lead to a dangerous broadening of the legal use of force principle at a time when a serious attempt was being made to restrict it. Such assessments would prove well-grounded notably over Vietnam, the Dominican Republic, Hungary and Czechoslovakia.

As with the League-sponsored attempt to see states voluntarily renounce the recourse to war in return for collective security, the UN Charter offered a similar deal without using that exact and discredited phrase. In Chapter VII, entitled: 'Action with respect to threats to the peace, breaches of the peace, and acts of aggression', the Security Council under Article 42 "may take such action by air, sea, or land forces as may be necessary to maintain or restore international peace and security. Such action may include demonstrations, blockades, and other operations by air, sea, or land forces of Members of the United Nations". Article 44 openly refers to this as the 'use of force' and Article 50 to 'preventive or enforcement measures'. Article 41 indicated that a prior step would be "measures not involving the use of armed force are to be employed to give effect to its decisions, and ... may include complete or partial interruption of economic relations and of rail, sea, air, postal, telegraphic, radio, and other means of communication, and the severance of diplomatic relations".

Leading legal authorities from the pre-war era hailed these developments. Collective security, so Quincy Wright stated, "defines the aggressor qualitatively by the illegal character of its acts, in the hope that future aggression will be deterred because of the disposition of states to enforce the law". Wright elaborated by stating that the concept of collective security "relate[s] the security of each state to the stability of the entire system [and] seeks stability through general observance of law" (1976: 81). Wright had hailed the forcible action by the 'United Nations' in 1941 as heralding a 'new world order' where aggression would be met by collective counter action similar to Stowell in 1918. He envisaged a future era where this became the norm (Sees U.S.-Britain Union For Peace 1941).

Given the core desire to limit states' recourse to force, it is unsurprising that the framers of the Charter did not place in it any other explicit pathways to legal use of force, including humanitarian intervention. Paradoxically then, the Charter gave a prominence to human rights with which the League's Covenant pales in comparison. While the conventions and agreements of the 19th and early 20th century had tended to deal with human rights only in the context of armed conflict, the post-1945 era focused on general human rights. The Preamble expresses its "faith in fundamental human rights" and Article 55 (c) states the aim of advancing "universal respect for, and observance of, human rights and fundamental freedoms for all without distinction as to race, sex, language, or religion".

The role of human rights was furthermore established quickly through a row of important agreements, most notably the Convention on the Prevention and Punishment of the Crime of Genocide (1948), the Universal Declaration of Human Rights (1948), and later the Covenant on Civil and Political Rights (1966), and the Covenant on Economic, Social and Cultural Rights (1966). The post-1945 era saw a boom in declarations and agreements furthering the protection of human rights, reaching from the protection of refugees and children to torture and equal remuneration. At no point was the right to use force to implement such rights raised. International peace and security, defined as the sovereignty of states, took precedence over human rights.

The use of force was an area heavily influenced by this development and the issue of humanitarian intervention, first mentioned in the literature by Hall in 1880, regained importance. The legality of it was, however, heavily debated. As mentioned earlier in this section, the Cold War period saw the rise of ideologically motivated interventions, coupled with a deadlock within the Security Council. It became obvious that the numerous loopholes which existed for states to resort to force were being used. Consequently, critics such as Schwarzenberger believed that "while humanitarian intervention is morally explicable it is illegal" (1976: 90). Opponents saw the official legalization of the use of force undertaken for humanitarian purposes or any extension of the right to use force as potentially opening Pandora's Box.

Proponents of a right to humanitarian intervention, such as Richard B. Lillich (1973), believed that in instances of the UN's inability to act, both collective and unilateral use of force for humanitarian reasons should be permitted. They held that the UN's deadlock meant that it was often not possible to put an end to human rights abuses through a much needed military intervention. This was particularly widely discussed following India's military intervention in Bangladesh (then known as East Pakistan) in 1971 in order to halt the violent oppression of the people by Pakistan's armed forces. Here a state acted unilaterally in light of the UN's inability (so India claimed) in order to protect human rights.

The post-1945 era saw the problem of how to balance a need for the protection of human rights with a continued limitation on the use of force. In addition, there was the problem of reconciling the UN's aim of protecting human rights with its respect for state sovereignty as reflected in Article 2(7) which states that "nothing contained in the present Charter shall authorize the United Nations to intervene in matters which are essentially within the domestic jurisdiction of any state".

The fractious politics of the Cold War and decolonization made states reluctant to accept either the concept of humanitarian intervention in areas where their interests were involved or establishing a universal approach to the subject. The Tanzanian invasion of Uganda in 1979, for example, was one of the few non-controversial cases of humanitarian intervention at the time. The Vietnamese invasion of Pol Pot's Cambodia (1978), on the other hand, attracted much Western condemnation because Vietnam was a Soviet ally. The end of the Cold War removed much potential for controversy.

There was no major challenge in state practice to the 'rules' mapped out in 1945. States, especially major ones like the US, the Soviet Union and the UK, may have intervened in numerous instances in the Cold War period but they always sought to frame their acts within the rules above. Of course, states often merely paid lip service to the rules, as examined in greater detail in Parts II and III, in order to give their actions a veneer of legality. Yet, there was no explicit rejection of the rules like that posed recently by the US, Britain and Australia over the Iraq war where officials suggested the 'rules of San Francisco' were out of date.

The 'rules' before and after 1945 were always out of date or out of touch with one part of the world – the colonized world. The rules had been designed by and for Europeans without much wider reflection. Even today, scholars of international law and relations, often Westerners, regularly neglect this dimension.

In an era of virtually absolute non-interventionism, an American legal scholar rightly referred to extra-territorial 'concessions' in sovereign foreign states, such as China and Thailand, as "foreign interventions in some form" (Millard 1925: 4). With post-1945 decolonization, three of the first armed conflicts after the Charter was adopted, in Vietnam (with France from 1945 and 1946), Indonesia (with the Netherlands in 1947 and 1949) and Malaya (with the British from 1948), did not fall into the 'rules' in terms of an 'armed attack' on a state let alone a Member. The three attacking powers did not justify it as self-defense and certainly not as an illegal 'armed attack' by themselves. None of the actions were Chapter VII authorized either. For all of them, these were internal not international actions described in some cases as 'police actions'.

Of course their opponents took another view. They clearly felt the 'attacks' were as unjustified as their own armed struggles were justified. Yet, there was no legal framework in which to place their perspective let alone their legal personality while in this interim limbo. In Vietnam and Indonesia the status of statehood was claimed. Vietnam wrote to the UN to no avail. Australia, with India involved, referred the Dutch actions in Indonesia as a 'breach of the peace' to the Security Council which actually acted without armed counter intervention.

No international doctrine of the rights of armed decolonization was developed. In 1960, the General Assembly only went as far as expressing the right of self-determination of colonized peoples without linking it to the provisions covering armed conflict and self-defense. In 1972 in the UN *Ad Hoc* Committee on Terrorism, the Arab and Nonaligned Movement stressed the need to include state terrorism in the definition of terrorism and the use of force as permissible in achieving self-determination. Western states replied that the subject was already addressed and several (South Africa, Israel and Portugal) strongly rejected the latter (Dugard 1974: 74). The 'rules' in that sense were as rapidly out of date as the permanent membership of the Security Council. The almost complete success of decolonization by the mid-1970s took the pressure off the call for change to the 1945's 'rules of war'. Newly independent states lost their vigor in support of the right of self-determination, fearing break up of their own newly sovereign territory, though former colonial states discovered a new attraction to the doctrine with, for example, Britain wanting to retain Gibraltar and the Falklands.

The Machinery of San Francisco

The successor to the League of Nations came into existence on the 26th June 1945 stating as its aim the need "to save succeeding generations from the scourge of war". The mechanisms envisaged to achieve this aim and uphold the rules outlined above included collective security, state self-defense and regional collective self-defense. The organization's Security Council, consisting of five permanent members as well as ten non-permanent members, was given the ultimate decision-making power regarding the authorization for the use of force by the UN, regional arrangements, *ad hoc* multinational coalitions, and, to some extent, even individual states.

Arguably, the framers saw the former becoming the main instrument for peace and security, supplemented at least in the short to medium term, by new regional organizations, while self-defense would fade out, if not altogether, at least only a secondary role of immediate self-help until the cavalry, in form of the UN's 'blue helmets', arrived. As we all know, things did not go according to this plan.

The surrender by states of a wide right to use force except in self-defense was always predicated on the provision of security by the UN. It quickly became clear, however, that the stalemate in the Security Council, created foremost by the US-Soviet rivalry, restricted that organ's ability to function properly. Without effective collective security, the pressure would increase for states to return to armed self-help albeit disguised in terms of the new 'rules' of individual or collective self-defense.

In the aftermath of the Second World War, Philip C. Jessup, a liberal American international lawyer and Truman administration official, still reflected the widely held hope that "the international society is now entering on the third period, wherein collective international measures are taking the place of [individual] state action" (1959: 175). Reality soon showed, however, that it was not exactly true, although unilateral interventions were rare. Once again, the international system had not been capable of totally outlawing the use of force. Instead, as Stone observed, "the liberty of states to resort to war under customary international law is still a substantial liberty" (1959: 303). While in theory the UN was viewed by Inis Claude, Professor of International Relations at the University of Virginia, as "a dispenser of politically significant approval" (1966: 376), state practice looked very different. Collective security action by the UN was limited to a few peacekeeping operations.

Jessup feared the continued use of unilateral intervention mainly due to the fact that, despite the establishment of the League of Nations, the Kellogg-Briand Pact and the UN, "the traditional legal foundations of unilateralism remain[ed] largely unshaken" (1959: 11). Although writing before the Cold War paralysis set in, Jessup acknowledged, like Hersch Lauterpacht, that some instances would not allow a state to wait for a UN decision. Consequently, following the robust path of his compatriots, Stowell and Wright, Jessup argued that states would have to be "the judge in [their] own cause" (1959: 164).

The first real test for collective security came with the Democratic People's Republic of Korea's (DPRK) 'invasion' of the Republic of Korea. The issue was complicated by doubt whether there were two states in Korea and therefore whether there had been an 'armed attack' invoking the right of self-defense. Due to Soviet opposition, an earlier attempt to send the troops using a Security Council resolution alone had failed. The absence of the Soviet Union allowed a disputed Security Council endorsement of UN intervention in Korea. Subsequently, an alternative pathway to intervention was opened. The General Assembly in Resolution 377 Uniting for Peace resolved that "if the Security Council, because of lack of unanimity of the permanent members, fails to exercise its primary responsibility for the maintenance of international peace and security in any case where there appears to be a threat to the peace, breach of the peace, or act of aggression, the United Nations General Assembly shall consider the matter immediately with a view to making appropriate recommendation to members for collective measures, including in the case of a breach of the peace or act of aggression the use of armed force when necessary, to maintain or restore international peace and security". The shifting voting balance in the General Assembly as more colonized territories, ultra-sensitive over intervention, gained independence, meant this potentially radical pathway was subsequently closed in practical terms.

There were no more instances of the UN's multilateral use of force excluding peacekeeping until Iraq in 1991, once the Cold War stalemate had ended. The Cold War era was to be largely dominated by the unilateral and limited collective use of force. States' military actions spoke one language, their legal dealings another. The international use of force continued to be undertaken even though non-intervention agreements were concluded left, right and centre by recently decolonized states. Bowett, of Manchester University, however, maintained a firm line that the international use of force without UN authorization is "entirely inconsistent with the system of collective security envisaged by the United Nations Charter" (1958: 273–74).

Post-war idealism about the total outlawing of the use of force had begun to vanish even before most of the events described above. In 1949 Belgian's foreign minister Dirk Stikker stated that "in retrospect, the signing of the Charter at San Francisco only four years ago is seen as a charming dream from which we had awakened gradually into a grey reality". Speaking at the signing of the NATO treaty, Stikker believed that "this treaty we are about to sign marks the end of an illusion: the hope that the United Nations would by itself ensure international peace" (Address by President Truman and Foreign Ministers 1949).

Regional organizations, not alliances were envisaged in the Charter as a welcome complement to the UN. With the paralysis of collective security many came to see them as a more practical alternative. Others, such as George Keeton (1950), of the University College of London, and Schwarzenberger (1949), questioned when regional organizations, including NATO, were compatible with the Charter and not a return to regional military alliances that many blamed for the expansion of the Great War. The US had been a driving force for them in view of the prior existence of the Pan American Union which served as a vehicle to oppose external interventions in the Americas while also, some would argue, eventually facilitating internal ones (Grenada and Panama).

The OAS was established in 1946, three years later the North Atlantic Treaty established NATO. Its constitutions and declarations tended to be based on the UN principles, as the Pan American Union's Report on the Draft Declaration of the Rights and Duties of American States showed. The Union, renamed the OAS, declared in Article 15 of its Charter that "intervention by one or more states, directly or indirectly, and for whatever reasons in the internal or external affairs of another state is inadmissible", a clear reflection of the Charter's Article 2(7). Article 5 of the North Atlantic Treaty invoked the language of Article 51 of the Charter about armed attacks and collective self-defense, reaffirming the need to report action to the Security Council, while making obligatory the response which was optional in the Charter. The Manila Treaty of 1954 establishing the South East Asia Treaty Organization (SEATO), the Australia, New Zealand and US (ANZUS) Pact of 1951 and the Baghdad Pact of 1955 establishing the Central Treaty Organization (CENTO) also invoked the Charter's language of collective self-defense.

The discussion of the Cold War period and surrounding regional organizations focused on the issue of what rights they should be given regarding the use of force. The UN Charter, in Article 53, states that "the Security Council shall, where appropriate, utilize such regional arrangements or agencies for enforcement action under its authority. But no enforcement action shall be taken under regional arrangements or by regional agencies without the authorization of the Security

Council". While the founders of the UN realized the need for regional arrangements to support the use of the organizations, they were reluctant to give them a *carte blanche* with regard to their ability to use force.

Opinions on the level of freedom given to regional organizations regarding the use of force varied. American Richard Barnet suggested in 1968, in the light of Vietnam, an outright prohibition of any international use of force taken outside of the UN. This includes not only unilateral action but also the collective use of force if undertaken by a regional organization. The reservation of those opposing the expansion of the permission to use force by regional arrangements were fundamentally grounded in two issues. The first was the experiences of the inter-war years which showed that the prohibition of the use of force based on voluntary adherence had been ineffective. Consequently, many perceived a need to limit the use of force strictly to the UN, thereby closing any legal loopholes as best as possible. The second concern was that the rejection of an expansion of the right to use collective force to regional organizations was based on the concern about the ideological influences of, at least, the two major regional defense arrangements of the time.

The debate about the role of SEATO in Vietnam was important here. Any intervention undertaken by NATO, SEATO or the Warsaw Pact during the Cold War years would have been bound to have been based on ideological and US/Soviet driven objectives rather than just out of interest to preserve regional peace and security. Hence there were the concerns raised in opposition to any potential right to military intervention by regional organizations.

Moore, however, provided an important, albeit harsh, counter-argument, describing Barnet's suggestion as "simplistic and unworkable" (1972: 268). Moore argued that due to the Cold-War induced deadlock of the Security Council, as well as the international defense interdependencies, the universal prohibition of non-UN intervention was not realistic. For practical reasons, he argued that action by regional organizations and, at times, individual states should be permitted. Moore saw regional arrangements as more likely to pursue paths and take action in the collective interest rather than for selfish reasons as unilateral action would (1972: 348).

The Soviet Union conducted its major Cold War interventions in Hungary and Czechoslovakia through the collective framework of the Warsaw Pact. The US, after Korea, tried to mobilize an *ad hoc* coalition for intervention in Indochina in 1954 with the consent of France. When that failed it organized SEATO. When Britain and France paralyzed SEATO action, the US announced in 1962 it regarded its SEATO obligations as "individual as well as collective". When it intervened in Vietnam openly from 1965 on, it dropped the reference to SEATO, while Australia featured it. SEATO, in fact, never authorized the intervention which is best described as an *ad hoc* coalition (Pemberton 1989).

If the major states acting outside the UN mainly acted through collective regional organizations, some states did not. American John Norton Moore suggests it was not just Western states using unilateral force. He points to other ideologically and revolutionary motivated movements, such as anti-colonial and self-determination movements, as well as those seeking regional or religious unity, or simply those seeking to improve or gain access to natural resources and an increase in their wealth (1972: 147–48). Moore seems to misunderstand anti-colonial struggles which can hardly be characterized as interventions in foreign states except on the rare occasions where conflicts crossed borders. Yet, he is right that unilateral intervention was by no means limited to major powers. Once anti-colonial movements became independent states, they often behaved the same way as the previous colonizers. Egypt's use of force in Yemen (1962); Indonesia in Dutch New Guinea (1963), Malaysia (1963–66) and East Timor (1975); and Libya in Chad (1980) are cases in point.

This continuation of unilateral intervention during the Cold-War era, says British Labour politician Evan Luard, "led to comparable demands for collective intervention to restrain it" (1984: 164). Richard Falk, a liberal New Yorker and frequent opponent of Moore, agreed with this position, believing that especially following the US' intervention in Vietnam it was important to "inhibit unilateral recourse to violence arising from contradictory and subjective national interpretations of a conflict situation" (1969b: 446). What dominated the international system first and foremost was the unilateral use of force based on, said Falk, the "ideological opposition to Communism and Communist influence as the main premise for military commitment" (1969b: 504). This is a dangerous issue in Falk's eyes.

It also reflects a still widespread belief regarding the legality of the international use of force. The UN sits at the top of the four tier stand, followed by regional organizations, individual states acting through *ad hoc* multinational coalitions, and, last of all, states acting unilaterally. Suspicion regarding the use of force undertaken outside the UN remained high throughout the Cold War period. Any external use of force by a state was seen, said Australian Don Greig, as "likely to be inconsistent with the general purpose of maintaining international peace and security or of promoting friendly relations between states" (1976: 871).

What concerned most writers of the time, such as Americans Michael Reisman and Myres McDougal, was the need to establish a set of guidelines or principles to supplement the UN Charter and to manage any use of force undertaken outside of the UN and without Security Council authorization. This is an issue which remains relevant but unresolved.

Conclusively, it can be said that the Cold War era showed that despite the limitations placed on the use of force by the UN Charter and other regional organizations, states had by no means "totally abjured self-executed force as an instrument of international policy" (Pennock 1958: 388). Instead, ideologically motivated interventions and a wish to establish a façade of stricter non-intervention regulations, circumvented to fit the respective state's interests, was common.

In the later post-1945 era the two major post-Vietnam interventionist policies of the time were the Brezhnev and the Reagan doctrines. Both ideologically motivated, the doctrines aimed at justifying their international use of force with the pursuit or spread of their respective political system. The Brezhnev Doctrine of 1968 purported to limit the sovereignty of states within the Warsaw Pact (and the Soviet sphere of influence) and aimed at combating 'anti-socialist' forces. The Reagan Doctrine's guiding principle during the 1980s was its embrace of the international use of force for the sake of assisting anti-Communist insurgents and the furthering of democracy. Yet, neither was implemented in a direct challenge to the established rules. The Soviet Union used a collective mechanism for Czechoslovakia and an intervention in Afghanistan. The US relied on covert support for non-state proxy forces in Cuba, Guatemala and Nicaragua.

The Definitions of San Francisco

Despite the seemingly watertight limitation on the use of force in the UN Charter, legal loopholes were soon found, partly because the key terms were still undefined. Some saw the necessity to clarify these terms in order to limit states' misuse. So, in 1947 the General Assembly asked its new International Law Commission (ILC) for a Draft Code on Aggression and in 1953 for a Definition on Aggression. It was to be another 21 years until the General Assembly passed Resolution 3314 on the Definition of Aggression.

This was a very slow and, for some, a pointless process. Many observers such as Kurt Wilk started to question the universality of international law as early as 1951, believing instead that the international legal order was merely divided into American-led and Soviet-led interpretations. Yet, despite similar initial skepticism, the developments in international war law in the pre-1945 era had by no means been pointless. This fact was reflected in the *Nürnberg* trials in which the principal charge against the Germans accused was the crime of "planning, preparation, initiation, or waging of a war of aggression or a war in violation of international treaties". The main international treaty referred to was the Kellogg-Briand Pact, a treaty in force until the current day. The *Nürnberg* trials reinforced what had been visible in the 1919–1944 period in treaties and, to a large degree state practice, namely that wars of aggression were crimes. This perception was also restated in the General Assembly Resolution Uniting for Peace (1950) which in Article 1 stated that "any aggression ... is the gravest of all crimes against peace and security throughout the world".

Aggression thereby was defined as "the use of armed force by a State against the sovereignty, territorial integrity or political independence of another State, or in any other manner inconsistent with the Charter of the United Nations" (Article 1). Aggression was said to include invasion, bombardment, blockades, attacks on armed forces, and the sending by or on behalf of a State of armed bands, groups, irregulars or mercenaries. It was furthermore and once again confirmed in Article 5(2) that war of aggression was a crime against international peace.

In the meantime, before the UN reached this point, Stone had published his key work, *Aggression and World Order* (1958). Its focus on the term 'aggression', however, like the General Assembly's, seems to have been overtaken by the Charter.

The main discussion had moved on to what constituted 'self-defense' and the related concept in Article 2(4) of 'armed attack' which gave the right to the former. Of the younger legal scholars, Bowett, whose major work had a more relevant title, *Self-Defence in International Law*, separated aggression and self-defense, taking an expansive view of self-defense which he believed was permissible in four instances, namely the protection of the right of territorial integrity, political independence, protection of nationals, and particular economic rights (1958: 270). Britain's fading imperial interventions, such as Suez in 1956, weighed heavily on his mind as two of his criteria were cited by Britain as justification for its action. Brownlie, in his *International Law and the Use of Force*, called for "the reservation of the right to individual and collective self-defense [to] be given a narrow interpretation" (1963: 113). He described Bowett's categories as "ill-defined essential rights ... arbitrary and vague" and argued that they "[involve] a virtual renunciation of all the developments in the law since 1920 and a return to a broad permission for self-help" (1963: 430).

The issue of 'collective self-defense' was even more controversial with many seeing in it the potential to unravel the tight restraints put around state use of force in the Charter. Surprisingly, Bowett took a critical view. "The duty of Members is to abstain from intervention until authorized to act by a competent organ of the UN. To concede a general right of intervention, without the authorization of a competent organ, would, in our view, be entirely inconsistent with the system of collective security envisaged by the Charter and, in particular, the delegation of primary responsibility for the maintenance of international peace and security by the Security Council. This limitation on the freedom of action of members cannot be overcome by relying on an extended interpretation of the right of 'collective self-defense'" (1958: 273–74). The apparent contradiction between his restrictive view of collective self-defense and expansive view of individual self-defense was not explained.

The concept of 'collective self-defense' became even more controversial from the 1960s onwards. The US government clearly felt compelled to make a comprehensive legal defense of its intervention in Vietnam from 1965. The State Department issued 'The Legal Basis for U.S. Actions against North Vietnam' on March 8, 1965 as the Marines landed. As the debate over the escalating commitment grew, the State Department's Legal Adviser submitted a lengthier Memorandum to the Senate Committee on Foreign Relations exactly one year to the day later. These strongly invoked the justification of 'collective self-defense'. Falk (1966) questioned the application of this justification to what he saw essentially as an internal conflict and to acts of force not amounting to armed attack. Interestingly, the Soviet Union invoked the same justification, though only the third of three, in support of its multilateral intervention in Czechoslovakia two years later (Union of Soviet Socialist Republics 1968: 298). For many legal authorities and small states, the justification of collective self-defense was the last refuge of a superpower.

State practice, at least by larger powers, showed a broad interpretation of the issue of when self-defense should be permitted. The US had built the collective self-defense principle into a number of its multilateral treaties. It invoked the principle along with others for its deployment of force in Thailand in response to developments in Laos in 1962; over its intervention in the Dominican Republic in 1965, Cambodia in 1970 and Grenada in 1983. Moore, who locked legal horns with Falk over Vietnam, generally supported this broader interpretation, especially if conducted by a regional organization, at least with respect to US actions in Vietnam and Central America (1967: 1087). The Soviet Union also invoked the principle over intervention in Afghanistan in 1979 (United Nations: 1980).

Not before time, a more forensic examination of the meaning of all these crucial terms was undertaken. In 1984 Nicaragua filed a dispute with the ICJ regarding military and paramilitary activities in and against Nicaragua by the US. Nicaragua was, amongst others, represented by British jurist Brownlie and French lawyer Allain Pellet, the US by Americans McDougal and Moore. The Court rejected the US' justification of individual and collective self-defense, in response to alleged requests by El Salvador, Honduras and Costa Rica to counter aggression by Nicaragua.

The Court, with the American and British judges dissenting, challenged the US' justification of collective self-defense by saying that "the exercise of this right is subject to the state concerned having been the victim of an armed attack" (1986: 93).

It thereby differentiated between types of the use of force, ranging from the most serious form, that is armed attack, to less severe action.

In its judgment the Court relied heavily on Article 3 (g) of the 1974 Definition of Aggression, describing it as reflecting customary international law. Based on this, armed attack was defined as "including not merely action by regular armed forces across an international border, but also (based on Article 3(g) of the Definition of Aggression) the sending by or on behalf of a State of armed bands, groups, irregulars or mercenaries, which carry out acts of armed force against another State of such gravity as to amount to *(inter alia)* an actual armed attack conducted by regular forces, or its substantial involvement therein".

The ICJ also concluded that third party or collective interventions were not justified by lower levels of aggression not amounting to armed attack.

American John Lawrence Hargrove claims that the Nicaragua judgment "left the law of force and self-defense a feebler, poorer thing than it found it: not just more poorly crafted, but, far more importantly, with weakened prospects for actual relevance to international life" (1987: 143). This writer believes, however, this is a questionable and overly harsh judgment. A determination under what circumstances self-defense was legal and what actually constituted an armed attack was vital for a legal environment dominated heavily by ideological pretenses and diversity in action. The Nicaragua judgment defined 'armed attack' in Article 51 in such a way as to challenge fundamentally some states' concept of the right of self-defense, individual and collective, by limiting its legal use.

Summary

At the outset of this chapter, Grewe's claim that the Cold War period merely constituted a continuation of the inter-war years regarding the development of international law, was cited. This claim is true in the sense that the doctrine of non-intervention was further strengthened through the restriction of the use of force to individual and collective self-defense and action authorized by the Security Council. At the same time, however, the doctrine of intervention was extended with the notion of collective security. This gave states the option to use force even if they had not been attacked themselves and was frequently employed by the US and Soviet Union. Both regularly used regional organizations, originally established to complement UN enforcement or *ad hoc* coalitions, as a guise for the use of force under collective self-defense. Smaller states used unilateral force outside the UN.

The loopholes used in existing international law were made possible foremost by the fact that some of the core concepts in the UN Charter such as 'self-defense', 'use of force' and 'armed attack' had not been defined. It was not until 1986 that the ICJ judged there were different levels of armed attack and that not all of them justified military intervention. Similarly, the Definition of Aggression a decade earlier helped limit the abuse or questionable interpretation of states regarding these core concepts. So when large states, most notably the US and Soviet Union, undertook military interventions, they did so within the existing legal framework. The Europeans used the colonial framework but these soon ended. Smaller states acted unilaterally but these had less impact. Whereas the motivations or intentions may have been different, states' justifications focused on individual and collective self-defense, therefore reinforcing rather than challenging the legal regime.

Chapter 4

The State of Play: Developments in the Contemporary International System

> As I said a year ago, we have reached a fork in the road. If you, the political leaders of the world, cannot agree or reach agreement on the way forward, history will take the decisions for you.
>
> Kofi Annan (2004)

The end of the Cold War in 1990 gave renewed hopes to those who believed in the principles on which the UN had been founded. As mentioned in the introduction to this book, there was the belief that a new world order would emerge. Most notably there was the hope that with the reduction of the importance attached to ideology, the use of force and intervention by states would be reduced dramatically. In addition, it was believed that the cessation of superpower rivalry would finally allow the Security Council to function effectively, establishing a working system of collective security: largely superseding the 'anarchical society' of self-help which had so bedeviled the older international system.

Based on these hopes and confronted by, at times, a somewhat different reality, the development of international law in the post-Cold War era saw a focus on five major issues: first, the changed interpretation of state sovereignty which in the post-Cold War era has been conditional rather than guaranteed; second, the move towards collective action, though not always UN-authorized, as a core legitimizing factor for the international use of force; third, the use of the 'just war' discourse in justifying military intervention; fourth, an increased focus on when intervention is permitted in the domestic affairs of states, most notably for humanitarian reasons; and fifth, the debate on whether the notion of individual and collective self-defense could be expanded to include pre-emptive action, counter terrorism, state responsibility for terrorism, and the use of force against rogue states. As the latter two aspects are to be examined in great detail in Part II and III of this book, the focus of this chapter will be on summarizing the development of the aforementioned three concepts: sovereignty, just war and the format of states' international use of force.

Sovereignty is not Virginity

> Sovereignty is not virginity, which you either have or you don't. (Geoffrey Howe 1990: 679)

The examination of state practice and its challenge to the long-established legal regime regulating the international use of force shows that sovereignty today is no longer, as argued by former British Deputy Prime Minister, Geoffrey Howe, clear cut. Sovereignty, once described as constituting absolute power and an unrestricted right to non-interference, according to Swedish Prime Minister, Göran Persson, today implies a sense of responsibility to all humanity through the international community (UN News Centre 2004). Intervention for both humanitarian reasons and security in the post-Cold War era has been therefore undertaken on two grounds: first, the belief that sovereignty is conditional; second, that conditions in or behavior of other states can constitute not only a local or regional but potentially an international concern which gives grounds for violating sovereignty. Consequently, as La Trobe University's Joseph A. Camilleri and University of Melbourne's Jim Falk (1992: 157) argue, the claim to sovereignty has become "politically more fluid and legally more ambiguous" in the contemporary international system.

Justifying the international use of force by referring to this seemingly semi-permeable state of sovereignty can, however, be a case of opening Pandora's Box. Whereas the international community and its cart horse, the UN, have to acknowledge that absolute sovereignty does not exist in order to advance the protection of human rights, such an acknowledgement can also lead to a lowering of the barrier of non-interference in general. A reinterpretation of the concept of sovereignty, most notably by individual states such as the US, UK and Australia, to allow the use of force based on the six additional justifications discussed in this book is the hallmark of sovereignty in the 21st century. Sovereignty is no longer viewed as an unquestionable attribute of states. Instead it is seen in a non-legal sense as a privilege which has to be earned and which can be suspended temporarily if the government of a respective state is seen to violate certain commonly upheld norms, newly and still vaguely defined.

The UN Charter focuses much more on states than individuals. Accordingly, it emphasizes the upholding of state sovereignty over individual rights. While the concept of sovereignty has been seen by most as essential for maintaining a basic order and stability in the international system, its existence has also increasingly been a hurdle to maintaining and, in some instances, restoring this order and stability. The paradox between the doctrine of intervention and non-intervention therefore continues.

Article 2(1) states that "the organization is based on the sovereign equality of its members" and reinforces the perception of the right to non-intervention in Article 2(7) by saying that "nothing contained in the present Charter shall authorize the United Nations to intervene in matters which are essentially within the domestic jurisdiction of any state". The principle of non-intervention has been confirmed in numerous declarations since.

Sovereignty today, due to the greater emphasis on the rights of individuals, is no longer so clear or absolute.

Murdoch University academic Samuel Makinda said that the UN was originally seen as "more of a resister, than a facilitator, of change in the practice of state sovereignty in the post-Cold War era" (1998: 103). As recent years show, the UN is moving increasingly towards tolerating the temporary suspension of sovereignty, albeit while ensuring it remains for humanitarian or security reasons and is undertaken or authorized by the UN as opposed to individual countries. Even though this section has shown that the concept of sovereignty faces clear challenges and is undergoing reinterpretation, it remains the "universal organizing principle for the management of the global system" (Clapham 1999: 537).

So while sovereignty gives states the right to partake in the international system, it also placed upon them certain duties and not just towards other states. When these duties cannot be fulfilled, argues the Secretary-General's High-Level Panel on Threats, Challenges and Change, "the principles of collective security mean that some portion of those responsibilities should be taken up by the international community" (2004: 17). Even though there are no official criteria which lead to a suspension or even derecognition of state sovereignty in a legal sense, it has increasingly been done not only in instances of humanitarian intervention but also in cases where force is used against 'failed states': a non-legal phrase which hints at some loss of full sovereign authority.

In the light of these issues, there has been a push for sovereignty to be temporarily suspended so that intervention in states is legally less controversial. The argument here is that sovereignty is viewed as being conditional on what Danish Professor of Political Science Georg Sørensen says is "the assumption that the states who have it can basically take care of themselves" (2004: 120). States which cannot do so, may relinquish their right to non-interference. The International Commission on Intervention and State Sovereignty (ICISS) argues, however, that "the suspension of the exercise of sovereignty is only *de facto* for the period of the intervention and follow-up, and not *de jure*" (2001: 44).

Most states continue to see sovereignty as elementary to their existence and right to non-interference: especially smaller and Third World States (African Union 2003). Egyptian representative, Ahmed Aboul Gheit, has expressed the traditional view held by many states that "intervention must not impact the territorial integrity or sovereignty of a sovereign state under any circumstances" (UN News Centre 1999). This is impossible if there is an intervention no matter how limited in scale and duration. So the ICISS insists that sovereignty is returned to a respective state once conditions of peace, stability and so-called good governance are seen to have been re-established (2001: 44).

The belief that sovereignty is conditional is reflected particularly in interventions undertaken for humanitarian reasons. There have been calls for sovereignty to be redefined to enable quicker international intervention: particularly in instances of large-scale killings, genocide and ethnic cleansing (Annan 1999b: 49). Although contemporary sovereignty, as defined by Americans Thomas Biersteker and Cynthia Weber, is a state's "externally recognized right to exercise final authority over its own affairs" (1996: 2), it is also understood that sovereignty entails the power and duty to do right by its people. Arising from this notion is the understanding that if its population is grossly mistreated, the government of that state loses some legitimacy and with it the right of freedom from interference by outsiders. Implicit in the Genocide Convention of 1948, this view was reiterated in the 2001 ICISS report and in 2003 by a number of heads of states attending the July 2003 Progressive Governance Conference.

By the end of the Second World War most people certainly accepted in theory, as American economist and sociologist Saskia Sassen said, that sovereignty "based on the will of the people had become established as one of the conditions of political legitimacy for a government" (1996: 2). Yet, this theory was only rarely extended into practice. With few exceptions, such as the Tanzanian invasion of Uganda and the Vietnamese invasion of Pol Pot's Cambodia, there were no humanitarian interventions. With the end of the Cold War and the occurrence of genocides such as in Rwanda and Bosnia, Kofi Annan (1999c) expressed an increasing belief that "surely no legal principle – not even sovereignty – can ever shield crimes against humanity". This belief was reflected in state practice during the 1990s and, to a lesser extent, in the 21st century.

During the Cold War, human rights were viewed largely through an ideological prism: for democratic states, communist states were abusers of their citizens' rights. The communist states held the reverse view. The doctrine of containment of communism meant force was to be threatened or used to prevent further communist governments. Yet, interventions in established communist or non-communist states by either side after 1945 were very limited in number, often covert or indirect, and almost never justified in terms of the non-ideological language of international human rights. Nuclear deterrence, with or instead of, law kept overt interventions to a minimum despite the heightened rhetoric over rights in the Cold War sense. Covert operations were more common. The doctrine of non-intervention and state sovereignty thus appeared more impermeable than today.

In the contemporary international system, the UN, as well as individual and coalitions of states, refer increasingly to the latter half of Article 2(7) which states that the principle of non-intervention "shall not prejudice the application of enforcement measures under Chapter VII". In the Somalia crisis of 1992, the Security Council seemed to shift from its long held disposition of giving preference to state sovereignty by permitting the use of force based on humanitarian grounds. There has been today what Norwegian academics Knut Nustad and Henrik Thune call "a shift from the primacy of states to primacy of individuals" (2002: 173). This means that a state's sovereignty and right to non-interference are conditional upon the extension of human rights to its own citizens.

While humanitarian intervention in instances of severe human rights abuses and genocide has reached an almost mandatory stage, there remain concerns regarding the concept's abuse by individual states in order to justify force. The use of force to counter perceived threats to international order, security and stability, as posed by, for example so-called rogue states, states supporting terrorism, and failed states, have also been difficult to justify under the UN Charter's recognition of sovereignty. These fears have been voiced most notably by smaller states and have led the DPRK to condemn, in particular, non-UN authorized humanitarian intervention as, what North Korean ambassador Li Hyong Chol (2000) called, "a dangerous concept that could beautify such act of highhandedness and eliminate the essential spirit of the UN Charter".

State practice from the 1990s onwards appeared to push for the suspension of sovereignty in instances of humanitarian crisis such as genocide. This trend amongst states towards tolerating the use of force and with it a temporary suspension of sovereignty, in instances in which states do not meet their responsibilities was clearly reflected by the High-Level Panel. The Panel argued that sovereignty "today clearly carries with it the obligation of a state to protect the welfare of its own peoples" (2004: 17). This is the case most notably when the government in question is either unable or unwilling to halt the large-scale loss of life, genocide or ethnic cleansing. This also has been applied to issues of self-defense.

American National Security Advisor Condoleezza Rice (2002b), in the aftermath of the September 11 attacks, argued that today "threats come ... less from strong states than from weak or failed states". She (2003) and George W. Bush (2002e) stated that the US' main concern with regard to failed states was their potential to act as a safe haven for terrorist groups.

The High-Level Panel (2004) also acknowledges this prospect. Australia intervened in the Solomon Islands in 2003 on the basis of it being a failed state: its main concern lying not so much with terrorism but rather money laundering, drug and people trafficking (Downer 2003b). When South Africa, Ethiopia and Mozambique intervened in Burundi in 2003, their main concern was the instability bought along by the warring factions within the state, including the issue of refugees and thus to re-establish political and economical stability in the country (African Union 2003).

The use of force for self-defense shows that states may also be viewed as not meeting their responsibility warranting a right to non-interference even if no humanitarian concerns exist. The focus here is on the argument that a right to non-interference does not exist as the state in question either does not adhere to recognized norms of international behavior (rogue states) or is unable or unwilling to exercise its responsibility of halting terrorist attacks emanating from its territory (counter terrorism). In both instances, it is claimed by some, pre-emptive force may be used. The use of force in these instances is reflective of today's interdependent world in which distances between states no longer make them immune from what takes place elsewhere. Globalization has led not only to shared interests and greater vulnerability but also to greater cooperation amongst states (Mingst and Karns 2000, Rotfeld 2000, Akihiko 2002).

The growing trend towards greater interdependence between states in the post-Cold War era has meant that collective or cooperative security has become one of the main aims, at least in theory, of states in the international system. This is first and foremost due to the fact that, as Harvard University's Robert Patman says, "many contemporary security threats ... are largely beyond the control of individual states and therefore require international, not national, responses" (1999: 4). These issues include, amongst other things, states themselves or conditions therein posing a safe-haven for terrorists, money laundering, drug-trafficking, refugee flows and proliferation of weapons. All of these can pose threats to states thousands of kilometers away from the place of action. According to Stockholm International Peace Research Institute (SIPRI) researchers Renata Dawn and Caroline Holmqvist, this means that it is "questionable whether any internal conflict [in an increasingly globalized world] can be devoid of international dimensions" (2005: 85). Consequently, in the 21st century if a state wants to preserve not only its national security but also the peace and order of the international system as a whole, as Blair implied, it has to take into account the fact that in the current interdependent world, the chain of the international community is only as strong as its weakest link (1999a). Bill Clinton characteristically captured this point in a folksy analogy: "in our global village, progress can spread quickly; trouble can too [and] trouble on the far end of town soon becomes a plague on everyone's house" (1995: 780).

Multilateral Fig Leaf

> The only possible argument against the substitution of collective measures under the Security Council for individual measures by a single state would be the inability of the international organization to act with the speed requisite to preserve life. (Philip C. Jessup 1959: 170)

The initial phase of the post-Cold War era looked promising for those who believed in the effectiveness of a system of collective security. When Iraqi forces invaded Kuwait in 1990, the UN, for only the second time in its history (after Korea in 1950) authorized an official peace enforcement mission. Louis Henkin, of Columbia University, however, argued shortly afterwards that the development of collective security enforcement through the UN could not be taken for granted. Indeed, it became increasingly clear that the international community would have to come to grasp Jessup's above observation on collective security.

The genocide in Rwanda showed that while the UN, at law, had the power to act, in practice it did not. This meant that disillusionment regarding both the UN and the international system's general ability to limit the use of force to such collective action revived. Alternatives to UN action would have to be debated. This recognition led some observers such as Nottingham University academic Dino Kritsiotis (1996: 176) to argue that apparent failings of the UN collective security arrangement improved "the prospects for a unilateral recourse to force". Not all agree. In light of the increasing perception that, as Professor of International Relations at the University of Ljubljana Zlatko Sabic argues, international security "can only be accomplished and sustained through a collective effort", states have focused if not exclusively on the UN authorized use of force then at least on collective action (2003: 493). This multilateral use of force is viewed as a more legitimate means of breaching state sovereignty.

Sabic countered that the majority of states did not want to abandon multilateralism for the unilateralism which has previously been more evident. This collective format of intervention is reflective of the fact that due to the growing interdependence caused by globalization, states are largely forced to embrace collective approaches to problems and threats. In an age of increasing interdependence, described by Kofi Annan as "the glue of common interest", the threats present in the contemporary international system are mainly of a transnational nature (2005a: 3). State boundaries alone do not protect countries from such dangers, implying that today "the collective interest is the national interest" including when it comes to security issues (Annan 1999b).

There are two principal ways of dealing with such threats: multilaterally (collectively) or unilaterally. The distinction between the two is, as Georgetown University's Christopher C. Joyner (2005: 167) rightly points out, not just one of numbers. Instead, it is "distinguished by the purpose and authority attributed to that use of force". Joyner describes the multilateral use of force as "the result of the decision of a competent international organization [which] is taken on behalf of the community at large" (Dixon 2005: 289). In fact, multilateral interventions can take at least three distinct forms: under Security Council auspices, as part of an established regional organization or as part of an *ad hoc* coalition not arising from any specific international organization. All three, in descending order of legitimacy, are widely seen as preferable to unilateral action. The inability of the UN to mobilize security action itself after Iraq (1991) meant most focus has fallen on regional organizations and *ad hoc* coalitions.

Brownlie claims that there has been a move by the Security Council to 'subcontract' regional organizations, *ad hoc* coalitions and individual states to undertake enforcement action (2002: 11). Chesterman refers to this as the privatization of the Security Council's responsibilities, most notably its 'duty' to maintain international peace and security (2001a: 164). This approach includes UN authorized action in Somalia (1992), Haiti (1994), the Great Lakes (1996), Sierra Leone (1997), East Timor (1999), and The Democratic Republic of the Congo (2003) to name just a few (Gray 2002). According to Chesterman, this trend towards regionalism is, however, coupled with the reduction of the importance attached to the UN Security Council's authorization. He claims that the UN today, "rather than operating as a source of legal authority [is] seen as one policy justification among others" (2001b: 169–70). Indeed, the Security Council was largely ignored with regard to NATO's use of force against Kosovo and the US actions in Iraq.

Kofi Annan has consequently argued that "the task is not to find alternatives to the Security Council as a source of legal authority but to make it work better" (2005a: 33). In the meantime, however, states are using alternatives to retain their use of force in the sphere of, if not actual then at least apparent, legality, by acting multilaterally and through regional organizations and *ad hoc* coalitions:

sometimes authorized or subcontracted by the UN, sometimes acting outside of the UN's framework.

The interventions in Korea (1950), Iraq (1991) and East Timor (1999) are examples of the first type. Australia, though not the US, invoked its membership of SEATO as part of the legal basis for its operations in Vietnam (1965); the Soviet Union invoked the Warsaw pact over Czechoslovakia; the OAS was invoked as the basis for US-led interventions in Grenada (1983) and Panama (1989); finally, NATO was invoked for the US-led action in Kosovo (1999). In no case was UN authorization given or sought. Examples of the third type include US intervention in Vietnam (1965), Afghanistan (2001) and Iraq (2003).

Chapter VIII of the UN Charter allows regional organizations to deal "with such matters relating to the maintenance of international peace and security ... provided that ... their activities are consistent with the purposes and principles of the United Nations". The use of regional organizations to uphold peace, prevent aggression and resolve conflicts was an issue also stressed in the UN Secretary General's 1992 report, *Agenda for Peace* (Boutros-Ghali 1992a).

Generally speaking, regional bodies and their member states would be both more aware of crisis in their specific region and interested in solving them. They are also more likely to be aware of local economic, political, strategic and cultural aspects and therefore better equipped to deal with these problems. Although organizations such as the OAS and African Union (AU) have more than thirty and fifty member states they are still smaller than the UN and therefore potentially less likely to find themselves in a stalemate which at times has marked this body. At the same time, however, regional organizations, just like the UN are dominated by major powers and their interests. In addition, they may be able to deploy troops to crisis areas more quickly but many organizations such as the AU or Organization of Eastern Caribbean States (OECS) often do not have the financial means to act. So while the UN has recognized the increased role regional organizations can play in upholding peace and security, the Report of the Secretary General (2000) also pointed out that this relationship largely lacked clearly defined rules regarding the authority and power, regional bodies were given.

Boutros-Ghali (1995) saw a real danger that UN-authorized or subcontracted states and regional organizations "may claim international legitimacy and approval for forceful actions that were not in fact envisaged by the Security Council when it gave authorization to them". Clarification of this issue is of particular importance when it comes to the use of force undertaken by regional organizations as such action, as stated in the UN Charter, is originally only permitted in instances of self-defense and if authorized by the Security Council. In the end, the credibility of regional organizations which become involved in the international use of force depends largely on the structure and membership of the body, the track record of the organization, the aim and outcome of the use of force, as well as whether authorization by the UN has been given.

The second group which have emerged as a major player in international politics are *ad hoc* multinational coalitions. Depending on the crisis or threat, individual states group themselves together in order to use force internationally. These coalitions are rarely identical for each instance. Instead they exist by the *credo* that, as Rumsfeld (2004) made clear, "the mission must determine the coalition and not the coalition the mission". With this in mind, one could say that *ad hoc* coalitions are the candy shop of the international use of force. Membership in an international or regional organization is more likely to generate a stronger obligation for members to become involved in military missions although they may have no vital political, economic or strategic interest in the issue. By contrast, *ad hoc* coalitions allow states to pick and choose areas of involvement as their interests suggest. These coalitions are adaptable, have the ability to be deployed within a short period of time and can also be withdrawn more randomly than UN troops or those of regional organizations which seem to be bound by a higher degree of accountability.

Swedish academic Peter Wallensteen observes that "major powers alone may have the power but their actions do not carry international legitimacy" (1997: 15). He adds that, at least initially, *ad hoc* coalitions often strive to receive authorization from an international organization such as the UN. This in return reinforces the view that despite their shortcomings regional and international organizations still hold a greater degree of legitimacy than *ad hoc* coalitions when it comes to the international use of force. Renata Dawn tries to point out a positive aspect of these *ad hoc* coalitions and suggests that states concerned with their sovereignty may feel that the use of force by a group of states, as compared to a regional or international body, is less intrusive (2001: 109). The claim that the use of force by *ad hoc* coalitions is less intrusive may be the case with military missions permitted by the respective state but would be doubtful with regard to the international use of force undertaken without permission. In any case, as mentioned above, *ad hoc* coalitions are not bound or held back by the established terms of agreement of international and regional organizations and thereby are more of a concern.

Dawn furthermore argues that the international use of force by *ad hoc* coalitions tends only to take place in areas in which regional organization do not exist or exercise limited influence. This was, for example, the case with the Australian-led intervention force in East-Timor in 1999. Consequently, according to Dawn (2001: 109), these coalitions "represent not so much an alternative to an existing regional institutional order as an effort to make up for its absence". Based on this view, the action taken by the 'Coalition of the Willing' in Iraq (2003) would be viewed as an initiative taken only on the basis of the absence of a regional organization in the Middle East. Instead, the League of Arab States had earlier "categorically rejected an attack on Iraq or a threat against the security and integrity of an Arab state" (Mahassani 2003). Consequently, and considering the amount of regional organizations in existence, the use of *ad hoc* coalitions does not always constitute a substitute but sometimes merely an alternative to regional organizations. Similar to the potential of using regional organizations to circumvent the UN, *ad hoc* coalitions may be used to circumvent regional organizations.

Regional organizations are also often used to disguise unilateralism. During the Cold War era the US established NATO as a potential vehicle to intervene in Europe. Similarly, the US and France established SEATO in 1954. Although a South-East Asian organization, the body included only two states from this region: Thailand and The Philippines. Though by no means a Middle Eastern power, the US also joined CENTO in 1958. As a member of varying regional organizations the US was therefore able to invoke the collective defense mechanisms inherent in their charters. The pursuit of national interests was disguised in form of regional and collective action.

While the Security Council may only be one among many justifications, it is still widely considered to be the crucial legitimizing factor (Voeten 2005: 528). The UN can by no means prevent the use of force outside its sphere but its principle organ the Security Council, according to Georgetown academic Erik Voeten "may raise the costs of unilateral action" (2005: 534). The use of force outside the UN framework tends to be viewed, at least initially, with great suspicion. States appear to prefer, according to Pallet (2000: 385), to tolerate the occasional ignorance of international law rather than fundamentally rewrite the long-established legal regime.

The failure of collective security arrangements with regard to preventing genocide in Rwanda, as well as putting a stop to the civil war in the former Yugoslavia and Somalia, meant that by the mid-1990s, some disillusionment had set in. The reality was that multilateralism was often not able to, as American academic Michael Glennon (1999: 5) said, "filter out the worst forms of national self-interest and keep them from playing a leading role in international intervention". States may not want to participate in intervention in which they have no specific political, economical or strategic interest. Similarly, some may want to intervene in countries which the international community as a whole does not view as a threat to international peace and security. Furthermore, some may wish to prevent intervention by other states. Yet, states still found it easier to organize intervention collectively, albeit largely through regional organizations and *ad hoc* coalitions, rather than the UN just as they had in the Cold War. For example, the US was able to lead NATO, not the UN into intervention in Yugoslavia.

A number of states believe that both current collective security arrangements under the UN and international law, are inadequate to deal with the threats and problems facing the international system. Consequently, they have resorted to collective force outside of the organizations – not always authorized. Individual states and groups of states have assumed for themselves the right now reserved to the Security Council, that is, to use force in instances other than self-defense following an armed attack. The practice of states in this area has challenged the long-established legal regime governing the international use of force.

The unilateral use of force, in contrast, is simply an intervention by a single state. Joyner's definition that it is "a unilateral decision ... designed primarily to achieve goals personal to the acting state" confuses the issue because such self-interested motives could also apply to states in any of the three types of multilateral interventions (Dixon 2005: 289). Examples of recent unilateral action include the Soviet Union in Afghanistan in 1979 (although controversially by invitation), Israel against Iraq (1981) and Lebanon (various) and the US strikes against Libya (1986), Sudan and Afghanistan (1998). More than 350 years after the birth of modern international law, it appears that collective action is seen as a crucial legitimizing factor regarding the use of force. Ruth Wedgewood, an adviser to the US Department of Defense and Professor of International Law at Johns Hopkins University, put it succinctly by saying that "unilateralism sits uncomfortably in a multilateral world" (1998: 726).

Cases such as NATO's intervention in Kosovo (1999) or the US-led *ad hoc* coalition in Iraq (2003) show that states go to great lengths to invest their actions with as much legitimacy as possible through the use of collective means. Such collective action through regional organizations and *ad hoc* coalitions is then accorded an additional appearance of legality, by invocation and interpretation of previous UN Security Council resolutions, the UN Charter and existing international law, as will be examined in Part II and III.

This development of acting collectively though in many instances outside the UN framework, has not been a recent issue as exemplified in previous chapters, but rather a trend which has been in existence since the end of the Cold War (Branch 2005: 104). The Iraq War has, however, brought to the forefront the debate as to whether or not states will opt increasingly for non-UN authorized military action or not. Kofi Annan argued that the "right to act unilaterally, or in *ad hoc* coalitions ... represents a fundamental challenge to the principles on which, however imperfectly, world peace and stability have rested for the last fifty-eight years". He furthermore states his concern that such logic would lead to the "proliferation of the unilateral and lawless use of force, with or without justification" (2003b). While criticizing non-UN authorized action, Annan acknowledges that it will not be possible to rule out of such behavior unless the situations and threats at hand can be dealt with effectively through UN collective means. According to South African academics Xego and Olivier, this means "stringed requirements for legality of such [unilateral] action [have to be laid down] in order to prevent a widening gap between law and practice" (2003: 101). The examination of this perceived gap will occur in subsequent chapters.

While seeing the need for occasional action taken outside the UN, Bruno Simma, a judge on the ICJ, believes that "the more isolated these instances remain, the smaller will be their potential to erode the precepts of international law, in our case the UN Charter" (1999: 4). Klaus Kinkel, former German Foreign Minister, agreed with this view. While supporting NATO action against Kosovo he also warned previously that the organization's decision "cannot create a precedent [and] we must not allow the Security Council's monopoly on the use of force to get on a slippery slope" (Deutscher Bundestag 1998). Generally speaking, collective action, as opposed to the unilateral use of force by states, is viewed as exercising a certain amount of restraint on actions taken. Yet, there continue to exist concerns when states act collectively but outside of the UN framework.

The current security arrangements favored and pursued by states are a reflection of a struggle not so much between multilateralism and unilateralism but between collective action undertaken through and outside of the UN. Multilateralism offers more legitimacy but is often difficult to arrange and can reduce the leading states' freedom of action. So, whereas in theory, cooperative security is viewed as "the most desirable and adequate concept for the challenges ahead" (Rotfeld 1994: 3), in practice states remain unsure how to best respond to the current threats to international peace and security.

Robert L. Hutchings (2003), Chair of the US National Intelligence Council, has argued that a 'crisis of multilateralism' has emerged since the decision by the US to act with the help of an unauthorized *ad hoc* coalition to intervene militarily in Iraq in 2003. Annan (2003b) indirectly described this decision as "very painful for those of us who believe in collective answers to our common problems and challenges". The international community witnessed a divide between those states which favored UN-authorized collective action and those who advocated the collective use of force outside of this UN framework if need be. Annan (2004) stated that a 'fork in the road' had been reached and that a decision had to be made whether the current institutions and rules were adequate to deal with the threats to international peace and security or whether changes were necessary.

This debate continues with a number of UN-authorized Commissions and Panels having made suggestions for the establishment of "new principles and norms adequate to the new needs and requirements" (Rotfeld 1999: 12) of the security environment of the 21st century. Today it seems as though the international community is confronted with a world it thought it had left behind and would not encounter again in the post-Cold War era. Instead of the unchallenged rule of law and the pursuit of the use of force through the UN, there has been a challenge posed to the rules governing the international use of force by state practice.

Just War or Martial Sins

> Established just war precepts, rather than being clear guides to action (or inaction), can be vague, malleable, and subject to self-serving manipulation by governments seeking both legitimacy and exculpation for their martial sins. (Gregory D. Foster 2004: 23)

Prior to the rise of international law in the 17th century, just war theory tended to fulfill the purpose of classifying the rightfulness of the use of force within the Christian world. It allowed the categorization of the use of force as 'just' and 'unjust' depending on whether the criteria of *jus ad bellum* (justice to resort to war) and *jus in bello* (justice in war) were fulfilled. The former include the principles of just cause, right intention, legitimate authority, reasonable chance of success, proportionality of ends and the use of force as an *ultima ratio* (last resort).

The rise of secular international law and, in particular, the rise of international collective security organizations such as the League of Nations and, later, its successor the UN should, in theory at least, have made the notion of just war obsolete. Instead, the challenge of recent state practice to the rules governing the international use of force has seen a partial re-emergence of just war theory. As the old argument of self-defense is less applicable to the types of action undertaken in recent years, states have occasionally resorted to the invocation of just war theory to justify the use of force. The application of just war theory occurs most notably in four core instances: the use of force against rogue states, failed states, states supporting terrorism and in instances of humanitarian intervention. The justification used for resorting to the use of force in these instances is not directly reflected in the UN Charter or customary international law.

The first explanation for the continuing relevance of just war theory lies in the changing nature of the international system since the establishment of the UN Charter in 1945. Some, most notably the US under Bush (2003a) and the UK under Blair, claimed that international law and the UN, in its current formats, do not deal sufficiently with the changes that have occurred in the international system. Admittedly, the focus of the UN and international law remain on traditional inter-state conflict and the prohibition of it, rather than internal conflicts. Humanitarian intervention, for example, may be illegal from an international law perspective but has increasingly been accepted under moral pretenses. Just war theory is therefore used by states to fill the gap between international law which determines which actions are legal or illegal and morality with its determination of actions as right or wrong. The problem with this use of just war theory is, however, that moral justification can merely be used as legal excuses and moral principles are more culture grounded than legal rules. This can be of particular concern as such justification are used more frequently on a non-UN-authorized basis. One has to ask whether the implicit superiority of Christianity over other religions been replaced by that of Western political values – including democracy – over other cultures?

Consequently, German philosopher Jürgen Habermas' view that "moral norms appealing to our better judgment may not be enforced in the same fashion as established legal norms" (1999: 270) has to be taken into the consideration of an overall assessment of such use of force based on what are essentially moral justifications. It is the issue of morality to which governments appeal by using just war rhetoric. Its revival in the post-Cold War era has been astonishing. The growing importance of just war rhetoric resumed with the Gulf War and its declaration as a 'noble cause' by George Bush Snr (1991: 67–8). Developments in recent years, most notably the rhetoric of 'just cause' and 'just war' with regard to the use of force in Kosovo, Afghanistan and Iraq, seem to confirm its continuing importance (Blair 1999b and 2001b, Howard 2003b, Koizumi 2003, Berlusconi 2003).

Bush, announcing the cessation of major combat operations in Iraq in May 2003, went so far as to argue that fallen US soldiers' "final act on this Earth was to fight a great evil" (2003e). Earlier, one week after September 11, Bush (2001a) told Americans "we will rid the world of evil-doers": a phrase which arose in

1487 with the publication of German inquisitors of the Catholic Church, Heinrich Kramer's and Jacob Sprenger's *Malleus Malificarum*. This invocation of an old Christian term, more than many others of Blair or Howard, reflects the religious roots of just war theory.

Just war theory is very much focused on unilateral action (and today non-UN authorized force) as it arose long before the modern state system or collective security organizations. Consequently, it tends to be used when UN-authorized action is sidelined. However, the 21st century has seen an interesting development, namely the consideration of the adaptation of aspects of just war theory and rhetoric on a multilateral basis. This development is the second reason for the continuing relevance of the concept.

Just war theory's embrace and use by a number of key players within the international system, particularly the UK and US, has made dealing with the issue on a multilateral basis essential. This is especially so because just war theory, as mentioned before, is largely used to justify the use of force for humanitarian reasons and on an expanded notion of self-defense. These instances are largely not covered by international law which has led some states to argue their case not on legal but moral pretenses.

The perception that current international law does not cater adequately for the use of force based on humanitarian grounds is reflected in the ICISS report which lists six criteria for military intervention in protection of human rights. They are not legal but rather moral criteria based on just war theory. The military principles outlined are identical to six criteria used for the determination of *jus ad bellum*: legitimate authority, just cause, right intention, last resort, proportional means and reasonable prospects of success (2001: 32). An examination of the reasons for the continuing relevance of just war theory consequently shows that like its original form, the theory is today also used in order to expand the grounds for intervention.

The first category of *jus ad bellum*, 'just cause', is widely viewed as the "essential weak link in just war theory" (Coates 1997: 147). As Harvard University academic Laurie Calhoun points out, such "rhetoric of morality is obviously not the prerogative of the righteous" (2000: 454). Although highly ambiguous, it is the category of *jus ad bellum* which is used most frequently to justify the use of force. Yet, the use of the 'just cause' criteria for determining the rightfulness of the use of force has led to confusing outcomes in which the same instance of the use of force, such as Kosovo, Afghanistan or Iraq, may be interpreted as 'just' by some and 'unjust' by others (Rau 1999, Falk 2001, Pryce-Jones 2001, Columbus 1999).

Regarding Iraq, Howard and Blair (2003) argued respectively that "Australian and British forces have fought together in a just cause" and that "it was a just cause, we thought it was the right thing to do".

According to the ICISS, the use of force only constitutes a just cause if it halts or reverts actual or apprehended large scale loss of life, including genocide, as well as ethnic cleansing (2001: 32). The report thereby limits the interpretation of 'just cause' to humanitarian issues which is an important difference to interpretations by individual states, regional organizations and *ad hoc* coalitions. These individual interpretations have included causes such as the spread of democracy, regime change, and halting the development or proliferation of weapons of mass destruction (WMD). The instance of the US-led intervention in Iraq is one of the most obvious examples for such diverging interpretations of the just cause principle. Bush argued that the planned removal of WMD was "serv[ing] a great and just cause" (2003d).

The second criterion of 'legitimate authority' is widely debated as it brings out, more than any of the other *jus ad bellum* criteria, the issue of sovereignty over the use of force in the international system (2001: 32). The ICISS argues that the UN is the "only organization with universally accepted authority to validate such operations" (2001: 49). Kofi Annan has supported this view by stating that the non-UN authorized use of force will always have its legitimacy questioned and have limited support (UN News Centre 2003). The Commission, however, acknowledges that action undertaken by a regional organization or any other form of collective action can be viewed as legitimate if it has been authorized by the UN. It also acknowledges that it is unrealistic for states not to become active in instances in which the Security Council, says the ICISS, "fails to discharge its responsibility in conscience-shocking situations crying out for action" (2001: 55). It therefore establishes a hierarchy of authority reaching from the UN, to regional organizations, *ad hoc* coalitions and individual states.

The third criterion of 'right intention' today implies the need for force to be based on altruistic rather than self-interested reasons. However, Canadian Professor of Ethics at the University of Waterloo, Brian Orend, observes that "one needs to acknowledge that purity of will is probably a pipe dream" (1999: 129). The belief that a mixture of altruism and self-interest may be sufficient to be called a right intention is also embraced by the ICISS (2001: 55). The Commission argues that in order for force to be classified as a right intention it should be undertaken multilaterally and done to "halt or avert human suffering" (2001: 35). This emphasis on improvable and unachievable purity of motive illustrates the problem here. With rules or laws motive is far less important and judgments of behavior more objective.

The fourth *jus ad bellum* criterion, that is the use of force as a 'last resort', can easily be described as an "endlessly receding horizon" (Baumann 1991: 150). It is true that unless a clear definition exists of what constitutes a last resort and when it is reached, this criterion could theoretically lead to a just war never being justified. Robert Phillips, Professor of Philosophy at the University of Connecticut, suggests that the criterion does not imply states being "locked into a series of steps beginning with the most pacific means and gradually escalating in the direction of force" (1984: 14). Such an interpretation is partially accepted by the ICISS. The Commission states that diplomatic and non-military means have to be undertaken before force is used and before it constitutes a last resort. However, the ICISS acknowledges that "this does not necessarily mean that every such option must literally have been tried and failed" before the halting of large scale killings is permitted (2001: 36). Even when non-humanitarian issues are at stake, government officials argue, as did Dick Cheney (2004), with regard to both Afghanistan and Iraq, that "the use of force is always our last resort".

The fifth *jus ad bellum* criterion of 'proportional means' entails essentially that the damage caused by the use of force must be less than the scale of damage it is trying to stop or avert. One of the problems with this criterion is the lack of definite ways in which to calculate such proportional means. This is also an issue reflected in the ICISS report, which only addresses the issue in a vague way, stating that "the scale, duration and intensity of the planned military intervention should be the minimum necessary to secure the humanitarian objective in question" (2001: 36). Generally speaking, proportional means can refer to a number of issues, including the damage caused to a state's infrastructure as a consequence of the use of force, as well as the duration of the conflict or the weapons used (ICISS 2001: 37). There is no simple way of conducting what Carl von Clausewitz viewed as the cost-benefit analysis of war (2007: 31–42). The interpretation of proportional means depends very much on the national interests at stake for a state.

The final criterion of *jus ad bellum* is the 'reasonable success' regarding the use of force. This can be seen as the most subjective criterion, the assessment of which rarely, if ever, speaks out against the use of force if the other criteria have already been fulfilled. Government leaders would not pursue the use of force if they were not convinced by the chances of its success. As with the issue of proportional means, the ICISS is again hesitant to draw up any clear guidelines on this criteria. This 'failure' can largely be attributed to the fact that criteria, such as the reasonable chance of success, are difficult to determine in the abstract. Following from this, the ICISS limits itself to saying that a reasonable chance of success means "halting or averting the atrocities or suffering that triggered the intervention in the first place" (2001: 37). It goes on to state that the use of force is not justified in instances in which the use of force on humanitarian grounds can lead to a larger conflict.

Such an instance has occurred in Iraq where sectarian violence has broken out since the removal of Saddam Hussein from power in 2003. To what extent the prediction of such events could have influenced the US calculations of a 'reasonable chance of success' can only be speculated. It furthermore indicates that the interpretation of what actually constitutes a success is also highly subjective. If it was the removal of Hussein, the US has clearly succeeded. If it was, however, to halt the suffering of the Iraqi population, who clearly continue to endure sectarian violence, then the use of force has clearly failed.

The interpretation of *jus ad bellum* criteria by individual states and the community of states, as represented by the ICISS, can diverge greatly. The subjectivity involved in the interpretation of the criteria clearly shows the danger inherent in just war theory when used to justify non-UN authorized use of force. This means, most notably, the disguise of the pursuit of national interests by referring instead to the pursuit of supposed moral and altruistic reasons such as humanitarian concerns as mirrored in just war theory.

The ICISS makes a respectable attempt at merging the gap between legality and morality in instances of intervention as interpreted by many states. The report tries to steer the application of just war theory into multilateral waters and thereby attempts to set up ways of controlling and limiting the challenge of recent state practice to the rules governing the international use of force. Just war is not, of course, incorporated into international law or the UN Charter. It is also highly unlikely that it will ever be. Just war theory, while used by some states to justify their use of force remains a discourse from the past, highly culturally-biased and separate from international law. The quasi-legal basis of just war theory finds it difficult to compete with the long-established legal regime regulating the international use of force.

Summary

In conclusion, it can be said that in the 21st century Jessup's 1950s comment is valid: unlimited sovereignty, which has developed since the Peace of Westphalia, is "no longer automatically accepted as the most prized possession or even desirable attribute of states" (1959: 41). While state sovereignty was close to absolute in the 19th century, territories which were viewed as 'non-civilized', 'barbarous', 'savage' or 'feeble' were not allocated the privilege of non-intervention (Lorimer 1872: 189). Today, sovereignty has been substantially softened and made conditional on the fulfillment of governmental responsibilities, most notably, the adequate treatment of citizens.

While the doctrine of intervention has consequently been expanded, this has been done on the *proviso* that the use of force is undertaken collectively. The League of Nations first institutionalized the notion of collective security which was later confirmed in the UN Charter. During the Cold War, however, the focus was not so much on global collective, but regional collective, security through organizations such as NATO, SEATO, CENTO, OAS, OECS and the Warsaw Pact. Today, collective action focuses on regional organizations and *ad hoc* coalitions. The first Gulf War promised the future reliance on formal multilateral means to combat new threats. Since the September 11 attacks and the intervention in Afghanistan, states have continued to resort to collective action through regional organizations and *ad hoc* coalitions: not always authorized.

According to Professor of Political Science at the University of California, Patrick M. Morgan, multilateralism is seen as "the source of legitimacy" and unilateral action tends to be viewed critically (1993: 346). Consequently, even those states acting outside the UN framework attempt to undertake force, argues Oxford's Montague Burton Professor of International Law Adam Roberts, "at least with a multilateral fig leaf" (1997: 128). This includes not only the establishment of *ad hoc* coalitions but also drawing on various regional bodies to give approval (Roberts 1997: 128). The examination of state practice in the post-Cold War era, which is to follow, will show that states' response to conflicts and threats, while largely collective in nature, appear, according to The Aspen Institute, to be "*ad hoc* and often inconsistent, born of the moment and the most recent experience" (1996: 9).

Just war theory remains relevant today, not so much because it continues to restrain the use of force, as claimed by American theologian John Courtney Murray (1960: 13) during the 1960s, but because it has been invoked to expand the grounds for the use of force beyond self-defense. It also takes the judgment of the legitimacy of an intervention away from the UN, which is either seen as hopelessly ineffective or hopelessly biased by its Western members, back to the European and especially English-speaking world. It gives that authority of judgment back to where it was when international law developed and was seen as a rule for the civilized not the uncivilized: back into Western hands.

Part II

For the Good of Humanity: The Use of Force for Humanitarian Reasons

The justifications given by states for the contemporary international use of force have centered, as explained in the introduction to this book, around two core categories: first, the use of force for humanitarian reasons; second, the use of force based on individual and collective self-defense. Part II of this book concentrates on the former.

Military intervention for humanitarian reasons can be further sub-categorized into three types: first, the protection of a state's own nationals abroad; second, the protection of foreign nationals, also better known as humanitarian intervention; third, intervention in so-called failed states, which are characterized by political instability, internal conflict and economic hardship.

The focus of the use of force in these instances is the protection of the individual within these states, rather than the protection of the intervening state's security. It appears that, in these instances the defense of human rights, in varying forms, is a core justification for military action. One cannot, however, ignore that there is great inconsistency with regard to the application of such interventions. Consequently, human rights are not forcibly protected in every case of gross abuse. Rather, the use of force tends to be linked to the position of the host state in the international system and the interests at stake of the intervening powers.

This part examines these three types of intervention for humanitarian reasons and assesses how state practice in these instances challenges the established rules for the international use of force. As with all six subsequent chapters the validity of these challenges will be appraised by examining state practice both prior to and post-1990. Only a comprehensive analysis of state practice during these different eras can enable an appropriate assessment of how and if the current use of force challenges international law.

Chapter 5
The Snail and the Slug: The Protection of Nationals Abroad

Of the three areas in which force is used on humanitarian grounds, the protection of a state's own nationals abroad has been amongst the least controversial. Prior to the Second World War such forcible protection was largely seen as a stand-alone customary right of states which often also included the protection of commercial interests and property abroad. In addition, nationals were rarely in genuinely 'foreign' countries. Instead, the protection of citizens centered largely on their presence in colonies and later mandated territories.

With the decolonization movement of the Cold War period, which reached its peak in the 1960s and 70s, the forcible protection of nationals began to be viewed in a different light. The international community was now very skeptical of states' invocation of this justification for military action. The core reason for this was that it was used by former colonial powers to justify intervention in newly independent territories. While the foreign governing structures in these new states may have disappeared, often the former colonial master's citizens had not. So when internal unrest emerged in these states, outside intervention would often be justified on self-defense, the protection of the former colonial power's nationals being an aspect of this.

Today, force is rarely used in so-called rescue missions abroad. Instead, there is a combination of forceful and non-forceful means, including the use of commercial airliners and buses, to organize the evacuation of nationals. Such action tends to be short-term in nature, often lasting only a few hours. Consequently, it has been a little debated topic in international relations and law, so much so that states do not even find it necessary to justify their actions on a legal basis.

This chapter will examine the surprising development of the forcible protection of nationals from a sole legal justification by states prior to 1945, to an aspect of self-defense during the Cold War period and, finally, the near absence of any legal justifications in its implementation since 1990.

Intolerable Cruelty

> Grotius had practically nothing to say in regard to the specific subject of the protection of the citizen abroad, primarily because the citizen for the most part stayed at home. (Frederick Sherwood Dunn 1932: 48)

The forcible protection of nationals abroad is, indeed, not an issue discussed in much detail by the classic writers of international law. This is largely due to the fact, as America's Dunn rightly stated, that subjects and citizens at the time rarely ventured outside their own countries' jurisdiction. While Aristotle had earlier explored the notion of citizenship in Greek city states, the concept of the citizen itself was not established until the emergence of the modern republican nation-state after Grotius' writings.

While Grotius (2001) does not refer specifically to the protection of nationals abroad, he does stress the importance sovereigns ought to place on their subjects, as well as the former's right to protect these subjects. Vattel, in the 18th century began to address the issue in more detail stating his belief that "whoever uses a citizen ill, indirectly offends the state, which is bound to protect this citizen; and the sovereign of the latter should avenge his wrongs [and] punish the aggressor" (1805: 224).

It was not until the 19th and particularly 20th century that literature on the subject of the protection of nationals abroad expanded (Clark 1912, Offutt 1928, Hindmarsh 1933).

In 1910, even before the word 'globalization', US Secretary of State Elihu Root correctly put this down to "the increase in facilities for transportation and communication [which] has set in motion vast armies of travelers" (1910: 517). It was, however, not only the industrial revolution but also the colonialization by states such as the UK, France, Netherlands, Spain, Portugal, Germany and Belgium, which led to a dispersion of nationals in what were, or became, foreign states. Many nationals moved abroad not just on an individual basis but as a group, taking with them the system of their home country, settling abroad on an often long-term or permanent basis. Much like a snail, many such nationals moved to these colonies and foreign territories with their house, that is the system and protection of their home country, in the form of colonial or concessionary jurisdiction. For these persons, their home country could forcibly protect them without it being an intervention. Some followed the interests of their state into what remained sovereign foreign jurisdictions.

The latter situation is reflected in a number of instances, among them the 1861 intervention by the UK, Spain and France in Mexico. According to Thomas Corwin, the US Minister to Mexico, "the archives here [are] full of complaints against the Mexican government for violations of contracts and spoliations and cruelties practiced against American citizens", as well as other foreign nationals (1861: 65). In the eyes of these states the conditions within Mexico justified the forcible protection of their nationals. Similarly, the 1898 American intervention in Cuba was based on a perceived threat to the well-being of US nationals. In this instance US President William McKinley claimed that "we owe it to our citizens in Cuba to afford them that protection and indemnity for life and property which no government there can or will afford" (1898: 757). In short, these were not interventions in the same way as protective actions of nationals in a colony or concession.

According to Hall and, later, Bluntschli the state was now entitled and indeed had the obligation to protect its own nationals, if necessary, by force.

Bluntschli saw this as being warranted where the foreign state did not oppose the ill treatment of the nationals in question, as well as in instances when the foreign state by its own actions caused injuries to such nationals (1874: 223). Of course, there was a strong element of cultural superiority here with the rules implicitly being about the right of 'civilized' European states intervening in less 'civilized' non-European states – especially in Asia, Africa and the Middle East. This parallels the way humanitarian intervention developed mainly as a basis for Christian European states intervening in Islamic territory.

Such claims were made by the respective countries in the aforementioned instances. It was particularly stressed in the Boxer Rebellion of 1900 in China. One of the few non-colonized countries of Asia, China opposed increasing foreign influence in the country, including the hated 'concessions', which in parts led to attacks on foreigners. Numerous states, amongst them France, declared it could not "evade the duty of protecting her citizens" (Delcassé 1900: 313). A sole intervention by the UK in June was followed shortly after by an alliance comprised of eight nations, amongst them France, Russia and Japan.[1]

The subsequent head of the Swiss League delegation, Edmond Pittard (1896: 1), building in a sense on Vattel, went one step further by claiming that the citizen was the essence of the state, a view which lead to the belief that in instances of mistreatment of nationals, the state itself has been attacked or an act of aggression has been committed against it.

This view reflected the fact that in republics the people were not subjects of a sovereign but were themselves the sovereign. This is an issue which rose to great relevance in the UN era and will be dealt with in more detail in the subsequent Cold War section of this chapter.

The potential for abuse of the justification of the forcible protection of nationals abroad, particularly with regard to Pittard's and Vattel's arguments, was clear. This manifested itself, albeit in a shady, convoluted way, in Japan's invasion of the Chinese province of Manchuria (1931) and Germany's occupation of Czechoslovakia (1938). Both instances were justified by the respective governments on the grounds of the protection of nationals abroad although in the latter case, despite the claims of ethnic kinship, the persons were not German citizens (De Lima 1971: 33). Adolf Hitler went so far as to state that the situation in Czechoslovakia had "become completely intolerable for the Sudeten German

---

1 The alliance of eight nations was comprised of Japan, Russia, Great Britain, United States, France, Austria, Italy and Germany; other, more controversial cases of intervention based on the justification of the protection of nationals include the French Blockade of Argentina (1838–1840), Great Britain's intervention in Abyssinia (1867–1868) and Honduras (1873), Great Britain's and France's intervention in Egypt (1876–79), France in Portugal (1893/94) and Turkey (1901), Great Britain, Italy and Germany in Venezuela (1902), Italy in Corfu (1923).

people and, in consequence, dangerous to the peace of Europe" (Carnegie Endowment for International Peace 1938: 437). He justified the invasion on the view that the Sudeten German people, actually Czech citizens, "are being oppressed in an inhuman and intolerable manner and treated in an undignified way" (Carnegie Endowment for International Peace 1938: 412). Similar to the instances in the 19th century, these cases were largely based on the intervening states claim or belief that, according to Edwin M. Borchard, of Yale University, an emergency situation existed "where the local government has failed, through inability or unwillingness, to afford adequate protection to the persons or property of the foreigners in question" (1915: 448).

States in this period largely used the protection of nationals abroad as their sole justification for the use of force. The establishment of the League of Nations and growth of international law, however, lead to an increased debate regarding the legality of such action. With the increasing restrictions on the use of force, both states and writers on the subject stressed the fact that the temporary use of force for the protection of nationals did not constitute intervention (Borchard 1915: 448, Dunn 1932: 19). Instead, such use of force was referred to as so-called 'interposition' which, said Stowell, constituted "a justifiable action undertaken by a state to induce another state to respect its rights under international law, including the rights of its nationals" (1921: 2). For many states, according to Oppenheim, the protection of nationals was viewed as a right originating from customary international law and not derogated by treaties that followed (1912: 182).

There were, nevertheless, two noteworthy instances which at least attempted to influence the use of force by states, particularly with regard to the forcible protection of nationals abroad. The first was the attempt by the Committee of Experts of the League of Nations to establish a declaration titled The Responsibility of States for Damages Caused in Their Territory to the Person or Property of Foreigners. The declaration was, however, not adopted due to the wide-held belief by states that the forcible protection of nationals abroad was a customary international right and that the subject was consequently "without question ... not ripe for codification" (Ralston 1931: 570).

The second instance was Article 11 of the Montevideo Convention of 1933, which tried to counter the issue of interposition by stating that "the territory of a state is inviolable and may not be the object of military occupation nor of other measures of force imposed by another state directly or indirectly or for any motive whatever even temporarily". The brief duration of an intervention, one of the major defenses by advocates of a right to the forcible protection of nationals, was supposed to no longer be a legally justifiable argument. This, however, had little impact on state practice which continued to believe that, according to American Jackson Ralston, "the writers tell us – and modern practice often sustains them – that nations have the right ... to protect their nationals abroad" (1931: 572). Until 1945, such justification for the use of force appeared to remain perfectly legal.

A Sacred Duty

> The right [of the protection of nationals abroad], like the right of self-defense from which it flows, is limited to such force as is necessary and appropriate to protect the threatened nationals from injury. (Monroe Leigh Nash 1976: 123)

The establishment of the UN and the commencement of the Cold War era saw a lively debate on the forcible protection of nationals abroad. The reason for this lies in two core developments. First, the restrictions placed on the use of force by the UN Charter and the widespread belief that the forcible protection of nationals was now illegal (Brownlie 1963: 298). Second, there was the decolonization process which erupted in 1945, disrupting long established ruling structures in the non-European world. With the achievement of national independence, the legal protective shell of colonialism was removed, commonly leaving many nationals of the retreating colonial power plus other Europeans, exposed in what were often strife-torn areas.

While former colonies such as The Congo, Indonesia and Vietnam achieved constitutional independence with the military forces of their former occupying powers withdrawn, large numbers of those imperial powers' nationals were left behind. Often these nationals were born or had lived in these former colonies for many years and had little interest in returning to their home country. Much like slugs they were now without the guaranteed protection of their house, that is their home state, as was the case pre-1945. Sometimes such nationals were not well treated by the new regimes or there was such strife that there was no strong local state mechanism to protect them.

Newly independent states suspected the forcible protection of nationals abroad was now beginning to be a major excuse for former colonial powers to continue or even reclaim (Suez, 1956) their influence and protect their interests under the guise of protecting their citizens. The latter used a type of force which equaled intervention but would not be seen or justified as such. American H. Scott Fairly consequently rightly observed that "the legal justification for the protection of nationals abroad was a direct product of nineteenth century imperialism" (1980: 33). The forcible protection of nationals abroad was largely undertaken by First World powers against Third World Countries which were often weak and lacked major military capacity or allies. Thus intervening states were able to undertake military operations without fear of effective defense or retribution.

Brownlie observes that with the UN Charter's limitation of the use of force to self-defense and action taken or authorized by the Security Council "only a minority of states have continued to assert [the] legality" of the forcible protection of nationals abroad (1963: 298). States which did so, amongst them most notably France, Belgium, the UK and US, sought to justify their resort to force within the new framework of international law. There are three main arguments which were brought forward by both writers and states alike to justify the forcible protection of nationals abroad in the Cold War era.

The first was expressed in the words of Henry Kissinger's State Department legal adviser, Monroe Leigh, in 1976. He argued that the right to protect nationals abroad flowed from the right of self-defense. While the Charter does not cover the forcible protection of nationals abroad, many states saw it as an act justifiable under Article 51, which permits individual and collective self-defense following an armed attack. This argument is closely linked to Pittard's earlier belief that the protection of nationals abroad is equivalent to the protection of the state itself. Critics raise two major problems over the use of Article 51.

Similar to Higgins (1961), Brierly had argued, during the interwar period that while a state should be interested in the fair treatment of its nationals abroad, it was "an exaggeration to say that whenever a national is injured in a foreign state, his state as a whole is necessarily injured too" (1995: 218).

This reflects the strong anti-interventionary sentiment of that time. More recently, India's Guha Roy agrees with this, saying that while citizens had a right to seek protection by the state at home, it was discretionary on behalf of the state if they resided abroad (1961: 875). His view, almost certainly shaped by his non-Western background, which saw the justification as a mere pretext and open to abuse, is shared by numerous other writers (Ronzitti 1985: 69). Indeed, state practice gave them numerous reasons to be skeptical. It illustrated the fact that the equation of a threat to nationals with a threat to the state had, said Canadian Jean-Pierre Fonteyne, "potential to incite states to disregard any notion of proportionality and to resort to force as soon as even a very small group of their nationals is endangered" (1974: 252).

The Suez Crisis of 1956, when Britain and France intervened forcibly in Egypt, was amongst the first instances of the forcible protection of nationals abroad. The intervening states justified the legality of their actions by referring to Article 51 and the right to self-defense. This was a rather clumsy attempt by former colonial powers, denied their previous colonial legal framework for intervention, to try and fit their intervention awkwardly into the new framework of international law. Selwyn Lloyd, British Secretary of State for Foreign Affairs, insisted that "there was an imminent threat to British Nationals, to British ships, and to the canal itself". According to the British government, referring to the UN Charter, "self-defense undoubtedly included a situation where the lives of a State's nationals abroad were in imminent danger" (House of Commons 1956).

Wright, however, saw the action by Britain as illegal as, in his view, it was not an instance which could be determined to constitute a case of self-defense following an armed attack (1957: 84). The US and most of the world shared Wright's view.

This second controversial aspect of using Article 51 was the issue of what actually constitutes an armed attack. This was particularly challenged by the Nicaragua judgment of 1986 which established different categories of what constituted armed attack (as explained in Chapter 3). Consequently it became clear that, according to British lawyer James E.S. Fawcett, "to regard the mistreatment of nationals ... as an 'armed attack' within the scope of Article 51 would be to empty that expression of any real meaning" (1961: 404). Although this was the perception held by numerous writers and states in theory, the practice looked different. Both before and after the Nicaragua judgment, the argument of the forcible protection of nationals as constituting an aspect of self-defense under Article 51 was the primary legal justification. Among these instances are four cases, which due to their controversy, are particularly noteworthy: the US interventions in the Dominican Republic (1965), Cambodia (1975), Grenada (1983) and Panama (1989).

Following a military coup in the Dominican Republic in 1965 to overthrow the government of widely viewed moderate Juan Bosch, civil war erupted. While there was substantial internal popular support for Bosch, the US took military action based, according to US President Johnson, on his belief that Bosch was a communist. The aim of the later-entitled Johnson Doctrine was the prevention of "the establishment of another communist government in the Western Hemisphere" (Johnson 1965a). This ideological stance was, of course, not a legal basis for intervention so it was not employed in this sense. Traditional legal justifications had to be appended to it. The US offered two.

The first, given by the US Representative to the OAS and supported by President Johnson (1965a, 1965b), was to "protect its citizens ... from violence in a situation where there are no authorities to insure their protection" (Bunker 1965: 740).

Critics questioned how more than 20,000 US troops were needed for a rescue mission which, the US claimed, was to protect a small number of American nationals. Further doubts regarding this justification emerged when US troops remained in the Dominican Republic even after the evacuation of American nationals.

Consequently, a belated second justification for the military intervention was brought forward. The US invoked the collective security arrangements inherent in the OAS Charter, organizing the deployment of a multinational OAS peacekeeping force under Article 19's provision for "maintenance of peace and security in accordance with existing treaties" and, argued the US, supported by the provisions of the UN Charter in Article 53.

This probably reflected US doubts as to the validity in international eyes of the 'protection of nationals' justification.

A similar issue arose with regard to the Cambodian situation when it appears to this author that the justification of the forcible protection of nationals was merely a shield for the motivations of the US. In May 1975 the Cambodian navy seized the American merchant ship *Mayaguez* and imprisoned the crew. The US described this incident as an act of piracy but also viewed it as an armed attack which, according to government official Philip Buchen, meant that "we have the right of self-defense, but only self-defense" (National Security Council 1975: 15).

Vice-President Nelson Rockefeller believed that the capture of the *Mayaguez* "will be seen as a test case [and] I think a violent response is in order" (National Security Council 1975a: 8). So, while government records show that the rescue of nationals was one objective, justified officially on the basis of self-defense, judging by Rockefeller's and Kissinger's remarks it was by no means the driving one (Ford 1975: 721–22, Scali 1975: 720, National Security Council 1975b).

The US intervened in 1983 in Grenada when the tiny Caribbean nation had experienced the armed overthrow of Maurice Bishop's government by a revolutionary group led by Bernard Coard. This was of great concern to the US because it feared Grenada under Coard would strengthen ties with Cuba and the Soviet Union. The US invaded Grenada together with member states from the Organization of Eastern Caribbean States (OECS).

The justifications in official US documents concentrate on two major issues, namely humanitarian reasons to protect American nationals and collective self-defense, following an invitation by Grenada's former Governor-General, as well as a request by OECS member states, based on Articles 8, 22 and 23 of the organization's treaty (Reagan 1983a: 67, Organization of Eastern Caribbean States 1983: 68, Shultz 1983: 69, Kirkpatrick 1983: 77).

Claiming its invasion lawful under international law, the Reagan administration must have been surprised when the General Assembly strongly disagreed, stating that it "deeply deplores the armed intervention in Grenada, which constitutes a flagrant violation of international law" (UNGA 1983).

Even Reagan's usually staunch British ally, Margaret Thatcher, criticized the invasion of a Commonwealth country.

The US response to this setback was to focus on the humanitarian justification for what Reagan now termed a 'rescue mission' including that of US students at a local medical college (1983b: 78). Critics remained doubtful in the face of the continuing military presence in Grenada after the nationals had been 'rescued'. The White House countered the General Assembly reaction to the invasion by issuing a statement saying that "we find it sad that the United Nations sees fit to deplore actions taken for humanitarian reasons, to save innocent lives, and to protect human rights, in full accord with the principles of the United Nations Charter" (1993: 78). A statement reiterated by US ambassadors Middendorf (1983) and Kirkpatrick (1983).

The US intervention in Panama in 1989 was the most controversial use of force justified, at least in parts, on the protection of nationals abroad (Bush 1989b).

Several thousand American troops were sent to Panama, arresting then head of state, General Manuel Noriega, on drug trafficking charges and establishing a new government. Earlier President Bush stressed the US commitment "to protect[ing] the lives of our citizens" as a major justification for the use of force (1989a: 70–71). In light of the large scale impact particularly on the political independence of Panama, the protection of nationals as a leading aim of the intervention was questioned by many.

Despite the aforementioned examples, state practice during the Cold War era shows that the protection of nationals abroad was largely seen as posing an exception to the prohibition of the use of force established by the UN Charter. Indeed, over the four decades of the Cold War period, only slightly more than a dozen uses of force regarding the protection of nationals occurred. Due to its potential for abuse, as reflected partly in the US cases, legal writers argued that certain criteria had to be fulfilled before the intervention could be considered legitimate. Both Lillich (1967: 347–51) and South Africa's Anthea Jeffrey (1981: 728) address this issue in some detail, listing five and three criteria respectively for such rescue operations in order to determine their legality.

These include the need for an imminent and actual danger to the lives of the nationals abroad, an unwillingness or inability of the foreign state to act (stressed in 1915 by Borchard), the dispatch of the lowest possible number of troops, their speedy withdrawal following the completion of the rescue mission, as well as the impartiality of the intervening state (Waldock 1952). Lillich and Jeffrey differ over the former's listing of the invitation of the foreign state as a criterion and the latter's insistence on the need for the intervening state to report its actions and justifications to the Security Council (Moore 1984: 154). Interventions undertaken on the above basis attained the perception of greater legality and were viewed, said Lillich, "either ... not [as] intervention at all or, if it is, [it] becomes a legally justifiable one" (1969: 209).

There are three further instances of the forcible protection of nationals abroad which are seen, at least largely, to fulfill the criteria of being a genuine case: the Belgian intervention in The Congo (1964), the Israeli intervention in Uganda (1976) and the US action in Iran (1980). The presence of Belgian nationals in The Congo was a result of colonialism. Israel has encountered the issue because of the high level of transnational linkages of its citizens who have migrated from other states and have sometimes held dual nationality. In the US case, its nationals were embassy and related staff, a situation faced by all states but usually protected by the host state's respect for diplomatic immunity.

Following the hostage taking of several thousand foreign nationals, predominantly Belgian, by a Congolese rebel group, the Belgian government, with support from the US military, launched a rescue mission. The Belgium government stated its belief that "no country would have been able to ignore its sacred duty to protect its citizens in extreme peril" (Reuters 1960).

Both Belgium and the US had attempted to solve the situation through a range of diplomatic options, including the attempt to achieve a resolution through the UN and the OAU. This attempt to pursue diplomatic means before resorting to force, together with the fact that several foreign nationals had already been killed, gave the Belgian operation greater legitimacy when it intervened to rescue the hostages without authorization by the Congolese government.

Israeli action in Uganda also related to the freeing of hostages and, similar to Belgian and French action in The Congo, was short term. A group of German and Palestinian 'terrorists' hijacked a plane with mostly Israeli nationals on board and demanded the release of a number of prisoners by Israel in exchange for the release of the hostages. The Ugandan government was not seen as neutral in the issue and Israeli forces intervened without the invitation of the government, killing numerous Ugandan soldiers.

The Israeli Ambassador to the UN, Chaim Herzog, stressed the fact that the mission, which lasted less than 24 hours, was a way of Israel "exercising its inherent right of self-defense", adding that the concept of state sovereignty was in this instance secondary to that of "man's liberty" (Shannon 1976: A1).

Thomas Krift, however, argues that the action nevertheless constituted a violation of Uganda's sovereignty, as well as an act of aggression (1977: 47–8). This is a discussion that was also brought to the Security Council's attention subsequent to the event with many states agreeing with Krift's interpretation. Israel, however, also received support for its actions, most notably by Monroe Leigh, Legal Adviser of the US Department of State, who stated that there existed a "right to use limited force for the protection of one's own nationals from an inherent threat or death" (Nash 1979: 123).

A further, albeit failed, attempt to rescue hostages through the use of force was the US actions in Iran in 1980. In November 1979, a group of students stormed the US embassy in Teheran, taking numerous American nationals hostage. The US, at first, attempted to find a non-forceful solution which included diplomatic pathways, economic sanctions and submission of the issue to the ICJ. The Court referred to the hostage taking incident as an armed attack but said no link could be established between the militants and the Iranian government (1980: 29).

Before the Court had handed down its judgment, the US in April 1980 undertook a failed armed rescue attempt, "ordered for humanitarian reasons" (The White House 1980: 38). President Jimmy Carter and other government US officials stressed the operation was only a rescue mission based on humanitarian concerns, not a military attack (1980: 5–8). The small size of the force confirms this was the case. In its report to the Security Council, the US additionally stated that the use of force had been undertaken "in exercise of its inherent right of self-defense with the aim of extricating American nationals who have been and remain the victims of the Iranian armed attack on our Embassy" (ICJ 1980: 18).

All three instances of the forcible protection of nationals abroad included the rescuing of hostages (i.e. a small number of nationals), low-level troop deployment, as well as short duration of military operations. Consequently, these instances met the criteria of legality argued by Lillich more closely than the previously mentioned operations by the US. While the forcible protection of nationals abroad was most often justified on the basis of self-defense as in Article 51, there are two further arguments which were used to support the primary one.

The first was the argument that the forcible protection of nationals abroad was not in contravention to the UN Charter as this type of use of force did not "threaten the territorial integrity and political independence of a state", as stipulated by Article 2(4). This is contradicted by both the Declaration on Principles of International Law Concerning Friendly Relations and Co-operation among States in Accordance with the Charter of the UN (1970) and the Declaration on Inadmissibility of Intervention in the Domestic Affairs of States and the Protection of their Independence and Sovereignty (1965). These state that armed intervention was synonymous with aggression and the latter declared in Article 1 that "no state has the right to intervene, directly or indirectly, for any reason whatever, in the internal or external affairs of any other state".

Numerous legal authorities from America and Britain, as well as states which supported this justification, had previously upheld the legality of the principle, especially in the early years after the Charter. Jessup was blunt and stated that it was "not in any manner inconsistent with the purposes of the United Nations" (1946: 93). They argue that such interventions should be limited to instances in which the foreign state is unable or unwilling to protect the nationals and was justified as a last resort, taking priority over the entitlement to territorial integrity" (Bowett 1957: 122).

Support for this view from American authorities continued in the Cold War. Moore agreed and said that in most instances of the forcible protection of nationals abroad there was "practically no real interference with meaningful self-determination and only low levels of violence or threats to international peace" (1969: 263). This would include the above mentioned cases of forcible interventions in Uganda, Congo and Iran which were viewed as having a minor or non-existent impact on the respective states' territorial integrity and political independence. Later John D'Angelo agreed with Bowett, arguing that "striking a theoretical balance in favor of protecting nationals seems fair because interventions to protect nationals usually do not disrupt the basic world order" (1981: 518).

Unsurprisingly, Canadian Fonteyne was less expansive than his American counterparts. He pointed out that "armed intervention will still inevitably constitute a temporary violation *de facto* of the latter's territorial integrity and, to a certain extent, of its political independence, if carried out against its wishes" (1974: 255). The adoption of the Definition of Aggression by the General Assembly in 1974 supported Fonteyne's rather than the American and British view. Resolution 3314 described aggression as "the invasion or attack by the armed forces of a State of the territory of another State, or any military occupation, however temporary". This, to an extent, pulled the rug out from under the argument that the forcible protection of nationals was not contrary to Article 2(4). The Definition of Aggression, however, did state "a determination that an act of aggression has been committed would not be justified in the light of other relevant circumstances, including the fact that the acts concerned or their consequences are not of sufficient gravity".

The second argument to support the forcible protection of nationals abroad on the basis of self-defense following Article 51, is the belief that such use of force is covered under customary international law. Under traditional law the protection of nationals was seen, said Britain's McNair, as an aspect of self-defense or preservation (1961: 210–19). Bowett went so far as to say that the right to self-defense does not belong to states "by grant under the Charter, but by virtue of pre-existing rights, and the Charter is only relevant in so far as it imports a restriction on pre-existing rights" (1957: 115). While this is an argument made by many legal writers, especially from common law countries like Britain, it has not been used much in state practice. Generally states have accepted the dominance of the UN Charter in dictating the rules for the use of force, rather than resorting to customary international law.

In conclusion, interventions undertaken for the protection of nationals abroad during the Cold War period appear to this writer and others to be largely a shield for larger scale military operations pursuing a number of other objectives.[2]

Such action tended to be justified primarily on self-defense under Article 51. This occasionally was supported by the argument that such a right existed under customary international law and that the action taken did not infringe upon the territorial integrity and political independence of the respective state.

The widespread rejection of the attempt to justify the forcible protection of nationals on the basis of self-defense shows that it is an issue which was viewed with skepticism during the Cold War era. Although the justification was employed in a number of both genuine and non-genuine cases, even Bowett conceded that it lacked "the degree of wide-spread support necessary for a customary right" (1986: 41). At the end of the Cold War authorities observed that generally states had rejected such intervention as illegal (Arend and Beck 1993: 110). Action by countries such as the UK, US, France and Belgium who chose to establish their right to the forcible protection of nationals abroad, have been the exception.

An Emergency Exit

> The international community, now more than ever in the post-Cold War period, is prepared to accept, endorse or, at the very least, tolerate the forcible protection of nationals abroad in appropriate cases. (Richard B. Lillich 1992: 222–23)

Lillich rightly observed that the protection of nationals abroad has been a less controversial subject since 1990. The Post-Cold War era is indeed marked by an interesting contradiction: that is, the large number of instances of the forcible protection of nationals abroad and the lack of their debate in the literature.

The majority of writers today only touch on the subject of the protection of nationals abroad in passing. Lillich, Israel's Yoram Dinstein and Britain's Christine Gray are some of the few who dedicate any substantial time to the issue. Neither Dinstein nor Gray, however, go beyond listing half a dozen incidents since 1990. The only post-Cold War publication which deals with the issue in any detail, including its history and current examples, is Lillich's posthumously published *Lillich on the Forcible Protection of Nationals Abroad.* It is often, however, the very absence of discussion in the literature and government statements which is more telling than the common occurrence of it.

Largely referred to as rescue missions or operations and evacuations, the use of force for the protection of nationals since 1990 has been limited to short-term,

2 Further Cold War interventions justified on the basis of the protection of nationals abroad include France in Mauritania in 1977–79, and France in Chad in 1978–79.

small-size force deployment. With regard to the main actors, the post-Cold War era shows a similar picture to the Cold War era with the US, France and Belgium being at the centre. At the same time, the protection of nationals abroad continues to show colonial traces. The use of force has centered, with some exceptions, on Africa and other territories formerly claimed as colonies, particularly Liberia, Rwanda and the Central African Republic to name just a few. A closer look at these instances shows that, while the majority of rescue missions nowadays may be genuine, there are still some which are seen as dubious. This is particularly the case with regard to action undertaken by France and Belgium, former colonial powers in Africa, intervening in now independent states.

During the 1990s, France continued to have more than 7,000 military personnel stationed across seven African countries and former colonies, including Senegal, Côte d'Ivoire, Gabon, Djibouti, Chad and the Central African Republic. During that time Chad alone was home to 160,000 French nationals, which is indicative of France's reasoning behind the forcible protection of nationals in these countries (Whitney 1997: 10). In some instances, such as Rwanda in 1994 and the Central African Republic in 1996, France and Belgium combined forces to intervene in the conflict.

Rather than merely rescuing its nationals, they engaged actively in the conflict by aiding the existing government and blocking rebel forces.

Such behavior, however, has decreased today and troops are largely used to evacuate nationals with withdrawal taking place immediately after the task is completed. This was the case, for example, with French troops in Gabon and Chad (both 1990), as well as French and Belgian troops in Zaire in 1990 and 1993, as well as the Central African Republic in 2003.

Other countries that were not colonial powers also intervened forcibly to protect their nationals abroad. New Zealand, for example, sent a Navy frigate to the Solomon Islands in 2000 to evacuate its own and other foreign nationals.

Similarly, Australia, deployed warships to Fiji in 2006 in anticipation of the possible need for an evacuation.

The US employed comparable short-term small-size deployments when it rescued its own and other foreign nationals from Liberia in 1990 as a consequence of fierce clashes between the government and rebel groups, as well as in the Central African Republic in 1996, Sierra Leone in 1997 and Côte d'Ivoire in 2002 (Henry 1990: A17).

There are two further core reasons, apart from the colonial legacy, which explain the occurrence of the forcible protection of nationals in the post-Cold War era. First, there is the increased international movement including migration of people. Globalization has both allowed and forced people to leave their home country and settle abroad. In some instances this has also lead to some nationals acquiring an additional citizenship. Second, there is the issue of tourism, international education and business travel, resulting in a large number of people visiting foreign countries and inadvertently becoming caught in the crossfire of either existing or emerging conflicts.

These two factors have been a key trigger for a number of rescue operations in the post-Cold War era. This said, it has to be pointed out that it rarely happens that only a single state's nationals are affected by such a situation. Consequently, there have been a number of incidents in which multinational rescue operations have been undertaken, most notably in Rwanda (1994) and Lebanon (2006).

As violence between the Rwandan government and the Rwanda Patriotic Front rebel group was increasing, a range of countries, amongst them Germany, Canada, France, Belgium and the Netherlands, decided on a joint operation to undertake the forcible protection and evacuation of their nationals (McFadden 1994: 1). In view of the worsening conditions and impending or actual genocide, it is one of the few operations where a long-term deployment of foreign troops to protect not only foreign nationals but also locals would probably have been widely accepted.

A further example of a multinational rescue operation was Lebanon in 2006. Following the abduction of two soldiers and the bombardment by *Hizbollah* of villages on the Israeli border with Lebanon, Israel responded with air strikes and a land incursion. More than 70,000 foreign nationals were evacuated from the crisis area (Conway 2006).

They included tourists and foreign workers from over 30 countries, most notably Canada, Australia, the Philippines, the US, UK, France and India, as well as Lebanese holding dual citizenship. The issue of dual citizenship, as mentioned earlier, was of particular interest in this case. The Australian government alone has recorded 25,000 dual Lebanese-Australian nationals living in Lebanon (Australian Broadcasting Corporation 2006).

Prior to 1945 the protection of nationals came as a package, that is the protection of people, property and investments. The use of force today tends to focus only on evacuation of nationals. In addition, evacuations, as in Lebanon in 2006, do not always take place through forcible means. While numerous warships from the US, UK, India, France, Canada, Greece and Italy were used in an attempt to evacuate nationals, there were also a number of civil measures undertaken, such as evacuating foreign nationals on chartered buses, cruise ships and commercial aircrafts.

State practice in the post-Cold War period consequently shows that there is a continued belief in a right to use force to protect nationals abroad. During the Cold War period, the protection of nationals was justified on self-defense and widely debated. Today, as Lillich said, there appears to be a "near complete absence of legal or other criticisms" (1992: 222–23). Indeed, America's Rex Zedalis rightly points out that UN practice with regard to the condemnation or acceptance of the protection of nationals is inconclusive (1990: 248). This is similar to individual governments who do not seem to oppose states protecting nationals forcibly, as long as such action takes place, said Georgetown University academic Wingfield, "as its most pure, [that is] a rescue operation, lasting no longer than the evacuation itself" (2000: 441). There now appears a consensus that, as long as the forcible evacuation takes the previously mentioned form, it violates neither Article 2(4) of the Charter, nor the territorial integrity or political independence of a state as reflected in Article 1 of the Definition of Aggression.

There are three core reasons for why the protection of nationals abroad in the post-Cold War era is now a less controversial and little discussed issue. First, states are now well aware that, as Lillich stated, "the longer troops remain in another country, the more their presence begins to look like intervention" (1967: 350). So for the protection of nationals to look like a genuine rescue operation rather than a pretext for an invasion based on other objectives, the deployment has to be short-term and include the bare minimum of force or troops necessary for a successful evacuation. As the next section will show, in the contemporary international system it is not so much the protection of nationals but rather humanitarian intervention which is seen as a figleaf for interventions pursuing other objectives.

Second, there is the view that rescue missions, said Dinstein, "cannot be counted as precedents if they are carried out with the consent of the government of the local state" (2001: 204). Indeed, very few governments have opposed states entering their territory for short-term operations related to the protection of nationals. One exception would be the US intervention in Liberia in 1990 where the latter did not give its express consent. Consequently, the issue has been rarely raised in the UN generally or the Security Council in particular. Again, the exception was Liberia where, however, it was not the Liberian government but the Cuban Ambassador who criticized the action before the UN (UNSC 1990a).

Due to the long held hostilities between Cuba and the US, this may have been more a political stance rather than a genuine belief as to the illegality of the action.

There is one important point, however, which has to be raised with regard to states objecting to the forcible protection of nationals taking place in their territory. While such objections may rarely occur due to acceptance of the concept, it has to be noted that this could also be due to uncertain governance situations. In failed states, often dominated by civil war (the topic of a subsequent chapter), for example, there is rarely a securely established government or a single party in control which would be able to give official permission for such forcible protection of nationals to take place in its territory.

In conclusion, it can be said that that the forcible protection of nationals has advanced to a wide-spread phenomenon and retreated to a little discussed issue. This is partly because of the fact that colonialism in its past form has largely officially ceased to exist. In the continuing instances, the deployment of forces has been short term without an obvious motive and has had the consent of the state in question. As a result, issues of legality are no longer at the centre of debates-either in the UN nor amongst individual states or regional organizations. Consequently, current state practice regarding the protection of nationals has challenged the rules governing the international use of force not because states are pushing for a change in the rules but due to their rejection of any detailed discussion of the issue.

Summary

The issue of the protection of nationals abroad has changed greatly over the last few centuries. Originally the concept was closely linked to colonialism and the wish of imperial powers to protect not only their nationals but also the property, business and investments established through the colonization process. During the 19th and early 20th century, nationals residing abroad consequently tended to enjoy large-scale protection by their home state. The belief was that a state was entitled and indeed had the obligation to protect its nationals residing abroad, regardless of whether this was in colonies or other non-Western states. States in this period largely used the protection of nationals abroad as their sole justification for the use of force.

This contrasts with the Cold War era which saw the rise of self-defense as the justification for the forcible protection of nationals abroad. States called on Article 51, as well as customary international law, to give their actions the appearance of legality. This was because the colonial framework was no longer legally or politically available in the decolonized world. Regardless of the justifications given, this remained a hotly debated topic during the Cold War era. The main reason for this was that during this period it often appeared to be merely a shield for military operations pursuing wider objectives. Its legality during the Cold War years was questioned by the majority of states. Such operations were not particularly common and when they were, they were supported or undertaken only by a small group of states, most notably the UK, US, France, Belgium and Israel.

In the contemporary international system a real turn-around seems to have occurred. While the above mentioned states have continued the practice, numerous other states have joined the ranks to undertake rescue operations. Such evacuations, however, tend to take place using a combination of both forcible and non-armed means. In the post-Cold War era, states tend to engage in short-term, low-level rescue missions which appear to have neither a pretext nor appear to be a shield for wider objectives. In addition, such operations tend to take place with the consent of the state in question.

As a consequence, the forcible protection of nationals abroad is today seen by many governments as an undertaking which either requires no or only limited legal justification. The majority of states rarely provide such justification and action is questioned neither by the UN nor other regional organizations. Current state practice has consequently managed to challenge the established rules governing the international use of force in one important matter. Rather than pushing for a change in the rules, current state practice has lead, so it seems, to a near universal acceptance of the concept, provided it takes place in what Zedalis (1990) termed, its 'purest form'.

It is quite extraordinary to this writer that state practice has managed to establish a section of the international use of force which appears to no longer require legal justification. To have such a situation in the post-Cold War period, an era in which states, like no other time in history, have struggled to provide legal justification for their international use of force (and other states, as well as international and regional organizations have demanded they do so), seems astonishing.

As the next section will show, however, the controversy which originally surrounded the issue has now moved to a subject matter closely linked to it, that is the protection even of foreign nationals. Oppenheim's contradictory observation that "a state cannot treat foreign citizens passing through or residing on its territory arbitrarily according to discretion as it might treat its own subjects" is now invalid (1912: 182). Instead, humanitarian intervention has advanced to a popular justification for states to use force in the contemporary international system.

Chapter 6

From Dawn To Dusk: Humanitarian Intervention

The concept of humanitarian intervention is where the gap between what is perceived as legitimate or actually legal – that is, between the spirit and letter of the law – is widest. The forcible protection of human rights involves debates regarding, says Britain's Jim Whitman, "the three most fundamental organizational systems of human social life: law, morality and politics" (2005: 259). This apparent conflict is based on the perception that the UN Charter and international law do not reflect the contemporary notion that respect for sovereignty and non-interference are conditional on the state's respect for human rights. According to the ICISS, this "long due internationalization of the human conscience" has left the UN struggling to find a way of balancing its two core values: the protection of state sovereignty and human rights (2001: 9).

The Danish Institute of International Affairs, in light of NATO's military action in Kosovo, defined humanitarian intervention as "a coercive action of states with the use of armed forces in another state without the permission of the state government, with or without United Nations Security Council authorization aiming at averting or stopping massive human rights or international humanitarian law violations" (1999: 11). Britain's Tony Blair is the state leader most associated with an expanded view of the right of humanitarian intervention. He described NATO's 1999 intervention in Kosovo as a "just war, based not on any territorial ambitions but on values" (1999a).

Originally, the forcible protection of 'human rights' was mainly reflected in the intervention of Christian states in Muslim ruled territory in order to 'protect' Christian minorities: or, as Fonteyne said, "restricted to the relations between 'civilized' and 'non-civilized' nations" (1974: 219). With the introduction of numerous human rights conventions following the Second World War, such rights began to claim a position equal, rather than subordinate, to state sovereignty. This ultimately culminated in the contemporary notion that humanitarian intervention is no longer a right but, as the ICISS has stated, a duty of states. With an estimated 170 million people killed by their own governments over the past few decades, there have been plenty of grounds in theory for states to protect human rights forcibly (Rummel 1994: 4). In practice, of course, this rarely occurred. When it did, it triggered furious legal and other debate.

Humanitarian intervention finds itself in a quasi-legal *niche*, viewed in some instances as morally right but legally wrong. No other justification for the use of force finds itself in such a contradictory position. There have been several questions which have dominated discussion from the beginning until now. Is there in international law a right or a duty of humanitarian intervention? What is the severity of human rights abuse necessary for military intervention to be justified? Is the required authorization and format for such a use of force unilateral or collective in nature? Is disinterestedness of the intervening powers, rather than motivation by economic, political and strategic interests, necessary and how is this to be assessed?

This chapter will examine the various views on these questions by governments, legal authorities and international institutions over the three identified time periods. The overall picture is the concept developed under the old, fading religious umbrella before 1914, was effectively outlawed in the inter-war years, tolerated in small doses in fact, if not principle, during the Cold War and finally, almost prescribed in the post-Cold War years.

The White Man's Burden

> It is virtually impossible to separate the humanitarian motives for intervention from the political motives and to assure the absolute selflessness of intervening states. (Antoine Rougier 1910: 525)

The origins of the modern concept of 'humanitarian intervention' arguably arose with the religious notion of just war as advanced by St. Augustine at the unification of Christian church and Roman state, when he asked "why ... should not the Church use force in compelling her lost sons to return" (Schaff 1887: 926). Nearly a thousand years later before that religious age ended, Aquinas echoed Augustine's writings against the background of the 11–12th century Crusades launched to halt and even reverse the expansion of Muslim rule, particularly in the Holy Lands. The traditional idea, of the later-entitled 'human' rights, was thus restricted to the notion of the support of Christendom everywhere and survived in a modified form into the 20th century.

The source of modern human rights lies with the Protestant Reformation and Martin Luther in the 16th century, advocating the idea of individual conscience in religion. With the Enlightenment period in Europe in the 17th and 18th century, this idea developed into the secular notion of so-called natural rights. With the secularization of the rules on the use of force, the just war doctrine of intervention lost its mandate.

Grotius promoted the concept of state sovereignty but expected a state to respect the fundamental rights of man. He relates this in some ways to the issue of humanitarian intervention when he states that "when a tyrant practices against his subjects atrocities which no just man can approve, the exercise of the right vested in human society is not precluded" (Lauterpacht 1943: 24). Vattel, a century later, argued that "if tyranny becomes insupportable, obliges the nation to rise in their defence; every foreign power has the right to succour an oppressed people who implore their assistance" (1805: 218).

It is questionable, however, whether either was referring to forceful as opposed to non-forceful means of support, such as diplomacy and asylum.

The rise of liberalism during the era of Enlightenment, calling for the establishment of universal individual 'rights', was reflected in two core documents born out of revolutionary republican circumstances, including the move away from religious and monarchical towards secular and republican systems of governance: the French Declaration of the Rights of Man and of the Citizen (1789) and the US Bill of Rights (1791). The concept of 'universal' rights at the time was, of course, anything but universal: being limited essentially to European males.

These declarations reflect the contemporary perception that human rights were best advanced and protected by the individual state itself – once republicanized. Enlightenment figures shared Kant's view that the universal establishment of republican democracies would achieve respect for rights as well as perpetual peace. This was thus a matter of national and not yet international law.

Despite the move from religious to secular justifications, the late 18th and 19th century witnessed interventions based on a combination of both religious and newer natural rights. The 1774 Treaty of Koutchouk-Kainardji provided for Imperial Russia's ministers making representations in favor of Orthodox Christians abroad. State practice was reflected in German lawyer and diplomat Georg Friedrich de Martens' belief that "vis-à-vis non civilised nations ... intervention by the civilised powers is in principle legitimate when the Christian population of those countries is exposed to persecutions and massacres" (Fonteyne 1974: 219). Britain, France and Russia accordingly forcibly intervened in Greece in 1827–30 to establish the country's independence following the massacre of Christian Greeks by the Ottoman Empire, claiming in the Treaty of London (1827) that they were motivated "no less by sentiments of humanity, than by interests for the tranquility of Europe". Under the Treaty of Paris of 1856, the Sultan was compelled to acknowledge his "generous intentions towards Christian populations of the Empire". France's unilateral intervention in Syria (1860–61), with a mandate from the UK, Prussia and Russia, was triggered by the massacre of Maronite Christians by Druze Muslims supported by the Ottoman Empire. In 1866, the Europeans, less Britain, made demands in favor of Greek-Cypriots seeking unity with Greece, on the Sultan who, rather than suffer armed intervention, accepted a British proposal for their more generous treatment. In 1876–78 Serbia and Montenegro declared war on the Ottoman Empire in support of oppressed Christians in Bosnia-Herzegovina and Bulgaria. When the Sultan rejected threats of European intervention unless he treated his Christian subjects better, Russia declared war stating it was "determined not to hesitate as long as the principles that have been recognized as equitable, humane, necessary by the whole of Europe have not received full execution of in effective guarantees" (Fonteyne 1974: 212). In 1887, European states again protested Turkey's treatment of its Christian subjects in Macedonia (Thornberry 1991: 33–4).

The treatment of Jewish minorities also arose as an issue. From 1867, Britain sought to persuade the new Romanian government to protect Jews from persecution, with the US and several European states remonstrating in 1872, making Jewish equal treatment a condition of recognition of Romanian independence under the Treaty of Berlin (1878). Russia's plea for exception from the treaty's provision that religious difference should not be reason for excluding persons from civil and political rights in Bulgaria, Montenegro, Serbia, Romania and Turkey was dismissed. Subsequently, in 1891, the US first criticized Russia for the treatment of its Jewish subjects and then a year later Romania. US President Benjamin Harrison stated that "the banishment, whether by direct decree or by any less certain indirect methods, of so large a number of men and women is not a local question" (1891–92: xiii). A decade later, his successor Theodore Roosevelt, stated that "chronic wrongdoing, or an impotence which results in the general loosening of the ties of civilized society may ... ultimately require intervention by some civilized nations" (1904: xii).

From the mid-19th century non-religious bases for intervention on the grounds of abuse of rights increased. The 1839 Treaty of London, recognizing Belgium's independence, provided that the signatories "would consider its duty to interpose its influence ... so as to ensure to the inhabitants ... protection against oppressive and arbitrary acts". Britain, France, Spain, Portugal, Italy and Austria protested but did not act to halt Russian suppression of a Polish uprising in 1863. In 1892 the US protested both Peru's treatment of indigenous workers and France's treatment of a rebellion in the Congo. The US intervention in Cuba in 1898 was an early example of non-religious intervention, directed against Spanish rule which included significant relocation of the rural population. US President William McKinley claimed to be acting "in the cause of humanity ... to put an end to the barbarities, bloodshed [and] starvation" adding as justification the protection of nationals, commerce and property, as well as a threat to the US's and the region's peace (1898: 757).

Clearly, there was a lack of consistency in the application of humanitarian intervention, both religious and secular. Legal writers were also divided. In late 19th century Hall wrote "for the most part the treatment which the subject receives from them is merely fragmentary, notice being taken of some only on its grounds, which are usually approved or disapproved of without very clear reference to a general principle" (1884: 266). While some legal scholars supported the use of force for humanitarian purposes, Fonteyne's (1974: 219) later claim that it was universally endorsed is incorrect. The majority of observers rejected the notion. There is also a pattern in the support and rejection of the concept between the British and European-American legal scholars.

We have seen, in aforementioned instances, the robust approach of US leaders. Henry Wheaton, a US lawyer and diplomat, also approved of the intervention in Greece, seeing it as "a further illustration of the principles of international law authorizing such an interference ... where the general interests of humanity are infringed by the excesses of a barbarous and despotic government" (1836: 91).

E.J. Phelps, was less ebullient, saying intervention by force of arms in Cuba would be a 'crime'. Yet, while he allowed only 'necessary self-defense' as a justifiable forcible intervention, he said the "sole and rare exception ... [was] to prevent unjustifiable slaughter and outrage in another country if it becomes absolutely necessary" (The Implied Covenant 1898: 6).

Sheldon Amos was also cautious, demanding a distinct 'purity of motives' regarding such use of force (1880: 15).

British common law tradition created less sympathy for codifying law both international and municipal. Lord Robert Phillimore, an English judge, vehemently opposed such interventions, saying that "as an accessory to others, this ground may be defensible, but, as substantive and solitary justification of intervention in the affairs of another country, it can scarcely be admitted into the code of international law, since it is manifestly open to abuses, tending to the violation and destruction of the vital principles of jurisprudence" (1854: 320).

Until Hall coined the phrase in 1880, such intervention was referred to as having been conducted 'in the interest of humanity' or for 'humanitarian concerns'. Hall was dismissive, considering its future significance only in a footnote, concluding that "international law professes to be concerned with the relations of states to each other [and] tyrannical conduct of a government towards its subjects, massacres and brutality in a civil war, or religious persecution, are acts which have nothing to do directly, or indirectly with such relations" (1884: 264). Later described by Stowell (1921) as a 'severe critic' of humanitarian intervention, Hall did concede that such interventions "whether armed or diplomatic, undertaken either for the reason or upon the pretext or cruelty or oppression ... would have had to justify themselves, when not authorised by the whole body of civilised states accustomed to act together for a common purpose" (1884: 266).

In America, Woolsey argued that states were authorized to intervene to protect individual rights when a "crime of a government against its subjects" had been committed (1872: 57).

Four decades later Borchard supported this view and wrote "where a state under exceptional circumstances disregards certain rights of its own citizens, over whom it presumably has absolute sovereignty, the other states of the family of nations are authorized by international law to intervene on grounds of humanity" (1913: 507).

France's Antoine Rougier, published in 1910 what Graham fourteen years later described as "the most important study ever ... of the theoretical bases of humanitarian intervention" (1924: 318). Still cited today, Rougier defined the concept as "the idea that it is legal to control a state internationally over its internal affairs when the latter are in violation of human rights and that it is legal to reorganise its legal functioning" (1910: 472). He argued that so-called 'barbaric' or 'semi-civilized' states which commit acts contrary to humanity can be told what to do by civilized states, including by armed intervention in response to violations of human rights, such as the right to life and freedom. Yet, Rougier remained deeply concerned about the potential for abuse and that this would never be an act of pure selflessness, instead, tending to be influenced by other motives. He warned that the concept of humanitarian intervention "appears to be a clever legal means to gradually eat into the independence of a state in order to push it progressively towards limited sovereignty" (1910: 526).

There were exceptions to the general divide between British and European/American views on the topic. John Westlake and Montague Bernard, both English legal scholars, supported humanitarian intervention, with Westlake stating that "laws are made for man and not creatures of the imagination, and they must not create or tolerate for them situations which are beyond the endurance, we will not say of average human nature, but of the best human nature that at the time and place they can hope to meet with" (1858: 320).

Bernard went further, arguing that while law may prohibit intervention, there are instances in which "it becomes a positive duty to transgress it" (1860: 34). Oppenheim acknowledged its illegality yet hoped that international law would eventually recognize "the rule that interventions in the interests of humanity are admissible provided they are exercised if the form of collective intervention" (1912: 194–95).

In Europe, Guiseppe Carnazza-Amari, an Italian lawyer, P. Pradier-Fodere, and I. Pereira, opposed the doctrine with the former stating that "the actions and crimes of a people within the limits of its territory do not infringe upon anyone else's rights and do not give the basis for a legitimate intervention" (Fonteyne 1974: 215). America's Dr William E. Lingelbach (1900) also disapproved of it.

The German violation of Belgian neutrality, guaranteed by the 1839 Treaty of London and accompanied by stories of supposed atrocities, led many, especially in America, to inject renewed enthusiasm for the doctrine. American Henry Green Hodges, echoing Stowell's public campaign in favor of US intervention, predicted happily that international law would eventually "sanction an ever increasing number of causes for intervention for the sake of humanity, where that cause is made the object of collective action on the part of a number of the larger powers" (1915: 91).

The assertion of war crimes by Germany towards the war's end and the condemnation of Turkey in the Treaty of Sèvres for its treatment of its own Armenian subjects in the war, raised the issue afresh. Yet, after the First World War, the focus of the League of Nations and the international community as a whole appeared to be on the avoidance of war, rather than the issue of armed intervention for humanitarian purposes. While the Covenant did not cover the issue, a fresh concern for the protection of human rights was reflected in its minority treaties and mandates. Signatory states of such minority treaties obliged themselves to grant equal rights of citizenship, freedom, religion and language to all their inhabitants.

Clearly one era had now ended. P.H. Winfield wrote that "mere religious persecution cannot now justify an intervention" (1924: 161). Yet, other secular grounds were widening. The League of Nations Committee did not believe that the new rights constituted so-called international rights of the individual while accepting the existence of rights "created by states for the benefit of their nationals or of foreigners" (1926: 182). The American Society of International Law at its Round Table Conference on the Codification of International Law in Respect to Nationality (1926) disagreed, stating instead that there was a right of the individual under international law. Colombian-born Professor of Political Science at the University of California, Malbone Graham, claimed the same year, that humanitarian intervention's "legality has been recognized through the development of new and enlightened standards of the social Law of Nations" (1924: 328). He believed that there would be an increase in the number of causes justifying humanitarian intervention (1924: 324). Winfield, while worried, felt the doctrine was "least likely to be abused where the majority of leading states exercise it collectively" (1924: 161–62). Graham agreed, predicting that it would be limited to action which is either undertaken directly or mandated by the organization (1924: 326–27).

There was not only abuse of rights after the foundation of the League, but also of the doctrine. In 1931, Japan claimed mistreatment of its nationals as grounds for intervention in Manchuria. Italy invoked Article 22 of the Covenant and a commitment to the abolition of slavery for its armed intervention in Abyssinia in 1935. The pinnacle of hypocrisy was reached with Nazi Germany's invocation of humanitarian grounds, that is, the protection and securing of minority German rights in the Sudetenland, of people who were not German citizens, when intervening in Czechoslovakia in 1938.

States and the League did little to stop external abuse, and even less to stop internal abuse, by these countries. In 1933, English Jew Norman Bentwich, Director of the League's High Commission for Refugees from Germany, expressed the belief that "the scope and deliberate atrocity of the persecution of Jews in Germany constitutes such a challenge to the established principles of religious and racial equality ... that the League cannot, without serious damage to its authority, stand aloof" (1933: 75). Yet, it did. Americans like Stowell agreed, saying in 1936 "the right of independence ceases when it is abused beyond the point which the people of neighbouring states can regard with tolerance" (1936: 105). Yet they also did. States were not interested in intervening, either unilaterally or multilaterally.

Yet, many came to accept that, according to Wright, "a rule of international law, which prohibits gross inhumanity and abusive exercises of power even in a state's internal administration, has been violated" (1938: 529). Toward the war's end in 1944, his compatriot, Manley Hudson, agreed that a state had a legal obligation to ensure that "conditions prevailing within its territory do not menace international peace and order, and to this end it must treat its own population in a way which will not violate the dictates of humanity and justice or shock the conscience of mankind" (1944: 35). These changing views reflected the scale of reaction to the full discovery of the Holocaust, leading to a surge in international human rights law from 1945. Charles C. Hyde prophesized "international society will ultimately evince an interest in the welfare of the private individual sufficient to cause the law of nations to restrict the freedom of a State in the treatment of its nationals" (1945: 211). This process was gathering pace.

The Cucumber Sandwich

> There is as yet no such thing as humanitarian intervention in international law and very little likelihood that there will be in the foreseeable future. (Robert H. Jackson 1987: 546)

The UN Charter mentions human rights more than half a dozen times, calling for their promotion and encouragement. The inclusion of the phrase 'protection of human rights' was, however, rejected (Schwelb 1965: 363). Such a phrase may have represented a more concrete 'legal' basis for humanitarian intervention (Dugard 1967: 185, Lauterpacht 1950: 120). Michael Reisman, nevertheless, claimed that the Charter's coverage of human rights and their subsequent strengthening in numerous conventions also reinforced the concept of humanitarian intervention (1984: 80). The Charter does not, however, define which rights and freedoms have to be abused and to what extent to justify such intervention.

The Inter-American Juridical Committee in the 1940s stated that it was only the circumstances of the Second World War and the repressive internal acts carried out by some governments which brought about a "realization by democratic governments that the adoption of a declaration of the rights of man was not merely an ideal of humanitarian conduct but a necessary condition of international peace" (1946: 105–106).

International law which, to date, had focused almost exclusively on the rights of states, now shifted its focus to include individuals through so-called human rights. According to Lauterpacht, recognition of the existence of crimes against humanity asserted "the existence of rights of man grounded in a law superior to the law of the State" (1948: 104). The *Nürnberg* trials established, according to British Chief Prosecutor Hartley Shawcross, that "there is a limit to the omnipotence of the state and ... the individual human being, the ultimate unit of all law, is not disentitled to the protection of mankind when the state tramples upon his rights in a manner which outrages the conscience of mankind" (Lie 1949).

Intervention over human rights prior to the Universal Declaration of Human Rights (UDHR) in 1948 largely centered on the protection of a state's own nationals abroad. Human rights conventions established under the UN extended, said McDougal and Bebr, "the protection of basic individual liberties, most broadly conceived, to levels of effective authority higher than the nation state" (1964: 603).

The ICJ's advisory opinion on Southwest Africa in 1950 confirmed the new emphasis on international obligations of states to human rights over their sovereignty (Rodley 1989: 332). The ICJ decided that, while South Africa did not have a duty to submit the former German colony of Southwest Africa to UN Trusteeship status, it nevertheless was under an international obligation under the League of Nations mandate. This included the submission of regular reports and transmission of petitions from the inhabitants to the United Nations Trusteeship Council (UNTC) (ICJ 1950: 19).

The ICJ further suggested the human rights provisions of the UN Charter, particularly Article 80(1) confirming the rights of inhabitants of mandated territories, were not a mere directive but a legally binding obligation.

The Convention on the Prevention and Punishment of the Crime of Genocide, adopted the day before the UDHR, was another major step. This defined genocide, a term coined by Poland's US-based ex-patriate Raphael Lemkin, as "acts committed with intent to destroy, in whole or in part, a national, ethnical, racial or religious group" (1944: 79).

Similar practices had been condemned in the past, yet, the dominant view, as noted by Oppenheim and Lauterpacht, was generally that human rights abuse was a matter within the domestic jurisdiction of a given state rather than a subject of international law.

This convention, however, deemed genocide "a crime under international law which [states] undertake to prevent and to punish".

This could be interpreted to say that genocide and other human rights abuses were matters not entirely within the domestic jurisdiction of states. France's representative at the Security Council's first session, Alexandre Parodi, certainly thought so. He said that, such a situation as existed in Franco's Spain, ceased to be a domestic affair when it had the potential to threaten world peace, stressing that Article 2(7) "does not refer merely to matters within the domestic jurisdiction of a state, but to matters 'essentially' within such jurisdiction" (Joyce 1956: 85). The ICJ soon confirmed this view of human rights and went so far as to declare that "all states can be held to have a legal interest in their protection" (1951: 24).

Looking back, Swiss-born Louis Rene Beres, judged this era as "the end of the idea of absolute sovereignty concerning non-intervention when human rights are in grievous jeopardy" (1988: 126). Intervention, of course, did not always refer solely to military interference. Instead, it had earlier also embraced situations in which the domestic affairs of another state was merely commented on by other governments. Intervention for the protection of human rights following the Second World War eventually covered a wide spectrum, ranging from political commentary, economic sanctions and the use of armed force.

These conventions raised the question, posed by Lemkin, whether the "moral right of humanitarian intervention [should] be converted into a right under international law" (1947: 145–46). Lemkin, a close associate of Pella and France's Donnedieu de Vabres in promoting the Genocide Convention, said such acts should be treated as crimes against humanity and pursued like any other criminal act. This occurred both with regard to the *Nürnberg* and Tokyo Tribunals. Pella's and Lemkin's call for an international criminal court to deal with both crimes against humanity and war crimes was, again, not yet realized (Pemberton 2008). Pella's idea of a universal law of extradition for international crimes also lay dormant.

The onset of the Cold War at the same time as the adoption of these foundational conventions, paralyzed further substantial progress in international human rights. After very little through the 1950s, it was not until the latter half of the 1960s that there were further major steps. American David S. Bogen observed that the "fundamental human rights involved are subject to modification according to mankind's increasing sensitivity toward the individual and human rights" (1966: 300). By this time the number of non-European members in the UN had increased substantially with decolonization. The International Convention for the Elimination of all Forms of Racial Discrimination (ICERD) of 1965 explicitly brought race into the frame of international human rights. In 1966 there were two more foundational covenants based on the UDHR, the International Covenant on Civil and Political Rights (ICCPR) and International Covenant on Economic, Social and Cultural Rights (ICESCR). The Proclamation of Teheran in 1968 claimed there was now "a common understanding of the peoples of the world concerning the inalienable and inviolable rights of all members of the human family and [it] constitutes an obligation for the members of the international community". This proclaimed, amongst other things, the equality of all people and their right to life, liberty, protection from slavery and torture, as well as a right to seek asylum. The expansion of international human rights did not necessarily lead to an expansion of the right of intervention in their name. The ICERD was used to criticize but not invade apartheid Rhodesia and South Africa.

Similar to the period after the Covenant, the Cold War era showed that the international community dealt cautiously with these issues, especially that of humanitarian intervention. Both the Soviet Union and the US were suspicious of international law encroaching on their domestic sphere, resulting in the former refusing to accept the UDHR and the latter declining the ratification of the Genocide Convention. Colonial powers feared these new rights encroaching on colonial rule. Australia, a close ally of the US, declined for ten years before ratifying the ICERD because of its implications for its indigenous populations in Australia and New Guinea, plus its immigration policy. The Cold War led the rival sides to see human rights in terms of the ideological divide with either belligerent seeing the other as an abuser of human rights. The Inter-American Juridical Committee's 1946 statement that a state which disregards its own citizens' human rights was the most likely potential threat to international peace and security, was obviously an attempt to discredit the Soviet Union and its allies through the new language of human rights.

In 1948 US Secretary of State, George C. Marshall, reiterated this sentiment saying governments which abused their own's citizens rights were unlikely "to respect the rights of other governments and other people and are likely to seek their objectives by coercion and force in the international field" (UNGA 1948: 36).

Yet, the stand-off of deterrence, nuclear and conventional, meant states did not have much room to conduct armed interventions for fear of triggering a wider war: human rights remained a war of words not weapons. If human rights abuses occurred in a Cold War ally, states turned a blind eye. When major civilian casualties were caused by armed interventions, like the US in Vietnam and Cambodia, the Soviet Union in Hungary and Czechoslovakia, and the Europeans in their colonies, the actions were seen as wars or 'police actions' and not matters of human rights abuse.

Quincy Wright was correct when he observed that superpower rivalry, combined later with the self-determination and decolonization process, resulted in a renewed focus on state sovereignty at the cost of the protection of human rights (1954: 47). Yet he claimed the two were complementary not exclusive: "the rights of nations can be assured only in a world which respects the rights of man" (1954: 50).

International lawyers remained divided. After the 1948 conventions, Lauterpacht argued that humanitarian intervention was now permissible "in cases in which a state maltreats its subjects in a manner which shocks the conscience of mankind" (1950: 32). American authorities mainly agreed: Ann and A.J. Thomas, especially so, for cases where the abuse was widespread rather than merely isolated (1956: 378). They said "if nations had wished to exclude humanitarian intervention from these prohibitions ... they would have done so explicitly" (1967: 7). Richard Lillich (1969) was also convinced.

The ILC argued that the doctrine of humanitarian intervention "appears to have been so clearly established under customary international law that only its limits and not its existence is subject to debate" (1970: 11). Reisman and McDougal (1973) went one step further and called on the Commission to draft what they referred to as a Protocol of Procedure for Humanitarian Intervention.

Yet, some English scholars were more doubtful as Britain receded from a global imperial role, with Bowett referring to this "uncertain right" (1957: 120). Brownlie's massive book devotes a little over three pages to the topic stating that "it is extremely doubtful if this form of intervention has survived the express condemnations of intervention which have occurred in recent time or of the general prohibition of resort to force to be found in the United Nations Charter" (1963: 340–41). Third world scholars feared the doctrine could be used to infringe their states' newly-won sovereignty (Manouchehr Ganji 1962: 43). The debate, however, did not heat up as states were not intervening on this basis.

Among those who supported the right or duty of humanitarian intervention, there was a realization that the right could be used by states to disguise aggression. Yet, Leiden University's John R. Dugard countered that such a "right should not be denied merely because it may be abused" (1967: 182).

Indeed, he argued the converse, that the prohibition of the use of force, including humanitarian intervention, had led "to attempts to clothe such interventions in the garments of self-defense" (1967: 177). The right of self-defense was more likely to be abused than that of humanitarian intervention. David S. Bogen argued in this context that "the value of preventing further outrage may outweigh the harm done by intervention" (1966: 302).

Supporters of humanitarian intervention saw the need for rules to prevent abuse. Falk said intervention should be undertaken collectively as "a way to refuse the absolute claims of internal sovereignty to override a higher commitment to a minimum standard of human dignity" (1959: 168). Wright disagreed arguing that "intervention does not gain in legality under customary international law by being collective rather than individual" (1957: 86). Leitel thought the authorization of collective action also had to be based on a common verdict of either the international or regional community (1970: 238). Moore, who usually disagreed with more liberal legal authorities like Falk, but invariably took a robust view over US military interventions, argued unilateral action was necessary until an effective international enforcement mechanism was established (Conference Proceedings Part I 1973a).

Jessup had cautiously said "the inability of the international organization to act with the speed requisite to preserve life" would be the only argument for individual state action as opposed to collective action taken under the auspices of the Security Council (1959: 169).

Falk thought if intervention was unilateral, the nature of the intervention was important: short duration in troop employment would give good indication whether intervention was genuine; long-term military occupation would indicate improper interference (1959: 176). Dugard supported such restrictions and explicitly excluded more ideological aspects of human rights from legitimate grounds for intervention, even such as establishing democracy (1967: 185).

State practice at this time did not follow the prescriptions of the above and indicated anything but a widespread embrace of the concept. The Cold War era showed, argued Americans Slater and Nardin, that "even when faced with serious violations of human rights, governments will usually find extremely weighty reasons not to engage in military intervention" (1986: 92). Non-intervention rather than intervention was the norm. Michael Walzer claimed that the abundance of severe human rights abuses during the Cold War was embarrassing, implying that there were numerous situations which would have warranted outside interference (2000: 101). This reflected the debate at the International Conference on Human Rights at Teheran in 1968 over how to enforce international human rights conventions.

The humanitarian catastrophe in the Nigerian breakaway republic of Biafra during the years 1967–1970, for example, did not lead to intervention; neither did the apartheid policies of South Africa or Rhodesia, although international sanctions were imposed. Some interventions in the Cold War period did have minor alleged humanitarian components: the Belgian and US intervention in The Congo (1964), the US in the Dominican Republic (1965), Israel's action in Uganda (1976), as well as US intervention in Grenada (1983) and Panama (1989). Yet, states did not invoke it as their primary justification, focusing on the protection of nationals, as well as individual and collective self-defense, even in the three instances where it seemed there was a substantial and persuasive case for so doing.

In 1971, India justified its intervention in East Pakistan not as humanitarian but self-defense against Pakistan's aggression (International Commission of Jurists 1972, UNSC 1971a). Fonteyne says India wanted to avoid inconsistencies between its action in Bangladesh and prior rejection of exceptions to the use of force including for humanitarian reasons (1974: 204). India did report to the Security Council that "we have on this particular occasion nothing but the purest motives and purest intentions: to rescue the people of East Bengal from what they are suffering" (Franck and Rodley 1973: 276): a matter on which they had previously expressed concern. Some viewed the Security Council's lack of condemnation, calling only for a ceasefire by both sides, as amounting "to a condonation of the intervention" (Sornarajah 1981: 73). This was not the widespread view (UNSC 1971b, UNSC 1971c, UNSC 1971d).

Others saw it merely as evidence of the Security Council's Cold War paralysis. The US, a SEATO ally of Pakistan and which saw India as Soviet-inclining, said that the events in East Pakistan, despite their tragic nature, did not justify the use of force. It said India had placed "in jeopardy the territorial integrity and political independence of its neighbor" (UNSC 1971c).

Even later legal scholars have judged India's intervention as launched only to "diminish the power and halve the territory of its fiercest political and military rival" (Bazyler 1987: 589).

The intervention revived the debate among legal scholars over the subject with previous concerns being reaffirmed. American authorities generally remained favorable with American Robert Chilstrom (1974: 132) asserting, questionably, such intervention was not outright inconsistent with Article 2(4) as it impaired neither the territorial integrity nor political independence of a state. Reisman and McDougal also took a broad view, arguing that if neither the UN nor regional organizations acted, forceful intervention by individual or a group of states was permissible, in general, and mandatory for genocide for signatories to the UN Charter and Genocide Convention (1973: 192).

Frey-Wouters and Lillich thought UN authorization desirable but, in view of UN passivity, Lillich (1969: 218) accepted unilateral action as legitimate if it met five criteria covering the immediacy and extent of violations, an invitation from appropriate authorities, appropriate scale of force and relative disinterestedness of intervening states (Conference Proceedings Part III 1973b).

Lillich's last point has always featured in debate over the subject. Brownlie continued to be suspicious of admitting a right so open to abuse, concluding any allowance for such use of force outside of the restraints of the UN would prove "a general license to vigilante and opportunists to resort to hegemonial intervention" (1973: 147–48).

Fonteyne questioned this, asking rhetorically if states were allowed to "'acceptably' break the law for humanitarian reasons, why should it not be equally tolerable to violate it for other, perhaps morally less commendable motives as well?" (1974: 249).

He suggested disinterestedness could be established if the intervention abstained from any unnecessary force and left governing structures largely intact.

Yet, he seemed to contradict himself, adding the "achievement of a lasting solution in such cases will usually require a change of government or even secession" (1974: 255), effected, perhaps he meant, not by the intervening power. The Netherlands' Bart De Schutter preferred intervention by multilateral organizations which he said "guarantees the strength of international support free from the pursuit of national interests or political goals" (1972: 31). University of Ottowa academic Laurie Wiseberg thought you could not avoid a convergence of national and humanitarian interests even if that was just governments being pushed into intervention by domestic pressure (1975: 303). Americans Thomas M. Franck and Nigel S. Rodley were the voice of opposition. They argued that the UN Charter clearly prohibits unilateral action and does not in any way imply an exception for humanitarian intervention of which they said, "on balance, very little good has been wrought in its name" (1973: 299).

Vietnam's intervention in Cambodia in 1978–9 was widely viewed with suspicion. According to some, it was based solely on the former's territorial ambitions. Cambodia called it an act of aggression (UNSC 1979a).

For Bazyler, Vietnam's installation of a 'puppet regime' meant the intervention could not be justified on humanitarian grounds (1987: 608). Yet, there is no doubt about the existence of gross human rights abuse even if there is debate as to whether it reached genocidal proportions (Wolf 1988, Klintworth 1989).

Governments' reactions divided predictably on then Cold War lines in support of Soviet-aligned Vietnam or China-aligned Cambodia. The majority, notably the anti-Soviet US, UK and France but also the German Democratic Republic, Kuwait and Sudan, condemned unjustified interference in Cambodia's domestic affairs, reiterating the primacy of political independence and territorial integrity (UNSC 1979b, UNSC 1981a).

Pro-Soviet Czechoslovakia and Hungary excused the overthrow of the Kampuchean government as internal change rather than external intervention. Even Bangladesh, having previously achieved independence through intervention, refrained from support (UNSC 1981a).

Ultimately, the Security Council and many states condemned Vietnam, leading Michael Akehurst to suggest there now existed a "consensus among states in favor of treating humanitarian intervention as illegal" (1984: 99). This judgment seems overly harsh and oblivious to the obvious ideological and political concerns behind states' respective positions.

The same year, Tanzania intervened in Idi Amin's Uganda, supported by the rebel Uganda National Liberation Army, following the killing of over 300,000 people and influx of thousands of refugees (Hassan 1981: 893–94). President Julius Nyerere did not claim humanitarian but self-defense grounds citing Uganda's earlier invasion (Ronzitti 1985: 102). He said he fought an aggressor, adding "the world owes me nothing" (Smith 1986: 78). Although hosting Uganda's ousted President Milton Obote, Tanzania withdrew its troops quickly and kept out of local politics though it established close relations with the new government (Donnelly 1984).

Although the intervention was raised officially neither in the Security Council nor the General Assembly, silence by states should not be taken as endorsement of the principle. The majority of states did not want to give weight to the legal principle on the basis that they were more likely to be recipients rather than perpetrators of such use of force. Yet, in the context of uncertainty regarding the quasi-legality of the doctrine, they were prepared quietly to allow "tolerance of 'acceptable' breaches of principles of law" where the morality seemed overwhelming and their interests were not threatened (Wolf 1988: 355–56). This intervention was not as colored by Cold War considerations.

Legal authorities were not so silent with the established positions being continued. At the end of the Cold War, the majority of writers doubted that a legal right of forceful humanitarian intervention existed (Pogany 1986).

American Robert H. Jackson and Carl G. Rosberg (1986: 25) worried about further interventions of this kind, stating that humanitarian intervention remained illegal under current international law.

Western liberals like Falk disagreed. Even some non-European scholars had moved to acceptance. India's Nagendra Singh seemed to go even further, arguing that for signatories the UN Charter contained "legal obligations in the human rights field" (1986: 28). Some conceded a limited right but no duty existed (Wolf 1988: 352). According to Farer, Third World states in the General Assembly recalled all too vividly when the phrase humanitarian intervention "served as a fig leaf for the crass thrust of imperial interest" (1987: 581).

Pakistan's Farooq Hassan quipped, the doctrine is not so much a right but a 'phenomenon of power' (1981: 911).

On the gravity of abuse required, Anthony D'Amato, later lead counsel for genocide-accused Serb Milan Kovaceciv at the International Criminal Tribunal for the former Yugoslavia (ICTY) in 1998, added slavery and widespread torture as abuses justifying humanitarian intervention but argued that "only the grossest abuses of human rights by a government against its own citizens would overcome the burden against external interference" (1985: 660). American Oscar Schachter (1984) demanded an equally high standard.

Falk (1981: 159) took a wide view counting genocide, official racism, state terrorism, totalitarian government, a government's refusal to meet basic human needs, ecocide, and war crimes as severe abuses.

On the authorization and format of such action, some made a requirement that intervention be conditional on the host state itself, with the UN, or other members of the international community, having given their consent or participating (Bazyler 1987; 604). Schachter (1984) noted this rarely had happened.

Bazyler was blunter, describing the record of both the UN and regional organizations as 'pitiable'.

On motives, Bazyler also argued that interventions should not be condemned "as non-humanitarian merely because the intervening power also has political, economic or social motives for intervening" (1987: 601).

Many Third World countries and former colonies continued to believe the doctrine was a guise for imperialism, rather than genuine external help (Fairley 1980: 63). Yet Hassan claimed that "the necessity of complete indifference has been rejected as both naïve and absurd" (1981: 897) as it is unlikely ever to exist with political, social, and economic prerogatives always playing a role in a state's use of force. Schachter (1984) and Levitin (1986) thought much the same.

American R. George Wright was also unconcerned with a lack of disinterest stating that if the doctrine of humanitarian intervention was a "mere pretext for imperialism, imperialism may readily find other suitable pretexts if deprived of this one" (1989: 441).

If the legal scholars were uncertain and divided, the ICJ in 1986 did not shed much light on the matter when it had a chance. In the Nicaragua case the US argued that its covert action had as one of its aims the protection of human rights. The ICJ questioned both the justification and the alleged methods, concluding "the argument derived from the preservation of human rights in Nicaragua cannot afford a legal justification for the conduct of the United States" (1986: 135).

The US claim was flimsy, its motives clearly ideological and the ICJ wanted to limit such broadening of the right to use force but the diverse body of legal authorities needed guidance from international institutions. Some observers thought the ICJ was virtually rejecting the concept altogether (Rodley 1989: 332).

The removal of the 'communist/anti-ideological' reflex from state policies with the end of the Cold war meant that a more flexible view could be taken. International crises would not be seen in such an automatically us-them way. In light of this, Wright thought that the previous "restrictive approach to humanitarian intervention is no longer appropriate ... given the current and foreseeable practical realities of world affairs" (1989: 435). Schachter (1984) agreed and thought there would never be an instance meeting all requirements at once.

Opinion was moving this way among scholars who were doing more than either international organs or governments to clarify the issue. Yet, the quasi-legal status the doctrine was achieving was described by Wolf as being "like a cucumber sandwich, ultimately unsatisfying" (1988: 355). The post-Cold War era consequently demonstrated the international community no longer believed that it was only genocide which justified outside intervention by states but also various other types of abuse and that states had a right, perhaps even a duty to intervene.

The Golden Age

> Humanitarian Intervention will remain at most in a legal penumbra – sometimes given legitimacy by the Security Council, sometimes merely tolerated by states. (Simon Chesterman 2001a: 87)

Falk (2003) says the 1990s were a golden age for humanitarian intervention, with University of Leicester academic Ahmad M. Ajaj observing that it "has never enjoyed as much legitimacy as it does today" (1993: 215).

Forcible protection of human rights took place in Liberia (1990), Northern Iraq (1990–91), Bosnia-Herzegovina (1992–95), Somalia (1992–93), Haiti (1994), Sierra Leone (1997–2000), Kosovo (1999) and East Timor (1999). Hyde's 1945 hopeful prophecy was finally if hesitantly being realized.

Instances of humanitarian intervention, however, were not always undertaken with Security Council authorization. Often, such as in Kosovo and East Timor, states referred to an alleged independent right to use force for humanitarian reasons.

The debate over a right to humanitarian intervention brought to the forefront the balance between sovereignty and the protection of human rights especially for the UN, which exists to protect both (Mamvig 2001: 267). Undersecretary-General to the UN, Brian Urquhart, has pithily termed it 'Sovereignty vs. Suffering' (1991: A23).

Figures from international organizations were expansive. Former Secretary-General Javier Perez de Cuellar, argued in 1991 that "it is now increasingly felt that the principle of non-interference within the essential domestic jurisdiction of states cannot be regarded as a protective barrier behind which human rights could be massively or systematically violated with impunity".

His successor, Kofi Annan said, in 1994 with regard to Rwanda, the international system was witnessing a "developing international norm in favor of intervention to protect civilians from wholesale slaughter". Acknowledging the doctrine had critics, Annan (1999b) called for balanced acceptance of this new willingness to no longer tolerate severe human rights abuse. Two years later the ICISS admitted the debate, saying humanitarian intervention has been "controversial both when it happens, and when it has failed to happen", but insisted that "state sovereignty implies responsibility" towards citizens (2001: ix, 1). Many but not all legal authorities and states now agreed on the principle if not the appropriate method (Charvet 1997: 47).

Some writers have gone so far as to claim the right to intervene, at least in the severe case of genocide, is now, potentially paradoxically, equal to the right to non-interference, an instance of *jus cogens*: a norm of international law from which no derogation is permitted (Ninčić 1970). Romanian-born American Edward Luttwak claimed "but for all its shortcomings, the new rule – whereby human rights outrank sovereignty – must still prevail, because the old rule is simply dead" (1999: 60).

Ravi Mahalingam, however, warned there has to be a balance in law and practice rather than the favoring "one to the practical exclusion of the other" (1996: 225). Michael Byers and Chesterman are less convinced of "the development of a new rule of customary international law" as "especially one with peremptory status, requires considerably more than a single partial exception in a half-century of non-intervention on humanitarian grounds" (2003: 184).

State practice has been less wholehearted than international organizations in embracing the concept (Secretary-General's High-Level Panel 2004).

States, unsurprisingly, still seem to need convincing that the abuse of others' rights affects them (Byers and Chesterman 2003: 202). In 1992–3 the international community at large remained indifferent to 300,000 deaths in Somalia until it was only shamed into action by UN Secretary-General Boutros-Ghali (Arniso 1993: 206). If lack of self-interest was one restraining factor, fear of abuse of a widened principle was another.

The majority of UN-member states, reflected in the Non-Aligned Movement also known as the Group of 77 (now featuring 130 states), in 2000 rejected "the so-called 'right' of humanitarian intervention" which they said had no legal basis in the Charter or general principles of international law.

China and Russia also remain largely opposed to the concept of state sovereignty being conditional on the respect for human rights (Bellamy and Williams 2006: 156). Smaller and Third World countries still fear that the concept will justify the use of force against them based on Western political and legal values (Janse 2006: 671, Orford 2003: 18–34).

Algerian President Abdelazia Bouteflika, a member of the Group of 77, said he supported action authorized by the UN but that many states remained "extremely sensitive to any undermining of our sovereignty, not only because sovereignty is our last defense against the rules of an unequal world, but because we are not taking part in the decision-making process of the Security Council" (Newland, Patrick and Zard 2003: 37).

According to India's Mohammed Ayoob this reflects the basic difference between Northern and Southern states' views on justice and order in the international system with the North placing a premium on justice within states and order among them and the South exactly the opposite (2002: 99).

Yet, it is worth noting Article 4(h) of the Constitutive Act of the African Union, framed in 2000 in the aftermath of Kosovo, which states "the right of the Union to intervene in a Member State pursuant to a decision of the Assembly in respect of grave circumstances, namely: war crimes, genocide and crimes against humanity". Dutch academic Steven Blockmans said that this signifies "many African states are becoming used to the idea that gross and mass violations of human rights have been removed from the sphere and have become matters of international concern" (1999: 778). Yet, the Union has proved reluctant to intervene beyond peacekeeping in the name of this right.

Some international organizations and committees have even suggested recently the protection of human rights not just as a right but responsibility of the international community (Danish Institute of International Affairs 1999, Secretary-General's High-Level Panel 2004).

In 2001, the ICISS also called the protection of human rights, through outside intervention if necessary, a duty. Its report said "where a population is suffering serious harm, as a result of unwilling or unable to halt or avert it, the principle of non-intervention yields to the international responsibility to protect" (2001: ix). The concept of the 'responsibility to protect' was adopted by states at the UN World Summit in 2005. Yet, NATO refused a June 2003 request by Annan to intervene in the five-year long civil war in the Democratic Republic of the Congo, despite the cost of thousands of lives and countless massacres and previous readiness to intervene in Kosovo, Afghanistan and Iraq at least partly on supposed humanitarian grounds. Annan, consequently, turned to the EU which deployed a French-led force.

Seybolt argues that states will largely see humanitarian intervention as "an optional action, not a universal cosmopolitan duty" (2007: 280). Despite NATO's refusal, humanitarian intervention in the post-Cold war era seemed to be moving from a permissive to an obligatory basis. This went too far for some. Mahalingam worried that a duty to intervene would result in sovereignty becoming 'meaningless' (1996: 261). The Security Council, however, has invoked states' security and not humanitarian concerns alone as justification in order to reconcile the two concepts.

Following the end of the Cold War, the Security Council (1991b) established a link between human rights abuses and a threat to international peace and security, condemning Iraq's repression of its population, particularly in Kurdish areas.

A year later a Security Council Summit declared that "non-military sources of instability in the economic, social, humanitarian and ecological fields have become threats to peace and security" (UNSC 1992b).

In the Somalia crisis of 1992, when the Security Council made the decisive shift from its long held disposition of giving preference to state sovereignty by permitting the use of force based on humanitarian grounds, it argued the situation was a breach of the peace under Article 39. States used the Charter's Chapter VII, covering breach of peace, threat to peace and act of aggression, to justify force in Rwanda, Haiti and Sierra Leone.

Since the end of the Cold War, the Security Council has declared threats to or breaches of international peace and security in internal armed conflicts (Yugoslavia, Liberia, Central African Republic), disruptions to democracy (Haiti, Sierra Leone) and humanitarian crises (Somalia, Rwanda, East Timor).

In eight of the nine there were UN-authorized humanitarian interventions with the UN peacekeeping mission in Bosnia-Herzegovina in 1995 the sole exception although it also had a humanitarian dimension. Chesterman (2001a) views the above development as a turning point in the development of humanitarian intervention.

Condoleezza Rice still clearly sees a distinction between security and human rights protection with security coming first, stating "there is nothing wrong with doing something that benefits all humanity, but that is, in a sense, a second-order effect" (2000: 47).

Other observers agree with this view arguing that state leaders have to be able to show that the use of force is not only in the common good but also in the state's own interest (Stedman 1993: 15). Maybe the emphasis on security weakens the principle of disinterested humanitarian concern but to the benefit of more effective action.

States' signing of human rights covenants certainly reflected acceptance of certain standards but the definition of what is the threshold of abuse that justifies intervention remained unclear (Heinze 2004, Teson 2006).

Annan stated that the Security Council should be prepared to act in instances of "systematic and widespread breaches of international humanitarian and human rights law, causing threats of genocide, crimes against humanity and war crimes" (1999a: 21), something reflected in the ICISS report.

The highest threshold of genocide is fairly clear but opinions differ on lesser criteria.

Post-Iraq, even staunch human rights supporter Falk cautioned that, genocide aside, state sovereignty should not be "overridden by unauthorized uses of force delivered in an excessive and inappropriate manner" (2004: 33). Nelson Mandela agrees (Adebajo and Landsverg 2002).

The ICISS regards large-scale loss of life, with or without genocidal intent, and ethnic cleansing, both actual or apprehended, as grounds for action, but only if the state in question is unable or unwilling to halt the atrocities (2001: xii).

The format of intervention also remains an issue which worries University of Queensland's Alex J. Bellamy in that the demand for strict criteria might prevent effective action (2005a: 33). Collective action remains the preferred format of most authorities including the ICSS and, if authorized by the UN, now attracts little controversy.

Some observers have viewed it as unlikely that the ICJ would condemn as illegal any use of force by the UN, including humanitarian interventions (Stein 2004: 23). De Schutter (1972) even said humanitarian intervention ought to be limited to the UN alone while the ICISS saw the Security Council as the preferred authority.

In reality, the continuing stalemate in the Security Council or indifference of states has largely prevented this. Its practice has been described as being '*ad-hocish*': such inconsistencies being unavoidable in an organ which reflects the interests of a multitude of core players (Österdahl 2005: 1).

Indeed, the UN has focused on peacekeeping rather than enforcement action with the Persian Gulf War of 1991 the only time the Security Council has authorized force against a sovereign state. The preferred option of dealing with humanitarian crises, particular since the Iraq War of 2003, has been peacekeeping rather than peace enforcement operations. The UN has deployed peacekeeping operations mainly to Africa including to Liberia, Côte d'Ivoire, Haiti, Burundi, Sudan, the Central African Republic and Chad. Operations tended to be undertaken with the consent of the host state and so were rarely controversial: 'intervention by invitation' is not prohibited under the UN Charter (Williams and Bellamy 2005a: 161). This move from coercion to consent is reflective of many of the obstacles facing both the legality of humanitarian interventions and the success rate of such operations. Yet, Somalia and Haiti have shown the shortcomings of UN peacekeeping where the ineffectiveness of the former led to UN-endorsed armed interventions. While peacekeeping is not the subject of this book, it is important to question its ability to successfully broker peace and end human rights abuses in light of its strict operational guidelines.

Somalia, Haiti, Rwanda and Kosovo have shown that while the UN may have the authority to intervene, it often lacks resources and ability to so do. So, when it does assess the need for forcible intervention, it has tended to 'outsource' the mission. The ICISS (2001: 46–55) accepts, should the Security Council be unable to act, the legitimacy of UN-authorized collective action in a hierarchy extending down through the General Assembly, regional organizations, *ad hoc* coalitions and individual states, especially when necessary to end severe humanitarian crises.

The former has the authority, the latter three the means. Legal experts such as Chesterman (2001a) and Reisman (2000) agree.

Rice argued in 2000 that, as the US would not be able to intervene everywhere, regional organizations and *ad hoc* coalitions carried an increasing responsibility to act if needed.

France's Operation Turquoise in Rwanda (1994) and the International Force East Timor (INTERFET) in 1999 are examples. Half of all multilateral peace operations since 1990 have been undertaken by regional organizations, followed by the UN which holds a third of the share. The remainder constitutes operations undertaken by *ad hoc* coalitions. (SIPRI 2009).

The 2004 Wilton Park Conference on Intervention consequently suggested strengthening cooperation between the UN and regional organizations in order to increase the likelihood of humanitarian intervention being undertaken and retaining a legal character.

This has led to both UN-authorized and non-authorized humanitarian interventions.

Working through established regional organizations with UN authorization is the format of the highest desirability for the UN. Yet, there seems to be reluctance for such organizations to act. The AU, for example, in 2000 explicitly expressed in principle support for humanitarian intervention but has, as Bellamy and Williams stressed, "neither the capability nor a political consensus to support serious interventionism" (2006: 157). The recent Darfur crisis in which AU peacekeepers suffered from grave underfunding, indicated a lack of commitment to go the higher stage of enforcement. In the absence of regional organizations conducting interventions, *ad hoc* coalitions have been the main operational and legal vehicle for humanitarian intervention in this period.

The UN-authorized, US-led operation in Somalia (1992–93) was, said Oxford University's Adam Roberts, "widely seen as a classic case of humanitarian intervention" (1993: 439). UN peacekeeping forces were already in the country overseeing a ceasefire agreement and securing the delivery of aid. When they proved unable to prevent the death of around 300,000 people, the Security Council authorized a US-led force to intervene (UNSC 1992d).

Boutros-Ghali (1992b) stressed that in the absence of a functional Somali government, the international community would not be able to act by invitation and the Security Council determined the situation to constitute a threat to peace under Article 39.

This was intervention not peacekeeping. Bush stressed that the mission was a strictly humanitarian and the US did not "plan to dictate political outcomes [and] respects your sovereignty and independence" (1992: 866).

This operation met all the agreed criteria for a humanitarian intervention and attracted criticism only of its effectiveness not legality. Humanitarian intervention in this form clearly was now widely acceptable.

If Somalia was an operational failure, it was a success in terms of entrenching the principles. Yet, the failure, including US troop losses, put in doubt further operations of this nature. When a greatly reduced UN peacekeeping force in Rwanda in 1994 was unable to prevent the killing of 800,000 people in three months, states were reluctant to intervene (Feil 1997, Kuperman 2001).

Eventually, the UN-authorized French intervention force did. The operation was viewed with suspicion by some as France had originally supported the incumbent government (Bellamy, Williams and Griffith 2004: 224–25). The international community's lack of political will to intervene militarily to halt mass killings, despite now having an agreed legal framework, was called by American Democratic Comgressman Solarz and academic O'Hanlon "one of the international community's greatest moral failures in the last half century" (1997: 10). After the false dawn of Somalia, Rwanda increased the push to clarify international law even further on the use of force to ensure one rule, non-interference, did not destroy the other, human rights. American Jill Stauffer said of the former, "a law that cannot save 800,000 people from being murdered in an overt genocidal campaign will not be a law capable of guiding anyone" (2007: 236).

As the century closed, further interventions revealed what Annan later referred to as the fork in the road for the international system. One response to failure in Rwanda was that states needed to develop better laws and processes to meet humanitarian crises with fully legitimate yet timely, effective collective intervention. The other response was to say the former would rarely be achievable and thus non-authorized action, unilateral if necessary but preferably multilateral, was the only effective path regardless of legality. A string of interventions went down the former path suggesting the new apparent growing consensus on the rules of humanitarian intervention would be strengthened.

A US-led *ad hoc* coalition intervened in Haiti in 1994 after a request to the Security Council by the country's democratically-elected President Jean-Betrand Aristide following his removal in 1991. The military *coup d'état* was condemned by both the OAS and the General Assembly. The Security Council itself did not become involved until 1993 when it imposed economic sanctions, declaring that the humanitarian crisis which had resulted from the forceful removal of the government constituted a threat to international peace and security.

The *junta's* subsequent agreement to allow Aristide to return was short lived, with violence between government and opposition forces resuming. The mandate of the Security Council-authorized coalition intervention was to use "all necessary means to facilitate ... the prompt return of the legitimately elected President and the restoration of the legitimate authorities" (Longchamp 1994, UNSC 1994a).

In 1996 the Security Council authorized a Canadian-led *ad hoc* coalition to intervene in Eastern Zaire which was host to hundreds of thousands of refugees from the previous genocide and general disarray in Rwanda and the scene of a civil war itself, which in return had led to refugees entering neighboring states. The situation resulted in massive humanitarian crisis. With the agreement of Zaire, the Security Council authorized an intervention with a mandate to use all necessary means under Chapter VII to "facilitate the immediate return of humanitarian organizations and the effective delivery by civilian relief organizations of humanitarian aid to alleviate the immediate suffering of displaced persons, refugees and civilians" (UNSC 1996c, UNSC 1996d).

In 1997, civil unrest erupted in Albania when government-sponsored investment funds collapsed, resulting in the majority of the population losing their life savings. Violent demonstrations and rioting swept the country resulting in substantial streams of refugees, particularly to Italy. The Security Council (1997a) viewed the situation with concern and consequently authorized an Italian-led multinational protection force to restore not only order but also most notably "to facilitate the safe and prompt delivery of humanitarian assistance".

In 1999, Indonesia was pressured by the international community, especially the US, to agree to an armed, Australian-led international intervention, subsequently authorized by the Security Council (1999b).

Unlike NATO's action in Kosovo this, said Australian Moreen Dee, was "a permissive, not uninvited, humanitarian intervention" (2001: 19). Many observers thought Australia would not have intervened without Security Council authorization (Wheeler and Dunne 2001: 808). This may, however, have been primarily due to its relationship with Indonesia rather than fear of appearing to act illegally. The fact this intervention followed and was succeeded by two UN peacekeeping missions respectively, added to its legitimacy as an UN-authorized intervention.

Critics claim the willingness of the EU to intervene militarily in the Congo in 2003 was driven less by humanitarian concerns than the EU's wish to present itself as a foreign policy counterweight to the US, which had refused to intervene. Perhaps this is true but this again demonstrated the international community was prepared to accept as legal, UN-authorized multilateral humanitarian interventions whether of an *ad hoc* or regional organization kind.

Yet, other events either side of this intervention were undermining the growing international consensus on humanitarian intervention.

UN authorization remains preferred not just for legal reasons alone. Operations authorized by the UN, on average, attracted more partners (Tago 2007: 202). Yet, the legal aspects remain uppermost. Annan (1999b) has expressed his concern that unauthorized military force outside the UN framework may undermine "the imperfect, yet resilient, security system created after the Second World War, and [set] dangerous precedents for future interventions". He stressed the need for the establishment of clear criteria regarding who may undertake such interventions and under which circumstances: demands partly met in the ICISS report. So while UN peacekeeping operations and UN-authorized multilateral interventions were gaining in popularity and legitimacy, enforcement action taken for humanitarian reasons without UN authorization remained highly controversial.

There were a number of instances where states went down that second fork in the road: unauthorized interventions. It is significant though that states in these unauthorized cases, are now inclined at least not to intervene unilaterally or perhaps even by *ad hoc* coalitions, but through established regional organizations in order to garner some vestige of legitimacy and avoid the criticisms of self-interested aggression.

The Economic Community of West African States' (ECOWAS) intervention in Liberia in 1990 sought but did not receive authorization from the UN which, five months later, suggested vague support without formal endorsement. ECOWAS' intervention in Sierra Leone in 1997–98 was authorized by the OAU and three months later did receive formal UN endorsement. These two interventions, taken through an established regional organization within its own region, significantly outside of any great power interest, sat in a limbo between legality and illegality. The situation was more clear cut and much more controversial over Kosovo in 1999.

After unsuccessful diplomatic attempts to resolve the situation where there was ethnic cleansing by Serbian forces in Kosovo, together with a substantial refugee crisis, NATO decided to intervene without seeking Security Council authority due probably to its fear of veto by Russia and China (Bellamy 2000, Henkin 1999).

Nor did it attempt to go through the General Assembly with the Resolution for Peace provision, again based on the uncertainty whether the Group of 77 would agree. After eleven weeks of aerial bombardment, the withdrawal of Serbian military forces and emergence of an 800,000-person refugee crisis, NATO deployed a peacekeeping force which was authorized by the Security Council (Arniso 1999: 287).

NATO countries defended their action on a number of grounds, mostly moral as opposed to legal (Solana 1999a). One of the few legal arguments advanced was the invocation of past Security Council resolutions condemning Yugoslavia's behavior and expressing concerns about the situation in Kosovo (UNSC 1998a, UNSC 1999d, Chirac 1999, ICJ 1999a).

In the ICJ, Belgium argued that this was not a violation of Article 2(4) as it had been directed neither against Yugoslavia's territorial integrity nor its political independence but primarily at the policies of the Yugoslavian (present day Serbia and Montenegro) government (ICJ 1999b, Solana 1999c).

Many questioned this, saying NATO maintained more than 15,000 troops, along with a UN transitional administration, in an operation which led to the creation of a newly independent state: undeniably a threat to the original Yugoslavia's territorial integrity (Chesterman 2002).

The Security Council's authorization of the NATO peacekeeping force and deployment of a transitional administration similar to East Timor, inevitably added some belated legitimacy to NATO's original armed intervention.

NATO contributing states blurred the line between legality and morality. NATO and the EU spoke of a moral duty to end the violence (Solana 1999b, European Council 1999).

Vaclac Havel (1999) said that "this is probably the first war that has not been waged in the name of 'national interests', but rather in the name of principles and values". A member of the UK's Foreign Affairs Select Committee on Kosovo (FASC) in 2000 argued that NATO members "sought desperately to articulate the legal justification which would encapsulate that moral imperative".

The UK argued that "in these circumstances [the failure of diplomacy], and as an exceptional measure on grounds of overwhelming humanitarian necessity, military intervention is legally justifiable" (UNSC 1999a).

The NATO force apparently viewed stopping the killings in Kosovo as a *jus cogens* superior to that of state sovereignty (Duursma 1999: 290).

Two years later the ICISS report reflected the opinion of the FASC and many writers that the NATO intervention in Kosovo demonstrated "a need to bridge a gap between legality and legitimization" (2001: 10).

The ICISS, similar to intervening states, also focused on the use of just war criteria as opposed to legal criteria in determining the legality of humanitarian intervention. The re-emergence of this concept was previously examined in Chapter 4 of this book. Schachter, as early as 1991, argued strongly that the use of force based on just war theory, as well as for human rights, democracy and self-determination is not legally acceptable.

This was a viewed shared by the Federal Republic of Yugoslavia, Russia and China which condemned NATO's use of force as an act of aggression and, together with the circumvention of the Security Council, a serious violation of both the UN Charter and international norms (UNSC 1998e, Milosevic 1999).

A number of writers thought the latter more serious (Charney 1999, Henkin 1999).

The ICJ, hearing Yugoslavia's complaint against ten states involved in the aerial bombings, dismissed the case in 2004 finding it had no jurisdiction. The ICJ did admit that it was "profoundly concerned with the use of force in Yugoslavia [and that] under the present circumstances such use raises very serious issues of international law" (1999c: 132).

Yet, the ICJ declined again to give clear legal guidance on the principle by not proceeding to judge the legality of non-UN authorized humanitarian intervention. The ICISS was equally undecided whether the bypassing of the Security Council or the ignoring of human rights abuses posed the greatest damage to international order (2001: 54–5).

The FASC report on Kosovo (2000) concluded that "NATO's military action if of dubious legality in the current state of international law, was justified on moral grounds".

The Independent International Commission on Kosovo (IICK), similarly contended that NATO action "was illegal, though legitimate" and supposedly expressing an 'international moral consensus' (2000: 4).

Even the ICISS report said that "only a thin red line [separated] NATO's action in Kosovo from international legality" (Simma 1999: 22).

Some legal writers have dismissed this half-way justification, doubting the legality of any non-UN authorized intervention (Henkin 1999). Others have rejected the moral argument: "the morality of the NATO intervention in Kosovo, understood as an illegal act directed toward improving the international legal system, is extremely doubtful" (Buchanan 2001: 704).

Bellamy, like others, is skeptical of the moral claim, suggesting self-interested concern over the potential extensive refugee problem, as well as regional stability, were among the real motives (2002: 3). Inconsistency of action, including NATO's inaction towards other humanitarian crises such as in Sierra Leone, according to American Michael Mandelbaum, confirms such an assessment (1999: 6).

The fall-out from Kosovo may not have been as damaging for the development of an effective legal framework for humanitarian intervention as some feared. Initial suspicions that states would be more willing to evade the Security Council in their use of force for humanitarian reasons, has not proved entirely true (Duursma 1999: 294). Yet, it may have encouraged states to use humanitarian grounds, unendorsed by the Security Council, as justification for non-humanitarian interventions, thereby degrading the integrity of the justification.

The danger of exploitation of humanitarian intervention by states to justify the use of force is evident in two cases which show that humanitarian concerns are rarely the sole motivation but instead have been used as excuses to give the action, if not legality, then at least legitimacy. The 2001 US-led multilateral military intervention in Afghanistan was deployed to oust the Taliban government and so deny this alleged safe-haven for terrorists. With the failure to bring order, the third stated aim, the rhetoric behind the intervention has increasingly been turned into a claim that it is a fight for the liberation of women (Kaldor 2003, Bush 2001c).

Clifford Owen said such retrospective humanitarian justifications could fuel the fears of certain states that they will be subjected by force to accept the moral values of the West (2006: 199). Humanitarian intervention not only on the grounds of gross abuses like genocide, but also for lesser abuses of the so-called third kind could be of grave concern to smaller, poorer countries, who possess stable governments and are not committing gross abuses, but have different values and are not sufficiently strong enough to maintain their right to sovereignty and non-interference.

The US-led use of force against Iraq is a similar case in which humanitarian issues have been pushed retrospectively to the forefront as justifications, especially in view of the inability to find weapons of mass destruction, the main original justification (Bush 2002c).

The coalition increasingly aired claims that approximately 300,000 Iraqis were killed by Saddam Hussein (Hudson 2003).

By presenting the liberation of an oppressed people as the reason for the use of force, actions were presented as altruistic, not just as a result of power dominance and pursuit of specific self-interest (Kelly 2003b).

Some authorities, even in the field of human rights protection, such as Kenneth Roth of Human Rights Watch, have said human rights abuses at the time of the intervention were "not of the exceptional and dire magnitude that would justify humanitarian intervention" (2006: 86).

There is even more controversy attached to unilateral rather than multilateral non-UN authorized intervention. Apart from self-defense, states and legal writers have relied on two grounds. The first is through reference to Articles 1(3) and 55 of the Charter which entail the demand for the respect of human rights. Allowing for the fact the UN is often inactive in cases of human rights protection, some argue states are merely implementing Article 56 which requires members to take "joint or separate action in co-operation with the Organization for the achievement of the purposes set forth in Article 55". Some argue the protection of human rights has been withdrawn from the Security Council's sole responsibility and is a matter for individual states.

The second argument is that the upholding of human rights is crucial for a stable and civilized global order and *jus cogens,* requiring no further legal authority. States then go on to argue that, in the frequent absence of specific Security Council authorization, it is legal to act under the authority of past Security Council resolutions. This was the case with NATO in Kosovo and the US-led coalition's intervention in Iraq in 2003. This is not an undisputed view. The ICJ in the Namibia Advisory Opinion had argued that "the language of a resolution of the Security Council should be carefully analyzed before a conclusion can be made as to its binding effect" (1971: 53).

Byers worried about the world order implications of such a justification. He thought in future states might "become significantly more cautious about supporting any Security Council resolution that might subsequently be interpreted so as to justify the use of force" (2002a: 40). Byers added that this may also result in an increased use of veto powers by permanent Security Council members, resulting ultimately in a weakened Security Council and an increase in non-UN authorized action. Annan (2001a) had no doubts; arguing "that it is for the Security Council to interpret its own resolutions".

Some observers have claimed the questionable use of humanitarian justifications for the use of force in Afghanistan and Iraq, together with an international focus on terrorism, have spelt "the end of an era of 'pure' humanitarian intervention as humanitarian motives are superseded with strategic national and international security targets" (Bellamy 2004: 132).

Falk (2003), who had hailed the 1990s as a 'golden age' for humanitarian intervention, argued that the use of humanitarian justifications in both Afghanistan and Iraq reflect America's approach towards humanitarian intervention after September 11 which had "morphed into *post hoc* rationalizations for uses of force otherwise difficult to reconcile with international law". Any real humanitarian benefit, according to Falk, was merely an unintended byproduct.

The Darfur Crisis confirmed this suspicion for many (Williams and Bellamy 2005b: 4). With estimated tens of thousand of dead and two million displaced, it was likened to Rwanda in 1994 (Roth 2006: 87). US Secretary of State Colin Powell, as early as 2004, acknowledged that genocide had been committed in Darfur, holding both the government and Janjaweed militia responsible. Yet, he added, that "no new action is dictated by this determination".

The Security Council did, however, refer the case to the International Criminal Court (ICC), as well as authorizing a hybrid peacekeeping mission with the AU. Bellamy and Williams link the international inaction to the alleged abuse of humanitarian justifications in the Iraq War. Western states also appear to have given more weight to security concerns in the war on terrorism than the humanitarian plight. In this the Sudanese government is an important ally. One critic said the lack of action proved that "the Axis of Evil will always upstage that of Misery" (Orwin 2006: 214). Russia and China have substantial economic interests in Sudan. There is also a fear that peace enforcement measures may jeopardize the Naivasha Agreement regarding the country's civil war (Williams and Bellamy 2005b: 37). Finally, the potential human cost regarding military forces might be seen, after Somalia, as too high. The Sudanese government had threatened that Darfur "would become a graveyard for any multinational force sent without its consent" (Badescu 2007: 72).

Summary

In light of recent developments American Thomas G. Weiss has stated that the war on terror and the questionable use of humanitarian justifications in Iraq and Afghanistan have led to a 'sunset' of humanitarian intervention (2004: 135). It appears that in the 21st century old doubts about such use of force, if not in theory then at least in state practice, have been revived.

As this chapter has shown, the protection of human rights by intervention was originally justified with the old notion of Christendom and the protection of Christianity. By the 19th century, amid general fading of a religious basis of international law, a hybrid notion of humanitarian intervention developed mixing the protection of Christians with the protection of newer secular rights. In the aftermath of the First World War, state sovereignty, as opposed to the protection of human rights, was of core concern.

The Cold War era, too, focused on deterrence and decolonization strengthened sovereignty as consolidated in the UN Charter. The simultaneous new emphasis on human rights, however, planted seeds of change. Yet, concrete provisions for humanitarian intervention did not exist. The force on humanitarian grounds was justified instead on self-defense.

The 1990s saw an easing of this Cold War provisory, witnessing a real development in the concept of humanitarian intervention. State practice during this period saw predominantly a focus on UN-authorized action, generally collective in nature. At the end of the 1990s and in light of intervention in Kosovo, Iraq and Afghanistan, old doubts about humanitarian intervention resurfaced.

These doubts are based primarily on the attempts by regional organizations, *ad hoc* coalitions and individual states to justify their use of force not on current international law but just war morality. This perceived need to act outside of the existing rules for justice led to the view that there also had to be a protection of sovereignty through the establishment of rules as to when such intervention may be permitted. According to Bazyler, for humanitarian intervention "to exist as a doctrine of international law, and not just a *post hoc* excuse for any armed attack, a simple, working set of standards must be formulated" (1987: 598). While the ICISS has established some guidelines around the notion of the responsibility to protect, confirmed by the UN World Summit in 2005, these principles are still far from being universally recognized or applied in practice. Humanitarian intervention is a policy that, while pursued theoretically, is not practiced in a consistent manner and instead has been likened to a hot potato with "all respectable nations [wanting] to touch it, but only to hand it off to others" (Orwin 2006: 215).

Tony Blair (1999a), in recent years, has claimed that the national interest in instances of severe human rights abuses must coincide with the interest of the common good. This means that states should feel obliged to intervene militarily as the protection of rights is not only in the international but also national interest. Ultimately, however, humanitarian intervention is likely to remain an exception rather than the rule when it comes to use of force by states. Nothing seems to confirm this more than the striking absence of large scale and genuine humanitarian intervention in the 21st century.

Chapter 7
The Uninvited Guest: Intervention in Failed States

The concept of so-called failed states, similar to rogue states, is characterized by high selectivity and subjectivity with regard to the use of force against such states. Although conflicts fought in failed states since the end of the Cold War have left eight million people dead and more than four million displaced, the problem is often ignored (Rotberg 2002a: 127). The reason for this is that the problem of failed states focuses mainly on the internal aspects of the states in question, that is, political instability, internal conflict and economic hardship. This contrasts with the concept of rogue states which deals with the external threat they supposedly pose. Intervention in failed states only tends to take place once these internal problems are perceived to go beyond the respective state's borders, posing a threat to international peace and security. Such threats occur most often in form of refugee flows, the spread of conflict to neighboring states, as well as the involuntary creation of safe havens for terrorist networks.

The concept of failed states was expressed at least as early as 1854 when Phillimore referred to the 'feebleness' of certain states meaning their sovereign rights were more conditional.

Americans Gerald B. Helman and Steven R. Ratner were the first to use the phrase in 1992 describing the emergence of failed nation-states as "a disturbing new phenomenon [of a state] utterly incapable of sustaining itself as a member of the international community" (1992: 3). They believed that state failure played a particularly controversial role in international relations as it is "anathema to the *raison d'être* of decolonization and offensive to the notion of self-determination" (1992: 4).

Initially, the concept of failed states only existed in a figurative sense. Colonies were viewed as being incapable of self-government and therefore automatically as failed should the colonial power withdraw. This only changed marginally during the decolonization process when many Western states feared the collapse of newly independent states. Frequently described as 'weak' with regard to internal order, stability and governmental structures, these states experienced intervention in a number of ways, including military and economic measures. In the post-Cold War era intervention in failed states remains highly controversial as it implies, in the eyes of many developing countries, cultural and political superiority of intervening powers. Indeed, the classification of a state as 'failed', and therefore incapable of existing without external interference, is reminiscent of past colonial practices, including the abuse of trusteeship obligations. Yet there is a real need for the international community to address the failure of its respective members.

Nursing the Infant

> The peoples left behind by the decomposition of Russia, Austria, and Turkey are mostly untrained politically: many of them are either incapable or deficient in power of self-government; they are mostly destitute and will require much nursing towards economic and political independence. (J.C. Smuts 1918: 11)

Similar to rogue states, the concept, if not the term of failed states, like 'rogue', is not entirely an invention of the post-Cold War era. Some of the literature on failed states suggests that the League of Nations mandate system, established under Article 22 of the Covenant, is an adequate parallel to draw with regard to earlier concepts of failed states. This is not entirely correct. Instead one has to take into consideration two further concepts, that of League plebiscites and colonialism. The territories in which such action was taken had, however, not (yet) failed. Rather they were seen as unable to sustain independent statehood to begin with.

Colonialism, which reached its pinnacle during the 18th and 19th century, saw the annexation and settlement of territories overseas by a number of core European powers such as Portugal, Spain, Belgium, The Netherlands, Britain, Germany and France. At the time of the First World War, the UK was the most prominent imperial power, having established the largest empire in history.

Colonialism generally gave native inhabitants either no or only limited say in the running of the occupied territory. Instead, the colonial power ruled and administered the given territory, regulating all core aspects of it, including resources, trade and settlement. Conservatives such as English writer Rudyard Kipling, and Cecil John Rhodes, founder of the state of Rhodesia (present day Zimbabwe) were strong believers in colonialism. Rhodes clearly believed in the existence of a 'civilized' versus 'uncivilized' world, arguing that "the more of the world [Britain] inhabit[s] the better it is for the human race" (Flint 1976: 248). It was widely believed that colonies would be unable to preserve any type of order, let alone establish any degree of self-government without the powers currently occupying them. Edinburgh's first Professor of International Law, James Lorimer, distinguished in the 19th century between 'civilized, 'barbarous' (Turkey and Asia) and 'savage' (e.g. Africa) humanity (1872: 101–102). The latter two being early expressions of rogue and failed states.

Although the late 18th and early 19th century saw settlers if not indigenous colonies in the Americas gaining independence, colonialism was not genuinely challenged until the end of the First World War. The issue of self-determination moved to the forefront of international relations, sparked by the assassination of Austrian Archduke Franz Ferdinand by Gavrilo Princip, a member of a Serb nationalist movement advocating the unification of Bosnia-Herzegovina and Serbia and their independence from the Austro-Hungarian Empire.

Woodrow Wilson, in an address to Congress in 1918, called for national aspirations to be respected, demanding that "peoples may now be dominated and governed only by their own consent".

Wilson's suggestions that self-determination was more than just a mere phrase, however, was not and could not be fully reflected in the partition of the Austro-Hungarian, German and Ottoman Empire's at the Peace Conference of Versailles, the Treaty of Sèvres (1920) and Lausanne (1923).

The people in territories formerly owned by these powers did not always receive the outright entitlement to be sovereign territorial states. Instead, fourteen overseas territories were entered into the League of Nations mandate system and in the care of victorious countries such as the UK, France, Belgium, New Zealand, Australia and Japan. Eleven of the disputed territories in Europe were accorded plebiscites.

This policy constituted neither a total end to colonialism nor a full realization of the concept of self-determination. It did, however, discontinue the earlier practice where an adversary's colonies were simply taken over by the victor state. Instead, South-African General, and later Prime Minister, J.C. Smuts, argued that, "reversion to the League of Nations should be substituted for any policy of national annexation" (1918: 12). While there was a recognition that self-determination had to be granted to a certain degree there was the simultaneous view expressed by Australian Oxford University scholar Gilbert Murray that the "ruthless application of the principle ... would produce a ... scattering explosion in our territories" (1922: 8). The League of Nations Mandate and Plebiscite System appeared to be the middle way, allowing the local population of the territories in question a greater say while at the same time allowing the mandatory powers to retain ultimate control.

These territories, said Article 22 of the League of Nations Covenant, were "inhabited by peoples not yet able to stand by themselves under the strenuous conditions of the modern world". The aim of the mandate system was to advance the interests of the inhabitants of these territories rather than the mandatory powers as demanded originally by Wilson in point five of his Fourteen Points. Article 22 distinguished between three classes of mandates, based on the developmental stage of the respective territories.

Class A applied to former Ottoman territories (Syria, Palestine and Iraq), seen to have reached "a stage of development where their existence as independent nations can be provisionally recognized subject to the rendering of administrative advice and assistance by a Mandatory until such time as they are able to stand alone".

Class B and C were former German colonies and territories, located in Africa and the Pacific. Here mandatory powers were responsible for the administration of the respective territory, ensuring freedom of conscience and religion, and prohibiting the establishment of military bases within these territories. Territories under Class C were seen as least likely to advance to the stage of self-government "owing to the sparseness of their population, or their small size, or their remoteness from the centres of civilisation".

These territories (German New Guinea, Nauru, German Samoa) were administered by Australia and New Zealand under the laws of the mandatory powers essentially as part of their territory. The mandatory powers were obliged to submit annual reports on finance, freedom of conscience, education, public health, and general administration of the territories which had been entered into their care (Hales 1939: 218).

James C. Hales saw the main merit of the mandates system as being "the triumph of the idea of self expression among formerly subjugated peoples and a denial of the idea of conquest" (1939: 203). In practice, however, none of the territories entered into the mandate system gained their independence for many decades. In fact, the only territory to be given sovereign statehood prior to the Second World War was Iraq in 1932 (Evans 1932). While the local population was given a greater say in the running of the territories and the League of Nations attempted to impose restrictions on the behavior of the mandatory powers, these territories in many ways continued to be quasi-colonies.

In addition to the mandate system, the League of Nations also proposed the establishment of eleven plebiscites. Oppenheim had previously argued that it was "doubtful whether the Law of Nations will ever make it a condition of every cession that it must be ratified by a plebiscite" (1912: 290).

But the post-First World War era revived it. The concept of plebiscites, recognizing the need for local population to have a say in their future, existed prior to the First World War. At the time of the French revolution, a number of territories were incorporated into France following plebiscites. These referenda were not seen ultimately as being 'free and fair' as armed troops were present at the time (Llewellyn-Jones 1933: 167).

The rise of the doctrine of self-determination, as mentioned above, gave increased importance to the involvement of the local population in the future of their territories. The Treaty of Versailles established plebiscites in the Saar Basin (Germany–France), the Klagenfurt Basin (Austria–Yugoslavia), as well as Upper Silesia (Germany–Poland), Allenstein and Marienwerder (Germany–Poland), and Schleswig (Germany–Denmark). The territories in question were claimed by two states and the population was given the option of choosing with which state to remain or, in case of the Saar Basin, whether to remain under the direct governance of the League. Plebiscites were seen as being strictly for only European powers who were viewed as having the capacity to self-govern or join an established state. The inclusion of non-European states in this principle was not seriously considered, unlike mandates where Japan was included.

Until a direct vote by the members of the plebiscite territories could occur, these areas were placed under mandate of an International Commission. While these commissions in some instances included states such as Norway, Sweden and Japan, their membership focused heavily on the victors of the First World War. Britain, France, to a lesser extent Belgium, and Italy were the core players administrating these territories. The International Commissions in most cases were supported by troop contingents, ranging from a mere 800 in Allenstein and Marienwerder to more than 10,000 in Upper Silesia (Macqueen 2006: 31–2). Such deployments, however, were not viewed as constituting an aggressive use of force contrary to the League Covenant. The action was therefore not viewed as a threat to the international order but rather contributing to its stability. Not everyone, however, shared this view.

D.P. Heatley, Professor of Political Science at the University of Edinburgh, called for the exercise of caution regarding the concept of plebiscites which he believed had the potential to constitute a "cannon against self-slaughter" (1921: 269). The plebiscite system was seen by some as potentially having a snowball effect, allowing minorities in states everywhere to separate from their current state. He saw the risk of "disturbing the being and stability of a state ... by inducing the loss of part of its population through secession or transference" as significant (1921: 269). The idea of a right to secession arising from the right to self-determination remained widely rejected. The League of Nations itself administered two territories, the Saarland (1920–1935) and the free city of Danzig (1920–1939). This concept of transitional administrations is reflected in many contemporary UN peacekeeping missions in which troops remain in a state until elections have taken place or, in the case of East Timor, until the transition to independent statehood has been achieved.

What both the mandate and plebiscite system had in common was the view that territories allocated to it were, in their present form, non-viable as individual sovereign states. While these territories, according to Hungarian Minister and lawyer Paul De Auer, did not "[possess] the attributes necessary to independence" (1920: 50), they were not seen as failed states as we understand the term today. Instead they were seen as not even having the potential to try out their hand at self-government, that is, failure was seen to be predisposed and therefore sovereign independence not considered.

The requirements for a state to be recognized as independent were established in the Montevideo Convention on Rights and Duties of States (1933). Article 1 asserted that "the state as a person of international law should possess the following qualifications: a) a permanent population; b) a defined territory; c) government; and d) capacity to enter into relations with the other states". As mentioned above, Iraq was the only territory or plebiscite which met these requirements, as well the conditions and developmental stage necessary to gain such status of self government. The independence of Syria, Lebanon and Trans-Jordan was recognized at the League of Nations Assembly's final session in 1946. The remaining territories, following the dissolution of the League of Nations, were transferred to the UNTC.

The Age of Consent

> Historically, mandates and international trusteeship are rooted in the decline and fall of empires, in the expansion of states into weak and backward areas. (H. Duncan Hall 1948: 15)

Following the end of the Second World War a quarter of the world's population continued to live in colonies and mandate territories (Office of Public Information

1963: 3). Consequently, the concept of self-determination increased its importance in international relations. While colonial powers such the UK had been under considerable pressure from the US to grant independence to its colonies through the Lend-Lease Agreement of 1942, it was also the economic toll experienced by core colonial powers as a consequence of the Second World War which rang in the age of decolonization. This process saw the member states of the UN grow from 51 in 1945 to 159 by 1989.

The achievement of independence was, as expressed in the introductory quote by Australian League official H. Duncan Hall, not necessarily viewed as being synonymous with such new states' capability of maintaining a stable internal order (1948: 15). Woodrow Wilson's son-in-law Francis B. Sayre, Harvard Professor of Law and US representative at the UNTC, controversially argued that these 'weak' states and territories were inhabited by "non-self-governing peoples who lack the power to control their own destinies or push progressively forward" (1948: 263). Sayre had been the last foreign policy adviser to Thailand where even this independent Asian state felt it needed European help to govern.

Interventions in such states were reflected in three distinctive ways during the Cold War era. First, some territories were placed under the UNTC, the successor to the League of Nations mandate system. Second, UN peacekeeping was in some instances used where new states struggled through the decolonization processes. Third, the development of weak or potentially failed states in Europe was prevented by large scale economic recovery plans and, in the case of Germany, Austria and Japan, the assumption of governmental authority by allied powers.

The General Assembly made its contribution to the realization of decolonization with the establishment of the UNTC which, according to Harvard Professor of International Relations, Inis L. Claude, had the task to "make the world fit for peace by launching a kind of international slum clearance project, and promoting the progressive development of peoples which have been left behind and pushed to the rear" (1959: 343). The ultimate goal, according to Article 76 of the Charter, was the establishment of self-government and territorial independence of the territories in question although many anticipated that goal was a long way off.

Although the UNTC supervised the move of these territories towards independence, the everyday overseeing of trust territories was undertaken by administering powers (Office of Public Information 1963).[1]

These powers had already administered the areas in question during the League of Nations period but were now confronted with even greater scrutiny on behalf of the international organization. Administering powers not only had to submit annual reports but also accept periodic visits by UNTC representatives to the trust

1 They included Cameroons (French and British administration), Togoland (French and British administration), Ruanda-Urundi (Belgian administration), Tanganyika (British administration), Western Samoa (New Zealand administration), New Guinea (Australian administration), Nauru (Australian, New Zealand and British administration), Pacific Islands Trust Territory (United States administration), Somaliland (Italian administration)

territories. The UNTC placed great importance on, so Article 88 of the Charter, "the political, economic, social, and educational advancement of the inhabitants of each trust territory".

The UNTC saw the transferal of eleven former mandate territories to its supervision. While former mandatory powers cooperated widely with this voluntary transferal, there was one exception. South Africa refused to transfer its mandate territory of South West Africa (Scott 1958). It was not until 1967 that the territory now known as Namibia was placed under the direct administration of the UN. By the end of the Cold War all but the Trust Territory of the Pacific Islands, comprising Micronesia, the Northern Mariana Islands, Palau and the Marshall Islands had gained independence due to the strategic importance the US placed on them. Some, however, accused the US of abusing its trusteeship by detonating atomic bombs on the Marshall Islands.

Trusteeship was a cautious and paternalistic device which balanced the right of self-determination with the administering power's desire for control. By 1960 there were more newly-independent states in the General Assembly and they pushed that balance closer to self-determination. The General Assembly played an important role in the decolonization process, calling in the 1960 Declaration on the Granting of Independence to Colonial Countries and Peoples (DGICCP) for "an end of colonialism in all its manifestations". This was not a view supported by certain key members (Britain and France) of the Security Council.

The attempt to achieve greater neutrality with regard to the working of the UNTC is reflected in its structure which consisted both of states administering the trust territories but also of the Permanent Members of the Security Council. The combined number of the two was then, according to Article 86 of the UN Charter, to be matched by an equal number of non-administering member states. Although the Declaration on the DGICCP stated that "inadequate political, economic, social or educational preparedness should never serve as a pretext for delaying independence" this did occur. The granting of self-government and independence of these territories remained a highly political affair.

Territories such as Australian administered Nauru did not gain independence until 1968. Australia and Britain maintained large economic interests in the territories, having established in conjunction with Britain and New Zealand, the British Phosphate Commission (BPC) in 1919. Giving Nauru independence, therefore could have jeopardized their interests. Following its independence and the purchase of the BPC in 1967, Nauru decided in 1989, to launch legal action against Australia at the ICJ. The claim was that Australia had breached its trusteeship obligations, most notably due to its failure to rehabilitate phosphate lands environmentally damaged as a consequence of large scale mining prior to Naunian independence (ICJ 1992: 242).

The case of Nauru shows that independence of trust territories was often postponed for a number of reasons, including strategic and economic. While there was an unwillingness to allow certain territories to achieve self-government, this was often not as controversial as expected due to a lack of military force involved. In some instances, however, intervention on behalf of the UN occurred. As discussed in Chapter 3, the UN aimed to pursue collective security through peace enforcement as envisaged in Chapter VII of the Charter. Due foremost to a deadlock in the Security Council, caused by the rivalry between the US and Soviet Union, this was not always possible and an alternative to peace enforcement, peacekeeping, was established.

Peacekeeping was not mentioned in the UN Charter and is nestled implicitly somewhere in between the Chapter VI and Chapter VII. The organizing principles for the UN Emergency Force to Sinai (1956), established to secure the withdrawal of French, British and Israeli forces from Egypt, also gave the core principles of future peacekeeping operations. Dag Hammerskjoeld, UN Secretary General (1953–1961) focused on three core principles, characterized by Bellamy, Williams and Griffith as the "holy trinity of consent, impartiality and the minimum use of force" (2004: 96).

The UN peacekeeping operations during the Cold War focused mainly on inter-state disputes and ceasefire monitoring. An examination of the seventeen incidents of peacekeeping until 1989 show that only two qualify for consideration as intervention in a destabilized or, to use the contemporary phrase, potentially 'failed' state: the UN Operation in The Congo (UNOC, 1960–1964) and the UN Transition Assistance Group in Namibia (UNTAG, 1989–1990).

Namibia had been made the direct responsibility of the UN, following the General Assembly's declaration that South Africa had failed to fulfill its mandate. The organization administered the territory to "enable the people ... to exercise the right of self-determination and to achieve independence" (UNGA 1966). As Namibia was already under UN administration, its peacekeeping operation UNTAG which was established to secure the overseeing of the election leading to its independence, can be see as a component of this.

The UNOC operation was the first instance in which the UN attempted to stabilize a state which had the potential to collapse, sending peacekeepers, says the Director of the *Brahimi Report* William J. Durch, "where none had gone before" (1993: 315). With a strength of up to 20,000 personnel at its peak, the size together with the tasks of the operations were unprecedented. The Republic of Congo, a Belgium colony until 1960, requested the UN peacekeeping force following military interference by its former colonial power attempting to retain control of its copper mining interests by fostering the secession of the province Katanga. The timing of the peacekeeping operations suggests it was not only about getting Belgium forces to withdraw but also an attempt to support the Republic of the Congo in its transition from a former colony to a newly independent state.

The Security Council Resolution (1961) gave the policies and purposes of the UN peacekeeping force as the maintenance of territorial integrity and political independence of the Congo, as well as assistance to the government in restoring and maintaining law and order, including the prevention of the occurrence of civil war and the withdrawal of foreign military forces.

The first two aspects are of particular interests as they, said University of Michigan Professor of International Relations Harold Karan Jacobsen, reflected the issue of state preservation and the UN's aim of keeping intact the state structure left behind by the process of decolonization "protecting it against the danger of imminent collapse" (1964: 76). UNOC attempted to protect not only the territorial integrity of the Congo but also aimed at maintaining important administrative functions and infrastructure, all aspects which comprise a functioning state.

The operation demonstrated that peacekeeping had the potential to be a real alternative to the UNTC in protecting states which were going through the decolonization process from collapse and leading them into sovereign independence. Thomas M. Franck described UNOC as an "injection of a United Nations presence to bring international law to bear in a situation of international chaos" (1962: 632). While the problems The Congo faced were mainly internal, they had the clear potential (as do conditions in failed states today) to acquire regional dimensions. This was an issue recognized by the UN which described the situation in The Congo as a threat to international peace and security.

Peacekeeping, as action undertaken with the consent of the host state, although rare during the Cold War era, involved few of the controversies peace enforcement did. Both the US and Soviet Union concentrated on political and financial means as well as military action to keep many newly independent states stable and, more importantly, on their side. To construct a non-communist state for all and then the later part of Vietnam, the US first funded the French through the *European Recovery Plan (ERP)*, then directly to France from 1950, directly by itself from 1955, used covert action from 1962 and finally open intervention from 1964. During this time period the core concern was not so much state failure as it was Cold War rivalry and securing the superpowers' respective sphere of influence.

In the immediate aftermath of the Second World War US Secretary of State George C. Marshall stressed the need for Europe to have "substantial additional help or face economic, social, and political deterioration of a very grave character" (1947: 1159). The devastation caused by the war gave rise to the real threat of many of the European powers turning into failed states. Economies had been shattered, vital infrastructure destroyed and famine was potent. US aid was already flowing through the multilateral mechanism of the UN Relief and Rehabilitation Administration but the US wanted greater control. The US Congress' *Economic Cooperation Act* of 1948 concluded that "the existing situation in Europe endangers the establishment of lasting peace", therefore recognizing that internal state failure could have an international impact.

Amongst the largest receivers of the $12 billion (1947–1951) *ERP*, better known as the Marshall Plan, were the UK, France, Germany, Italy and The Netherlands (Harris 1948). This support program stopped the European states involved from disintegrating by rebuilding not only their economies but in the case of Germany and, due to a similar program, Japan also their political systems. This was meant not only to revive American markets but also bolster them as anti-Soviet bulwarks. The US also provided aid indirectly through the Marshall Plan and directly to

European countries to support their attempt to construct 'friendly' post-colonial states in their colonies especially in opposition to anti-colonial local forces.

Germany, according to the Declaration Regarding the Defeat of Germany and the Assumption of Supreme Authority by Allied Powers (1945) had "no central Government or authority ... capable of accepting responsibility for the maintenance of order [and] the administration of the country". According to Hans Kelsen Germany therefore ceased to exist as a sovereign state (1945: 521). The powers, represented in the Allied Control Council by the US, Soviet Union, UK and France assumed all powers possessed (originally) by the German government, including law-making functions. The allied powers, however, stressed that this did not amount to annexation and was, instead, temporary in duration. The Potsdam Protocol stated that the allied forces, by assuming governmental powers, intended to give "the German people ... the opportunity to prepare for the eventual reconstruction of their life on a democratic and peaceful basis". This occurred with the election of Konrad Adenauer as West Germany's first Chancellor in 1949.

The international community during the Cold War era faced the challenge of both large scale decolonization, as well as rebuilding following the end of the Second World War. It was no longer only former colonies which were seen to be in need of external support to guarantee their survival. Instead, core Western powers such Germany, Austria, the UK and France were in need of large scale support in order to prevent the collapse of state structures.

The new situation and changing international environment meant there was a reliance on a continuation of both new and old methods. Preventing state failure was undertaken by placing territories under the UNTC, as well as deploying peacekeeping forces. The assumption of governmental powers and large scale economic support was seen as a solution for Western powers emerging out of the Second World War.

The doctrine of non-intervention, reflected in numerous declarations and treaties since its first inception at the Peace of Westphalia, was not a major issue during the Cold War with regard to preventing territories and states from collapse through external intervention. The explanation lies in the three core aspects. First, territories placed under the UNTC were not seen as sovereign independent states. Rather they were former colonies and mandate territories on a long road to eventual independence. Consequently, the doctrine of non-interference did not apply to them. The situation with Germany in 1945 was slightly different. While Germany was recognized as constituting a sovereign state, including a permanent population and defined territory, it lacked a further core criteria for statehood: a government. Following its defeat in the Second World War, there was little opposition to the Allied forces' temporary assumption of governmental powers. The situation was seen as constituting an aspect of post-war politics and the transition of Germany into a new democratic state. The third explanation for the lack of controversy regarding the prevention of state collapse through external interference lies in the nature of peacekeeping. As mentioned earlier, the core organizing principles include the aspect of consent from the government and all (warring) parties. As this had occurred in the instance of the UN peacekeeping operation in The Congo and UNOC was deployed at the request of the Congolese government, the issue of non-intervention was not relevant.

Overall, there was the growing recognition during the Cold War era that internal unrest and potential state failure was not only a local problem but rather an issue of international concern. This was magnified even more in the post-Cold War era where weak or lacking governmental structures have led to human catastrophes and the unintentional support of international threats such as transnational crime (drug trafficking, money laundering) and terrorism.

Staying Alive

> There is a beginning and an end to the state, as to everything else. States are born and die, and the determination of these two facts is precisely the proper function of international law. Whatever the claims and aspirations of existing states, it would be legally unsound and historically untrue to affirm their immortality. (Krystyna Marek, 1968: 5–6)

The post-Cold War era has seen the emergence of numerous so-called failed states, a phrase which encompasses varying degrees of the spectrum, ranging from weak through to failing, and collapsed. Weak states may be interpreted as experiencing distinct challenges to order and stability, such as economic decline or human rights abuses. Failing states experience more substantial challenges, often on a range of issues, usually including internal unrest and external intervention. Collapsed states tend to lack a functional government all together, as is the case with Somalia. Jean Germain Gros (1996) goes so far as to distinguish between five types of so-called failed states: the anarchic, the phantom, the anaemic, the captured and the aborted. An exact and internationally accepted definition of these classifications, however, does not yet exist. Instead they continue to merely evoke, in the words of Harvard University Professor of Public Policy, Robert I. Rotberg, "an amorphous sense of dysfunction" (2009: 91).

In order to determine state failure, it is assumed that a state should fulfill certain basic criteria and that deviation from this idealized form can help to determine when and to which extent a state has failed. The UN Charter suggests basic criteria on which nations are supposed to be based on, namely "respect for the principle of equal rights and self-determination of the people". The Charter also calls for the promotion of conditions of stability and well-being, indicating a preference for democratic forms of government.

While the UN Charter and international treaties such as the UDHR indicate a preference for democratic governance structures stating that "the will of the people shall be the basis of the authority of government", including 'periodic and genuine' elections, sovereign equality is bestowed even to those states which do not have these characteristics (UNGA 1991b). Nevertheless, failed states, in the eyes of the Fund for Peace (2006), diverge from these above mentioned basic criteria of an idealized state by not being able to deliver goods and services to their population, uphold infrastructure, maintain law and order, as well as control the state's territory and, to what German sociologist and political economist Max Weber, famously referred to, as the legitimate monopoly over the use of violence (1966: 27). According to Ira William Zartman, Professor of Conflict Resolution at Johns Hopkins University, a state which fails to meet these criteria loses its right to govern (1995: 5).

By failing to display either some or all of these "recognizable signs of sovereign statehood", states are considered to be in one of the stages of a failing state, ranging from weakness, as in Georgia, to total collapse, as in Somalia (Devetak 2001: 179). Collapsed states are the most extreme end of the scale, argues Rotberg, a "mere geographical expression, a black hole into which a failed polity has fallen" (2002b: 90).

The British Department for International Development (DID) draws up four categories of what it calls weak states: relatively good performers; states that are weak but willing; states that have the means but not the will; and those with neither the will nor the way to fulfill the basic functions of statehood (2005: 8). Military interventions, as will be examined, only appear to take place in the second (which includes states such as East Timor) and fourth category (states such as Haiti and Sudan).

David Carment, Professor of International Affairs at Ottowa's Carleton University, refers to this spectrum of state failure as "a non-linear process of relative decay", implying that rather than gradually processing from one stage to the next, conditions can change rapidly (2003: 409). Indeed, often a natural disaster, economic downturn or ethnic conflict, as has been the case in Kenya most recently, are enough to move already weak states into a downward spirale of failure.

The *Failed States Index* (2005) estimates that around two billion people, a third of the world's population, live in states which occupy varying positions in this failed state spectrum. As mentioned, the phrase failed state is used to denote varying degrees of failure, ranging from weakness to total collapse. Similarly, the phrase also tends to be used in cases of both the failure of the state and of the government. This will also be the case in this book in order to limit confusion and avoid unnecessary repetition. Whereas state and government failure often go hand in hand, failure can also be restricted to just one area. Zimbabwe, for example, represents a case of failed government due to its economic mismanagement and inability to feed its population. The Former Yugoslavia, on the other hand, can be classified as a failed state, in the very sense of the word, as its territory has disintegrated along ethnic lines and has been replaced by a number of new states.

As was outlined in the previous chapter on humanitarian intervention, sovereignty today is increasingly conditional and dependent on a state's performance in a range of areas. Yet, states continue to be the base building blocks of the international system. The Montevideo Convention (1933) declares states to be "a sole person in the eyes of international law". Consequently, the suggestion that a state may die or even be 'put down' rather than re-established or kept alive artificially through outside intervention, may shake the foundations of the international system. Indeed, Nii Lante Wallace-Bruce, Ghana-born lawyer and academic, believes that "international law would be spelling out its own doom if it were to readily issue death certificates for states" (1996: 477).

This is not to say, however, that such a decertification of states is unheard of. The US government currently has such a process of decertification of states if they are seen as being unable or unwilling to enforce both local and international laws. This process, however, is limited very much to counter-narcotics performance. It is also highly subjective and political, including states such as Libya and Cuba which rank relatively low in other failed states indexes. Nevertheless, America's Jeffrey Herbst points out that this could be a possible approach for the international community to take. On an international basis, however, there is no process to certify that "a state has died, if it ever lived, and that something else has taken its place" (1996: 124).

As a consequence, some states may not exhibit any of the criteria necessary for it to be a genuinely sovereign state but are nevertheless recognized as such. These states, amongst them Somalia, exist only, as argued by University of Cambridge's Professor of International Relations, Christopher Clapham, because "dominant states of the global order deemed that they should be permitted to do so" (1998: 144). In the case of Somalia, this strict adherence to traditional state boundaries has meant that Somaliland has not been recognized. Even though the area has more solid administrative structures, governance and infrastructure than the officially recognized state of Somalia, it has been refused recognition by states (Menkhaus 2006). Georg Sørensen claims that this is due to the fact that both the UN and major powers gave post-colonial and newly independent states a 'certified life insurance', guaranteeing them their right to sovereignty and independence (2007: 364).

What consequently appears even more disturbing to some observers, as indicated in the introductory quote by Geneva Professor of International Studies Marek, is the dominant unwillingness of the international community to admit the actual or potential mortality of states. Instead, in the eyes of these critics, economic aid and, in extreme circumstances, military intervention, are used as 'life-support systems', keeping failed states artificially alive.

This phenomenon of failed states is being increasingly recognized as a major problem for the international community. The *NSS* states that "America is now threatened less by conquering states than we are by failing ones" (2000: 1), a view confirmed by many others including Rice (2005) and former French President Jacques Chirac (Reuters 2004). Kofi Annan (2005c) stressed that "ignoring failed states creates problems that sometimes come back to bite us". The impact of failed states on both regional and international peace and security was also the motivating factor for the establishment of the State Failure Task Force by the US in 1994. The government commissioned and financed group, claiming nevertheless independence of their views, consists of academics and other experts. Its aim is to identify "measurable characteristics of countries around the world that affect the risk of serious political instability" (Goldstone, Gurr and Harff 2000: iii).

Since then, numerous other governments and organizations have established groups and written reports regarding state failure, attempting to enable better prediction of state decline and countries at risk. Too numerous to be named in their entirety, the groups and reports include the US' National Intelligence Council's *Instability Watch List*, the Commission on Weak States and National Security, the British DID's Report, the World Bank's *Low-Income Countries Under Stress Assessment*, as well as the Fund for Peace's *State Failure Index*. Depending on the source, numbers (and names) of failed states range from as low as 30 to over 60.

While many organizations and states alike may have individual lists of failed states, the countries on these and the criteria used to establish their degree of failure, tend to overlap. The State Failure Task Force (2000: v), for example, defines states' failure to include four events: revolutionary wars, ethnic wars, adverse regime changes, as well as genocides and politicizes. The Fund for Peace's *State Failure Index* uses twelve indicators to determine countries at risk of state failure.[2]

This is an appropriate variety of criteria, including social, political and economic measures, which help to demonstrate that state failure is a multi-faceted phenomenon.

The absence of civil war and a government with an iron grip on power alone, such as is the case in Zimbabwe, by no means guarantee a stable state. Consequently, states with weak or non-existent governments such as Somalia and states with a strong government in charge can equally be candidates for failure.

The underlying reason for state failure in the 21st century is largely a consequence of ethnic, religious, nationalistic and tribal fragmentation within the territory of a given state. In the contemporary international system, state failure occurs most often in Africa, the former Soviet Union and Near East (Goldstone, Gurr and Harff 2000). According to Canadian scholar Michael Ignatieff, this current wave of disintegration, represents the fifth wave since the end of the First World War and is characterized by an attempt to "correct failures of previous episodes of state formation" (2002: 116).[3]

Many states now categorized as being in one of the stages of state failure have owed their demise to the withdrawal of major funding by Western powers in general and the US and Soviet Union in particular since the end of decolonization and the Cold War. Sierra Leone, for example, whose government revenue stood at

---

2 These criteria include: demographic pressures, refugees and displaced persons, group grievance, human flight, uneven development, economic decline, delegitimization of state, public services, human rights, security apparatus, factionalized elites, external intervention.

3 The preceding four waves of state fragmentation are: 1919 – The dismantling of the European empires after Versailles; 1945 – The creation of the so-called people's democracies in Eastern Europe; 1947–1960 – The decolonization of Africa and Asia; 1989–1991 – The independence of former Soviet satellites.

$10 million in 1999, a mere 4 per cent of what it had been twenty years earlier, was faced with utter economic collapse (Krasner 2004: 92). Many states, particularly in Africa, were supported heavily both financially and militarily due to their strategic position. Once the ideological tensions of the Cold War era had ceased, aid became increasingly conditional on issues such as human rights, economic reforms and democratic developments (Adam 1995). States such as Sierra Leone and Somalia are prime examples of high aid dependency and the adverse result of its sudden withdrawal.

State failure is also often due to a struggle for power by a number of ideologically opposed groups within a state, as well as leaders abusing resources to advance their individual interest while letting the population suffer. The most common causes of state failure are seen as being 'regime change', as well as ethnic and revolutionary wars (Goldstone, Gurr and Harff 2000: 29). Ignatieff claims that many newly independent states, especially those arising from the break of former colonies and other artificially created states, "won the right of self-determination on the cruelest possible terms: they have been simply left to fend for themselves" (1993: 8). Left with inappropriate governmental and administrative structures, these states have often struggled for survival. This vast proliferation of nation states, having now almost quadrupled since the establishment of the UN in 1945, is a further reason for the increased number of failed states. It is usually, however, a combination of mismanagement in the social, economic and political arena which is necessary for a state to fail, or in the worst case scenario, to collapse.

Hans-Henrik Holm, Danish Professor of International Politics, argues that most states which fail are "perceived as geographically and culturally distant", meaning there is little direct interest to incur financial or (in the most extreme instances) military loses to stabilize such a state (2002: 459). Most states in dire straits are, says Eric Laroche, UN humanitarian co-coordinator for Somalia, merely a 'forgotten emergency' (Bloomfield 2007). Although it may be easier to stabilize states rather then allowing them to collapse totally, preventative measures are often not taken (Von Einsiedel 2005: 14).

Looking at the number of weak, failing and collapsed states, it becomes clear that the international community largely fails to take an interest in the situation. Although Blair warned that permitting the rise of failed states would result in the eventual necessity to deal with them, action against failed states is often not taken until the impact has been disastrous, requiring the most extreme form of outside interference: military intervention (British Broadcasting Corporation 2002a).

Such action is, however, not always necessary as Zartman points out in his observation that state collapse is a "long-term generative disease ... whose outcome is not inevitable [with] cure and remission [being] possible" (1995: 8). Indeed, the British DID in 2005 estimated that each £1 invested in conflict prevention would save the international community the equivalent of over £4. The World Bank, too, has published information, suggesting that the cost of failure to the respective state and the international community as a whole amounts to a staggering $82.4

billion (Patrick 2006: 44). So why does inaction rather than action appear to be the preferred response of the international community?

One of the core reasons is that the traditional way of dealing with failed states, that is, entering them into a trusteeship, no longer appears acceptable. While some observers advocate trusteeship, viewing it as a radical but necessary step, it remains largely rejected (Langford 1999: 59). Observers like Ruth Gordon believe that "the concept should remain buried ... because trusteeship is a form of colonialism" (1997: 420). The UN Charter in Article 77 and 78 limits trusteeship to former League mandates and those detached from enemy states as a result of the Second World War. It states explicitly that the "trusteeship system shall not apply to territories which have become Members of the United Nations". Therefore, an amendment of the Charter would be necessary to revive the UNTC which suspended its work in 1994 after the last of its 11 trust territories, Palau, gained independence (UNSC 1994b).

The concept of transitional UN administration, as recently in Kosovo, Cambodia, and East Timor, has been described by former US State Department's Director of Policy Planning Stephen D. Krasner as "the one recognized alternative to conventional sovereignty [and which] is explicitly not meant as a challenge to the basic norms of sovereignty" (2004: 92). UN transitional administrations oversee the given territory of the respective state, exercise legislative and executive authority and build capacities for eventual self-government (UNSC 1999e). Such administrations are authorized and established by the Security Council but consent by the host state is required (one of the previously mentioned three core principles of traditional peacekeeping). While less controversial than the issue of trusteeship, such operations remain rare. The reason for this is that state-building exercises of this kind are not only very time- and labor-intensive but also require large funds, often where there is no political or economic interest for potential donors. The aim of transnational administrations is the reconstruction of an entire state, rather than just a quick fix. The latter is an option usually pursued by many other military interventions of a non-UN nature which aim to halt immediate threats to regional or international security, rather than addressing underlying issues which have led to state failure.

Such instances of military intervention by regional organizations and, in particular, *ad hoc* coalitions and individual states in failed states, have been far more controversial than UN transitional administrations. Looking at the State Failure Task Force's Table and the Fund for Peace's Index one can see that military intervention in one form or another has taken place against states in which the consequence of their failure has no longer been limited to within their respective borders. It is precisely when problems have spread to neighboring states, most notably in form of fighting and refugees, that states rise in prominence. In some cases, the chaos and anarchy in failed states, such as Afghanistan, have also provided a basis for terrorist groups and have advanced to posing a global threat.

There are five core ways in which failed states pose an actual or potential threat to both regional and international security: transnational crime, terrorism, refugees, internal conflict and humanitarian crisis. All of these aspects, individually or combined, can effect international peace, security and stability. As the issues of intervention on the basis of terrorism, internal conflict and humanitarian reasons are discussed at length in other parts of this book, it is sufficient to merely have a brief look at the issue of transnational crime.

Criminal activity in form of drug and human trafficking, as well as money laundering occurs in many failed states. This is, however, neither always a concern for the international community nor a consistent reason to intervene militarily. While force was used in Afghanistan, the producer of nearly 90 per cent of the world's heroin, this was not done on the basis of its transnational criminal implications. Instead the reason, as is well known, lay with the government's harboring of the terrorist network *Al-Qaeda*. Burma, the world's second largest producer of opium, has been largely ignored by the international community (Bush 2005). While economic sanctions are in place, events and conditions in this small state appear of little interest or, at least, not of sufficient interest to warrant international intervention.

This is also an issue reflected in Australia's intervention in the Solomon Islands in 2003 which came only six months after foreign minister Alexander Downer described any such action as 'folly in the extreme', a view also reflected in the Australian *Foreign and Trade Policy White Paper*. The reason it took Australia five years to intervene in the 495,000-person small nation is simply due to the lack of interests at stake. Only John Howard's recent concerns over the Solomons possibly becoming a "haven for terrorists, drug runners and money launderers", have led to consideration by Australia to use its forces to re-establish order (O'Callaghan 2003: 1). In the 2003–04 federal budget Australia allocated $175.8 million in financial aid to the South Pacific, including $37.4 million to the Solomon Islands (Australian Government AusAid 2003a and 2003b). In light of this and the view that the region, Downer added, "will not change direction as long as largely unconditional aid flows make it unnecessary", there is a clear and officially stated interest of the Australian government to get 'value for money' (Wade 2003).

So even with regard to the different problems caused by state failure there is list of priorities with transnational crime (if it occurs in geographically remote states) not always being a crucial criteria for intervention, being it economic, political or military.

One of the major problems of failed states is that the five above mentioned issues are often not contained to the respective state itself but spread across borders. The conflict in Sudan/Darfur has spread to Chad and the Central African Republic in form of rebels and refugees. Similarly, more than fifteen years of fighting and instability in Somalia has led refugees looking for shelter in neighboring Eritrea, Ethiopia and Kenya. Afghanistan and its instability, outside the capital of Kabul (and particularly in the Northwest of the country), reflected most notably in the production of opium. Drug trafficking and associated crime and disease have effected its neighboring countries such as Pakistan, Turkmenistan, Uzbekistan,

Tajikistan and even Iran (Fund for Peace 2007: 62). In some instances of state failure, such as Haiti, there has been little impact on external states.

America's Rosa Ehrenreich Brooks goes further to suggest that failed states also contribute to regional and indeed international instability by posing a fundamental legal challenge. They do so by being unable to sign or adhere to treaties on a wide-range of issues ranging from trade to human rights, the environment and political issues (2005: 1159–1160).

In the light of failed states gradually posing a greater threat to world peace and international stability, the UN has acknowledged that, in principle, failed states have to receive help to re-establish order (Annan 2001b). As with other instances examined in this book, the problem lies, however, in the fact that certain individual states have increasingly taken matters into their own hands, tending to take action against failed states on a multilateral although non-UN authorized basis.

Non-UN intervention against failed states tends to take place either in form of action through regional organizations or *ad hoc* coalitions. While there are some instances where the consequences of state failure have an international impact, they are usually limited to the state's respective region. Neighboring powers are therefore more likely to take action as can be seen with ECOWAS' intervention in Liberia (1990), the OAU's in Burundi (1994) and, in recent times, Sudan. In the absence of regional organizations (or their unwillingness to act) *ad hoc* coalitions have been established, such as the 2,000-strong intervention force from Australia, New Zealand, Fiji, Tonga, Samoa and Papua New Guinea to the Solomon Islands in 2003. Similarly, France sponsored the Inter-African Mission, consisting of Burkina Faso, Chad, Gabon, Mali, Senegal and Togo, in 1997 to oversee the implementation of the *Bangui Agreements* in the Central African Republic.

Action by individual states, on the other hand, only tends to occur in support of an already established UN peacekeeping force which may be unable to undertake certain action or may be temporarily absent or postponed. This was the case with the US-led Unified Task Force in Somalia (1992) and French Operation Turquoise in Rwanda (1994). The cost and time of rescuing failed states means that a job-sharing option is usually viewed as preferable.

Action against failed states, outside of the realm of UN-authorization, has been justified in two major ways. First, there is the view that as long as states are members of the UN, they enjoy all the rights given to them in the Charter, most notably the right to sovereign-equality and non-intervention. By embracing the view of Aja Agwu (2000), a research fellow at the Nigerian Institute of International Affairs, that "the government is a crucial factor in the existence of statehood, if it fails, the state has invariably failed", it is argued that these rights no longer apply. Lacking a single legitimate authority to govern the entire territory and having no longer a monopoly over the use of force, a failed state is seen as not being a political entity anymore and, consequently, in one sense no longer a state.

The second option of trying to legitimize military intervention and the use of force against a failed state is following an invitation of the state, as was the case, for example, with the Solomon Islands. Australia deliberately excluded the UN from the intervention, claiming that the organization was perceived to have shown very little interest in the issue and predicted that a UN resolution was bound to fail (Kerin 2003). By merely notifying the UN and using the Solomons government's request for assistance as the legal basis for the intervention, the validity of Australia's action has been questioned by a number of Pacific states, especially as the authority of Allan Kemaketa's government is doubtful due to accusations of corruption.

Often such intervention by invitation is dubious as the government or authority issuing the invitation does not necessarily represent a given state, as is the case in civil wars, or it does so under pressure, as was the case with Czechoslovakia and the intervention by Warsaw Pact forces in 1968 and by the US in Grenada in 1983. In these cases a failed states' sovereignty is, at least formally, still respected and merely a temporary ceding of it is requested in order to allow intervention.

In cases in which states do not have a real strategic interest and prefer non-interference, similarly questionable arguments are made which are essentially a reversal of the above, showing how it is possible to twist, turn and interpret existing laws and rules to suit one's best interest as long as there is no definite law to control the concept of failed states.

Zimbabwe is just one of many examples in which failed states have become "victims of the [lack of] political will when vital interests ... are not at stake" (Editorial 2003). Showing many characteristics of a failed state, such as lacking the ability to provide the population with sufficient food, and having a collapsed economy with 300 per cent inflation and 70 per cent unemployment, the international community's interest in intervention has been small. Powell (2003) has argued instead that change has to come from within, endorsing the concepts of sovereignty, non-interference and self-determination.

The legitimacy of military intervention in failed states outside the area of UN-authorized action is questionable and, at the time of writing, not covered by international law which still primarily serves to control conflicts between sovereign states and lacks coverage of intra-state conflicts such as in the former Yugoslavia or Liberia. The UN has in the past referred to Article 39, which gives the Security Council the authority to determine what constitutes a breach of the peace, to legitimize action in failed states. Most notable is Resolution 841, issued in 1993, with regard to the serious political instability in Haiti, which expressed the belief that a government incompatible with democratic values constituted such a breach of peace.

The ICISS promotes intervention in failed states if conditions in there have led to large scale loss of life, actual or apprehended. The report claims that failed states "are quite likely to generate situations which the international community simply cannot ignore" but says realistically at the same time that "there must be real doubts about the willingness of governments to provide those kinds of resources, other than on a very infrequent and *ad hoc* basis" (2001: 43). The report *We the Peoples* also stresses the need to "strengthen the capacity of those states to govern, not undermine them further" (Annan 200b: 13).

Military intervention, however, does not necessarily have a stabilizing effect as long term failure in Somalia has exemplified. Interventions in other states such as Afghanistan, the Democratic Republic of the Congo and Haiti have shown that both UN and non-UN interventions may have been what the *Failed State Index 2005* refers to as peacekeeping (or interventions) on the cheap. These states continue to rank in the top twenty of failed states with intervention not having changed much, often due to a lack of strength of the troops deployed or lack of will of states to commit long term. Indeed, Gros argues that military intervention merely provides temporary relief from what he refers to as "the harmful effects of state decay" (1996: 466).

America's Cato Institute scholars Logan and Preble predict that achieving what they term 'ambitious goals' often requires far greater number of troops than currently deployed. This includes up to 1.2 million troops in the Democratic Republic of the Congo and 800,000 troops in the Sudan (2006: 19). The recently established UN Peacebuilding Commission (2007) tries to counter this ineffectiveness by focusing on post-conflict recovery of states, aiming to organize resources and advice on reconstruction and institution-building. The concept of post-conflict peace-building was already put forward by Bourtros Ghali in his 1992 report *An Agenda for Peace* but its implementation has largely been stifled by lack of political will.

The principle of non-intervention is amongst the larger obstacle facing the universal acceptance or even just tolerance of the use of force against failed states. This is particularly true for the Group of 77 at the UN which is opposed to any compromise on this principle. The Group is already strongly opposed to humanitarian intervention, as discussed in Chapter 6, and views intervention in instances of state failure in similar terms. Some observers claim that due to their often small economies and populations, many of the member states, view their sovereignty as one of their last bastions.

Calls for greater interventionism, which some see as a new kind of imperialism, in order to deal with the issue of failed states has consequently sparked widespread outrage. Too familiar are the memories of foreign domination of former colonial states and those used as satellite states by the US and the former Soviet Union during the Cold War. Being forced to give up their hard-fought sovereignty in exchange for re-establishment of powerful order by individual or groups of states smacks of neo-colonialism. In the post-Cold War era, non-military means such as trusteeship are equally as controversial as the use of force when it comes to interference in and attempted rescue or reestablishment of failed states.

Summary

Failed states, argues Brooks, are "not the exception in many parts of the world, they are the norm" (2005: 1164). This is unlikely to improve in the future with predictions suggesting a UN membership increase to 400 states (Ryan and Lumley

2000: 233). Many of these would be unlikely to survive without external support of one kind or another. If such predictions about UN membership are correct, the issue of failed states will remain a crucial issue for many decades to come. Yet such states have often been likened to "the uninvited guest at a party: the overwhelming impulse [being] to ignore it, to treat it as insignificant, and to hope it will go away" (Woodward 1999: 55).

Somalia, which has been a failed states for the past fifteen years and is viewed as "the world's foremost graveyard of externally sponsored state-building initiatives", is the prime example that failed states will not simply disappear if ignored (Menkhaus 2006: 74). Gilbert Ware in 1965 predicted that should Somalia in any way contribute to regional or international instability, it would challenge the UN's credibility regarding its attempt to transform 'underdeveloped' into states (1965: 184). Many observers see this confirmed today.

Indeed, in the face of long-term failed states such as Somalia, Haiti and Afghanistan, there is a real necessity to establish legal criteria to determine and define when a state has lost its status of statehood. Similar to the inconsistent lists and classifications regarding terrorist organizations (Chapter 9) and rogue states (Chapter 10), there is no exact consensus or internationally accepted catalogue of failed states.

Considering the impact state failure can have on both regional and international security and stability, there is a real need to establish procedures of what to do when "the state itself, as a legitimate functioning order, is gone" (Zartman 1995: 1). Many of the core failed states of the decade such as Liberia, Sierra Leone, Sudan, Angola, Burundi and the Democratic Republic of the Congo continue to survive, at least as a shell (Rotberg 2002b: 90). However, critics question if it is wise to retain a state's sovereignty without questioning its viability. This is an issue which goes to the core of international law and its placement, says Cambridge academic Thomas D. Grant of "a premium on rules giving the aim to stabilize the identity and territory of states" (2004: 58).

Attempting to reestablish structure and order in a state through outside intervention is not always successful. America's David Rieff goes so far as to argue that, as can be seen in current state practice, "*ad hoc* responses to state failure and humanitarian catastrophe are rarely, if ever, successful" (1999: 1). What is needed is long-term dedication and effort by states rather than just the above mentioned quick fix. For any substantial commitment to state rebuilding to take place, substantial interests have to be, however, at stake. As this is not always the case, intervening states have little interest in establishing principles guiding the use of force against failed states. The existences of such criteria might oblige states to take action when no vital interests are at stake, rather than leaving them with the liberty to act *ad hoc* and as circumstances demand.

Part III

For the Good of the State: The Use of Force for Individual and Collective Self-defense

The preceding chapters in Part II of this book have examined the three categories of military intervention for humanitarian reasons. Part III will examine three categories of the use of force based on individual and collective self-defense, including an often expanded notion thereof.

Military intervention for individual and collective self-defense can be further sub-categorized into three types: first, the pre-emptive use of force against imminent or future threats; second, the use of force to counter terrorism in instances in which it is both harbored and sponsored by states; third, the use of force against so-called rogue states which are seen to violate what are perceived as standards of acceptable international behavior.

The focus of the use of force in these instances is the protection of the intervening state's security, either on an individual or a collective basis. It appears that in the contemporary era, individual self-defense and unilateral action in general are viewed with suspicion. Consequently, military intervention is often justified not so much on the protection of an individual state but rather presented as being undertaken for the securing of international peace and security in general. Similar to the use of force for humanitarian reasons, military intervention tends to be taken as collective in nature.

This part examines these three types of intervention based on individual and collective self-defense, assessing how state practice in these instances challenges the established rules for the international use of force.

Chapter 8
Bolt from the Blue: The Pre-emptive Use of Force

The concept of pre-emptive self-defense is the only category of the use of force analyzed in this book which is used to justify its practice on an anticipatory and not present event. The origins of the idea of pre-emptive action can be found in a very simple idea: to protect itself most effectively, a state may claim not only that it has to defend itself against an actual attack but also that it has to take preventive measures against those potentially using force against it in the future. Reisman defines pre-emptive self-defense as "a claim of authority to use, unilaterally and without international authorization, high levels of violence in order to arrest a development that is not yet operational and hence is not yet directly threatening, but which, if permitted to mature, could be neutralized only at a high, possibly unacceptable, cost" (2003: 143).

The view that one has not only to consider temporary but also future threats and do the utmost to nip them in the bud is not, as Robert Byrd suggests, a "radical new twist on the traditional idea on self-defense" (Chace 2003: 3) but something already suggested by the likes of Grotius and Machiavelli. It is questionable, however, how far to apply historic notions of anticipatory self-defense with new processes and technologies.

As the use of force by states remained largely unrestricted until the 19th century there was no real reason to justify the resort to war, neither in anticipatory nor reactive terms. This changed with the League of Nations Covenant (1919) and Kellogg-Briand Pact (1928) which attempted to oblige signatories not to use force against each other. Consequently, the use of force in general and pre-emptive action in particular had to be justified and was done so, primarily from the 1920s and especially from 1945, on the grounds of self-defense.

Viewed strictly from the aspect of security, pre-emptive action against possible threats is surely the most efficient way to deal with the issue of securing a state's safety, especially in view of the alleged absence of effective collective security mechanisms. This is an argument famously made by Donald Rumsfeld (2002) who quipped that "the only defense ... is to take war to the enemy [and] the best defense is a good offence".

This concept of pre-emption is criticized because current international law is based on the differentiation between potential and reality, between intention and action. In a law-based society people are prosecuted for what they have done, not for what they could have done or for things one considers them capable of doing. Even criminal intent is an actual not future thing. Hence, the justification of the use of force based on asserted intentions and not actions of the enemy has always been disputed. In the contemporary international system, the division is between those, like former French Foreign Minister Dominique de Villepin, who support the continued contraction of the grounds for the use of force and think that "war is always the sanction of failure" (Sutherland 2003: 15) and those who see it as necessary, in the US government's words, to "forestall or prevent ... hostile acts [by] act[ing] pre-emptively" (Government of the USA 2002: 15).

When states do use anticipatory self-defense they stress the immediacy rather than remoteness of a threat. In this context a difference has been made between pre-emptive action (that is against immediate threats) and preventive action (against more distant threats). It is often impossible to make a precise differentiation between prevention, preemption and anticipatory action because, as France's François Heisbourg observes, "the public discussion of the new national security strategy uses them, more or less, interchangeably" (2003: 77).

This section examines state practice with regard to the issue of anticipatory self-defense. It shows that even though the concept is highly controversial and much discussed, it is rarely applied or openly embraced by states. Such public support for anticipatory self-defense appears to be a gamble which few players in the international system are willing to take. The stakes are too high, with governments fearing that an embrace of anticipatory self-defense could one day lead to hostile states using this very justification against them.

Overwhelming Fear

> A Nation has the right to resist an injurious attempt, and to make use of force and every honest means against the power that is actually engaged in opposition to it, and even to anticipate its machinations. (Emerich de Vattel 1805: 216)

De Vattel's statement, similar to Grotius' view that "it is permissible to kill him who is making ready to kill" (1925: 176), is often taken out of context or at face value. Vattel, for example, makes his support for anticipatory defense conditional on the need for clear evidence of impending danger or threat, suggesting that if action was taken "upon vague and doubtful suspicions" a state would run the risk of becoming an 'unjust aggressor' (1805: 216).

The right of anticipatory self-defense, particularly in the inter-war years, was often linked and compared to the notion of self-defense in criminal law. The argument here was that a person was not obliged to wait until they had been physically attacked to defend themselves but rather that one was, according to British lawyer J.M. Spaight, "justified in anticipating it, provided [one acts] under a reasonable apprehension of serious violence" (1932: 23).

This notion of imminency is reflected best in the classic case of pre-emption, or anticipatory self-defense as it is often referred to, the *Caroline* incident of 1837. According to Byers (2002c) this was a fundamental step in international law which "drew a legal line of differentiation between war and self-defense". The *Caroline*, a ship owned by US nationals, was allegedly providing assistance to Canadian rebels fighting the UK. The ship was set on fire in US waters by British troops and several Americans killed in, what the British authorities claimed to be, an act of self-defense (Arend and Beck 1993: 18). As mentioned in Chapter 1 of this book, US Secretary of State Webster, challenged this perception, stating that in order for the use of force to be considered self-defense "it will be for the government to show a necessity of self-defense, instant, overwhelming, leaving no choice of means, and no moment for deliberation" (1857: 1137–1138).

Essentially, however, international law was still in its infancy and restrictions on a state's sovereignty and use of force remained minimal. Phillimore clearly accepted the concept in 1854 as a measure against armed bands in another state. International law writers of the time such as Westlake (1904) and Woolsey (1872: 191) reflected this view stating that "a wronged nation, or one fearing sudden wrong, may be the first to attack, and that is perhaps its best defense". Self-defense in all its forms, that is following an armed attack or prior to an attack having occurred, appeared acceptable.

The need to justify the resort to force with adherence to the so-called *Caroline* criteria of necessity, proportionality and imminency regarding self-defense was complicated by the establishment of the League of Nations (1919) and the Kellogg-Briand Pact (1928). Both limited states' sovereign right to wage war, strengthening instead the doctrine against aggression. Despite the restrictions imposed, there was one prominent exception to the renunciation of war: the permission of the use of force for self-defense purposes. Some observers, amongst them Borchard, saw this as a weak spot, particularly in light of the fact that no specific definition of self-defense existed. Borchard (1928) believed that "it would be difficult to conceive of any wars ... that cannot be accommodated under these exceptions".

Indeed, the new developments in international law did not entirely prevent states from using force and representing it as the need for self-defense, particularly by anticipatory action, on an individual basis. Amongst the most prominent instances of the time was the German invasion of Denmark and Norway (1940) and the Soviet Union (1941), justified controversially as anticipatory self-defense (International Military Tribunal for Germany 1946b). The *Nürnberg* trials later used the *Caroline* criteria to judge the German claim, stating that "all the alleged intelligence reports contain no information which comes within miles of justifying an anticipatory invasion based on the doctrines of self-preservation" (International Military Tribunal for Germany 1946a). While the principle of anticipatory self-defense as such was not rejected, the assessment of Germany's claim and facts on hand suggested Germany did not meet the *Caroline* criteria. It also highlighted the concepts inherent potential for abuse. The British attack on the French ships in 1940 in Mers-el-Kébir (Algeria) to stop them being captured by the Germans was not justified as pre-emptive defense but the outraged reaction suggested further little support for such operations.

The major problem with regard to pre-emptive action prior to 1945, was that there was neither a definition of self-defense nor aggression. Without clarification of these issues it was difficult to determine what exactly constituted an actual act of aggression, let alone an impending or immediate threat justifying anticipatory self-defense.

Anticipating Evil

> To permit anticipation may virtually destroy the rule against the use of force, leaving it to every nation to claim anticipation and unleash the fury. (Louis Henkin 1963a: 151)

Although the UN Charter prohibits the threat and use of force, it stresses that states have maintained their "inherent right of individual or collective self-defense if an armed attack occurs against a Member of the United Nations". Article 51, however, makes this exception conditional on the matter being immediately bought to the Security Council's attention and self-defense measures being limited until the Council takes action.

During the Cold War this narrow interpretation of self-defense was the favored stance of governments. The notion of pre-emptive self-defense was almost rejected, so it appears, due to two core issues. First, there was the use of the concept by Germany during the Second World War, condemnation thereof at the *Nürnberg* trials and the realization of the concept's potential for abuse. Second, there was the bipolar balance of power in the international system and the fact that an embrace of the concept of anticipatory self-defense by either one of the superpowers had the potential to turn a cold war into an active one. Yet, the emergence of nuclear weapons in 1945, suggesting a state would suffer unacceptable losses by either a first attack or even a retaliation, raised the issue of pre-emption to a new height.

In 1953, US President Dwight D. Eisenhower, however, emphatically rejected the suggestion the US might use force pre-emptively against the Soviet Union. Eisenhower (1954) associated this type of action with Nazi-Germany, adding that he did not believe that it was an appropriate policy to take and that he "wouldn't even listen to anyone seriously that came in and talked about such a thing". State practice during the Cold War era actually starkly opposed anticipatory self-defense with only three instances been seen as constituting such action and only one being justified as such by the executing state.

US President John F. Kennedy, similar to Eisenhower, avoided justifying the US action during the 1962 Cuban Missile Crisis, limited to a naval blockade and quarantine, as self-defense, pre-emptive or otherwise. Yet, it is often mentioned in the literature as a potential instance of anticipatory self-defense (Mallison 1983: 177). Kennedy himself described the stationing of offensive weapons by the Soviet Union in Cuba as threat to the US and the international community as a whole, stressing that "we no longer live in a world where only the actual firing of weapons represents a sufficient challenge to a nation's security to constitute maximum peril" (1962: 716).

Ultimately, however, the discovery of missile bases in Cuba was only declared a threat to the US under Article 52, instead of Article 51, of the UN Charter which states that "the existence of regional arrangements or agencies for dealing with such matters relating to the maintenance of international peace and security". The US decided to work through the OAS in enforcing the naval blockade, reserving the right of the OAS to use force if deemed necessary (Cheyes 1962). Justifying the use of force as pre-emptive action in light of a potential future threat to the US through the possible launch of missiles from the Cuban basis was not viewed as a serious option for Kennedy, as it would have been likely to provoke a military counter reaction by the Soviet Union.

On the one hand, as we have seen, the massive destruction threatened by nuclear weapons raised the idea of the necessity of an anticipatory strike despite of massive destruction by retaliation. On the other hand, the deterrence dynamic drove both superpowers explicitly to reject such a doctrine for fear of provoking such an anticipatory strike. Indeed, the later International Law Association's *Report of the Committee on the Use of Force in Relations among States* rightly argued that "the existence of nuclear missiles has made it even more important to maintain a legal barrier against pre-emptive strikes and anticipatory defense" (1985–86: 203).

The second instance which is often seen as constituting an incident of anticipatory self-defense is the so-called 'Six Day War' between Israel on one side and Egypt, Syria and Jordan on the other (Greig 1970: 681). Following the gathering of Egyptian forces in the border region of Israel, the latter decided to bomb Egyptian airfields along with their grounded aircraft. Originally, this action was justified as repelling a previous armed attack by the Egyptians with Israel merely acting in self-defense. The representative of the United Arab Republic, as which Egypt was known as between 1958 and 1971, rejected this suggestion claiming that it was Israel which had acted with "treacherous premeditated aggression". This meant Egypt, Syria and Jordan now had the right to defend themselves in accordance with Article 51. In the same Security Council meeting Indar Jit Rikhye, Commander of the UN Emergency Force in Sinai, supported the United Arab Republic's statement with his report that it had been Israeli aircrafts which had originally violated Arab airspace (UNSC 1967a).[1]

Israel, however, maintained that "in accordance with its right under Article 51 of the Charter, the victim defended itself, alone and successfully" (UNSC 1967c).

Due to the conflicting versions of the states involved, the Security Council at the time did not condemn any state as an aggressor and merely called for hostilities to cease (UNSC 1967b). So, while Israel may have acted in anticipation of an

---

1 Egypt and Syria unified as the United Arab Republic in 1958. Only three years later Syria seceded from the union. Egypt continued to be referred to as the UAR until 1971.

aggressive act by its Arab neighbors, it did not justify its actions on pre-emptive but rather defensive grounds following an actual armed attack. Although the exact reasoning for this cannot be ascertained with certainty, it can be assumed that the choice of the Israeli justification was based on the likelihood than any endorsement of pre-emption could trigger such action by its enemies.

The third instance was when Israel attacked the Osirak nuclear reactor in Iraq (1981). This was the only case which used the justification of pre-emptive self-defense. Israel claimed that intelligence received indicated that nuclear bombs were to be developed at the facility and used against Israel. Sigvard Eklund, Director General of the International Atomic Energy Agency, however, stated that "the Agency has inspected the Iraqi reactors and has not found evidence of any activity not in accordance with the Non-Proliferation Treaty" (UNSC 1981b). The Security Council consequently condemned the Israeli use of force as a violation of the Charter, clearly rejecting the concept of anticipatory self-defense and likening it to an act of aggression rather than defense (UNSC 1981c). The President of the Council, speaking as the Representative of Mexico, added to this by stating that the concept of anticipatory self-defense had been abolished by the UN Charter (UNSC 1981b).

Israel, however, maintained its stand, interestingly basing the justification of pre-emptive action on the literature in the field and statements by legal scholars, rather than actual state practice. During the presentation of the case to the Security Council, the Israeli representative referred to the likes of Stephen Schwebel, Myres McDougal, as well as Humphrey Waldock, British lawyer and judge on the ICJ (1973–1981). Waldock, was cited saying "it would be a travesty of the purposes of the Charter to compel a defending state to allow its assailant to deliver the first and perhaps fatal blow" (UNSC 1981b). This was, however, said in the light of the Suez Crisis of 1956. This instance, while officially being justified by Britain under the notion of self-defense, extended to the protection of nationals abroad rather than pre-emptive action, as has been examined in previous chapters.

Israel's reliance on the assertion of a right of anticipatory self-defense in the debate in the literature rather than actual state practice gives credit to Henkin's pithy observation that "pre-emptive war as 'anticipatory self-defense' has been hypothesized by many professors but asserted by few governments" (1971: 545). As reflected in the three instances often claimed to be examples of pre-emptive action, the notion has largely been rejected by both states and the UN alike. The ICJ, too, has been reluctant to comment on the legality of anticipatory self-defense. In the Nicaragua case the ICJ acknowledged that Article 51 was a reference to customary international law but that the phrase 'inherent right' with regard to the use of self-defense "applies in the event of an armed attack" (1986: 94). It therefore makes the legality of self-defense conditional on an armed attack having occurred rather than just merely being anticipated.

So while states, international organizations and judicial organs seem to reject the legality of anticipatory self-defense, legal scholars have been divided into two camps with one side favoring a restrictive interpretation of Article 51 and the other a permissive reading. Oppenheim (1969), Jessup (1959), Kelsen (1964), Wright (1963) and Brownlie (1963) believed that self-defense can be invoked "only if, and that implies after, an armed attack occurs" (Kelsen 1964; 914), limiting the use of force to an actual as opposed to anticipated attack.

Bowett, Reisman, McDougal and Waldock, on the other hand, stress that there continues to exist a right of anticipatory self-defense based on Article 51, believing that "the rejection of an anticipatory right is, in this day and age, totally unrealistic and inconsistent with general state practice" (Bowett 1972: 4). The argument here is also that the inclusion of the phrase 'inherent right' in Article 51 refers to customary international law and the survival of the right to pre-emptive action. While the Tokyo International Military Tribunal (1948) embraced the view that "the right of self-defense involves the right of the state threatened with impending attack to judge for itself in the first instance whether it is justified in resorting to force", the observation by Bowett and others is not entirely correct as both the above examined case studies and ICJ judgment show.

Proponents of this permissive view claimed that the developments in military technology justify a right of anticipatory self-defense. While representatives of the restrictive reading of Article 51 rejected such a claim, they in some instances acknowledged the fact that such use of force is likely to occur notwithstanding, if that state fears it is faced with annihilation. Henkin argued that while "anticipation in that case may have to be practiced; it need not be preached" adding that "the Charter need not make a principle of it; the law need not authorize or encourage it" (1963b: 532–33).

This rejection of the incorporation of the issue into international law is reflective of the attitude of many opponents of pre-emptive action who appear most concerned about such behavior creating a new rule, rather than an exception to the rule. Franck, for example, believed that a rule which "permits a pre-emptive strike whenever a nation regards itself as 'intolerably threatened' is so subjective as to be no rule at all" (1970: 821).

Indeed, it is the difficulty, if not impossibility of determining with exact certainty "if the danger to a state is demonstrated to be real and imminent, not deemed to be hypothetical and potential" which is of major concern (Joyner 1984: 134). This makes states, international organizations and judicial organs alike reluctant to embrace the concept as a justification to resort to force internationally.

Israel's attack on the Iraqi nuclear reactor made clear that the concept of pre-emptive force could be applied not only to imminent threats but also to three other instances as described by Zedalis. These include the invocation of anticipatory self-defense against prospective but distant threats, against situations which potentially threatened the balance of power, particularly in the military sphere, as well as threats presented, said Zedalis, by another state's defensive military systems (1987: 173).

By expanding the concept of pre-emptive self-defense, the concept is likely to develop a life and momentum of its own. France's Austrian-born Stanley Hoffman raised the dangers of this in the immediate aftermath of the 1981 event by stating that "anticipatory self-defense ... can be even more of a source of self-serving claims than self-defense against an armed attack in progress" (1981: 153). The use of the concept of self-defense following an armed attack was in many instances during the Cold War dubious enough. A widespread embrace of the concept of anticipatory self-defense, or its inclusion in international law, would have stretched the realms of false implementation even further.

The concept received a new lease of life in American foreign policy during the mid-1980s, particularly following the 1986 bombing of a German discothèque frequented by American military personnel. The US government was quick to describe the act as one state-sponsored terrorism. Missile strikes against Libya followed, justified on the basis of self-defense but mixed with a claim of pre-emptive measures. Although the US use of force was condemned by the General Assembly, Reagan (1986) told Americans that "this pre-emptive action against terrorist installations will not only diminish Colonel Qadhafi's capacity to export terror, it will provide him with incentives and reasons to alter his criminal behavior". He added that Libya had a well established pattern of terrorist activities and was therefore likely to act again.

This stance followed from the so-called Shultz Doctrine launched three months prior to the bombing. Concerned with the growing number of terrorist acts in the international system, the US Secretary of State George P. Shultz announced that "a nation attacked by terrorists is permitted to use force to prevent or pre-empt future attacks, to seize terrorists, or to rescue its citizens, when no other means is available" (Gwertzman 1986: A1). This was a policy which was continued in the Department of Defense's *Report to the Congress on Security Arrangements in the Persian Gulf* (1986). In a speech almost twenty years later, Shultz (2002) re-stated his stance but acknowledged that his views were strongly criticized and dismissed by others. This embrace of anticipatory self-defense with regard to countering terrorism is also one of the hallmarks of the post-Cold War era as the next section will show.

Deception and Defiance

> We must adapt the concept of imminent threat to the capabilities and objectives of today's adversaries. (…) The greater the threat, the greater is the risk of inaction – and the more compelling the case for taking anticipatory action to defend ourselves, even if uncertainty remains as to the time and place of the enemy's attack. To forestall or prevent such hostile acts by our adversaries, the United States will, if necessary, act pre-emptively. (National Security Strategy, 2002: 15)

The literature on anticipatory self-defense in the post-Cold War era shows how clearly the concept is linked with the issues of proliferation of WMD and particularly terrorism. Prior to the September 11 terrorist attacks there was little debate about the issue of using force pre-emptively. As will be shown in this section, it has only arisen previously with regard to the 1998 military strikes by the US against targets in Afghanistan and Sudan.

While the issue of pre-emption has been debated more widely than in previous decades, this writer questions Swedish judge Ingrid Detter's observation that "anticipatory force has in recent years become more acceptable in practice" (2000: 87). To the contrary, even states embracing the doctrine in theory, if not in practice, such as the US do not see it to be, as Kissinger (2002) observed, in their "national interest to establish pre-emption as a universal principle available to every nation".

The *NSS 2002*, is the *mot d'jour* when it comes to discussing the doctrine of pre-emption in the post-Cold War era. Rather than being a bolt out of the blue, this doctrine has been of increasing importance since the Reagan administration, as outlined in the previous section.

The end of the Cold War demonstrated that traditional deterrence, most notably in form of mutually assured destruction, may have been effective in containing rival states but did not work well against terrorism (including state-sponsored and harbored), as well as rogue states (Bush 2002b). Incidents such as the World Trade Center Bombing (1993), the Tokyo Subway Station Attack (1995), the September 11 attacks (2001), the Bali bombings (2002 and 2005) and the Madrid Train bombings (2004) demonstrated that the subjects of pre-emptive action were primarily terrorist groups. Shultz (2002), recently reiterated his 1987 position on terrorism cited above, stating that America ought to reserve the right to act against such networks in anticipatory self-defense and arguing that it was "not just hot pursuit [but] hot preemption" which was necessary.

The Iraq war, as will be examined later, was reflective of considerations to also use pre-emption against rogue states, most notably the 'Axis of Evil' (Iraq, Iran and North Korea) as defined by Bush (2002a). Many observers, amongst them Dinstein, however, question the argument that the changing nature of threats and weapons on which anticipatory self-defense justifies a renunciation of the limitations set in place by the Charter. Dinstein believes that "the inference that Article 51 is only operative under conditions of conventional warfare cannot be substantiated" (2001: 168–69). Yet, this is one of the core arguments embraced by *NSS 2002* in its section *Prevent Our Enemies from Threatening Us, Our Allies, and Our Friends with Weapons of Mass Destruction*. Before discussing this with regard to pre-emptive action and its relation to the Iraq War, a previous instance claimed to incorporate aspects of anticipatory self-defense will be examined.

In 1998 the US embassies in both Nairobi (Kenya) and Daressalam (Tanzania) were bombed, an act linked to Osama Bin Laden's terrorist network *Al-Qaeda*. In response, the US undertook missile strikes against Sudan and Afghanistan claiming they were "to prevent and deter additional attacks by a clearly identified imminent and concrete terrorist threat" (Clinton 1998: 1464). The aim of the military action was not only to destroy terrorist bases in Afghanistan and a pharmaceutical plant in Khartoum, suspected of producing VX nerve gas, but also to discourage the two states' support for and harboring of terrorists (Barletta 1998). Bill Clinton (1998) said that "these strikes were a necessary and proportionate response to the imminent threat of further terrorist attacks". The US told the Security Council it was acting in self-defense, adding that the type of force used, a missile attack, complied with the rules of necessity and proportionality (Richardson 1998). These criteria were first outlined in the *Caroline* case of 1837.

This stand on terrorism and the possible need to counter it through pre-emption was also reflected in the US *National Security Strategy for a New Century* which stated that "the United States must act to deter or prevent such attacks" (1998: 7). It is, however, the *NSS 2002* which is probably the most important official US security document of the post-Cold War era as it openly and extensively embraces the concept of anticipatory self-defense.

The core of the *NSS* is its claim that "nations need not suffer an attack before they can lawfully take action to defend themselves against forces that present an imminent danger of attack" (2002: 15). The entire report takes this interpretation beyond traditional notions of anticipatory self-defense, implying that proof of the immediacy of a threat, one of the three *Caroline* criteria, was not necessary to justify the use of force. US Secretary for Defense Paul Wolfowitz (2002) supported the gist of *NSS*, stating that "the notion that we can wait to prepare assumes that we know when the threat is imminent". Chris Bordelon claims that removing the requirement to prove the existence of an imminent threat leaves "no principled means by which the law can distinguish force used in self-defense from aggression" (2005: 144).

It is particularly this latter issue and the US' indication that it is displaying little willingness to act through the UN with regard to the preventive use of force which, says Falk, "threatens to a degree the sovereign rights of every state" (2002: 333). Indeed, the *NSS 2002* does not discuss collective security or the UN as an option for dealing with imminent threats. Instead, the White House has argued "the United States will not hesitate to act alone, if necessary to exercise our right of self-defense by acting pre-emptively against such terrorists, to prevent them from doing harm against our people and our country" (2002: 6). While going strongly on the rhetoric of pre-emption, the US exercised a certain degree of caution by adding that it "will not use force in all cases to pre-empt emerging threats, nor should nations use pre-emption as a pretext for aggression" (NSS 2002: 15). This clearly shows that even states embracing the concept, most notably Israel and the US, do not want it to become a generally accepted norm. Rather, there is a preference for it remaining an exception to the rule of a limited interpretation of the notion of self-defense: an exception only they will be justified in taking.

This is particularly evident with regard to the final legal justification given by the US and its allies for the use of force against Iraq in 2003. Prior to presenting the legal justifications to the Security Council, the US was adamant in portraying the threat Iraq posed to both the US and the international system as a whole. The two major claims were outlined in the US government's report *A Decade of Deception and Defiance*. The findings centered around Iraq's alleged connection to and support of terrorism and alleged possession of WMD (with intent of proliferating them to terrorist groups).

The first claim brought forward by the US was an alleged connection between Iraq and terrorist groups, in particular *Al-Qaeda* (UNSC 2003b). If concrete evidence could have been established proving that Iraq had sent *Al-Qaeda* members to the US to undertake attacks, self-defense would have been possible. As examined in Chapter 3, the Nicaragua judgment's definition of armed attack included "the sending by or on behalf of a State of armed bands, groups, irregulars or mercenaries, which carry out acts of armed force against another State of such gravity as to amount to (*inter alia*) an actual armed attack conducted by regular forces, 'or its substantial involvement therein'" (1986: 93). No such connection was then established with regard to Iraq. Germany's Michael Bothe said that the likelihood of an impending and direct armed attack on American soil by Iraqi forces, the scenario which would have made a right to anticipatory self-defense less disputable, was also far fetched (2003: 240).

The issue of self-defense and terrorism will be more closely analyzed in the next chapter. So, it is sufficient here to raise the difficulty of applying traditional criteria of anticipatory self-defense, that is imminency, necessity and proportionality to the threat of terrorism. Bordelon argues that proportionality, for example, "becomes virtually impossible to measure as to pre-emptive force, because no attack has occurred, is occurring, or is planned as to which the use of force must be proportionate" (2005: 142). Indeed, Haass highlights the difficulty of obtaining accurate intelligence needed to assess the extent of the potential threat, as well as anticipating the reaction of the state on whose territory the attack takes place (1999: 52).

The second US claim was Iraq's possession of WMD, an assertion which was not supported by the UN-sponsored investigations and reports into Iraq's weapons capabilities. The infamous 2002 British dossier, *Iraq's Weapons of Mass Destruction: The Assessment of the British Government,* even went so far as to suggest that Iraq was capable of deploying chemical and biological weapons within 45 minutes. Later searches also failed to find any WMD, thereby undermining the reliability and accuracy on which the US had earlier relied. The fact that states do not have "the benefit of *post factum* wisdom" is a further deterrent for the embrace of pre-emptive action (Dinstein 2001: 173).

Critics such as Pakistani academic and lawyer Niaz A. Shah have stated in the light of questionable intelligence that "the mere possession of these dangerous weapons should not in itself be a ground for reaching a conclusion that the attack is imminent" (2007: 103). Otherwise most large powers, including the five permanent members of the Security Council, would have to consider themselves potential subjects of pre-emptive action.

For many, including Shah, the Iraq invasion laid the foundations for the doctrine of pre-emption. Ironically, in the end, the use of force may have been motivated by the doctrine of anticipatory self-defense but not legally justified as such. The rules were thereby not challenged. The arguments of WMDs and support for terrorism originally brought forward by the US for the invasion of Iraq and supported by its two key allies, Australia and the UK, received little support within both the Security Council and General Assembly, with only eight countries sharing the view that the use of force in its proposed form was justified (UNSC 2003c). Largely, the justification was, in the words of Kenya's Jackson Nyamuya Maogoto, a "confusing jumble of arguments that were long on rhetoric and short on substance" (2004: 12).

In the end the US itself did not rely on the doctrine of pre-emption to justify the use of force, a concept increasingly seen as a 'political liability' in light of having difficulties in getting other states to accept the necessity of action taken under its auspices (Verdirame 2004:100). The intervention was officially justified on the grounds of implementing UN resolutions. The US claimed to the Security Council "these operations are necessary in view of Iraq's continued breaches of its disarmament obligations under relevant Security Council resolutions" (Negroponte 2003). As will be discussed in Chapter 8, the coalition focused particularly on Security Council Resolutions 678 (1990), 687 (1991) and 1441 (2002) in their legal case for the war.

The US core coalition partners, Australia and the UK, have embraced the concept of pre-emption to varying degrees. Australia under the administration of John Howard almost unequivocally mirrored the US stance on the subject. Howard (2002) firmly embraced "the principle that a country which believes it is likely to be attacked is entitled to take pre-emptive action is a self-evidently defensible and valid principle". It was a view also reiterated in *Australia's National Security Strategy: A Defence Update 2003*.

The UK has been less enthusiastic about embracing the concept even though Blair has since stated that "the one thing we have learned post-11 September is that to take action in respect of a threat that is coming may be more sensible than to wait for the threat to materialize and then to take action" (Committee on Foreign Affairs 2002). Deciding to side with its coalition partner, the British government publicly supported the doctrine (although less expressly so than the US or Australia). What is telling, however, are the contents of a leaked secret memorandum by Peter Goldsmith, British Attorney General to Blair. Having been asked to present a legal opinion on the impending invasion of Iraq and possible legal justifications, Goldsmith (2002) stated with regard to pre-emptive self-defense that "if this means more than a right to respond proportionately to an imminent attack (and I understand that the doctrine is intended to carry that connotation) this is not a doctrine which, in my opinion, exists or is recognized in international law". So even Britain's chief law officer rejected the doctrine.

So while both Australia and the UK gave vocal support to the doctrine of pre-emption, Britain did not view it as a viable legal justification. Like the US, both countries wrote to the Security Council outlining that, with regard to the use of force against Iraq, "the objective of the action is to secure compliance by Iraq with its disarmament obligations as laid down by the council" (Dauth 2003, Greenstock

2003). The use of force in order to implement Security Council resolutions was viewed as the more secure and credible legal basis.

As mentioned in the introduction to this book, in order for state practice to fundamentally challenge or even change established international law, its application has to be widespread, consistent and made with a belief it is legal. It is therefore crucial to assess the stand states other than the US and its two core coalition partners the UK and Australia have taken on the issue of pre-emptive self-defense. Their failure to invoke it as a legal justification over Iraq is telling.

States which, to varying degrees support the doctrine of pre-emption include the UK, Israel, Russia, Australia, Italy, and to lesser extent Japan and Taiwan. The strongest opponents of the doctrine, at least when it came to vocalizing dissent, were France, Germany, and (following its withdrawal from Iraq) Spain supported by the UN and other regional organizations such as the EU. The Islamic Conference of Foreign Ministers (2004) also condemned "the principle of pre-emptive military strikes against any country under any pretext whatsoever".

Israel, as the preceding section has shown, is a longstanding supporter of anticipatory self-defense, arguing that it "reserves its fundamental right of self-defense, both preventive and reactive, including where necessary the use of force, in respect of threats emanating from the Gaza Strip" (Knesset: 2004). India, in light of its arch enemy Pakistan's recently acquired nuclear capabilities, has also jumped onto the pre-emption bandwagon stating that "pre-emption or prevention is inherent in deterrence [and] where there is deterrence there is pre-emption" (Krishnaswami 2002).

Taiwan embraced the doctrine to a lesser degree with specific regard to China, suggesting it could be implemented should there be any sign that China was planning to invade (Wu 2003). China, in return, has been a traditional opponent of US pre-emption, referring to it as the logic of the powerful and claiming it as relying mainly "on subjective judgments, and is very easily abused and used as a pretext for war" (Reisman and Armstrong 2006: 544). With regard to Taiwan, however, it has made somewhat of an exception, passing the Anti-Secession Law of 2005 which left open the possibility of pre-emptive action should Taiwan overstretch its secessionist aims. Japan stated that it would use force against the DRPK if there was evidence that it was going to launch a missile attack (British Broadcasting Corporation 2003).

Interestingly enough, supporters of the doctrine can also be found within the camp of states usually opposed to the US. Russia began favoring pre-emptive action following the Beslan school siege of 2004 in which Chechyen separatists took more than a thousand hostages. In the aftermath of the event, Colonel Yuri Baluyevsky said that Russia would "[carry] out preventive strikes against terrorist bases, [and] will take all measures to liquidate terrorist bases in any region of the world" (Walsh 2004). President Vladimir Putin attempted to stress Russia willingness to adhere to international law, including reporting to the Security Council should such action be resorted to (Agence France-Presse 2004).

The DRPK felt it had a particularly strong case when it argued that it may be the next target on the list of US military action after Iraq. It therefore warned that "pre-emptive strikes are not the exclusive right of the US" (Kui 2003). The inability to limit the permissive nature of the doctrine to a particular state is especially a problem. Although Rice (2002b) warned that the US Doctrine "does not give a green light – to the United States or any other nation – to act first without exhausting other means", the embrace of the concept by one state makes it inevitable that other states will follow. The doctrine allows for the tables to be turned and for states advocating pre-emption to be confronted with their own demons, that is Pakistan taking pre-emptive action against India or Syria against Israel. Some observers like Germany's Dietrich Murswiek consequently warn that should the doctrine be generalized "the stability of the state system would suffer a severe blow, and the general prohibition of the use of force would practically make way for a general entitlement to pre-emptive use of force" (2003: 12).

This has been an issue which has been of particular concern to regional and international organizations such as the EU and the UN. They, more than individual states, are aware that extending the right to use force, regardless of whether it is in the area of humanitarian intervention, failed states or pre-emptive action, applies to all states, rather than just a select few.

The EU *Security Strategy 2003*, often viewed as a counterpart to the US *NSS*, does not mention or discuss the issue of pre-emption, let alone debate its legality. The European Parliament (2002) had previously already "asserted that pre-emptive strikes were not the most effective approach in the fight against terrorism". Annan has also been strongly critical of the doctrine of pre-emption stating that that non-UN authorized action undertaken unilaterally or through *ad hoc* coalitions was a "logic [which] represents a fundamental challenge to the principles on which, however imperfectly, world peace and stability have rested for the last 58 years". Annan (2003a) adds that a widespread adoption of anticipatory self-defense "could set precedents that resulted in a proliferation of the unilateral and lawless use of force, with or without justification".

Two core reports, *The Responsibility to Protect* and *A More Secure World*, also reject the concept of pre-emption. The former report has been interpreted by some as being supportive of the notion of anticipatory self-defense. This perception is based on the report's endorsement of the concept by stating that "military action can be legitimate as an anticipatory measure in response to clear evidence of likely large scale killing" (2001: 33). The ICISS, however, clearly limits this exception to the prevention of genocides, rather than writing out a *carte blanche* regarding the usage of pre-emptive action.

The second report, similarly, acknowledges that there may be situations which warrant preventive military action but fails to clarify under which circumstances this may occur. It says that any preventive use of force should be authorized by the Security Council stating that considering the numerous and diverse threats "the risk to the global order and the norm of non-intervention on which it continues to be based is simply too great for the legality of unilateral pre-emptive action, as distinct from collectively endorsed action, to be accepted. Allowing one to so act is to allow all" (Secretary-General's High-Level Panel 2004: 63). This section of the report concludes with the strong statement of support for Article 51 as it stands and does not favor its rewriting or reinterpretation.

The belief that the UN can determine a situation and threat and act, if necessary, pre-emptively is a view also reflected in the Secretary-General's report *In Larger Freedom*. Here Annan stated the belief that "where threats are not imminent but latent, the Charter gives full authority to the Security Council to use military force, including preventively, to preserve international peace and security" (2005a: 33). This is supported by Franck (2001) who argued that if credible evidence of an impending and destructive attack by a state or terrorist organization exists, the use of force by regional or international organizations will be tolerated.

The ICJ has refrained from making a specific ruling on the legality of pre-emptive self-defense. While the ICJ has avoided the issue of preemption, it has dealt with the issue of self-defense, most notably in four cases: *Nicaragua* (1986), *Oil Platforms* (2003), *Armed Activities in the Congo* (2005) and the advisory opinion regarding the *Palestinian Wall* (2004). The latter focuses on the issue of self-defense with regard to armed attacks and non-state actors which will therefore be dealt with in the next chapter.

As mentioned in Chapter 3 of this book, the Nicaragua judgment ruled that "the exercise of this right [of self-defense] is subject to the state concerned having been the victim of an armed attack", thereby interpreting Article 51 in a narrow way (1986: 93). Its subsequent judgments and advisory opinions have followed this restrictive pattern. The *Oil Platforms Case* (Iran vs. US) added further pressure on the state exercising self-defense by stating that "the burden of proof of the fact showing the existence of an armed attack rests on the state justifying its own use of force as self-defense" (2003: 161).

In its most recent judgment the ICJ was asked to rule on the issue of whether Uganda's claim of self-defense against the Democratic Republic of the Congo had been lawful. The ICJ argued that neither the rebel movements nor their activities could be directly linked to the Congolese government, reminding Uganda that "Article 51 of the Charter may justify a use of force in self-defense only within the strict confines there laid down [and] it does not allow the use of force to protect perceived security interests beyond these parameters" (2005: 54). For action taken outside these boundaries, recourse to the Security Council was available.

The Democratic Republic of Congo vs. Uganda case has been criticized for not attempting to define what actually constitutes an imminent threat, a determination crucial for examining the validity of any instances of anticipatory self-defense. Shah argues that the ICJ should have ruled on the matter of what constitutes and imminent threat as "its guidance would have been informative and timely given the fact that self-defense is used as a main argument in the current war on terror" (2007: 100). Director of International Security Studies at Harvard, Litwak (2003), similarly, argues that once 'imminent threat' was defined it would pave the way for addressing such threats through effective collective action, most notably the

UN, rather than individual states or group of states. Indeed, while the Nicaragua case attempted to define the concept of armed attack, subsequent judgments have been reluctant to examine other aspects regarding the legality and wider interpretation of self-defense. This, however, has not necessarily been viewed as negative and some observers have been less concerned about the reluctance of the ICJ to speak out on these issues, claiming that this silence was a stance in itself, confirming international law on self-defense as it currently stands (Ochoa-Ruiz and Salamanca-Aguado 2005: 524).

Sean D. Murphy, Professor of Law at George Washington University, argues that Iraq, more than the 1998 US missile strikes, showed the two core problems inherent in the doctrine of pre-emptive self-defense. The first was, as examined in this section, the inability to gain widespread support for the doctrine. In the end, the US itself did not think it a strong enough argument for use as a legal justification. Secondly, there was the risk of relying on faulty or doubtful intelligence (Murphy 2005: 747).

It was particularly the failure of the 'Coalition of the Willing' to achieve a stable peace in Iraq, following the war, that made former coalition members such as Spain, question the doctrine of pre-emption (Associated Press 2004). Even former staunch supporters of the Iraq War and its justification on pre-emptive self-defense, such as American neo-conservative Richard Perle, spoke out against the doctrine. Perle, six months after the end of official combat hostilities in Iraq, stated that he disagreed with the view held by some high-ranking American officials that "if ... international law doesn't permit unilateral pre-emptive action without the authority of the UN, then the defect is in international law" (Burkeman and Borger 2003). Instead, the defect was increasingly seen to lie with certain states' wish to stretch, said Bellamy, "the term [self-defense] so far that self-defense and aggression become indistinguishable" (2003: 499).

In light of the lack of endorsement it received both during the Iraq War and in its aftermath, Reisman and Armstrong observe that the US in its *NSS 2006* has "already softened its claim to a right of pre-emption in practice, if not in policy – particularly with regard to Iran and North Korea" (2006: 532). It appears that similar to the US approach during the 1990s surgical strikes are the favored option regarding action against terrorism compared to full-scale military invasion. While the *NSS 2006* reaffirms the US willingness to act pre-emptively, it states that this will not always be the case and that non-military means are the preferred option of dealing with such threats. The *NSS*, possibly in light of potential abuse of the doctrine by other states, reaffirms similarly to previous governmental documents that "no country should ever use pre-emption as a pretext for aggression" (2006: 18).

America's Michael Lacey argues that anticipatory self-defense becomes "nothing more than a slippery slope of naked aggression ... without the *sine qua non* of necessity, proportionality and immediacy" (2000: 294). It is, however, the difficulty of meeting these criteria with regard to reliable intelligence on terrorist networks and so-called rogue states which makes the endorsement of the concept difficult.

Summary

The observation that the American strategy of pre-emption will work neither in practice nor in principle due to its fundamental challenge to the rules governing the use of force was very much linked to the failure of the coalition in Iraq. Critics like China's Gu Guoliang argue that in order for such a doctrine to be effective, the intelligence regarding "the rival nation's capabilities and intent" has to be watertight and pre-emption will have to be used as the actual legal argument (2003: 136). While states continue to shy away from this, as the US did most recently with regard to Iraq, the doctrine of pre-emption is unlikely to establish itself as an accepted fixture in the realm of legal justification for the use of force. The concern that anticipatory self-defense, says Britain's James Pattison, "is far more likely to undermine the prohibition on the use of force and lead to abusive intervention" then to strengthen the international order is one of key oppositions the doctrine faces (2007: 313).

The Iraq war was driven apparently by motives of anticipatory self-defense but justified on the grounds of implementing UN resolutions. The opposition to it exemplifies this widespread rejection of both pre-emption and the unilateral use of force. The relative non-use of it as a legal justification by the intervening powers attests to the fact there is not yet as full-blooded challenge to international law on it. The dominant view seems to remain the fact that in the absence of such an armed attack having occurred, it is only the UN which can take action. The lack of success in getting other states to embrace the doctrine is also based, as this chapter has shown, on the arbitrariness of linking terrorist activities with so-called rogue states such as Iraq, the DPRK and Iran.

For many, says Bellamy, the risk that "pre-emptive self-defense blurs into aggression" is too great a risk a take (2004: 145). Indeed, one of the main hurdles of anticipatory action is that by extending the right of self-defense states, said Dutch-born former Clinton advisor Ivo H. Daalder, "[erase] any viable distinction between the offensive and defensive purposes of military action [a distinction which] the legitimacy of using force depends crucially on" (2003: 177). Distinguishing between aggression and defense was, as Chapter 1 of this book has shown, one of the first core accomplishments of the international law in the area of the use of force. Pre-emption also leaves "the assessment of danger entirely in the hands of a self-interested actor, the state claiming the right to pursue a preventive war", making it a doubtful legal justification (Brunnée and Toope 2004: 410).

Arend, Professor of Government and foreign service at Georgetown University, argues against this suggesting that should the UN Charter be interpreted as "no longer accurately [reflecting] existing international law, then the Bush Doctrine of pre-emption may, in fact, be lawful – even if it is politically unwise" (2003a: 89). Based on the above examination and stands taken by the ICJ and international organizations this, however, appears unlikely. Yet, the inability to reject totally pre-emption is evident in some UN reports, as well as statements by Annan, as discussed above. John C. Yoo, legal adviser to the US Department of State, said that "while nations must not use pre-emption as a pre-text for aggression, to be for or against pre-emption in the abstract is a mistake" (2004: 730). The UN, for example, has acknowledged this inability to reject preventive action all-out by embracing pre-emption in order to halt impending genocide. There is a strong interest, however, in limiting it to action by the UN. A widespread acceptance of the concept, let alone explicit permission thereof in the UN Charter is, however, highly unlikely. Rather the prohibition of the international use of force remains, said Kenya-born James Gathii, "of extremely high normativity and, as such state practice inconsistent with it confirms the norm against non-use of force in the absence of widespread and representative repudiation" (2005: 70).

To many states, self-defense is the last true bastion of the permissible use of force in the international system. Not only is there a wish to defend it but also to adapt it to the circumstances if need be. However, such expansions of the concept have always been viewed with great suspicion because the potential detrimental effects appear to outweigh the benefits. Pre-emptive action since 1919 has been mainly seen, as American lawyer and diplomat Covey Oliver stated, "a temptation to the impatient, the angry and the nervous, always to be handled with the greatest care" (1963: 375).

Chapter 9
The Remains of the Reign: The Use of Force to Counter Terrorism

The rules governing the use of force in the international system were primarily designed with respect to armed conflict between states. As will be shown, some consideration was given at an early stage to the subject of attacks on a state by 'armed bands' or what we could call today in a formal sense – non-state actors – or, more politically, 'terrorists'. Yet, this was never a major focus. Increasingly since 1945 and, especially, since 2001, rules governing a state's rights in countering terrorism have moved to a central place in international affairs (Pilgrim 1990: 173–74).

The term 'terrorism' is among the most debated in international relations. There is as yet no agreed international legal definition of the term and there are significant differences between the respective legal definitions of states: it took around sixty years for states to agree on an international definition of 'aggression' following the trigger event of the First World War. There have been calls for multilateral action against what is now called terrorism since at least 1881. An international legal definition was drafted in 1935 but has never been widely approved. There are even wider differences in the definitions of scholars.

Bellamy (2005b: 284) notes the existence of four core elements in most definitions of terrorism, expressed succinctly as: politically motivated violence conducted by non-state actors against non-combatants with the aim of creating fear beyond the actual victims itself and society in general. Australia's Gregory Pemberton agrees, adding that, increasingly since the First World War, states often used or threatened (i.e. nuclear deterrence) force in much the same way, that is targeting civilians to create terror, as terrorists. The fact of being a non-state actor is therefore the key source of distinction (Pemberton forthcoming). Although civilians have increasingly become terrorist targets, the original targets, state leaders and their officials, remain under attack.

The absence of an international definition and diversity in states' definitions allows considerable debate as to which groups are or are not 'terrorist'. Not even states allied in the 'war on terror' have the same lists of terrorist groups. Pemberton distinguishes between three types of organizations to which the term 'terrorist' is frequently if inconsistently applied: nationalist groups pressing for change of state borders usually by creating a new state (e.g. ETA, Tamil Tigers) or by breaking from an original state and joining another (e.g. IRA); revolutionary groups aiming to achieve great internal change (not just a *coup d'état*) in the government but not necessarily altering the borders of a state (e.g. Nepal); and, finally, transnational groups operating in and against a variety of states aiming to change their policies or perhaps governments (e.g. anarchist, some Marxists and now Islamic groups like *Al-Qaeda*). Of course some groups combine these elements. For example, post-war anti-colonial movements such as in Vietnam sought to establish a new state combined with revolutionary (republican socialist) internal change.

Pemberton further identifies three inevitably overlapping yet distinct time periods during which the different types of terrorist groups have been most prominent: first, the period from the 19th century up to 1920 mainly witnessed anti-monarchical, republican groups, which sometimes combined national separation, with a small amount of transnational anarchism; second, the period 1920 to 1975 which witnessed republican national-separatist, often socialist and many anti-colonialist groups; third, the period from the 1970s to today which has seen more transnational terrorism, briefly Marxist at first and increasingly Islamic, which in some instances is also national-separatist in nature (Pemberton forthcoming). A number of groups from the first and second periods have continued in the third era.

Some 'terrorist' groups, especially those seeking only change either within a state or to its borders, are of limited concern to most unaffected states unless their activities spread further into the territory or citizenry of those states or into international matters like air and maritime navigation. This partly explains the continuing limits on multilateral counter terrorist action including a definition of the term.

Compared to statistics on international armed conflict, as well as other humanitarian catastrophes like famine and starvation terrorism, University of Sydney's Ben Saul claims, "commands disproportionate attention relative to the harm it causes" at least in terms of immediate destruction (2006: 134). That might be true. The important issue under study here is states' reactions, exaggerated or not, to terrorism, especially some attempts to expand the doctrine of self-defense under Article 51 to counter non-state armed attacks thereby challenging the long-standing rules over states' use of force.

The European Disease

> It is the duty of every state neither to encourage nor tolerate on its territory any terrorist activity with a political purpose. (Council of the League of Nations 1935: 554)

The term 'terrorism' was originally used with reference to state not, unlike today, non-state behavior. During the French Revolution *Jacobin* leader Maximilian Robespierre and *Girondist* Georges Danton used the term '*terreur*' (1793–94) to describe the republican government's campaign in which perceived enemies of the government, on the left and right, were executed on a large scale, resulting in a general atmosphere of fear. Robespierre later explained: 'Virtue without terror is powerless.' Hence the Jacobins embraced the word *terreur*: their Thermidorean opponents attacked them in 1794 with the pejorative terms '*terrorisme*' and '*terroriste*' accusing them of establishing a '*règne*' or '*système*' of '*terreur*' (Pemberton forthcoming). The terms reached English in 1794, a year prior to the date mistakenly claimed by the Oxford English Dictionary, and German by 1796.

The English usage of the term quickly changed to refer to actions of individuals or those associated with nationalist or revolutionary organizations seeking a change from monarchical to republican government (as in Russia and Prussia), independence of their region (as in Ireland), or the more undefined goals of anarchism or revolutionary Marxism. These actions manifested themselves primarily in the assassination of leading public figures. The actors were often referred to as terrorists or anarchists (Schroeder 1919). From 1883 the term 'dynamiter' was also often used, referring to the methods used by these early 'terrorists' (Pemberton forthcoming).

The origins of the types of political violence called terrorism lie in the popular political forces released and expressed by the French and associated republican revolutions. Carl von Clausewitz was the first observer to theorize the new military phenomenon of 'peoples' war' which then became harnessed to radical politics. Theorists of Marxist and/or anarchist revolutionary violence, departing from the peaceful anarchism of one main mentor, France's Pierre-Joseph Proudhon, began to proliferate in Europe around the middle of the 19th century, just before and especially after the unsuccessful 1848 revolutions. In 1842 Saxony's Edgar Bauer published *Bruno Bauer and his Enemies;* Karl Marx's and Friederich Engel's *Communist Manifesto* appeared during the revolutions and, German Karl Heinzen's article *Der Mord* (1849) soon after. Those inspired by such works looked either to sudden mass revolutionary actions or single acts of terror.

International law writers began from this date to debate the matter with a noticeable difference between Europeans and the English-speakers. The former asserted a strong duty of states not to tolerate not just armed violations by private persons, foreign or otherwise, on their territory against another state but also lesser activities such as agitation. The latter only saw the duty applying to armed actions by private persons in another state but still certainly took a robust view on the injured state's rights in such matters. Phillimore, referring to Vattel's earlier work and the 1837 *Caroline* case in support, said an invaded state should first remonstrate but, if the host state, "whether from favour to the rebels, or feebleness of the executive", did not redress the 'evil', then the injured state "is warranted by international law in crossing the frontier, and in taking the necessary means for her safety, whether these be the capture or dispersion of the rebels, or the destruction of their stronghold" (1854: 189).

Five years later, in the light of the attempted assassination of Napoleon III, Liberal Home Secretary, Sir George Cornewall Lewis wrote that a state "is bound to prevent political refugees and other aliens from using its territory as a place for the preparation of measures hostile to another State, and that permission to foreigners to use its territory for such purpose is not only a breach of amity, but even of neutrality" (1859: 70). He also spoke of a state's obligation to prevent its territory from being used "as an arsenal in which the means of attack against a foreign government may be collected and prepared for use" (1859: 70) but he did not address whether this gave a state a right to intervene. Cornewall saw the matter as essentially criminal and argued only for extension of extradition treaties.

As these 'private persons' were non-state actors, the issue of international use of force by a state against another state arose only when another state was involved as host, wittingly or otherwise, to or in support of terrorists. Indeed, as most of these incidents took place internally within a state, they remained merely an internal criminal matter. Of course, the possibility and reality of movement by such actors before or after the act, raised the issue of them operating outside the jurisdiction of the state in question. This did raise international issues, as that state would have to rely on extradition treaties to return the accused to the jurisdiction of their home state, if such a treaty existed between the two states. For the extradition regime is essentially bilateral, relying on individual treaties between states. Moreover, most extradition treaties excluded political offences from extraditable crimes due to a strong European tradition of sanctuary, originally religious for Protestants and eventually asylum on secular political grounds.

The attempted assassination of Napoleon III led to the Belgian *clause d'attentat* which sought to exclude, from political crimes in Belgian extradition treaties, "an attack upon the person of the head of a foreign government or of the members of his family, when this attack takes the form of either murder, assassination, or poisoning" (Dugard 1974: 68). As a consequence, the extradition of assassins was possible in more cases.

Revolutionary thought continued to grow in Europe especially with the foundation of the International Workingmen's Association (IWA) in 1864 in Geneva. Russia's Sergei Nechayev issuing of the *Revolutionary's Catechism* (1869) and Mikahail Bakunin's 1870 call for violent revolutionary struggle in opposition to Marx's support for peaceful social change at the 1872 IWA conference at The Hague, lead to an anarchist conference in Switzerland the same year. Irish nationalist violence also became prominent in the UK.

Assassinations of public figures continued, including US President James Garfield and particularly the Russian Tzar Alexander II in 1881, which led to a call by the Russian government for combined action against regicide or, as the *New York Times* put it, "the suppression of terrorism". The German government not only discussed new measures to protect the public against explosives but also sought agreement with other European states to restrict the right of asylum in order to prevent its abuse 'by foreign revolutionaries'. This second proposal for multilateral counter terrorist action was described as "common means for combating the evil" (Suppression of Terrorism 1881).

No concrete steps were taken and assassination of state leaders seemed to be the order of the day in the late 19th century. The publication of Russian Peter Kropotkin's *Revolutionary Government* in 1892 presaged a new wave of terrorist incidents. There were a series of anarchist attacks in France. Attacks by the Irish Republican Fenian brotherhood continued including an attempt on the Queen in

1887. An anarchist bomb exploded at the Greenwich observatory, London, in 1894 the same year French President Sadi Carnot was assassinated by an Italian anarchist for executions of other anarchists. Four years later in 1898 another Italian anarchist assassinated Empress Elisabeth of Bavaria of Austria-Hungary. That year European states finally acted and held the International Anti-Anarchist Conference "to forge", says Jensen, "weapons that might control and suppress what was then perceived as society's fiercest and most intractable enemy, anarchist terrorism" (Jensen 1981: 323). France, Germany and Belgium had already implemented national anti-anarchist laws but some states also felt the need to address the issue on a transnational level.

One of the major outcomes of the conference was the recognition that information on perpetrators and suspects would have to be shared between the police forces of different countries. Assassination of further public figures, most notably US President William McKinley in 1901, further strengthened the conference's intentions. They were affirmed in the Secret Protocol for the International War on Anarchism or St. Petersburg (1904) which called for greater cooperation between the law enforcement agencies. This led, after the interruption in international cooperation wrought by the First World War, to the establishment of the International Criminal Police Organization in 1923 (Bach Jensen 1981: 334).

Long before this, terrorist violence continued with such frequency that London-based writer Joseph Conrad published the fact-inspired novel *The Secret Agent* in 1907. A year later France's Georges Sorel argued for terrorism in *Reflections on Violence*. The next year terrorism opened a new frontier when Japanese Prime Minister Ito Hirobumi was assassinated by a Korean nationalist. This 'European disease' was spreading across the world. In 1914, terrorist violence crossed another threshold with states going to world war over it.

As stated earlier, terrorist violence had been seen essentially as an internal matter of domestic criminal law rather than an international issue involving the use of force by one state against another. This changed with the assassination of Austrian Archduke Franz Ferdinand by an ethnic-Bosnian Austro-Hungarian subject and member of the *Black Hand*, a Serbian nationalist movement. Vienna, represented by Minister for Foreign Affairs Leopold Berchtold (1914), correctly held Serbia responsible for "acts of terrorism, [and] in a number of attempts at assassination, and in murders" because the "movement ... came into being under the very eyes of the Serbian Government [and] subsequently found expression outside of the territory of the Kingdom". Perhaps this was the first condemnation of an act of state-sponsored terrorism. Serbia's rejection of Austria's demand that it investigate the matter on Serbian territory led to war.

The focus on German 'war guilt' after the war meant no effort was put into examining how this new problem could be handled. The main concern of states and the League of Nations on limiting recourse to war meant that states were unlikely to develop a doctrine of armed intervention in the case of state-sponsored terrorism nor, initially, to cooperative peaceful measures for all states to prevent such acts re-occurring. Meanwhile, terrorist incidents returned at the war's end with political violence in defeated Germany and Hungary and bombings in New York in 1919–20. More restrictive gun laws followed in parts of Europe but not yet counter terrorist laws.

The matter was not entirely ignored by the international community. When the legal secretariat of the League called in 1926 for all member states to consider legal issues suitable for greater international codification Romania, whose new civil code already contained counter terrorist measures, nominated terrorism. This initiative, instigated by Pella, was ignored although the newly re-formed International Association of Penal Law (formerly *Union Internationale de Droit Pénal)* discussed the matter in a series of its annual conferences from 1931 driven mainly by Pella and Lemkin. The League made some progress towards codifying laws against piracy which included a political component.

The assassination of Yugoslavian King Alexander I and French President Louis Barthou in Marseilles in October 1934 by a member of the Internal Macedonian Revolutionary Organization, seeking independence from Yugoslavia, revived the shadow of Sarajevo. Yugoslavia, ironically, like Austria in 1914 accused a state, in this case Hungary, of complicity, stating to the League "the assassination was organised and executed with the participation of those terrorist elements which had taken refuge in Hungary and which have continued to enjoy the same connivance in that country as previously" (Kuhn 1935: 90). Hungary denied the allegations, stating it had only granted asylum to refugees, accidentally issued some passports and did not have any role in the assassination. Unlike the catastrophic events of 1914, this did not come down to an armed state versus state confrontation. The League's Council steered the parties into an international discussion and law making process which led in 1935 to the drafting of the first international law against terrorism which was presented to states in 1937.

Article 1 of the Convention for the Prevention and Punishment of Terrorism defined terrorism as "criminal acts directed against a state and intended or calculated to create a state of terror in the mind of particular persons, or a group of persons or the general public". Like previous usage, the convention largely limited acts of terrorism to those causing death or grievous bodily harm to heads of states, members of their families and other public figures. Destruction or damage to public property, endangerment of the lives of members of the public, as well as "the manufacture, obtaining, possession, or supplying of arms, ammunition, explosives or harmful substances" with the aim of committing an act of terrorism were also deemed criminal offences under Article 2 (League of Nations 1938: 23).

In the end, however, many states were reluctant to allow the convention to compromise their sovereignty. Numerous countries, amongst them the US and UK, continued to believe that terrorism could be dealt with under domestic legislation or was irrelevant to their societies, thereby rejecting the need for the establishment of international rules. Consequently, the convention was merely signed by 24 states and ratified only by British-India, which had long faced armed resistance by locals to British occupation before Gandhi's non-violence took root. A peaceful cooperative pathway to countering terrorism was thereby stalled.

The discussions deliberately did not address the crucial and politically sensitive issue of state responsibility, focusing instead on getting states to agree to international law defining acts of terrorism and providing for extradition of perpetrators to a proposed international criminal court. This was to avoid heightening tensions between Yugoslavia, Austria-Hungary and their respective supporters. By so criminalizing such acts, the League hoped to avoid another and future 'Sarajevos', thereby preventing such wars. Kuhn, a contemporary writer, said the discussions showed "the extent to which a government is responsible for preventing or repressing subversive or revolutionary activity by persons or groups within its territory directed against the peace and order of a foreign state, is not well settled in international law" (1935: 89). Article 1 of the convention did stress the duty of states to refrain from encouraging terrorist activities and to prevent terrorist acts.

This development stalled with the Second World War. During this time period the term 'terrorism' was used mainly by Germany with reference to the acts of the underground resistance to German occupation, particularly in France (Malinowski 1944). Obviously, there was no prospect of international agreement to see or deal with this as a common threat during the war. Meanwhile, the Marxist concept of armed popular struggle was moving to the mass populations of the colonized, rural sphere with huge implications for international order.

A Cheap Means

> The main ingredient that singles out this new era is that state-sponsored terrorism, where governments support acts of violence designed to terrorize peoples and destabilize governments of other nations, has become commonplace in many parts of the world (Yonah Alexander 1987: 144).

The Cold War era was immediately preceded by the foundation of a dramatically re-designed international legal system conceived in the 'spirit of San Francisco' and expressed in the UN Charter. The overwhelming aim of the Charter's draftees was to limit states' recourse to war. Therefore it is not surprising that only the narrowest of grounds were left to states to use force: in self-defense against armed attack.

The issues raised by terrorism – attacks by non-state actors and whether a state sponsoring terrorism or even conducting its own terrorism below the violence level of what normally would be considered an armed attack – were simply not addressed. The new ICJ, in one of its first judgments, the *Corfu Channel Case*, confirmed the narrow view of the Charter, saying a state's control of territory and waters did not automatically mean "that state necessarily knew, or ought to have known, of any unlawful act perpetrated therein, nor yet that it necessarily knew, or should have known, the authors" (1949: 18). This was not about terrorism but it set a high threshold before a state's unlawful actions, potentially including support for terrorism, could be considered an armed attack.

The word and deed of terrorism had largely disappeared from the international stage during the war. The term was used from 1945 initially, overwhelmingly and ironically, by Jewish groups and the British with reference to radical Jewish organizations such as *Irgun* in Palestine fighting the British for an Israeli state. Occasionally, it was also used to describe repressive internal past and present policies of Fascist and Communist states.

Sporadically, at first, and then almost exclusively it was harnessed by Western states for the Cold War to describe communist or other left-wing movements fighting their established governments notably in Spain, Italy, Greece, Germany, the Philippines, China, Korea, Japan, Cuba, Costa Rica and Nicaragua. Sometimes communist governments such as Rumania used it in reverse. Slowly, at first, with reference to Indonesia, Indochina, Burma and India, then from 1948 for Malaya, terrorism was used to describe the armed struggles against European colonialism and rural insurrections including in Latin America. The US preferred the term 'communist', whether exactly accurate or not for such movements, because it denied the nationalist and anti-colonial aspects of these struggles with which it should theoretically sympathize. For the Europeans, where 'communism' was not as negative a term, terrorism was more often used. The British neatly straddled this divide by employing for Malaya the term 'communist terrorist', which hardly otherwise appeared before and after the Cold War (Pemberton forthcoming). Terrorist as a term faded from extensive use in the anti-colonial dimension of the Cold War though states with legitimate communist parties continued to use it as France did in Indochina and Algeria.

A new legal framework adding to or challenging the Charter's rules on the use of force, depending on different viewpoints, was developing under this screen of political rhetoric. In his famous 1947 'Truman doctrine' speech, the US President revived the phrase 'indirect aggression' which the Soviet Union had first included in its 1933 anti-aggression pact and then used to describe Nazi Germany's methods just before the Second World War. Now other US officials took up Truman's phrase repeatedly to argue the Soviet Union was getting under the Charter's narrow 'armed attack' definition of aggression by using supposed non-state actors within targeted European countries to take over their governments for communism and/or the Soviet Union (the two were deliberately conflated).

From the Korean War that year, US officials also applied the term to Asia and then increasingly the Middle East. In 1953 Secretary of State John Foster Dulles threatened the US would retaliate (implicitly with nuclear weapons) in Asia, especially Indochina and Korea, to aggression "by whatever means", understood as direct or indirect aggression. The term 'indirect aggression' sought to portray all communist movements as direct agents of the Soviet Union or China and deny the internal dimension, which outside Europe was very genuine, thereby opening the legal door to intervention as collective self-defense. There was a stalled and half-hearted attempt to modify international law to take account of this supposed phenomenon.

During UN debates in 1950 the US and its allies but not the Soviet Union pushed for the term's inclusion in an expanded definition of aggression. In 1952 Kelsen, who had witnessed Hungary enter the Nazi and then Soviet orbit through purportedly externally-inspired internal change, argued that states' support of terrorist incidents "were itself the aggressive attack" (1952: 62). Yet, the US weakened its own position by not including the phrase in its string of new security treaties including NATO, ANZUS, US-Japan, SEATO and CENTO. The US did not want too low a threshold committing itself to armed collective self-defense especially when its military doctrine was by then based on 'massive retaliation' with nuclear weapons.

The 1954 Draft Code of Offences against the Peace and Security of Mankind considered as a crime "the undertaking or encouragement by the authorities of a State of terrorist activities in another State, or the toleration by the authorities of a State of organized activities calculated to carry out terrorist acts in another State". This was not connected, however, to the Charter's strict rules on grounds for self-defense. This statement overlooked the fact that most of the armed struggles of this period were genuinely internal, often anti-colonial, and not directed, even if often supported, from the outside.

'Indirect aggression' arose again dramatically over accusations by Lebanon's government in 1958 against the United Arab Republic, with the suggestion of Soviet involvement. The following year the term was next employed to characterize *Pathet Lao* guerrillas in Laos with the deliberately vague implication, as there was no proof, that an outside state, with China the only possibility, directly involved. Haiti accused the Dominican Republic of indirect aggression in 1963, a charge echoed by the US two years later in partial justification of its intervention there. It was also used to justify the US deployment of forces in Thailand in 1962. Indirect aggression was becoming a serious problem confronting the Security Council.

Ultimately, the US claimed its bombing of the Democratic Republic of Vietnam (DRV) was justified under international law because it was collective self-defense against what it explicitly termed, an 'armed attack'. 'Indirect aggression' faded from public use after brief mutual accusations by the US and Soviet Union over Afghanistan in 1980. For all the rhetoric, the US never 'retaliated' against the Soviet Union or China for their alleged 'indirect aggression' – nuclear weapons not law was the restraint – though the weaker DRV was bombed on this basis.

Leaving aside related crucial legal issues of whether there were two states in Vietnam and the actual level of DRV armed operations, there was by this time some limited authoritative legal opinion supporting this expansion of the Charter's armed attack to include the type of action implied by 'indirect aggression'. Writing around the time of the Lebanon crisis, Brownlie (1958: 731) and later Higgins (1963) supported such a view based on what Germans called *Nadelstichtaktik* (needle prick tactic) which argues it is not the individual but totality of attacks which accumulate to constitute an armed attack justifying self-defense.

In November 1965 the Soviet Union attempted to have the UN condemn interference in the internal affairs of other states so as to mobilize an attack on US policies in Vietnam and the Dominican Republic. The US mobilized opposition though not only from its allies but also from Third World countries fearing a return of colonial interference or even their own domestic problems. The final resolution sponsored by 37 states declared no state "shall organize, assist, foment, finance, incite or tolerate subversion, terrorist or armed activities directed to the violent overthrow of the regime in another state, or interfere in civil strife in another state" (Middleton 1965: 1). Apart from reaffirming a principle of non-support of non-state armed forces acting against another state, this resolution demonstrated that 'terrorism' was only seen as a tactic of intervention rather than a form of international political violence in its own right. So no specifically anti-terrorist policies resulted.

This soon changed. By the end of the 1960s, the anti-colonial and rural insurrectionary wave of struggles was coming to an end but a different type of non-state political violence was emerging. In Western countries small groups, loosely Marxist-inspired, began to emerge: Red Brigade (Italy), Red Army Faction (Germany), Anti-Fascist Resistance Group (Spain), Black Panthers, Afro-American Liberation, United Freedom Front, Weatherman, Symbionese Liberation Army (USA), Japanese Red Army (Japan), *Action Directe* (France) Revolutionary Organization November 17 (Greece) and Revolutionary People's Liberation Front (Turkey). There was virtually no known external state role except from shared Marxist ideology and the fact some of these non-state actors occasionally cooperated across state borders even with newer Arab groups. Small and elitist, these groups were relatively easily dealt with by their respective states without having much international impact (Coll 1987: 300).

There was a second more international aspect to the new terrorist wave. The anti-colonial movements between the 1940s and 1970s may often have articulated a transnational Marxist ideology. In reality, they pursued goals limited to national liberation and by means which rarely extended beyond this arena. They seldom took their political violence abroad, including even to their particular colonial state. This was different with regard to secular pro-Palestinian and anti-Israeli Arab groups which began to emerge at the end of the 1960s after Israel's victory in the 'Six Day War' of 1967, notably the Palestine Liberation Organization (PLO), Popular Front for the Liberation of Palestine (PFLP) and Black September.

There were several reasons for the change. Although Marxist ideology was theoretically transnational, under colonialism it usually assumed a mainly nationalist approach. Yet, Marxism, which stressed international proletariat solidarity, suggested workers of colonial countries should not be held responsible for their state's transgression. So rarely was anti-colonial violence returned to the *metropole*. This was not just a question of lack of technology though the growth of international air and sea travel certainly created more opportunity. It was more the transnational nature of the target – Jewishness – and the perception Israel existed only because of international Western support that political violence against it assumed such a transnational form.

The new wave opened with attack on *El Al* in Athens in 1968 and was followed by attacks in Zurich, London, Kuwait, Sudan, Beirut as well as Israel itself. The attack at the Munich Olympics in 1972 highlighted this new international battlefield. International travel, especially air but also sea, was a new major target. In 1974 the Japanese Red Army combined with the PFLP. In 1976 an Air France aircraft was hijacked by the PLO and German group *Revolutionäre Zellen*. The hijacking of the Italian cruise ship *Achille Lauro* in 1985 was the crest of this wave.

The UN attempted to provide leadership in an international counter terrorist campaign. Cold War politics meant a 1969 Soviet proposal that terrorism be included in the definition of aggression, supported by some small non-communist states, was not successful. The next year, however, the Declaration on Principles of International Law concerning Friendly Relations and Co-operation among States outlined the duty of countries to "refrain from organizing, instigating, assisting or participating in acts of civil strife or terrorist acts in another State or acquiescing in organized activities within its territory directed towards the commission of such acts".

The spate of air hijacks led to the adoption of The Hague (1970) and Montreal conventions (1971) extending airline security concerns from the Tokyo Convention of 1963 to cover terrorist hijackings. The General Assembly established a 33-member *Ad Hoc* Committee on Terrorism in 1972 to define and examine the causes of and preventative solutions to terrorism. There was large disagreement between the members especially Arab and non-aligned states: the former stressed the importance of addressing state terrorism, meaning Israel. Western states rejected this, arguing that any use of force exercised by states was already covered under existing international law (Franck and Lockwood 1974: 74). Recently independent states, a majority of committee members, argued that the use of force by non-state actors was permissible in achieving self-determination which was rejected for obvious reasons by South Africa, Portugal and Israel (Dugard 1974: 74).

The 1974 Definition of Aggression nevertheless helped clarify the issue with Article 3(g) classifying as acts of aggression "the sending by or on behalf of a State of armed bands, groups, irregulars or mercenaries, which carry out acts of armed force against another State of such gravity as to amount to the acts listed above, or its substantial involvement therein". Yet, while the definition of aggression was now finally agreed upon, by 1979 the Committee on Terrorism, still unable to reach consent on its key tasks, stressed in its report the continuing need for states to join both regional and international counter terrorist conventions leaving specific responses largely to states.

There was a mixed response from regional organizations. In 1970, the OAS, largely concerned with rural guerrilla movements which gave the region the second highest number of terrorist incidents during the Cold War, adopted the Convention to Prevent and Punish the Acts of Terrorism taking the Forms of Crimes against Persons and Related Extortion that are of International Significance. Western Europe adopted in 1977 the European Convention on the Suppression of Terrorism and the Agreement of the Application of the European Convention on the Suppression of Terrorism. Organizations in two other hotspots of terrorist incidents, Africa and the Middle East did not follow suit. Members of the Organization of the Islamic Conference (OIC) and Arab League were more concerned about alleged 'state-terrorism' undertaken most notably by Israel (Dugard 1974: 74). In Africa ECOWAS, the Southern African Development Community (SADC) and the Intergovernmental Authority on Development (IGAD) focused on socio-economic issues rather than security.

Legal writers generally advocated a moderate response. Falk, writing after the Israeli raid at Beirut airport in retaliation for the attack in Athens, suggested a framework to assess claims of legitimate forceful retaliation against terrorist attacks. This framework was to include initial pursuit by non-forceful means, placement of the burden of proof on the state retaliating, a state's need to prove its actions to be defensive rather than aggressive, keeping the force proportional and directed strictly against military and paramilitary targets, as well as informing immediately both the Security Council and the target state of the reason for the action (1969a: 441). Rosen and Franck accepted that with the absence of Security Council collective security, states should rightfully resort to self-defense under Articled 51 of the Charter (1975: 68). For Israel's Feinstein, even minor armed attacks were sufficient for this (1976: 540). Most writers, however, agreed with Falk's cautious approach. America's Fred C. Pedersen insisted there had to be 'substantial' complicity by a state with terrorists for forceful retaliation to be legitimate (1976: 220). Manuel R. Garcia-Mora argued the scale of the terrorist had to be a full-scale invasion by armed bands to justify armed self-defense (1962: 119). John F. Murphy, Professor of Law at Villanova University, saw attacks like Israel's in Lebanon as illegal reprisals and of greater danger to international peace and stability than terrorist acts supported by states (1978: 565).

Not all states felt the danger allowed them to be so restricted in armed unilateral responses. Israel had destroyed 13 Lebanese aircraft in retaliation at Beirut in 1968. In 1973 it intercepted an Iraqi civilian aircraft on the suspicion of it carrying a terrorist suspect, an assumption which proved incorrect. Israel had been undertaking military strikes against PLO bases in Lebanon, established under the 1969 Cairo Agreement, which had attacked Israel, something the Security Council repeatedly condemned. In 1982, following an attempt by the Abu Nidal Organization (ANO) to assassinate an Israeli ambassador, Israel invaded and occupied southern Lebanon, stating that if the country was "either unwilling or unable to prevent the harboring, training and financing of PLO terrorists ... then Lebanon must surely be prepared to face the risk of Israel's taking the necessary countermeasures to stop such terrorist operations" (UNSC 1982a). The PLO denied any involvement with the ANO's act, a claim even the UK seemingly supported. Lebanon condemned the action, stressed non-involvement of its nationals and argued that it could not be held accountable, and "no principles of international law can justify Israel's violent aggression" (Tueni 1982).

So Israel now justified its forcible self-defense as reaction not so much to a single event but rather to a 'campaign of terror' of over 150 alleged PLO attacks from Lebanon in one year. Self-defense was justified on Bowett's (1972) 'accumulation of events' theory. Israel also claimed Lebanon's provision of refuge was sufficient to warrant forcible self-defense against a harboring state, a view supported in principle by two ICJ judges Jennings (1986) and Schwebel (1986), as well as Moore (1987).[1]

Gross argued that following civil war and nationwide instability, the Lebanese government could not be held responsible (1983: 459). The Security Council (1982b) rejected Israel's argument, calling instead for an end to hostilities and Israel's withdrawal in respect of Lebanon's territorial integrity, sovereignty and political independence. The Security Council similarly condemned Israel's 1985 strike against the PLO in Tunisia. As the 1980s experienced a 45 per cent increase in terrorist incidents, compared to the previous decade, with fatalities tripling, this relatively passive and restrictive Security Council approach was likely to come under challenge (Memorial Institute for the Prevention of Terrorism 2008).

The US initially was more passive than Israel. From 1979 even as the Cold War was reviving for its last phase, a new global conflict was becoming apparent. The Soviet intervention in Afghanistan was initially seen as only part of the Cold War between the West and the Communist *bloc*. Yet, it was actually the beginning of the challenge of militant anti-Western Islamic fundamentalism. The Iranian revolution the same year confirmed this. The US established a list of states supporting international terrorism in its Export Administration Act of 1979 imposing controls on exports of dual-use goods and technology [that is civilian and military] "based on strategic relationships [and] threats to U.S. national security". In 1981 US officials first used the phrase 'state-sponsored terrorism': they were referring to the new Islamic Republic of Iran not the Soviet Union. When the US embassy and military barracks in Beirut were bombed in 1983, an act by the Islamic Jihad Organization based in Lebanon but allegedly connected to the Iran, the US did not respond militarily.

The US concern over terrorism was growing even with, or because of, the Cold War thaw once Mikhail Gorbachev came to power. In 1985 the US Department of State began to publish an annual list of state-sponsors of terrorism – often criticized as "a legally imprecise term" (Rowles 1987: 314) – notably including Libya, Iran, North Korea, Cuba, Nicaragua and Syria (Sabasteanski 2005). The mix included Cold War and new enemies. The next year the US defined the term as "the deliberate employment of violence or the threat of use of violence by sovereign states ... to attain strategic and political objectives by acts in violation of law intended to create overwhelming fear in a target population larger than the civilian or military victims attacked or threatened" (Senate Subcommittee on Security and Terrorism 1986: 82). While originally rejecting Israel's retaliation for terrorist attacks, by now the US argued that "the ability to take such action in

1 Also see UNSC Resolutions 228 (1966), 248 (1968), 265 (1969) and 316 (1972).

carefully defined and limited circumstances is an aspect of the inherent right of self-defense recognized in the United Nations Charter" (UNSC 1986a). The US actually followed an Israeli precedent, forcing an commercial aircraft to land in Italy where the perpetrators of the *Achille Lauro* hijacking were arrested.

Meanwhile, the UN exhibited some greater concern as terrorist acts increased. The General Assembly (1985a and 1985b), acting on the Report of the Sixth Committee, adopted a resolution which "unequivocally condemns, as criminal, all acts, methods and practices of terrorism whenever and by whomever committed ... calls upon all states to fulfill their obligations under international law to refrain from organizing, instigating, assisting or participating in terrorist acts in other states, or acquiescing in activities within their territory directed towards the commission of such acts". This general prohibition did not address the crucial issues arising from the terms of a legitimate armed response to terrorism – including the severity of attack and degree of state responsibility – possibly because the UN still hoped responses would remain criminal law enforcement not armed self-defense. This did not prove so.

In 1986 the US held Libya responsible for the bombing of a Berlin nightclub frequented by American military personnel and claimed that the missile strikes in reaction had been undertaken in self-defense but also to discourage future attacks, stating that this was "only the latest in an ongoing pattern of attacks by Libya" (Okun 1986). Ronald Reagan (1985) had earlier said "these terrorist states are now engaged in acts of war against the government and people of the United States": as a victim of such aggression the US was entitled to defend itself not only against the current attack but also for past ones, citing the 'accumulation of events' theory and potential future attacks (Stuesser 1987).

Although, Libya had a history of, said South African academic Khanya Motshabi, "voluntarily and, at times, unintelligently, [making] admissions implicating herself in the sporadic violence of which she has been accused" (1987: 674), the country's representative to the UN denied any involvement: "we shall never initiate aggression, nor shall we ever do anything to threaten peace and security". Libya further stated that it reserved its right to self-defense in the event of recurring strikes by the US, thereby positioning itself as a victim of aggression rather than the perpetrator (UNSC 1986b). The General Assembly condemned the US strikes as reprisals, both a violation of the Charter and international law, particularly as they had been undertaken against Qadhafi's residences, in civilian neighborhoods, risking civilian deaths and aimed deliberately to kill Qadhafi and members of his family (UNGA 1986, Boyle 1987). The US was outraged, referring to the law on terrorism as "not merely flawed (but) perverse" (Sofaer 1986: 902–903) and claiming that the ambivalence of the international rules on the subject "equates the criminal with his victim" (UNSC 1986b).

This was the background to the final conclusion to the ICJ's two year hearing of *Nicaragua v United States of America* by which it clarified at least some of these issues. Proceeding from the Definition of Aggression the ICJ, with the US and UK judges dissenting, argued that, for the conduct of the *Contras* in Nicaragua "to give rise to legal responsibility of the United States, it would in principle have to be proved that that State had effective control of the military or paramilitary operations in the course of which the alleged violations were committed" (1986: 65). The financing, training, arming and support of armed groups or, as an extension of this terrorists, while illegal was thereby not necessarily equivalent to an armed attack justifying armed self-defense. The mere tolerance of such activities was not considered sufficient justification. Proof of state responsibility and its level was required, the burden of which lay with the state undertaking armed self-defense (Frowein 1989). The ICJ (1986: 136) also indicated that the scale of the attack had to be of a certain severity, which it did not define comprehensively, but said was not reached in the respective US and Nicaraguan actions to justifying forceful self-defense.

As the Cold War drew to a close, legal authorities remained divided though among Western, especially American writers, there seemed to be a shift towards broadening the right to armed self-defense, in various forms, against terrorists and their state-sponsors. John Rowles warned that the terrorist threat must be addressed through international law while "taking care not to weaken them in ways that open the gates to the wider use of force under the cover of legal justification" (1987: 317). He allowed that "large-scale, continuing campaigns of terrorists attacks ... could give rise to the right of self-defense but ... only within the limits of necessity and proportionality" (1987: 314). Some definitely ruled pre-emption as 'virtually outlawed' if only because the difficulty of predicting terrorists' actions (Ofri 1984, Sullivan 1986). America's Jeffrey McCredie, argued for a high level of 'state responsibility' before self-defense was justified (1985: 94). Even Lewis Paul Bremer, fifteen years prior to becoming US administrator of Iraq, seemed reluctant to go down the armed path against terrorists, stating that terrorists were criminals and consequently "a major element of [US] strategy has been to delegitimize terrorists, to get society to see them for what they are – criminals – and to use democracy's most potent tool, the rule of law, against them" (1988: 48).

The alternative view was growing stronger. David Turndorf saw state-sponsored terrorism, as others had seen communist 'indirect aggression', as just "a cheap means of waging war" to get under the barrier of illegal armed attack (1988: 218). By using a third party, said Jenkins, states could avoid full-on confrontation with the target of attack and instead ensure the lowest possible degree of involvement in the acts of aggression (1984: 12). Predictably, Moore had no doubt terrorist incidents supported by states constituted an aggressive attack (1988: 441). Franz W. Paasche even predicted pre-emptive strikes would form "an important component of an effective" counter terrorism policy (1987: 394). Italian jurist Antonio Cassese also thought in instances of direct support of terrorism the use of force in form of self-defense by victim states was permissible but he thought the law less certain with regard to indirect support (1989: 598).

British lawyer and academic Christopher Greenwood said the General Assembly's rejection of the US justification for striking Libya did not mean that it was illegal. He thought the failure of the international community to establish clear rules of when force may be used against terrorist groups meant that "it is better than international law should adapt to take account of state practice than continue to set a standard which is ignored in practice" (1987: 956). In the light of the ineffectiveness of UN collective security against terrorism, Greenwood predicted an increase of actions like that of the US and judged that it probably "reflects the direction in which the law of self-defense is evolving" (1987: 960). This prediction would be tested in the post-Cold War years.

Apocalypse Now

> I have never since my childhood supported a shooting war in which the United States was involved [but] the war in Afghanistan against apocalyptic terrorism qualifies in my understanding as the first truly just war since World War II. (Richard Falk 2001)

In the post-Cold War era states continued to respond to terrorist attacks in two main ways each of which had two complementary or alternative paths. First, action was taken against the terrorists themselves by criminal law enforcement measures, including arrest or extradition, prosecution and punishment. This was sometimes supported by the UN. The other path was direct, limited military action against the terrorists inevitably and secondarily on the territory of another state. Second, action was taken primarily against another state which was seen by the injured state or states as either hosting, supporting or even sponsoring terrorism or committing state terrorism. Governments sought to do this unilaterally or multilaterally, by *ad hoc* coalitions, outside the UN.

The UN did not support such measures although in some instances it sympathetically avoided overt criticism. The key legal issues over the use of force in response to terrorism continued to be what gravity of the violence and what degree of state involvement in them met the standard read into the Charter's 'armed attack' by authorities and, thereby, what level if at all of armed intervention in self-defense was justified when lacking Security Council approval.

The *MIPT Terrorism Knowledge Database* reveals a staggering increase in terrorist incidents, as well as injuries and fatalities, from the late 1960s onwards. Between 1968 and 2007 there were slightly more than 35,000 terrorist incidents. Measured by decades, around a tenth of these incidents took place in the 1970s and more than two thirds in the 2000s. This severe increase explains the growing concern that terrorism and its counter has played in international relations and law. The following three sections will examine how states have addressed this challenge in form of criminal persecutions, armed force and UN collective security mechanisms.

Germany's Wolfgang Hetzer (2007) reflects the views of many when he argues that terrorists are clear-cut criminals, nothing else. Leaving aside the debate over whether at law or in political analysis this view should be accepted, in terms of state responses to terrorism, it means prosecution through municipal criminal law rather than through international armed force. Norway's Geir Ulfstein argued "the more effective the efforts to combat terrorism through combating crime, the less pressure there will be to use military force" (2003: 165). The failure of the 1937 conference on terrorism denied states an international criminal pathway with an international law criminalizing terrorism and international criminal court to try them. Yet, there were some successes with this approach in the post-Cold War period using national courts and the UN supporting injured states with sanctions.

US and UK criminal investigations of the 1988 explosion on a Pan American airliner which crashed into the Scottish town of Lockerbie, killing 243 mostly Americans, led in 1991 to the indictment of two Libyan intelligence agents. The UK's Security Council representative demanded their extradition stating that Libya must "surrender for trial all those charged with the crime [and] accept complete responsibility for the actions of Libyan Officials" (Hannay 1991). Following Libya's refusal, the Security Council (1992c) declared its "failure to demonstrate by concrete action its renunciation of terrorism" a threat to international peace and security.

Unlike the Berlin bombings, the US and the UK did not resort to force in alleged self-defense against Libya's terrorism or to enforce extradition. Instead both implemented economic sanctions, supported by UN sanctions (UNSC 1999c). In 1998 a settlement was achieved, resulting in the extradition of the suspects to a Scottish Court, established in the Netherlands, to meet Qadhafi's demands for neutral judicial ground (UNSC 1998b). One was convicted, the other acquitted. Libya then accepted responsibility for the agents' action, paid compensation and renounced terrorism, which led to the lifting of UN sanctions (UNSC 2003d). Despite missing an ICC, some delegates to the 1937 conference would have cheered.

The US approached the 1998 embassy bombings in Kenya and Tanzania in a somewhat different way. Armed force was used although the US also undertook criminal proceedings indicting Osama bin Laden and eighteen others with extradition sought for those residing in the UK. The UN demanded the Taliban "turn over Usama bin laden without further delay to appropriate authorities in a country where he has been indicted". In the absence of a response, the Security Council imposed sanctions to support US criminal proceedings (UNSC 1999c, UNSC 2000). In 2001 convictions were recorded for those arraigned. Bin Laden's residence in Taliban-ruled Afghanistan made a similar outcome unlikely though another factor was undoubtedly the weakness of evidence of direct involvement which may not have convinced a court.

When the *USS Cole* was attacked by suicide bombers in the Yemeni port of Aden in 2000, resulting in the death of seventeen sailors, the US response was more muted than previously. Unlike 1998, the outgoing Clinton administration did not respond with limited force, stating the US would launch an investigation to establish those responsible (Burns and Myers 2000: A1). The evidence linking bin Laden's *Al-Qaeda* to the attacks appeared incomplete, weakening the case for using force or criminal prosecution. The matter was left to the new Bush administration to handle, which it did, belatedly and very differently after September 11.

The initial response of the Bush administration to the September 11 attacks suggested it may also follow the criminal prosecution path. The US demanded extradition of *Al-Qaeda* leaders and access to training camps to ensure they were closed. This was rejected by the Taliban which demanded conclusive evidence linking bin Laden to the attacks for the Afghan supreme court plus approval of his surrender by all member states of the OIC (Bush 2001b, Abraham and Hopkins 2002). At this point the US chose the path of major armed force as detailed below. Whether the domestic imperatives behind US policy would have accepted a long drawn out legal process with an uncertain and relatively unspectacular conclusion, even if there had been signs of the Taliban making concessions, is doubtful. There is reason to suspect the use of force was probably favored from the outset (National Commission on Terrorist Attacks 2004, Greenwood 2002).

On the other side of Bush's very different approach over the September 11 attacks, the terrorist attacks by Islamist group *Jemaah Islamiyah* on the Indonesian island of Bali in 2002 were also handled through criminal law enforcement. The Australian and UK governments, which had the greatest share of the more than 200 mainly foreign nationals killed, did not react to the events militarily but instead left matters to the fully cooperative Indonesian authorities who arrested, charged, tried and convicted the suspects.

Similarly, the bombing of commuter trains in the Spanish capital of Madrid, killing more than 190 people, was also addressed only through criminal law channels. Investigations suggested the *Al-Qaeda*-linked *Abu Hafs al-Masri* Brigade as the culprit and in 2007 Spanish courts found the majority of individual defendants, including from Syria, Morocco and Lebanon, guilty (Barrett 2007, Hamilos 2007). Where appropriate, foreign states cooperated in the criminal process and the issue of state responsibility did not arise.

The UN has played a supportive role in some of these law enforcement cases through moral pressure or economic sanctions when, unlike with Indonesia and Morocco, states do not cooperate in criminal proceedings. This was the case with Libya (1992), Sudan (twice in 1996) for refusing to extradite persons suspected of attempting to assassinate Egyptian President Mubarak, as well as Afghanistan (1999).[2]

The UN also had an important if incomplete legal leadership role in adopting international criminal law against terrorism to guide states. Four conventions adopted since 1990 included, on the Marking of Plastic Explosives for the Purpose of Detection (1991), for the Suppression of Terrorist Bombings (1997), for the Suppression of the Financing of Terrorism (1999), and for the Suppression of Acts of Nuclear Terrorism (2005). All focus on judicial process, including extradition and prosecution of offenders. The Security Council (1999d)

2 Security Council Resolutions 748 (1992), 1054 (1996) and 1070 (1996), and 1267 (1999) respectively.

unequivocally condemned "all acts, methods and practices of terrorism as criminal and unjustifiable, regardless of their motivation": thus excluding armed struggle for self-determination desired by some post-colonial states. Just before this it reconstituted the *Ad Hoc* Committee on Measures to Eliminate Terrorism (1997) which had been tasked with drawing up the previously mentioned conventions, as well condemning terrorism on numerous occasions (UNGA 2005).

The UN's Counter Terrorism Committee, similar to the Policy Working Group (PWG) on the United Nations and Terrorism, in 2001 failed to define terrorism but worked to find a largely non-forceful way of suppressing it. The PWG suggested strategies included dissuading groups from embracing terrorism, denying them the means to do so and ensuring international cooperation in counter terrorism. Similar to Kofi Annan (2002 and 2005b) the PGW conceded that it "does not believe that the UN is well placed to play an active operational role in efforts to suppress terrorist groups, to pre-empt specific terrorist strikes, or to develop dedicated intelligence-gathering capacities" (2002: 3). In 2003, as part of Resolution 1456, the Security Council urged states to adopt international and regional conventions relating to terrorism, share information, collaborate regarding extradition and prosecution of suspects and suppress terrorists' access to financial sources.

The absence of a universally accepted definition of terrorism remained a problem. In this absence, the Security Council "encouraged states to unilaterally define terrorism in national law, permitting wide and divergent definitions" (Saul 2005: 141). The High-Level Panel decided, however, that the "lack of agreement on a clear and well-known definition undermines the normative and moral stance against terrorism and has stained the United Nations image" (2004: 51). A year after the invasion of Iraq the Security Council (2004a) generically defined terrorism as "criminal acts, including against civilians, committed with the intent to cause death or serious bodily injury, or taking of hostages, with the purpose to provoke a state of terror". This definition has, however, not been accepted universally, including by the OIC.

The limitations of the UN's role in the non-forceful criminal law path to counter terrorism, for which the 1937 conference had hoped to provide, is illustrated by American Professor of Law Mary Ellen O'Connell's comment that the September 11 attacks "involved the intentional killing of so many innocent people that they qualify as crimes against humanity, which are universal jurisdiction crimes" (2002: 906). The figures which pushed for the creation of crimes against humanity saw terrorism as a separate category of such crimes. Yet, they did see terrorism as potentially one. Universal jurisdictional crimes are not new: with piracy being one of the oldest (Wheaton 1836: 112–13). Terrorism has never been covered by *ius gentium* which would allow every country to try the accused in their jurisdiction regardless of where the alleged crime was committed.

The international machinery is lacking as well. The ICJ has no criminal jurisdiction, dealing only with states. The ICC was not then established and, when it was, terrorism was not included in its mandate. There was no suggestion of creating an international criminal tribunal, similar to Rwanda and Yugoslavia and, as they have been sitting for fourteen years, it is doubtful, as suggested above, the US would have waited that long (Greenwood 2002: 305). The Lockerbie, Bali and Madrid bombings show judicial proceedings were successful but very slow. Political pressures on governments do not always encourage patience. In several cases states have turned to international force to punish and deter terrorists and states linked to them.

Most states pursue terrorism through judicial procedures and covert operations, rather than the use of force in self-defense. There have been notable exceptions and thereby a debate over the lawfulness of such action. Inevitably, armed counter-action against non-state actors will take place in violation of the territorial integrity and sometimes the citizens of other states.

America's Liam Murphy (1991) argues law enforcement through extradition is not an effective way to deal with terrorism, leaving force as the sole solution. Brooks agreed it was becoming increasingly difficult to ascertain a clear difference between crime and armed conflict: "in the future there will be more and more *al-Qaedas*, organizations that have something in common with criminal gangs and something in common with armies" (2004: 718). This has led, as Oxford University's Andrew Hurrell has noted, to "the blurring of the language between waging war and pursuing criminals" (2002: 192).

In the *Advisory Opinion: Legal Consequences of the Construction of a Wall in the Occupied Palestinian Territory* the ICJ left no doubt that "Article 51 of the Charter ... recognizes the existence of an inherent right of self-defense in the case of armed attack by one state against another state" (2004: 12). While not absolutely stating that an attack must emanate exclusively from a state to constitute an armed attack, Judge Kooijmanns said this "has been the generally accepted interpretation for more than 50 years" (2004: 230). Judge Rosalyn Higgins was more unequivocal arguing that "self-defense is available only when an armed attack is made by a state" (2004: 215). University of Queensland's Andrew Garwood-Gowers has questioned the claim that the international responses to 9/11 "have given rise to a new principle of customary international law that permits the use of force in self-defense in response to 'armed attacks' committed by non-state terrorist organizations" (2004: 11). Yet, both ICJ dissenting judges in the above case and observers like Hebrew University's Michla Pomerance argue the suggestion that terrorist attacks may not legally constitute armed attacks justifying self-defense as "illogical in an era when the worldwide terrorist threats stem primarily from non-state actors" (2005: 26).

The US was not the only state to pursue this path. In 1995 Turkey intervened militarily in Iraq in pursuit of cross-border activities by Kurdish groups. Turkey told the Security Council Iraq had not been able to exercise authority over the northern region of its territory for several years and that, as a consequence, "Turkey cannot ask the government of Iraq to fulfill its obligation, under international law, to prevent the use of its territory for the staging of terrorist acts against Turkey". Turkey claimed that declaring Iraq unable to meet its responsibilities, meant that it was not attacking Iraq itself and so its use of force could not be considered a violation of Iraqi territory (Maleski 1996). Iraq, however, protested calling Turkish action an act of aggression and asked the Security Council to intervene (Al-Kadhe 2002a, 2002b).

The US, in response to two embassy bombings in Africa (1998) linked to *Al-Qaeda*, as well as judicial proceedings, used missile strikes against a pharmaceutical plant and terrorist training camps in Sudan and Afghanistan, respectively. The US claimed to have acted in self-defense and pre-emptively to deter the states from continued support of terrorism (Clinton 1998, Richardson 1998). Similar to the 1993 strikes against Iraq, Western states largely refrained from criticizing the US. Yet, Gray argues the "failure to condemn the USA should be taken to indicate sympathy and understanding rather than acceptance of a legal doctrine which destroys the distinction between [illegal] reprisals and self-defense" (2004: 164). Arab states, non-aligned states, Pakistan and Russia condemned this force (Drozdiak 1998, Said 1998). Annan criticized both the missile strikes and their unilateral nature (Agence France-Presse 1998). Nevertheless, the Security Council (1998f) declared itself as just concerned about the use of Afghan territory as sanctuary for terrorists and demanded that the Taliban stop the provision of such sanctuary and alleged training for such groups.

The Bush administration appeared to favor, more than Clinton's, a "new, more aggressive strategy against *Al-Qaeda*", which included increased counter terrorism funding for national security agencies, suggesting the law enforcement and limited strike pathways would be superseded by larger armed responses (UNSC 1998f). In 2002, after September 11, the US belatedly undertook missile strikes against *Al-Qaeda* members in Yemen suspected of involvement in the attack on the USS Cole (Downes 2004: 277). Like the strikes of 1993 and 1998, justifications included the claim that as "territorial boundaries or regimes are not changed or directly disrupted", at least permanently, this was not an illegal use of force (Paust 2002: 536).

Armed intervention, if kept proportional, primarily against terrorists but, inevitably, in the territory of another state seemed to be accepted. Armed intervention, directed primarily against a state for acts of either state-sponsored or state terrorism, remained more controversial. Chris Downes thinks the international community will become "increasingly responsive to the formation of modified paradigm for the use of force against terrorists". He was speaking of targeted killings but this also applies to major armed intervention (2004: 294).

The use of UN collective security mechanisms is seen as the third method of countering terrorism. The UN was established to restrict the use of force by government based on assumption that the illegal force would be, firstly, employed by states and, secondly, it would have severity (then undefined) amounting to an 'armed attack'. The UN Charter is silent on the use of force by non-state actors notwithstanding the clear position in customary international law, as we have seen, making some provision for a right of self-preservation by states against such non-state attacks. The Charter did not define the severity necessary for an action to be termed 'armed attack' and thus whether it included acts of state-terrorism.

So, in no instance has the Security Council considered collective enforcement action against a non-state actor for use of armed force or the state from where terrorist attacks occurred, were sponsored or directed. The closest thing to such action, was the economic sanctions imposed on Libya after 1988 and even then it was based on an assumption that these were actions of the Libyan government not non-state actors. Nor has the UN taken forcible action against states who have taken recourse to such non-state attacks or state-terrorism.

The role of the UN in such cases has been limited to approval or disapproval of the actions of the participants in any such conflict. In 1993 the Security Council, unsurprisingly, did not condemn and many of the permanent members sympathized with, the US missile strikes against Iraq's Military Intelligence Headquarters in Baghdad in response to an alleged foiled assassination attempt by the Iraqi intelligence service on former President George Bush.

Despite having previously recognized a general link between the Taliban and *Al-Qaeda* when it imposed sanctions against Afghanistan in 2000 and, again, in 2002, the Security Council initially did not attribute the September 11 attacks to Afghanistan (2001a, 2001c, 2002a). Shortly afterwards, however, the Security Council (2001e) condemned the Taliban for "allowing Afghanistan to be used as a base for the export of terrorism by the Al-Qaida network ... and for providing safe haven to Usama Bin Laden, Al-Qaida and other associated with them". There was, however, once again no explicit permission for the US and its coalition partners to use force.

In 2001 the Security Council acknowledged the US's right to self-defense, something which it had not done before with regard to terrorist attacks (Beard 2002: 565). On 12 September, the Security Council (2001a) recognized "the inherent right of individual or collective self-defense in accordance with the Charter [and] regards such acts, like any act of international terrorism, as a threat to international peace and security [and] stresses that those responsible for aiding, supporting or harboring the perpetrators, organizers and sponsors of these acts will be held accountable". The Security Council expressed readiness to take all necessary steps but not the use of force explicitly in response to the attack. Subsequently the Security Council (2001c) reaffirmed the right to self-defense and called on states to prevent and suppress the financing of terrorism, deny such organizations safe havens and increase exchange of intelligence on terrorism. This was too little, too late.

While the Security Council refrained from referring to an armed attack, its invocation of the right to self-defense logically must presuppose its recognition of the acts as constituting an armed attack. Yet, the ICJ (1986) has ruled that "states do not have a right of 'collective' armed response to acts which do not constitute an 'armed attack'". Ireland's Marianne Bogue agrees, stating that the Security Council's omission of the phrase 'armed attack' meant the body had "refused to extend the number of situations in which an individual state could cite its inherent right to resort to self-defense unilaterally", leaving aside the need for such action to be multilateral in nature and authorized by the Security Council (Bogue 2004:

204). America's John Quigley disagreed, saying the silence of the Security Council "must mean that it has exercised its power in the direction of concluding that the use of force was lawful" (2003: 544).

Many thought the nature of the September 11 attacks and the Security Council's recent condemnations of terrorism as threat to international peace and security meant the organ would have authorized the use of force if asked. The US together with its coalition partners, however, decided to act outside the UN on the basis of self-defense. The Charter recognizes implicitly self-defense may initially be taken prior to Security Council authorization but the two states had already raised the terrorist attacks within the UN. India's V.S. Mani argued unilateral self-defense is not permitted "once the Security Council is already in the picture" (2003: 66). The Security Council eventually called for and authorized a multinational peacekeeping force for Afghanistan. Led initially by the UK and from August 2003 by NATO, the 40 country-force's establishment could be taken to suggest either the UN was or was not fully accepting of the US-led intervention.

The Security Council was less tolerant in 2003 when Israel attacked alleged training camps of Palestinian terrorist organizations in Syria as a response to the bombings in the Israeli city of Haifa (Israeli Ministry of Foreign Affairs 2004). The Security Council (2003d) condemned the action, describing it as a violation of international law including Syrian sovereignty. In 2006 it took a very belated and more neutral stance when Israel launched a bombing campaign and subsequent intervention in Lebanon following the abduction of its soldiers and rocket attacks by Lebanon-based *Hezbollah*. The Security Council (2006) neither condemned nor supported the attacks, calling instead for the end of conflict.

In view of this ambiguous and quiet passive approach, even traditionally strong supporters of the UN have questioned its relevance in these matters. Falk (2001) said the UN "lacks the capability, authority and will to respond to the kind of threat to global security posed by this new form of terrorist world war". An opponent of all previous US military actions since 1945, he said after September 11 that it would have been unreasonable to have expected the US to rely on the UN to undertake forceful measures against Afghanistan in its defense. This meant supporting the right of the US to self-help in this instance: in the form of self-defense against an alleged armed attack.

The failure of the US and UK to seek prior UN authorization for its invasion of Afghanistan is a main reason why some legal writers reject its legality (Farer 2002: 359). Byers argues that the US has chosen to act both unilaterally with limited armed actions and multilaterally with *ad hoc* coalitions, rather than through the UN, "as a strategic decision directed at loosening the legal constraints on the use of force to the ongoing advantage of the US" (2002b: 410). This might be designed to allow for greater freedom of response when the level of attack and state-sponsorship is not as high. The *NSS 2002* advocated unilateral and pre-emptive force against terrorist groups and states that harbor or support them. Realizing this would never be accepted by the UN, the US may have decided to establish a pattern of action outside it.

The justification of such action raises several issues. For state terrorism, where a state is clearly the author of an attack, the crucial issue is whether the severity of the violation is equal to 'armed attack' as cited in the Charter and defined somewhat by cases such as *Nicaragua*. For state-sponsored terrorism, the issue not only includes severity but also the level of state responsibility to convert a non-state actor attack into a Charter-defined 'armed attack' implicitly only by a state.

In 1993 the US claimed state terrorism when Madeleine Albright, Permanent Representative of the US to the UN, justified missile strikes against Baghdad as a measure of unilateral self-defense based on "clear and compelling evidence regarding the involvement of Iraq in the attempted assassination" of former President Bush. The action was therefore both a reaction to what the US viewed as an actual and future potential armed attack. Iraq rejected charges of involvement as a US concoction and declared the force an act of aggression (Hamdoon 1993). While states of the non-aligned movement in the UN voiced moderate concerns regarding the missile strikes, Western states agreed with US actions. British Foreign Secretary Douglas Hurd said "the operation was a justified and proportionate exercise of the right of self-defense, and a necessary warning to Iraq that state terrorism cannot and will not be tolerated" (House of Commons 1993). This, of course, did not address the legal issues of whether there had been an armed attack in terms of severity.

The US initially pursued the criminal enforcement pathway to the September 11 attacks. Soon, in the face of Taliban recalcitrance, it turned to armed intervention. The US rejected the Afghan's governments counter claims (Bush 2001b). Both the US and UK then claimed before the Security Council self-defense under Article 51 with the US alone referring to an armed attack (Negroponte 2001, Eldon 2001). This latter claim was supported by the US's allies with NATO, ANZUS and the OAS all invoking collective self-defense clauses which are conditional upon the occurrence of an armed attack (NATO 2001, Howard 2001, OAS 2001). While this interpretation was also widely accepted by other states, the use of force against Afghanistan was rejected by Iraq, Iran and Malaysia, amongst others (UNSC 2001d).

The gravity of the 9/11 attacks was an issue taken up in the justifications by the US for the invasion of Afghanistan. One criteria later cited by the ICJ was clearly met in that for a state to have a right to self-defense under Article 51, the armed attack had to be against the territory not just citizens of a state (Maggs 2006: 156). On scale, Dinstein suggested that while the attacks alone may have not been sufficient taken on their own, viewed in light of past *Al-Qaeda* attacks and possible future action, the 'pinprick theory' applied (2001: 182). Israel and the US have previously used Bowett's 'accumulation of events' theory, arguing that while the individual attacks alone may not justify the use of force in self-defense, the whole action taken together did. Yet, the ICJ in the 2003 *Oil Platforms* case said "even taken cumulatively ... these incidents [concerning Iran] do not seem to the court to constitute an armed attack on the United States, of the kind that the court ... qualified as a 'most grave' form of the use of force". So the mere accumulation of attacks does not automatically justify the use of force in self-defense unless a certain gravity has been suffered.

The US claimed the gravity of the September 11 attacks was severe enough to constitute an armed attack by itself: saying it was "certainly akin to that of a military attack" and, combined with possible future action by *Al-Qaeda*, justified military action (Murphy 2002: 47). Rumsfeld said the scale of the attack meant "nothing is needed by way of additional authorization [and] every country has the right to self-defense" (Weisman 2002). Unlike previous terrorist attacks, the US clearly stated these were "on a scale that has created a state of armed conflict that requires the use of the United States and armed forces" (Bush 2001d). Quigley's (2003) argument that the US was no longer suffering armed attack at the time of its response cannot be used to deny legitimate self-defense as planning of large scale military responses and gathering of evidence take time. Yet, it does raise the vagueness of the legal difference between a reprisal for a one-off terrorist attack and self-defense against ongoing state attack.

There was a need to attribute the attacks to another state for major self-defense to be invoked on the grounds of state responsibility for a terrorist attack (Garwood Gowers 2004: 6, Byers 2005: 65). Legal writers agree state support of terrorism is rarely a straightforward issue with various levels of involvement some of which many agree could amount to an armed attack invoking self-defense and others not (Byman 2005). The ICJ in its *Nicaragua* judgment and International Criminal Tribunal on the former Yugoslavia (ICTY) have even disagreed somewhat. The ICJ, anxious to minimize recourse to armed self-defense, suggested that what was needed for state involvement to be considered an armed attack was 'effective control' by the state of the terrorists. The ICTY, anxious to secure a criminal prosecution, argued for the lower standard of 'overall control'. The ICTY (1999) explained that "control required for those powers to be considered *de facto* State organs goes beyond the mere financing and equipping and involves also participation in the planning and supervision of military operations. However, it is not required that specific orders or instructions relating to single military actions be issued".

The UN's ILC argued in October 2001 that actions undertaken by individuals or groups should under international law be viewed as an act of the state "if the person or group of persons is in fact acting on the instructions of, or under the direction or control of, that State in carrying out the conduct ... is in fact exercising elements of the governmental authority in the absence or default of the official authorities [and] to the extent that the state acknowledges and adopts the conduct in question as its own". All these bodies suggest clearly that the mere presence of terrorists on a state's territory is not sufficient to invoke state responsibility, particularly if such a state is unable to control its territory. This does not mean lesser direct armed action against the terrorists on the state's territory would necessarily be illegal as Phillimore long ago argued.

In the *DRC v Uganda* judgment of 2004 the ICJ, ruled that attacks by armed groups acting from Congolese territory against Uganda were not attributable to The

Congo as the government had been unable to control its border regions. The Court invoked Article 3(g) of the 1974 Definition of Aggression, which includes an act of aggression to be "the sending by or on behalf of a state of armed bands, groups, irregulars or mercenaries, which carry out acts of armed force against another state" but decided to drop the reference to the state's substantial involvement within such acts. The Congolese government therefore had its state responsibility waived and Uganda consequently had no right to use force in self-defense. Some legal writers disagree with this distinction for 'failed' or 'feeble' states (Reisman 1999, Paust 2002, Gazzini 2005).

The *Oil Platforms Case* also stated that the burden of proof showing the existence of an armed attack lay with the state wishing to act in self-defense. Yet, University of Pittsburgh's Jules Lobel, criticizing the 1998 US missile strikes against Sudan and Afghanistan argued that "international law cannot allow a nation to attack another based on a self-serving, unilateral characterization of facts not subject to multilateral investigation" (1999: 539). Some argued the evidence of responsibility must come from the Security Council (Cassese 2001: 1000). Yet, with little intelligence mechanisms, the Security Council would have to continue to rely on evidence provided by member states. The actual need for hard evidence has been rejected, not only by some writers on the subject, but also the US. The *NSS 2002* argues for pre-emptive action against terrorist groups, refusing to wait for what America's Gregory Maggs refers to as "perfect proof [which] may negate [states] right of self-defense altogether" (2006: 164). There was little controversy over the source and reliability of evidence in 2001; that would change after the invasion of Iraq.

NATO Secretary-General George Robertson (2001) claimed there was 'clear and compelling' evidence linking *Al-Qaeda* to the attacks. The US and UK both offered evidence which many accepted did meet the "clear and stringent evidentiary standard designed to assure the world community" (Lobel 1999: 547) required by the *Nicaragua* judgment and international lawyers said is required before the use of force (Blair 2001a, Negroponte 2001). This probably explains the lower level of controversy regarding the non-UN authorized nature of the intervention. Having quickly attributed responsibility to *Al-Qaeda*, the connection between *Al-Qaeda* and Afghanistan was assumed on simple fact the former was located there and openly tolerated. The Taliban government only provided sanctuary in return for large financial payment. There was no suggestion by the US or anyone it controlled *Al-Qaeda* or directed the attacks. Yet, Bush warned that "from this day forward, any nation that continues to harbor or support terrorism will be regarded by the United States as a hostile regime" (2001b) and again, "if you harbor terrorists, you are terrorists. If you train or arm a terrorist, you are a terrorist. If you feed a terrorist or fund a terrorist, you are a terrorist, and you will be held accountable by the United States and our friends" (2001e). The level of Afghan involvement was at the lower end of the scale of responsibility but US action still did not cause much controversy.

The use of force against Afghanistan also clearly went beyond the traditional limits – in time and scale – of incursions into the territorial integrity of another state in order to eliminate terrorists, similar to limited interventions in failed states and for humanitarian reasons (Travalio 2000: 166). The intervention led not only to a change in government but also resulted in a long-term military occupation of the country of almost a decade to date. In strict terms, this was a fundamental violation of political independence, at least in terms of the Taliban government, leaving aside whether it was justified. Prior to 2001, only Pakistan, Saudi Arabia and the United Arab Emirate had recognized the Taliban government and they severed diplomatic ties with it after September 11 (Walker 2002: 504–505). As there was little international support for the Taliban, there were few objections to its overthrow.

The use of force against Afghanistan has undoubtedly resulted in the notion of self-defense being "a broader, more uncertain concept than it was previously" (Garwood-Gowers 2004: 18). This has happened not only by the interpretation of terrorist attacks as constituting armed attacks under Article 51 but also by lowering the level of control by a state over a terrorist group for state responsibility to be invoked. Some legal writers support taking a broad view. Maggs (2006: 173–74) claims that both the UN and ICJ have since 1986 attempted to impose 'dangerous' restrictions on state's right to self-defense with Wedgewood likening the limitations to a straightjacket (2005: 61). University of New South Wales academic Devika Hovell questions the novelty of the terrorism threat and challenges the need for a "reinvention, or even abandonment, of the current international legal order" (2004: 399) J.M. Beard strongly disagrees with this position concluding that for self-defense to have any meaning in the contemporary international system "international law should not be interpreted to prohibit the United States from exercising its inherent right of self-defense" against not only terrorists but also states which support them (2002: 590).

Yet, a number of observers believe that further use of force against such states without authorization by the Security Council or a regional organization would be impermissible and "risks undermining the foundations of the international public order which the reaction intends to protect" (Dupuy 2004: 16). The Austrian reaction to Sarajevo's terrorism caused a world war: some fear this could happen again.

The US use of force against Afghanistan might have received wide-spread support amongst both writers and governments. Yet, it appears that rather than creating new customary law, this was an exception to the rule: states being unlikely to accept such an action again unless perhaps a similar spectacular incident occurs. State practice following the invasion of Afghanistan reflects the view that, unless terrorist acts are of a large scale and directly attributable to a state, which has neglected its responsibility to restrict terrorist activities on its territory or itself uses terrorism, the use of force is not seen as acceptable.

Russia, following the bombing of Moscow apartment buildings (1999), a hostage taking in a Moscow theatre (2002), the seizure in a school in Beslan (2004) and further attacks, began to mirror the US's and Israel's claim to a right to self-defense in response to terrorist attacks (Lavrow 2004). Russia also echoed the US' assertion of a right to use force pre-emptively, vowing to use all "necessary means ... to avert the terrorist threat" (British Broadcasting Corporation 2002b). Moscow's particular focus remains on Chechen groups based in Georgia, a US-friendly state in a region of growing competition for important energy reserves. Ironically, the US has warned Russia not to use force against this state thereby lessening the chance of a Russian action which might reinforce the legitimacy of the US claim to a right of pre-emption (Sestanovich 2002: 14).

Even the US's practice since Afghanistan suggests it has drawn back from challenging the rules on the use of force on the grounds of terrorist attacks. In the lead up to the invasion of Iraq, the US certainly mentioned Iraq's alleged state support of terrorism. Bush (2002d) stated "as a condition for ending the Persian Gulf War, the Iraqi regime was required [among other things] ... to stop all support for terrorist groups". Days before the invasion, Bush also said "the regime ... has aided, trained and harbored terrorists, including operatives of Al-Qaeda", arguing that terrorists could use chemical, biological and nuclear weapons acquired through the support of the Iraqi government to kill large amounts of people in the US and elsewhere. Bush implied direct cooperation between the Iraqi government and terrorist organizations, arguing that inaction of the US and international community would allow the alleged allies to begin a deadly conflict. Consequently Bush (2003b) states that the US would "choose to meet that threat now, where it arises, before it can appear suddenly in our skies and cities". Yet when the invasion was launched, this rhetoric served only as a background political not legal justification, which instead relied essentially on Iraq's defiance of Security Council resolutions.

Summary

Terrorism, in its various forms, has been of concern to states for more than two centuries. Yet the international community continues to struggle with ways of addressing the issue. During the 19th and early 20th century the focus remained on domestic law enforcement mechanisms, with varying degrees of success. The First World War demonstrated, however, that terrorism often had a distinct transnational nature to it. This development increased in the post-Cold War period with numerous left-wing and national-separatist movements. Consequently, the first international regulations regarding terrorism came into existence. The understanding of what actually constituted an attack justifying self-defense, however, continued to differ greatly. As a result states, particularly in the post-Cold War era, began to counter terrorism using a number of approaches, including criminal procedures, armed force and in few instances action through the collective security mechanism of the UN.

University of Cambridge academic Kimberley N. Trapp argues that state practice today reflects the international community's recognition of a right to self-defense "targeting non-state actors in foreign territory or to the extent that the foreign state cannot be relied on to prevent or suppress terrorist activities" (2007: 156). Other observers agree, claiming that the right to invoke Article 51 against states supporting or harboring terrorists is increasingly being recognized as 'applicable law' (2002: 67). Following the scale of terrorist attacks (such as September 11) over the last decade and the continuing threat of future incidents support for an expanded right of self-defense to counter terrorism is supported by many. The actual use of force and threat thereof against alleged terrorist groups by Israel and Russia, however, has found less widespread support.

Particularly since the end of the Cold War state practice has substantially challenged the existing rules by using force, often through large-scale military operations, to counter terrorism. American Tom Farer completely opposes this development stating that with regard to using military means against terrorism "there is simply no cosmopolitan body of respectable legal opinion that could be invoked to support so broad a conception of self-defense" (2002: 359). There indeed continues to be a widespread perception, that the military use of force, says US academic Greg Travalio, "inevitably carries with it the risk of escalation" (2000: 179). So far states attacked as part of counter terrorists strikes either have not had the ability to react forcefully (Afghanistan and Lebanon) or have refrained from so doing (Syria). This is something which, however, cannot be taken for granted. Thus it is likely the UN and the majority of states will continue to uphold a restrictive view of the right of self-defense in the case of terrorist attacks, sponsored or not.

Chapter 10

The (Un)Usual Suspects: The Use of Force against Rogue States

While the use of force against so-called rogue states is a rare occurrence, the phrase has, in all its variations been used in international relations since 1918 as, says Robert S. Litwak, "an efficient political shorthand that leaves no doubt about a country's place in the world of nations" (2000a: B3). The term, however, can be rather misleading as it is not so much the state's population which is rogue but, rather, its government. By equating a rogue government with a rogue state, the use of force against such a country has been justified.

Known as revisionist powers during the inter-war years, rogue states (or nations as they are sometimes referred to) are a label which associates states with inherently negative characteristics, alienating them from other members of the international system. Exactly what these characteristics are, depends on the circumstances of the respective era. They range from a states' wish to reverse the territorial *status quo* during the inter-war years to their support for terrorist groups, as well as the possession, development, pursuance or proliferation of WMD in the contemporary international system. What all these characteristics have in common, is the implication such revisionist and, later, rogue states violating what are perceived as standards of acceptable international behavior of the time. International standards today are seen as being those norms defined in the UN Charter, as well as other international treaties and law.

Since the end of the Cold War the phrase rogue states has been actively embraced as an important corner stone of US foreign policy under both the presidencies of Democrat Bill Clinton (1992–2000) and Republican George W. Bush (2000–2008). There is a wide-spread claim in the literature on the subject that the concept of rogue states has merely replaced one enemy image (that of the former Soviet Union) with a new one. This view is reflected in the US government's own *NSS* (2002) where the concept was officially endorsed and acted upon the following year with the use of force against Iraq by a US-led *ad hoc* coalition. While this intervention has been the only instance of the use of force against a rogue state to date, examining action against these types of states is crucial.

This is due to the concept being a crucial aspect of one of the world's most powerful countries and particularly because of Bush's (2002b) announcement to "oppose them [rogue states] with all our power". This, at least initially, implied the possibility of the US using force against more than just one so-called rogue state.

This chapter aims to examine the development of the concept of rogue states, looking at its origins and then focusing in particular on its usage in the post-Cold

War era. While the phrase has received much attention, it is a concept which currently really only is embraced by the US and, to a lesser degree, its allies in the war against Iraq, notably the UK and Australia.

The subjectivity of the concept, as well as its narrow embrace by the international community, means the future use of force against such types of states will be questioned. While state practice, as has been shown in previous chapters, is capable of challenging the established rules governing the international use of force, to do so it has to be embraced by numerous states, used frequently and implemented consistently, with a notion that it is legally justified.

Unless the international community finds a widely accepted definition of what exactly constitutes a rogue state, other than the vague assessment that they are states, said former British Foreign Secretary Jack Straw (2003) "who know no rules" and according to the *NSS* "hate the United States and everything for which it stands" (2002: 14), the use of force against such countries stands on shaky grounds. As this chapter will show the use of force against rogue states may rattle the cage of the established rules for the international use of force but by no means threatens to topple it.

Reforming a Killer

> [Germany] is a rogue nation, so bad that it has forfeited its right to live and the rest of humanity should not feel called upon to take the risk and assume the task of reforming an incorrigible and incurable killer. (Westbrook Pegler 1942: A)

The *Oxford English Dictionary* dates the first mention of the phrase 'rogue state' to the article *Confrontation in Lebanon* in *The Washington Post* in 1973 in reference to Syria. This is incorrect. The phrase 'rogue nation', which tends to be used interchangeably with the one of 'rogue state', makes its first appearance in a 1942 article of *The Los Angeles Times*. That description of Germany as a rogue nation, its character and behavior being described as "incorrigible and incurable", bears many similarities to the current understanding of rogue states (Pegler 1942). Until the end of the Second World War the reference to Germany as a rogue nation remains the only usage of this phrase. More widely used were the idioms of 'bandit' and 'outlaw' nations, as well as the less prejudicial revisionist powers, a phrase particularly popular in the 1920s and 1930s. Originally, the idea of the sovereign equality of states was qualified by the frequent suggestion non-European states were not equals. Lorimer's notion of civilized, barbarous and savage humanity was already being rooted. 'Savage' humanity relates to 'failed' states today. 'Barbarous' humanity relates to 'rogue' states today (1872: 101–102).

While Britain, as a participant in the Boer War, was described by the German media as the "bandit nation of the world" (Editorial 1899), it was largely Germany for whom this phrase was used (Always a Bandit Nation 1917). According to Philip Marshall Brown, Professor of International Law at Princeton writing during the

First World War, Germany was an outlaw nation which "knows no law except the law of his own will". The war, said Brown, therefore had to be fought in defense of international law and order, a status threatened by Germany (1918: 165).

Following the end of the First World War, bandit and outlaw states were viewed as states acting in disregard of the League of Nations Covenant and other important treaties such as the Kellogg-Briand Pact. Former US President William Howard Taft (1919) referred to such states as covenant-breaking nations, stressing the widely held belief that there was a need to boycott such offenders and, if necessary, use force against them. Amongst others, Italy was referred to as an outlaw state following its invasion of Ethiopia in 1935 (Gibbslondon 1935).

The phrases bandit and outlaw nations, as well as revisionist powers and, later, rogue nations, only gained meaning through the establishment and codification of international law. When this process started, it was non-European states – the Ottoman Empire and China – which were seen as outside 'civilized' international law. Within Europe, the concept of a 'barbarous' state was slower to develop.

Prior to the Geneva Convention of 1864, the Hague Conventions (1899 and 1907) and the League of Nations Covenant, in particular, states' coercive behavior in international relations did not tend to be regulated. Without existing rules, no violations could take place. States could not be condemned as outlaws if there was no international law to break. Once states, according to American Professor of Law at the University of Texas Charles G. Haines, found "a justification for the primacy of international law in the existing legal relations between states" it was possible to classify a state to be acting outside of or in violation of the laws (1936: 858).

The violation or challenge to one piece of law, the Versailles Treaty of 1919, pre-occupied states and legal scholars alike. The defeated of the First World War, most notably Italy, Germany, Austria, Hungary and Bulgaria, felt that the Versailles Treaty had been a dictated rather than a negotiated peace.

Germany, having been accorded the sole responsibility for the First World War in Article 231 of the Versailles Treaty, bore the brunt of the settlement's regulations. While the territorial concessions of Versailles resulted in the loss of former colonies and the withdrawing of state boundaries, it also included clauses, which according to John Hopkins University's Valentine De Balla resulted in "one-sided disarmament, and economic strangulation" (1932: 24).

As the five core defeated states of the First World War began to voice their dissatisfaction with the conditions of the 1919 peace settlement, the phrase 'revisionist powers' was introduced to refer to them (De Balla 1932: 49). This idiom described states challenging the conditions of the Versailles Treaty, in particular its territorial clauses, and calling for a revision of the agreement. Due to their territorial ambitions revisionist states were also sometimes referred to as expansionist states (Varè 1936).

Germany found it particularly difficult to meet the reparation payments stipulated in the treaty and together with its unequal treatment as a member of the international community, grew more resentful. Together with Italy, it was amongst the biggest proponents of treaty revision, a move opposed by the anti-revisionist bloc made up of France, Belgium, Poland, Czechoslovakia, Yugoslavia and Rumania. These states feared both the rearmament and renewed expansion of Germany (leading to a loss of territories allocated to them under the Versailles and associated treaties) and therefore endorsed the view that "revision means war" (Callender 1933).

The tension was diffused temporarily in 1925 when Germany's Foreign Minister, Gustav Stresemann, embraced the necessity for his country to join the Locarno Pact. Stresemann saw the main aims of Germany as including the amendment of its Eastern frontiers and "a settlement of the reparation problems in a manner tolerable for Germany and safeguarding peace" (Steed 1933: 126–27). The agreement, signed between Germany, France and Belgium, with the UK and Italy acting as guarantors, was essentially a non-aggression pact. In addition, its Article 1 restated "the maintenance of the territorial *status quo*" regarding Germany's western borders, an issue particularly important to France and Belgium, it did not restrict Germany's claim on it eastern borders. While it was not an all-out win for Germany, the Pact paved the way for Germany to regain admittance to the society of nations, joining the League in 1926. For a brief period this led to a normalization of relations between revisionist and non-revisionist states. Indeed, the importance attached to the Locarno Pact as a means of improving diplomatic relations was reflected in the award of the Nobel Peace Price to the Pact's key negotiators Austen Chamberlain (1925), Arisitide Briand and Gustav Stresemann (1926). Following Locarno only Russia was viewed as a bandit nation (Editorial 1926).

The Great Depression of 1929 added to Germany's economic hardship as it struggled to meet reparation payments. Combined with the restrictive political (disarmament) and territorial clauses of the Versailles Treaty, German Chancellor Heinrich Brüning (1930–1932) stressed the need for his country to emerge "from the dishonorable condition of legal and factual inferiority to equality and freedom with the community of nations" (Editorial 1932). Many states and legal scholars appeared sympathetic to Germany's plight, *The Times* acknowledging that "there will be no real tranquility in Europe until the question of revision has been boldly faced and settled one way or another" (Editorial 1933).

When Adolf Hitler became Chancellor in 1933 Germany began to pursue a more forceful path towards treaty revision, starting with its withdrawal from the League of Nations. According to Sisley Huddleston (1934), a British journalist later accused of collaborating with the Vichy regime, Germany had grown "tired of being promised jam tomorrow but never jam today".

The further step in the new path towards treaty revision was the signing of the Four-Power Pact of 1933. A watered down version of Benito Mussolini's original proposal, France, Britain, Italy and Germany confirmed their adherence to the League of Nations Covenant and enforcing aspects of it which related "to such matters as preservation of nations' integrity, sanctions and treaty revision" (Press Wireless 1933). It aimed not only at treaty revisions but also at disempowering the smaller states in the League of Nations. The UK, through Prime Minister Austen Chamberlain, argued, however, that in light of the German regime's persecution of Jews, "this is not a Germany to which we can afford to make concessions" (Callender 1933). He was pessimistic regarding the peaceful intentions of the revisionist states.

In order to once again avoid potential military confrontations, the UK and other major powers entered the Munich Agreement of 1938 which transferred the Sudetenland to Germany. Observers at the time appeared optimistic about this move suggesting that Chamberlain had "recalled the pronouncement of outlawry" and had ensured that "there are no bandits nations [instead] they are restored to grace and fellowship" (Chamberlain Accepts the Dictators 1938). In the end, however, the aspirations of the revisionist states resulted in the resort to force. French writer Romain Rolland's warning of 1931 that "Germany, rubbed raw ... is starved and will not bear this repression more than a year or two without social and national convulsions that will make the Western World tremble" became a reality a year after the Munich Agreement (1931: 445).

With Nazi-Germany's invasion of Poland in 1939, its description as a revisionist power no longer appeared sufficient. Instead, it had gone beyond the mere revision of the territorial *status quo* imposed on it following the First World War. Hitler-led Germany had launched an all out war not only against other states in Europe and abroad but also against its own people, persecuting religious and political minorities, as well as any group which did not comply with its view of a 'national socialist' society.

Germany, as one of initially many revisionist powers, was called the world's first rogue nation. It had not adhered to the legal regulations of the day which included arbitration as a preclude to the use of force and the prohibition of aggressive wars. During the inter-war year, it was revisionist states which resorted to force, rather than force being used against them by other members of the international system, as is the case today.

Misfits and Looney Tunes

> We're especially not going to tolerate these attacks from outlaw states run by the strangest collection of misfits, looney tunes, and squalid criminals since the advent of the Third Reich. (Ronald Reagan 1985: 9)

The Cold War era, for its first thirty years, was marked by the absence of the concept of rogue states. Writing in *The Los Angeles Times* in 1961 America's Alexander Holmes stated the belief that "to most of the world, Germany is still a rogue nation which has not changed its cruel, criminal nature" (1961: B5). Apart from this reference, it is not until the 1970s and the crisis in Lebanon that the phrase regained more widespread usage. *The Washington Post*'s 1973 Article *Confrontation in Lebanon* appears to be the first written usage of the term 'rogue state' as opposed to rogue nation. In the article Syria is described as a "rogue state which once again has sponsored an invasion of an Arab neighbor", referring to its support for Palestinian groups located in Lebanon. Even then the term rogue nation or rogue state is a little found phrase during the Cold War period.

A search of US newspapers, including *The New York Times* and *The Washington Post*, shows that there are a mere fifteen mentions of the term 'rogue state(s)' during the Cold War, a number which skyrockets to more than 500 in the era from 1990–2003 alone. The term 'rogue nation(s)' appears eleven times during the Cold War and more than 200 times in the post-Cold War era. *The Times* reflects a similar picture with small numbers during the Cold War era, and a substantial increase post-1990.

The explanation for this is rather simple. During the more intense periods of superpower rivalry between the US and Soviet Union, the opposing sides and their allies were referred to as Communists or Capitalists/Imperialists, not rogues. Each was the others enemy but they were in a group of states and so were not 'rogue'. With the relaxation of relations between the two superpowers in the 1970s, an era known as *détente*, the phrase 'rogue state' (often used interchangeably with 'outlaw states') resurfaced in international relations along with the new term 'pariah state'.

There was a certain need to appear more restrained when condemning actions and behavior by states, while seen as Soviet allies, by declaring them rogue or outlaw states instead of linking them directly with the Soviet Union. In addition, there was the need to find a term for states attempting to acquire WMD, in particular nuclear weapons, and sponsoring or harboring terrorists. The term 'pariah states' became popular during the 1970 and early 1980s before attention was shifted to a new breed, the rogue or outlaw state.

America's George H. Quester defines a pariah state as "a regime winning little or no sympathy in the outside world, while being threatened with an imminent military conquest by neighbors" (1981: 223). Amongst these so-called pariah states in the 1970s and 1980s were the non-Communist states South Africa, Taiwan, South Korea, Israel and to a lesser degree Pakistan (Harkavy 1981: 136). These states, having no rear alliances and faced with grave security threats, were seen as seeking to acquire nuclear weapons for their defense (Dowty: 1978: 115).

Kurt Waldheim, former UN Secretary-General (1972–1981) disagreed with the widely held belief that these so-called pariah states, most notably South Africa, criticized by the international community for its apartheid policy, should be dealt with through ostracism. Waldheim believed that "the United Nations has nothing to gain by the creation of a class of pariah states", lobbying instead a need to establish a dialogue with them "however indefensible [their] conduct [may be]" (1984: 102–103).

Pariah states and their pursuit of nuclear weapons presented a particular problem in the 1970s as the US and Soviet Union worked towards an agreement on arms control. While the superpowers aimed at limiting the spread of nuclear weapons, most notably due to their need for reducing the cost of defense and fear of random strikes, pariah states fell out of line by wanting to expand the spread of such weapons. This raised awareness of the need, argued America's Alan Dowty, to go beyond the focus on conventional military balances and towards "the problems of isolated 'pariah' states in antiproliferation strategy" (1978: 79). Indeed, agreements such as the *Test Ban Treaty* (1963), *Non-Proliferation Treaty* (1968) and *Strategic Arms Limitation Talks* (1969–1972; 1972–1979) would lose significance if so-called pariah states pursued nuclear weapons, thereby upsetting the bipolar power balance favored by the US and Soviet Union. Falk, writing about the need to establish a no-first-use pledge regarding nuclear weapons, predicted that "pariah states may prove more reluctant than superpowers to make such a declaration, as only the former face a severe security threat and lack the national capacity to evolve any substitute for nuclear weapons" (1977: 87).

With the exception of Israel, which came under attack from Egypt and Syria in 1973, in what came to be known as the Yom Kippur War, force was not used against pariah states. Although their pursuit of nuclear weapons proved irritating at times, the major and regional powers, as well as regional organizations and UN, did not consider them a threat sufficient enough to use force against them. Instead, there were "widely-held external perceptions of [a pariah state] as a temporary state scheduled for history's rubbish heap" (Harkavy 1981: 139).

The end of *détente* in 1979, ushered in by a change in US government (Reagan), as well as the Iranian Hostage Crisis and Soviet invasion of Afghanistan, saw the substitution of the fear about pariah states with the one of rogue or outlaw states even as the Cold War revived. The core concern now appeared to be state-sponsored terrorism and the possibility of WMD being passed on to such terrorist groups by rogue states.

The core rogue states of the 1980s according to Reagan included non-Western orientated Libya, Iran, North Korea, Cuba, Nicaragua and Syria (1985: 9). The latter was removed from the list after its President Hafez al-Assad's negotiated the release of American hostages in Beirut following the hijacking of a plane on route from Athens to Rome in 1980. Prior to that, Syria had been accused by the US as a state-sponsor of terrorism, particularly focusing on its involvement in the politics of Lebanon and support of Palestinian organizations (Fisk 1986). While Syria, Cuba and Nicaragua featured on the US list of rogue states against whom covert action was undertaken, overt force was only used with regard to Libya and Iran.

Iran did not really feature on the list of states with which the US was concerned until the Iranian revolution of 1979 which saw the ousting of the US-supported Shah Mohammad Reza Pahlavi and the establishment of an Islamic republic under Ayatollah Khomeini. The same year the US-embassy in Teheran was stormed by a group of radical students who took staff hostage, holding them captive for more than eighteen months. In light of the Iranian government's reluctance to secure the hostages release, Carter launched a failed rescue attempt in 1980 (as discussed in Chapter 5). The unsuccessful operation and, said American academic Robert H. Kupperman, the US' "diplomatic and military failures in dealing with the terrorist tactics of that rogue nation resulted in national humiliation" (1982: C5). It also resulted in this incident being the only attempt by the US at using force against Iran, a state it now considered a rogue.

Libya's status as a rogue state was coupled strongly to its alleged involvement in two core terrorist attacks during the 1980s. Amongst them was the bombing of a disco in Berlin, frequented by American servicemen (1986), and the Lockerbie bombing (1988). For years following these incident Qadhafi was seen as, said American journalist Brian Duffy, an "international outlaw, condemned for his wide-ranging support of terrorism" (1986: 26). In response to the Berlin bombing Reagan authorized air strikes against military installations and suspected terrorist facilities in Libya. The state was accused of supporting a number of terrorist organizations, amongst them Palestinian groups, a sponsorship viewed as "weapons of 'proxy' war by states seeking cost-effective and secret means of weakening enemy states" (Wilkinson 1978: 12). These connections also gave rise to a fear of weapons acquired by such rogue nations being passed on to terrorist organizations supported by them (O'Toole 1979, Nye 1982). Despite these concerns the use of force against Libya remained limited to a number of interdictions by US military forces in 1986 and again in 1989.

While the main concern with states such as Libya, and to some degree, Syria and Iran, focused on their alleged connections to terrorist groups, there was also the US-held perception that these states were also Soviet 'clients' (Singer 1989, Kissinger 1986). Therefore, the term rogue or outlaw states was used not only to refer to countries which were allies of the Soviet Union but also to those sponsoring terrorism or attempting to acquire WMD (and possibly passing these on to terrorist organizations).

The Cold War era demonstrates that, while force was used against states considered as rogues, namely Iran and Libya, the format was limited to interdiction, rather than full-blown intervention. This changed with the use of force against Iraq in the post-Cold War era. The next section will examine not only this incident but also show how the denomination of rogue states can change. Once a rogue state does not mean always a rogue state, as both Syria and later Libya experienced, provided these states no longer, said America's Kupperman and Van Opstal, "refuse to adhere to the most basic covenants of international relations-abound" (1983: 74).

Walking Sticks and Weapons

> It is impossible to distinguish between offensive and defensive nuclear missiles and aircrafts as between offensive and defensive walking sticks. The offensive or defensive character never lies in the weapon, but in its use. (Georg Schwarzenberger (1963: 8)

The concept of rogue states was embraced even more intensely after the end of the Cold War due to the absence of the former prime enemy, the Soviet Union. Indeed,

Clinton in 1996 declared that "defeating these organized forces of destruction [rogue states] is one of the most important challenges our country faces at the end of this century and the beginning of the next". This move towards a new image of the enemy formed a corner stone of US foreign policy not only under Clinton (1992–2000) but also Bush (2000–2008).

Antony Lake, Special Assistant to Clinton for National Security Affairs, played an essential part in forming this policy stance, stating that US policy "must face the reality of recalcitrant and outlaw states that not only choose to remain outside the family but also assault its basic values" (1994: 45). Madeleine Albright (1997a, 1997b) also described rogue states as a serious threat to the international system. Based on this perceived menace, the US Congress in 1998 established the Commission to Assess the Ballistic Missile Threat to the United States, headed by Rumsfeld. The Commission concluded that "concerted efforts by a number of overtly or potentially hostile nations to acquire ballistic missiles with biological or nuclear payloads pose a growing threat to the United States, its deployed forces and its friends and allies". This included the estimation that there was a real possibility that within the near future, North Korea and other rogue states would be able to launch Intercontinental Ballistic Missiles (ICBM) against the US.

As a consequence of this assessment, Clinton proposed the establishment of a National Missile Defense (NMD) system to counter such possible missile attacks, particularly by the three core rogues North Korea, Iraq and Iran. This NMD proposal appeared very reminiscent of Reagan's 1983 Strategic Defense Initiative (SDI), more widely known as 'star wars'. Ultimately, however, the decision to establish such a NMD was not made during the Clinton administration and was left to the Bush government.

By the late 1990s, it appeared that Cold War defense policies, aimed this time at rogue states instead of the Soviet Union, had made a comeback. Rogue states, in place of the second former superpower were now held responsible for the continuing arms race. This condemnatory language, however, changed temporarily towards the end of the Clinton presidency. In June 2000 Secretary of State Madeline Albright announced that the phrase rogue state was to be substituted with the more subtle idiom of 'states of concern'. This shift was based on a perceived need on behalf of the US to recognize certain steps undertaken by rogue governments, such as the elections held in Iran and Libya's cooperation regarding the Lockerbie bombing trial (Boucher 2000). When America's Michael Klare pronounced that the previous seven years had been the "golden age of the rogue doctrine", he was unaware of the significance it would play under the Bush administration, climaxing ultimately in the use of force against the rogue state of Iraq in 2003 (1998: 13).

In his State of the Union Address in 2002, Bush had declared the three core rogue states, Iran, Iraq and North Korea as constituting an 'Axis of Evil', "arming to threaten the peace of the world [and] by seeking weapons of mass destruction, these regimes pose a grave and growing danger". Very much a reflection of Reagan's language and his classification of the Soviet Union as an 'Evil Empire',

Bush (2002a) stressed the possibility of an attack resulting from these rogue states, stating that "the price of indifference would be catastrophic".

The Bush administration's intent to act forcefully, if need be, against such rogue states became clear when in the same year it withdrew from the *Anti-Ballistic Missile Treaty* (1972), concluding that it hindered "our government's ability to develop ways to protect our people from future terrorist or rogue-state missile attacks" (Bush 2001g). This belief was strongly supported by Colin Powell, Chairman of the Joint Chiefs of Staff, in his call for the necessity of a missile defense shield to protect both the US and its allies from rogue states (Osborn 2001).

The Post-Cold War era, in many ways, can be seen as a continuation of the previous two decades with regard to the denomination of rogue states. The list of rogue states includes the 'usual suspects', namely Iran, Iraq, North Korea, Libya and (to a lesser extent) Cuba. It furthermore continues to focus on two core alleged policies of these states, that is the acquiring or development of WMD, as well as the support or sponsorship of terrorism. Despite these consistencies the term now, more than ever, said Litwak (2000a), "has become an elastic catch phrase that is used to demonize behavior and rally political support".

Critics of the US' use of the concept have argued that since the violation of acceptable standards of international behavior is seen as the smallest common denominator in the classification of rogue states, every country disregarding such standards of behavior should be classified as a rogue (Chancellor 2002). This would include, argue some, countries such as Australia under John Howard, for demanding concessions to the Kyoto Treaty on the prevention of global warming, or the US for opposing the ICC (Forsythe 2002).

Seeing that the definition leaves room for interpretation, the classification of states as rogues often lies in the eye of the beholder. The US, for example, currently views states which "hate the United States and everything for which it stands" (Government of the USA 2002: 18) as rogues and, hence, as threats to both their national security and world peace. North Korea, in return, views the US as the "most rogue and scoundrel state in the world" (Chol 2000).

This arbitrariness or political nature of definition can be seen as the core problem of the concept and is something also raised by its critics such as Fidel Castro (2002). The deciding factor for justifying the use of force through the concept of rogue states is that in international relations, as in other areas, things are rarely black and white or universally agreed upon. Why should, objectively speaking, Iran be condemned as a rogue state for pursuing a nuclear energy program and the UK not? Why is the rhetoric used to describe some state leaders pursuing nuclear weapons, for example Saddam Hussein's portrayal as a "homicidal dictator who is addicted to weapons of mass destruction" (Bush 2002d), different to that of other leaders of nations, such as India or Pakistan, which possess nuclear weapons?

The literature on the concept of rogue states reveals three core studies which have been undertaken to shed light on these questions by attempting to establish the classification, policies and behavior of such states.

Paul Hoyt (2000), looking at official documents and statements by American policy makers in the period 1993–1998, including reports such as *Proliferation Threat and Reponse* establishes the existence of five core rogues, that is Iran, Iraq, Libya, North Korea and Cuba. America's Mary Caprioli and Peter Trumbore go one step further by differentiating between what they describe as rhetorical rogues and objective rogues. Rhetorical rogues are states identified as such by policy makers while objective rogues meet 'objective' terrorism and WMD criteria as reflected in documents such as the US governments *Patterns of Global Terrorism*, as well as publications and data from the Carnegie Endowment for Peace and SIPRI (Caprioli and Trumbore 2005: 780).

The states categorized as rhetorical rogues are identical to Hoyt's (2000) list. Expanding the list to include objective rogues, however, one suddenly finds incorporated not only many US foes (Syria) but also allies or friends. This includes states such as Israel, India, Pakistan and South Korea. Consequently, Caprioli and Trumbore's study shows that "the relationship between state behavior and the application of the rogue label ... is neither automatic nor absolute [and is instead] based on the idiosyncratic views of these states amongst policy-makers" (Hoyt 2000: 310).

Nothing makes this clearer than an examination of the US *NSS* 2002's classification of rogue states. This identifies as rogue, states which are seen to disregard international law, sponsor terrorism, acquire WMDs, as well as reject basic human values. While these criteria appear, at least at first glance, as more or less 'objective' measures, it is the final one which mirrors the subjectivity of the concept. The call to classify states which dislike the US and its values as rogues is one which is unlikely to find acceptance outside of the very country which proposed it.

Generally speaking one concludes from the three studies and policy documents such as the *NSS 2002* that rhetorical rogues have a number of issues in common. They are mostly Arab, led by authoritarian regimes and, as America's Ehsan Ahrari (2001: 86) points out challenge the *status quo* in their region. Ahrari's assessment bears many parallels to the situation of revisionist powers during the 1920s and 1930s and their wish to challenge the victors of the First World War and the territorial, economic and political conditions imposed on them.

Having identified which states classify as rogues both rhetorically and objectively, it is also important to examine their policies. Hoyt divides the policies pursued by rogue states, in order of relevance, into four categories: the development of WMDs, posing of a regionally or global military threat, involvement in international terrorism, and challenging international norms (2000: 303).

As the development of WMDs is closely linked to the posing of a threat and the challenge of international norms, K.P. O'Reilly's 2007 study appears more helpful for this section. He, following in Hoyt's footsteps, focuses only on two policies of rogue states, that is the acquiring and/or development of WMD and the support and/or sponsorship of terrorism. His study shows that the acquiring or developing of WMD, constituting the policy associated with rogue states in 84 per cent of the cases, is clearly the main concern (2007: 306). It is, however, not so much the actual threat of the possession of such weapons which is the issue. Instead, in the mind of (particularly American) policy makers, says O'Reilly "concerns about the future threat posed by rogues far exceeds that of current power capabilities" (2007: 311).

The study also analyses the behavior of rogue states, finding that threatening and outlaw behavior are the two core characteristics of such states with which policy makers are concerned. Consequently, the main power held by rogue states is implication. Such states says Oxford University's Glen Segell "invoke fear and terror by appearing that they have something to hide" (2003: 484). So while Caprioli and Trumbore's study shows that rogue states "are not more aggressive, at least in terms of conventional military action, that other types of states", it is the 'fear of the unknown' which characterizes the threat stemming from such states (2005: 784).

A state's classification as a rogue, as both the past and present show, does not, however, have to be permanent. In 1999, for example, the US stopped labeling Libya a rogue after it surrendered two secret agents who were deemed responsible for the Lockerbie incident of 1988. Following the terror attacks of September 11, Libya furthermore offered its support to the US, signed the International Code of Conduct against Ballistic Missile Proliferation (2002) and in 2003 admitted that it planned to give up its secret WMD program.

Pakistan, too, aligned itself with the US in 2001, announcing that it would crack down on terrorist activities in its territories and assist the US in its war against terror. King's College London academic Alison Pargeter sees this behavior or change in attitude as motivated by a "need to restore international credibility in order to bring investment" (2005: 6). Israeli professor Barry Rubin (1999a) had earlier argued the success of non-forceful means in returning such outcast states from their "international equivalent of incarceration or commitment to a mental institution".

Consequently, the states listed by the US as rogues have been keen on ridding themselves of this status and have been largely attempting to do so (Sung 1991, Permanent Mission of Libya 2001a and 2001b, Khatami 2002). Iran has (at times at least) condemned terrorism. North Korea, who Brookings Institute's Joel Wit says is "the poster child for rogue states", has been stating disarmament and abolition of WMD are vital for ensuring peace (2001: 77). Despite these efforts to be welcomed back into the family of the international community's 'good' nations, their attempt has, so far, been fruitless. The primary reason for this being that the two states pursue a carrot and stick strategy. At times they make concessions to the international community before again resorting to sabre-rattling.

The concept of rogue states, it has to be stressed again, is one which is not generally recognized, neither by international law nor the international community as a whole. It is a propaganda 'soundbyte' rather than a legal or policy concept. According to America's Colin Dueck, while the concept "does capture certain undeniable realities ... it has more to do with American political culture than with international law" (2006: 224). Consequently, policy action toward these states varies depending on whether they originate from and are undertaken by the UN or the US.

The UN has taken a more generalized approach, addressing the problem of the proliferation of WMD rather than the idiom of rogue states. Similar to Kurt Waldheim's statement with regard to the UN's attitude towards pariah states, the international community generally speaking continues to believe that "the language of the rogue state ... inhibits constructive dialogue" (Rankin 2003: 52). Despite this reluctance to ostracize certain governments through the use of such language, the UN recognizes the need to deal with states who refuse to comply with the regulation, monitoring and verification aspects of the Non-Proliferation Treaty and various other agreements. In 1992 the President of the Security Council, on behalf of the members of the council, stated that "the proliferation of all weapons of mass destruction constitutes a threat to international peace and security" (UNSC 1992a). This was confirmed in Security Council Resolution 1540 which requires states to criminalize the proliferation of WMD, focusing particularly on the need to prevent the passing of such weapons to non-state actors.

In addition to these general policy statements, the UN has focused on sanctions, described by Chesterman and Pouligny as being "somewhere between statements and soldiers", as one core way of dealing with non-compliant states under the collective security framework (2003: 516). Sanctions which can be diplomatic, economic and military in nature, have enabled the UN to reprimand not only states declared as rogues by the US but also those not listed but nevertheless acquiring WMD, such as India and Pakistan (UNSC 1997b).

While the core states of concern remain Iran, North Korea and originally Iraq, all of which have had sanctions placed on them, this framework allows a more comprehensive penalizing of governments which exhibit internationally unacceptable behavior. According to Harvard University's Meghan O'Sullivan "sanctions mandated by the United Nations also carry the weight of international condemnation, which rarely provides a 'rogue' leader with the political tool that unilateral American denunciation does" (2000: 58–9).

While the UN has focused on diplomatic and economic sanctions to discipline states which acquire or proliferate WMD, the US has tended to focus on a whole range of strategies. Dueck (2006), building on Litwak's strategies, lists five such ways of dealing with rogue states: appeasement, engagement, containment, rollback and non-entanglement.

In addition to its establishment of a missile defense shield, the US has focused largely on the containment and engagement options with regard to governments it declares rogues (O'Reilly 2007: 309). The aim of using these strategies is to use political and economic means to create levels of cooperation with rogue states (engagement), as well as containing them through the creation of military and diplomatic counterbalances and generally quarantining them from the international system as a whole (Dueck 2006: 225–27). Rollback, that is the use of military force is often seen as appropriate for dealing with a rogue state which "does not react predictably to deterrence or other tools of diplomacy and statecraft" (Rubin 1999a: 72).

Klare predicted that the US would eventually be forced to back up such military rhetoric with action, suggesting, however, that "it would be a terrible mistake to assume that the next Desert Storm will produce as rapid and lopsided a victory as the last one did" (1995: 628). This prediction is eerily reflected in the current Vietnam-like quagmire situation in which the US finds itself in Iraq.

Until the use of force against Iraq in 2003, the rollback option involving military force was only used in form of interdiction. These included armed strikes on two occasions: first, against Sudan on suspicion of having a chemical weapons factory (1998); and secondly against Iraq (1998) for its refusal to continue cooperating with UN weapons inspectors.

The reason for the lack of armed responses to rogue states lies in the fact that they are, says Dueck, "most costly and risk prone (and when such action) fails, it tends to fail spectacularly" (2006: 228–29). While the US emerged largely unscathed from the first two instances of armed force against a rogue state, it was not so lucky the third time round.

The use of force in March 2003 against Iraq by the US, UK, Australia and Poland, was justified on the grounds of disarming a rogue state in terms of WMD (Howard 2003, Blair 2003, Bush 2003c). By linking terrorism to countries pursuing or possessing weapons of mass destruction, Bush (2001f) managed to portray Iraq as a source of violence in the international system, the removal of which was depicted as enhancing international security and stability and, thereby, world peace.

As part of arguing their case for the use of force against Iraq, the US government, as well as countless politicians, political scientists and the media, used the concept of rogue states to conjure up images of the Second World War and the consequences which appeasement, in terms of lack of action against potential threats, can have (Bush 2002c, Eccleston and Wilson 2003). This is convenient as the crimes of the Second World War are largely associated with individuals such as Hitler or Mussolini. Contemporary rogue states, too, are identified with one core leader. The personification of evil and the comparison of Hussein, Qadhafi or Kim Jong Il to the likes of Hitler is achieved. The threats associated with Hitler or the Second World War are conjured up. Interestingly enough, the opposite has also been the case with the Coalition of the Willing being likened to the coalition between Germany, Italy, Japan and, to a lesser extent the Soviet Union, in 1939 (Moir 2003). As a consequence, the use of force against rogue states quickly becomes more about removing an illegitimate and evil ruler rather than breaching another country's sovereignty, right to non-interference or world peace.

Although the logic of ridding the world from rogue states could, theoretically, be understandable, what further diminishes the credibility of the US' embrace of the concept, is the clear lack of consistency, even within the US specific definition, in its application. Why was force used against Iraq on what, today, seems false allegations of WMD? Why was the use of force not directed against other rogue states such as North Korea which has been accused of drug trafficking and has admitted to having nuclear weapons ambitions? Why has there been a lack of military intervention in Syria which has been accused of supporting radical groups such as *Hezbollah* and *Hamas*, as well as possessing chemical weapons and where the threat of proliferation of WMD to terrorists seems much greater?

The answer appears to lie in the simple fact that Iraq was "the weakest link in the axis of evil and, therefore, much easier to deal with" (Shumilin 2003: 33). Starting with Security Council Resolution 687 which demanded that Iraq "shall unconditionally accept the destruction, removal, or rendering harmless all weapons of mass destruction", the Hussein government had a long history of defying UN Resolutions. This disregard towards international norms reached, in the eyes of the US, its climax when Iraq did not comply fully with the Security Council Resolution 1441 (2002) which called for the full and immediate compliance by the Iraqi regime with its disarmament obligations.

Following more than a decade of containment policies which included a permanent military presence in the region, the creation of no-fly zones, the sending of UN weapons inspectors, economic sanctions, and the financial and material support of Hussein opponents, the US decided in March 2003 to opt for military measures and full-blown intervention.

Dueck argues that due to the containment policies pursued since 1991 Iraq "was in no condition to threaten or attack its neighbors" (2006: 231), a view opposed by the Bush administration. In his address to the nation prior to the intervention in Iraq, Bush (2003b) stated the government's belief that "peaceful efforts to disarm the Iraqi regime have failed again and again" and that in case of inaction "in one year, or five years, the power of Iraq to inflict harm on all free nations would be multiplied many times over".

The use of force against Iraq was initially seen by many as an "ideologically perfect result" by combining an end to the threat Iraq supposedly posed to world peace with the hope of deterring other rogue states from acquiring weapons of mass destruction (Pfaff 2001). One can assume that the US government was hoping for a follow-on effect, namely that the use of force against Iraq would serve as a warning and result in other rogue states changing their behavior. Paul Kelly, an Australian journalist, reflected this view well in his assessment of North Korea's possible reaction to the use of force against Iraq: "Imagine what the paranoid Pyongyang mob thinks as it watches footage of US troops in the ruins of Hussein's palaces. It's obvious: we're next!" (2003a: 11). While the use of force against Iraq must have clearly effected states such as Iran and North Korea, the reaction, six years after Iraq, appears to be a converse one of increased pursuit of WMD as a way of guaranteeing non-interference in its affairs, rather than their surrendering.

This reaction of other rogue states, together with the revocation by the US of the original threat assessment regarding Iraq, admitting that the Iraq Survey Group, as well as a bipartisan commission and a number of congressional investigations had found that "pre-war intelligence estimates of Iraqi WMD stockpiles were wrong" (NSS 2006: 23), means further use of force against rogue states is unlikely.

It almost appears as though the US only had, in every sense of the word, one shot to fire to establish the credibility of its concept of rogue states. In light of this 'backfiring' and the Vietnam-like quagmire which has now developed in Iraq, it is unlikely that the US will consider using full-blown intervention against another rogue state (Bush 2003g). Instead, the US administration will probably show an increased focus on diplomatic solutions, economic sanctions, covert action and, on rare occasions, minor interdiction.

The use of force against Iraq showed that, according to Segell, "the mere alleged acquisition, without any stated intent, of WMDs and delivery systems ... designated a threat to local, regional and global stability and security" does not appear sufficient to warrant the use of force (2003: 479). The risk of receiving false information and becoming involved in a long-term armed conflict now appear too high.

Observers of the concept of rogue states disagree with regard to its chances of survival. Whereas Rubin (1999b) says the concept is far from losing its importance, French philosopher Jacques Derrida (2003) predicts that its end is near, stating that "the concept has reached its limitations, its time has come".

Strange as it may seem both may be right. Whereas no definite conclusion can be drawn, in the long term the concept of this type of state is unlikely to have a future and establishing itself as a permanent and accepted justification for the use of force, let alone leading to changes in international law or the UN Charter to accommodate it.

The reason for this is that the concept is, to an extent, a simplification of complex situations in international relations by dividing the world into good and evil and is, due to its arbitrary definition and inconsistent application, primarily used to justify and further the narrow interests of specific countries. In addition, the rogue state, as an image of the enemy, is likely to fail. While international arms control is not the focus of this book, it is important to point out that the concept of rogue states is not an adequate one to deal with the problems in this field and non-compliance to such control. As Jennifer Rankin points out that "naming and shaming countries such as Iraq, Iran, Libya and Cuba did not alter their behavior, except perhaps to make them more hostile to the US" (2003: 51).

The supposed irrelevance of the phrase in the short term is also questionable. It is too easy to identify state sponsors of terrorism, as discussed in Chapter 9, as rogues and use them as rationalization not only to further national interests but also to deny the fear and panic over the fact that threats in the contemporary international environment can no longer be controlled or moderated by a single state or possibly even states in general. This is something reflected not only in US policy towards Iraq and other accused rogue states but also, for example, Russia's threat to label Georgia a 'rogue' unless it committed itself, says the official version issued by Mikhail Margelov, to oppose terrorism seriously (Georgia May End up as Rogue State 2002).

It shows that the concept of rogues is still widely used in international relations in the 21st century.

The US is continuing to use the concept but it is confronted with two core problems. First, the lack of support this concept is receiving from the international community (especially in the aftermath of the Iraq War). Second, the fact that, as Klare points out, many see states which are declared as rogues by the US as being "insufficiently menacing [and have not] engaged in unambiguously aggressive behavior since 1990" (1998: 14).

As implied in the introductory quote to this section by Schwarzenberger, the mere possession of WMD is not automatically equivalent to their future offensive use. While the label of rogue states may be equivalent to what Rubin (1999a) calls "a certificate of political insanity", with leaders hostile to the international community as a whole and the US in particular, they are nevertheless strategic and are likely to "weigh the costs and benefits of their own behavior within a given international framework" (Dueck 2006: 240).

This section has shown that the concept of rogue states used to justify the use of force outside the established one of self-defense stands on shaky grounds. This is due to its unclear definition, inconsistent application, as well as the dated parallels it draws and images it uses. If there was a desire to make the concept more appealing internationally and implemented more widely and consistently, there would be a need, says Arend, "to develop a set of rules relating to the use of force that will truly criminalize the behavior of rogue regimes" (2003b: 752). This bears great similarities to other issues raised in this book, most notably the need to establish a definition of terrorism and major human rights abuses, in order to make the international use of force in such instances more acceptable and justifiable. The establishment of any such rules, of course, argues Arend, presupposes the need for states to accept the universality of such regulations and to "understand that a rule-bases regime must apply to them (democratic states) as well" (2003b: 752). Whether governments are willing to do this instead of establishing their own definitions to suit their respective policies is questionable.

Summary

As a consequence of the emergence of modern international law there have always been a group of states which, based on their behavior, have been ostracized from the international community. Originally referred to as barbarous, outlaw, bandit or revisionist powers, as well as pariahs and rogues, these states have been a constant component of international relations for the past century. By either disregarding international law or challenging the status quo regarding the power distribution in the international system such states are classified as rogues. Rogue states tend to be on the receiving end of the use of force, rather than exercising it itself. An exception to this, however, also exists when in the 1930s the revisionist powers Germany and Italy resorted to force to reverse the territorial and political status quo.

The Cold War era only experienced the use of the concept of rogue states from the 1970s onwards when relations with the Soviet Union were relaxing and a new enemy image was employed. While embraced by the US, it was an idiom rejected by the UN which stressed the need for dialogue rather than exclusion. Since the 1990s in general and the use of force against Iraq in particular it has become increasingly clear that the concept of rogue states, says Caprioli and Trumbore, "seem to be at best a questionable foundation on which to build general foreign policy and defense policies" (2005: 788).

The concept of rogue states is so highly politicized that including it in any substantial manner into international law appears impossible and doomed for failure. While the US maintains a selective approach to the subject, says journalist Mike Clough (1999), "harshly denounc[ing] some dictators and cautiously woo[ing] others" it will be difficult to build international support for the concept.

Admittedly, as Condoleezza Rice stated, the US never strove for a one-size-fits-all policy (Emperor, Shedding Clothes 2003). However, treating rogues which seemingly pose a greater threat in different ways, supports claims by critics that the US' use of the concept to justify the use of force also serves a number of other policies, such as the pursuit of a NMD System and the government's defense spendings in general (Glaser and Fetter 2001, Eland and Lee 2001). In addition, it is seen as a way of legitimizing a global order as envisaged by the US and its wish for a "balance of power which favors freedom" in which the US continues to play a hegemonic role (Rice 2002). A term also previously used by former US President Johnson to justify the war against Vietnam (1971: 43). By arguing that other countries opposed to this role and disliked by the US cannot possess WMD, the US position of supreme military strenght and as the world's sole superpower, can be sustained.

Conclusion: The Road (Not) Taken

> Two roads diverged in a wood, and I –
> I took the one less traveled by,
> And that made all the difference.
>
> Robert Frost (1916: 9)

At the outset of this book George H.W. Bush was cited in 1990 when he welcomed and predicted a new world order in which the established rules of state conduct would be obeyed. This book concludes that the past two decades have reflected a very different reality.

The nature of current armed conflict suggests interesting implications for the international rules covering the use of force. The current legal regime developed with the notion that the prevalent form of armed conflict was between states. Instead, the post-Cold War era is dominated by intra-state conflicts, meaning those rules are often not the most relevant. Although conflict between states is rare, if it does occur, as was the case with the US-led intervention in Iraq, such use of force can have substantial repercussions for the rules as the analysis in Parts II and III showed.

The controversy surrounding the challenges to the long-established legal regime on the international use of force is captured nowhere better as in the former German Foreign Minister Joschka Fischer's statement. Made in response to Rumsfeld's case for war against Iraq Fischer clearly declared "Excuse me, I am not convinced" (Connolly 2003). Fischer was not persuaded by the evidence and reasons tabled by the US Secretary of Defense for intervening militarily in Iraq. Germany, which held the presidency of the Security Council at the time, like many other states, remained deeply skeptical not only with regard to the evidence but also the legal justifications presented. Annan agreed, stating in the aftermath of the war, that he believed "it was not in conformity with the UN Charter from our point of view, from the charter point of view, it was illegal" (British Broadcasting Corporation 2004).

The introduction to this book outlined that for state practice to be defined as custom, according to Brierly, it must "in its legal sense [mean] something more than mere habit or usage; it is a usage felt by those who follow it to be an obligatory one" (1963: 59). For state practice to be accepted as such it must furthermore be viewed by other states as constituting legally obligatory action. If state practice does not achieve wide-spread acceptance, it will merely be viewed as an attempt at unilateral law-making and, indeed, law breaking. The acceptance or rejection of state practice and its challenge to the long-established legal regime, however, is not always as clear as in Fischer's and Annan's statements.

As discussed in the body of this book a government's or organization's lack of condemnation regarding certain state practice does not automatically denote its acceptance of the action. Similarly, a government refraining from using such justifications itself does not consequentially indicate its rejection of such state practice. Indeed, the ICJ's predecessor, the PCIJ, in the *Case of the S.S. Lotus* argued that, "for only if such abstention were based on [states] being conscious of having a duty to abstain would it be possible to speak of an international custom" (1927: 28).

Governments' acceptance of state practice as constituting a new customary rule or legal behavior is therefore reflected most clearly if a combination of criteria are met: first, the practice is not rejected as illegal by the majority of states, particularly powerful ones; second, other governments embrace the practice of the state or states in question by undertaking it themselves; third, international and regional organizations endorse the practice either in statements or in action. This acceptance is conditional on state practice being viewed as either filling a gap or rectifying a perceived deficiency in existing international law. Acquiescence is also dependent on the practice being seen as furthering the stabilization rather than eroding of world order by allowing individual states to breach the law.

This book has shown that the international community is witnessing an interesting phenomenon. States' justifications for the use of force on humanitarian grounds, largely based on the argument that it represents not so much a legally but a morally binding obligation, have been more widely accepted than the use of force on expanded notions of self-defense. Here, state practice was largely undertaken in the belief that it constituted an extension of an existing legal regulation and was therefore permissible; a belief not embraced by the majority of states or international and regional organizations.

Part I examined the development of the regulation of violence from the 17th century through to the post-Cold War era. The religious notion of just war was replaced by the rules of secular international law. While state practice during this time was usually guided by the legal regime, it did not necessarily always coincide exactly with these rules, as is the case today. Instead, the arrival of the concept of sovereignty lead to the paradox between doctrines of interference and non-interference.

Prior to the First World War, the main concern of rules of war was with the restraint of violence in war rather than the use of force itself. With the commencement of the First World War there was a wide recognition that it was necessary to also establish a framework determining the legality of states' resort to force. At the forefront of this development was the push towards the establishment of an arbitration process. There was a further suggestion by some states that wars of aggression constituted a crime.

The interwar years witnessed the further development of international law on the use of force, most notably in the form of non-intervention and renunciation of war treaties. The establishment of the League of Nations and signing of the Kellogg-Briand Pact represented the two most important events of the time. The

League, however, did not totally outlaw the use of force. The notion of self-defense was established as a legal resort to force but remained undefined. The concept of collective security existed but no machinery for it was created.

Terrorism, on the other hand, was defined but its convention not ratified with the exception of British India. Similarly, the international legal regime had no practical framework for controversial humanitarian interventions which occurred. International law, during the two world wars, moved the justifications for the use of force from political to legal grounds. Yet, the significant rules established were supported by states more in theory than in practice. Nothing exemplified the disregard for the legal regime more than the commencement of the Second World War.

The Cold War era saw the restriction of the use of force to a never before seen level. Military action was now only allowed in instances of individual and collective self-defense and if authorized by the Security Council. This, again, constituted a paradox: to replace self-help as the doctrine of non-intervention was both strengthened and challenged by the enhancement of the notion of collective security. This concept was also reflected in the establishment of regional organizations which were aimed at complementing UN enforcement action. Due to superpower rivalry and the resulting stalemate in the Security Council, collective security, however, was not as successful as originally anticipated. Instead, the US and Soviet Union acted outside of the UN, always multilaterally, in most instances within the framework of regional organizations such as the Warsaw Pact, OAS or OECS. Some other states like Israel, Tanzania, India and Vietnam acted unilaterally. Despite the questionable use of the justification of individual and collective self-defense, such rationalization actually confirmed states' acceptance of the existing legal regime. State practice during the Cold War period did not explicitly reject the legal rules mapped out in 1945, operating instead within their confines.

Overall, the post-Cold War era has seen a substantial softening of the concept of sovereignty. While the notion was never truly absolute in the sense that it was sometimes seen as not applying to 'non-civilized' and 'feeble' territories, today's interpretation differs from those of the past. Sovereignty in practice is no longer a guaranteed attribute of states. Instead the right to non-interference is conditional on a state's behavior, most notably the adequate treatment of its citizens. Sovereignty may furthermore be 'suspended' in effect, if the government itself or conditions within the state, constitute a threat to international peace and security. The doctrine of intervention has consequently been expanded but made conditional on the use of force being collective.

Following the period immediately after the end of the Cold War, there seemed to be clear signs of a shift towards and growth of multilateralism including under UN auspices. The prime example cited in this latter respect was the multinational and UN-authorized use of force against Iraq in 1990. With the end of superpower rivalry, which had regularly led to a deadlock in the Security Council, collective security and with it multilateralism was seen as have been given a new lease on life albeit not as broadly as first envisaged at the start of the 1990s. Regional organizations have also had some greater effectiveness with NATO intervening in Yugoslavia in 1999. Where the first two multilateral paths have been seen as impossible or undesirable, *ad hoc* coalitions have been used such as the US-led interventions in Afghanistan and Iraq so as to give at least a *patina* of legitimacy in an world which frowns on unilateral uses of force.

Despite the recognition that sovereignty is conditional and collective action desirable states have, through the use of these six additional justifications, come up against the restrictions of established international law. They have therefore moved their justifications to a different discourse: just war. By using just war language to 'muddy the waters', intervening states have attempted to assign to their actions if not legality then at least a degree of legitimacy. A wider field of justifications reflects the wider field of threats in the current international system. While some of them are, as examined in Part II and III of this book, justified on an expanded interpretation of the legal right to self-defense, others are on the moral basis of humanitarian reasons.

A Road across a Vacant Land

The reaction to the use of force for humanitarian reasons, depending on which of the three respective sub-categories has been used, has ranged from seemingly complete acceptance, to apparent indifference and wide-spread controversy.

In the contemporary international system the forcible protection of nationals abroad is a little debated topic. Over the decades, the protection of a state's citizens has developed from a controversial intervention by former colonial powers to an undertaking the principle of which, no longer requires legal justification. It is also an action which tends to be questioned neither by the UN nor other regional organizations. This change is closely linked to the altered nature of such interventions. Today such action is usually termed a rescue mission, combining both forcible and non-armed means, for short term and low-level troop deployments. In addition, it tends to take place either with the consent of the host state or in the absence of an existing and functional government capable of granting such permission. Current state practice has consequently managed to challenge the established rules governing the international use of force in the sense that the protection of nationals abroad is not viewed as violating the territorial integrity and political independence of a state. Rather, it appears to be a low-level use of force which slips under the radar screen of Article 2(4). The protection of nationals abroad, rather than attacking the validity of the doctrine of non-intervention, attempts to confirm it by limiting the extent and time force is used.

State practice in this instance largely reflects the character of customary international law as described by Charles de Visscher, a Belgian academic and judge on the PCIJ. He argued that the "slow growth of international custom has been compared to the gradual formation of a road across vacant land". He continued, initially, "the tracks are many and uncertain, scarcely visible on the ground. Then most users, for some reason of common utility, follow the same line; a single path becomes clear, which in turn gives place to a road henceforth recognized as the only regular way, though it is impossible to say at what precise moment the latter change took place" (1968: 147). The lack of controversy which has surrounded the treading of this path regarding protection of nationals in the post-Cold War era has been very different to the one of humanitarian intervention.

Whereas there have been attempts by governments to stress that the use of force based on the justification of humanitarian intervention does not impinge on the territorial integrity and political independence of the respective state, practice presents a very different picture. Instances of humanitarian intervention tend to result either in a change of government or in some instances, such as Bangladesh and Kosovo, in the creation of a new sovereign state. The use of force in these cases consequently represents a fundamental challenge to Article 2(4) which is not only a core component of the UN Charter but also *jus cogens*. Not only do states attack this peremptory norm of general international law, they also do not concentrate exclusively on justifying their practice as *opinio juris*. Intervening states do not necessarily claim that their behavior is undertaken on the basis that it is a legal obligation but rather because it is a moral necessity. Objectively speaking, this means that such state practice would not have any chance of being accepted as a new customary rule. Instead, humanitarian intervention is one of the few justifications for the use of force which has found increasing acceptance by the international community, so much so that the UN at its 2005 World Summit adopted the principles of the ICISS report.

Humanitarian intervention in recent years has been elevated to being an almost mandatory, rather than a prohibited or permissive, use of force. Since 2001, however, this progress in legitimizing, if not legalizing, humanitarian intervention has not been met by state practice. Instead, governments have exhibited caution regarding the use of force in such instances following the contested use of the concept in Iraq and Afghanistan. States appear to have been restricting their own behavior following the perception that the attempt at establishing a customary law has possibly occurred too quickly.

The concept of humanitarian intervention has successfully challenged, nevertheless, Article 2(4) and Article 2(7) by states arguing that: first, the protection of human rights is equal, if not superior, to state sovereignty; second, large scale killings, genocide and ethnic cleansing are of international concern and no longer matters which are essentially within the domestic jurisdiction of a state. Rather than viewing states' entitlement to non-interference as an unquestioned right, it is seen as being conditional on a government's adequate treatment of its citizens. In instances in which this is not the case, either because a government is not able or willing, the state forfeits its right to non-interference and Article 2(4) is 'suspended' to halt or avert the large scale loss of life. Considering the pre-eminence of the doctrine of non-intervention this constitutes a substantial, albeit largely accepted, challenge to the long-established legal-regime on the international use of force.

The metaphorical road of humanitarian intervention may have been, in the words of American poet Robert Frost, the 'one less traveled by' in the 21st century. Yet, it is still in existence and maintained by states in theory if not necessarily in practice. Of course, the principle in practice is applied more often to weaker and smaller rather than large strong states.

The use of force in so-called failed states presents a similar picture to humanitarian intervention. Conditions in such states, however, tend to remain ignored until they have reached international proportions through cross-border flow of refugees, criminal activities or the use of their territory as a safe havens by terrorists. In addition, intervention is closely linked to a humanitarian crisis being in existence. The use of force in failed states therefore displays a substantial overlap with the issues of both counter terrorism (discussed below) and humanitarian intervention.

The doctrine of non-intervention and, with it, Article 2(4) is not only viewed as being temporarily suspended due to the humanitarian crisis in question. It is also considered as not necessarily applying to failed states. This a concept but not a phrase international law has recognized since the 19th century at least. Such states are seen as no longer meeting all four criteria of statehood as outlined in the Montevideo Convention of 1933. While they may still have a permanent population and a defined territory, they often do not have a central government which is in control over the entire territory and population with the capacity to enter into relations with other states. Failed states can therefore often neither endorse nor reject interventions into their territory. Yet, intervening states attempt to allocate their use of force legality by attaining the consent of either the government if it exists or in the absence of it, the major warring factions.

So while the use of force in failed states constitutes an attack in terms of Article 2(4), such action has tended to be covered either under the justification of humanitarian intervention or the use of force by consent. The failed states in question often do not have the means to voice their rejection or concern, meaning intervention in such states is not a widely debated topic. Instead, intervening states have had little interest in officially challenging the legal regime with regard to failed states and have preferred to operate in an *ad hoc* fashion. Rather than questioning the doctrine of non-intervention, intervening states view their actions as an exception to the rule undertaken in instances in which states, lacking effective government or allowing gross human rights abuses, temporarily do not hold sovereignty and with it a right to non-interference. Yet, even the assumption that it is up to individual governments or groups of states to determine whether a state is entitled to a right to non-interference, is alone a challenge to the established legal-regime and world order. This controversy, however, has largely been overshadowed by the fact that intervention in failed states is: first, closely linked to the justification of humanitarian intervention; second, often undertaken by (sometimes controversial) consent; third, frequently accompanied by peacekeeping operations undertaken either by the UN itself or regional organizations.

Challenging the Establishment

The use of force for self-defense in instances of pre-emption, counter-terrorism and rogue states has been undertaken in the belief that it is a mere expansion of the already existing legal rule of self-defense. The existence of the law itself is not questioned, only its scope. Yet, by pushing for an expanded notion of individual and collective self-defense, states have challenged three fundamental rules of international law: first, Article 2(4) which prohibits the use of force; second, Article 51 which makes self-defense following an armed attack the only exception to this rule outside Security Council authorization; third, Article 39 which leaves it to the Security Council, not individual states, to determine the existence of any threat to the peace, breach of the peace, or act of aggression.

These three articles form, with customary international law in the background, a clear framework within which violence by states has been largely conducted for the past sixty years. The maintenance of world order has relied on it significantly. The challenge to these rules by state practice, most notably by powerful states and particularly over the past decade, has been viewed with great skepticism and concern. The core reason for this is that such acts have constituted a fine line between alleged defensive and aggressive measures. The latter has been considered a crime since the end of the First World War. States are consequently, eager to present their actions as *opinio juris* rather than driven by selfish political, economic or strategic concerns. The use of force in instances of pre-emption, counter terrorism and rogue states has, however, not been accepted as constituting a legally binding action by the majority of states.

The concept of pre-emption has received wide-spread verbal endorsement by US policy makers but found little practical implementation. Pre-emption, as one of the cornerstones of the 'Bush Doctrine', was controversially advocated in the lead-up to the Iraq intervention. While the belief in the legitimacy of the concept was a clear driving force behind the decision to intervene, it was not put forward as a legal justification. While the US leadership clearly believed in the existence of such a right, it appeared to view its use as a sole justification as too high-risk. This was due to two reasons: first, it was not a concept which enjoyed wide-spread international acceptance, resulting in the high likelihood of its legality being questioned; second; the use of the concept could have opened the door to the few states which did embrace it (at least partially), Russia, India and Pakistan, also employing it as a legal justification. The US was, instead, focused on ensuring that pre-emption remained an exclusive right which only it could invoke. Such an attempt at unilateral law-making is highly unlikely to be accepted in the interdependent world of today. This is something even the US itself must have recognized.

In the end, the detrimental effects of pushing for an incorporation of pre-emption into the existing legal regime for the use of force appeared to outweigh the benefits. State practice, particularly by the US, therefore appeared self-regulating, not least of all because of the intelligence on which the first 'pre-emptive intervention' in Iraq was based, challenged and largely discredited the concept. Together with the two above mentioned reasons, practical experience removed much of the credibility from the concept of pre-emption, let alone a push for its incorporation into international law. What may have initially been planned as a substantial attack on the rules, quickly fizzled out to a temporary challenge. While it cannot be ruled out that such pre-emptive action will occur again, it is likely to be confined to the targeting of specific installations or terrorist camps, rather than full-out intervention as was the case in Iraq.

The use of force to counter terrorism, both against terrorist groups and states supporting or tolerating them, has re-emerged as an important issue in the 21st century. Usually states focus on taking criminal law enforcement measures and in some instances direct limited military action against terrorists. Intervention in the territory of another state, on the basis that it has not fulfilled its responsibility to stop terrorist attacks emanating from its borders, is less frequent though its legality has a long respectable pedigree. When it does occur, as has been the case with Israel in Lebanon and to a lesser extent the US-led intervention in Afghanistan, it is controversial. The reason for this lies particularly with the intervening states' interpretation of Article 51.

In order to justify the use of force against a state accused of supporting terrorist groups, either directly or indirectly, three core legal issues must be addressed: first, whether attacks by non-state actors actually do constitute an armed attack; second, what gravity of violence is necessary to constitute an armed attack; third, what degree of state involvement is necessary to meet the standard of self-defense following an armed attack.

The ICJ has indicated that the invocation of Article 51 is based on such an armed attack emanating from a state rather than a non-state actor. The majority of states have embraced this view, concentrating on criminal law enforcement means to persecute terrorists rather than the use of force. This is also the avenue, together with sanctions the UN has taken, if direct state involvement or support can be established. Terrorism is largely viewed as a criminal matter rather than one which permits the invocation of Article 51. In some instances, limited targeted strikes are, if not openly endorsed, then at least silently accepted.

The large-scale intervention undertaken in Afghanistan is likely to remain the exception. States appear to accept that an expanded notion of both armed attack and self-defense to counter terrorism forcefully bears substantial risks. To date, states which have been the subject of intervention or strikes either have not had the ability to react forcefully or refrained from so doing. The outbreak of the First World War over claims of state-sponsored terrorism shows, however, that the use of force to counter terrorist attacks can potentially lead to more large scale conflicts. The majority of states therefore uphold a restrictive view of the right of self-defense in such cases.

The use of force against so-called rogue states has been similarly controversial, least of all because the concept is highly subjective. While generally speaking the term applies to states which disregard international law, the concept appears primarily focused on states which challenge the *status quo* regarding the regional or international distribution of power. Rogue states is an idiom rejected by most, including the UN, which instead stresses the need for dialogue with rather than exclusion of such states. In some instances, there is a perceived need to employ sanctions as a sign of disapproval for a state's behavior. Military means are, however, rarely embraced. Consequently, the concept of rogue states, while used as a basis for foreign policy, is not used as a stand alone justification for the use of force. Instead and similar to pre-emption, it is used in connection with a disregard for UN resolutions, alleged aggressive behavior or disregard for human rights.

The highly politicized nature of the concept has meant that even states endorsing it, most notably the US, have not attempted to push for its official incorporation into international law. There are two core reasons for this: first, apart from Australia under Howard and Britain under Blair, few states have endorsed the doctrine; second, as the concept is highly subjective, states endorsing it prefer fluid criteria rather than clearly established legal principles on the concept. The former enables states to legitimize global order as they see fit, rather than using force according to 'objectively' established criteria. The use of the concept of both pre-emption and rogue states with regard to the use of force is viewed, even by exercising states, as an exception to the rule rather than a wish to attack fundamentally the doctrines of non-intervention and self-defense. In the end, their protection rather than undermining is far more advantageous to states.

Under Attack

Writing on the unilateral use of force outside of the UN framework, Byers and Chesterman argue that "the greatest threat to an international rule of law lies not in the occasional breach of that law ... but in attempts to mould that law to accommodate the shifting practices of the powerful" (2003: 203). The challenges by state practice to the long-established legal regime governing the international use of force have naturally been posed by such powerful states, most notably the US and UK. While the international legal regime often has scope for the accommodation of the use of force, reflected in the six additional justifications, action through the UN framework this is not always the preferred option of states. Instead, by declaring the UN unable and unfit to deal with the new principles for the recourse to force, as well as the 'threats of a new era', states challenge the rules for the use of force (Bush 2003a). Consequently, often it is not so much the legal system which is the problem but the political will of states which has led to the under-utilization or abuse of existing rules.

In conclusion, states do not always act within the framework of established international law but in some instances prefer to go down the road 'less traveled'. With regard to the justifications for the use of force on humanitarian grounds, this has made all the difference. State practice has challenged the legal regime by showing gaps in its framework and attempting to plug these, albeit often through the use of the just war discourse rather than law. The justifications based on an expanded notion of self-defense, have been viewed critically and are likely to remain paths only traveled occasionally and by a small number of states. These justifications are viewed as violating existing law rather than establishing new rules.

As demonstrated in this book, there has always been an uneasy dynamic in the relationship between the established international rules and state practice. In theory, of course, the two should coincide. In reality they regularly do not. State practice in the post-Cold War era has undoubtedly challenged the established rules for the international use of force. States have not, however, been able to attack fundamentally the long-established legal regime in the sense that the Charter has not been rewritten. The majority of states accept that the legal regime in existence is crucial for the upholding of international order. They believe that substantial attacks on this order are more detrimental than beneficial.

This stance was, perhaps, reflected in a very symbolic way with the award of the Nobel Peace Prize to US President Barack Obama in 2009. The Nobel Committee announced that the prize had been awarded for Obama's "extraordinary efforts to strengthen international diplomacy and cooperation between peoples". The fact that the US President had only been in office ten days prior to the nomination deadline, implies the prize was awarded more for the intentions voiced by Obama, rather than any actual accomplishments. While this has resulted in much criticism, the message entailed is powerful. Voicing support for Obama's values and attitudes, most notably his promotion of multilateral diplomacy and a central role for the UN, is not even an implied but an explicit criticism of the previous Bush administration's policies. It reflects the awkwardness with which the international community at large has grappled including but not limited to the way Bush previously challenged the framework within which violence by states has been largely conducted for the past sixty years.

Yet, even Obama in his Nobel lecture questioned the adequacy of the established legal regime in countering 'new' security threats. He argued that force, particulary on humanitarian grounds, is sometimes necessary, stating that "instruments of war do have a role in preserving peace". While calling upon states to adhere to the 'standards' governing the use of force and to strengthen the UN Charter framework, Obama did reserve the US' right to act unilaterally if necessary. A change of government alone, as the President's speech demonstrated, does not stop the relevance of the 'old architecture', that is the old legal regime, from being questioned.

Consequently, the issue of how to effectively address many of the current threats to the international system within an advocated multilateral and UN regulated framework alone, remains largely unresolved. This applies both to military and non-forceful means.

What is needed, as Falk rightly argues in his foreword, is a 'new agreed discourse on international force' and the consistent implementation of such rules. As long as the existing rules continue to be viewed by some as lacking in effectiveness or appropriateness and until these concerns have been addressed more successfully, states will continue to challenge the present legal regime. Therefore international law regulating the use of force will remain, for the foreseeable future and to varying degrees, ‘under attack’.

Bibliography

1881. The suppression of terrorism: the movement for combined European action spreading. *The New York Times*, 30 March, 1.

1917. Always a bandit nation. *The Los Angeles Times*, 16 June, II4.

1938. Chamberlain accepts the dictators. *Chicago Daily Tribune*, 19 April, 12.

1941. Sees U.S.-Britain union for peace. *The Baltimore News-Post*, 8 December.

1949. Address by President Truman and Foreign Ministers at signing of North Atlantic Treaty Pact. *The New York Times*, 5 April, 6.

1973. Confrontation in Lebanon. *The Washington Post*, 8 May, A22.

2002. Georgia may end up as rogue state. *Pravda* [Online, 7 August] Available at: http://english.pravda.ru/cis/2002/08/07/34034.html [accessed: 19 July 2007].

2003. Emperor, shedding clothes? Foreign policy. *The Economist* [Online, 18 January] Available at: http://www.economist.com/world/unitedstates/displaystory.cfm?story_id=E1_TVPRNTJ&source=login_payBarrier [accessed: 28 March 2008].

Abraham, G. and Hopkins, K. 2002. Bombing for humanity: The American response to the 11 September attacks and the plea of self-defence. *The South African Law Journal*, 119(4), 783–801.

Ad Hoc Committee on International Terrorism. 1979. *Report of the Ad Hoc Committee on International Terrorism*, A/34/37, New York: United Nations.

Ad Hoc Committee on Terrorism. 1973. *Draft Report of the Ad Hoc Committee on Terrorism*, A/AC.160/L.3, New York: United Nations.

Adam, H.M. 1995. Somalia: A terrible beauty being born? in *Collapsed States: The Disintegration and Restoration of Legitimate Authority*, edited by I.W. Zartman. London: Lynne Rienner Publishers, 69–90.

Adebajo, A. and Landsberg, C. 2002. The heirs of Nkrumah: Africa's new interventionist. *Pugwash Occasional Papers, No.1* [Online, January] Available at: http://:www.pugwash.org/publication/op/opv2n1.htm [accessed: 23 March 2007].

African Union. 2003. Communique of the ninety-first ordinary session of the central organ of the mechanism for conflict prevention, management and resolution at ambassadorial level. *African Union* [Online] Available at: http://www.africa-union.org/News_Events/Communiques.htm [accessed: 7 May 2007].

Agence France-Presse. 1998. Kofi Annan faults states 'individual actions' against terrorism. *Agence France-Presse*, 21 September.

Agence France-Presse. 2004. Putin says Russia 'seriously' preparing preventive strikes, rejects talks. *Agence France-Presse*, 17 September.

Agwu, A. 2000. Militants reign because the state has failed. *Lagos Post Express*, 24 July.

Ahrari, M.E. 2001. Rogue states and NMD/TMD: policies in search of rationale? *Mediterranean Quarterly*, 12(2), 83–100.

Ajaj, A.M. 1993. Humanitarian intervention: second reading of the Charter of the United Nations. *Arab Law Quarterly*, 7(4), 215–36.

Akehurst, M. 1984. Humanitarian intervention, in *Intervention in World Politics*, edited by H. Bull. Oxford: Oxford University Press, 95–118.

Akihiko, T. 2002. *The New Middle Ages: The World System in the 21st Century.* Tokyo: The International House of Japan.

Al-Kadhe, A.M. 2002a. *Identical Letters dated 14 January 2002 from the Charge d'Affaires A.I. of the Permanent Mission of Iraq to the United Nations Addressed to the Secretary-General and to the President of the Security Council*, S/2002/61, New York: United Nations.

Al-Kadhe, A.M. 2002b. *Identical Letters dated 5 February 2002 from the Charge d'Affaires A.I. of the Permanent Mission of Iraq to the United Nations Addressed to the Secretary-General and to the President of the Security Council, S/2002/150*, New York: United Nations.

Albright, M. 1993. *Letter dated 26 June 1993 from the Permanent Representative of the United States of America to the United Nations Addressed to the President of the Security Council*, S/26003, New York: United Nations Document.

Albright, M. 1997a. International economic leadership: keeping America on the right track for the Twenty-First Century. *Secretary of State* [Online] Available at: http://secretary.state.gov/www/statements/970918.html [7 September 2006].

Albright, M. 1997b. Secretary of State Madeleine Albright address before the Council on Foreign Relations. *Secretary of State* [Online] Available at: http://www.secretary.state.gov/www/statements/970930.html [accessed: 24 September 2006].

Albright, M. 2000. Transcript: June 19 interview of Albright on Diance Rehm Show. *Embassy of the United States Tel Aviv, Israel* [Online] Available at: http://telaviv.usembassy.gov/publish/peace/archives/2000/june/me0619a.html [accessed: 17 September 2006].

Alexander, H. 1961. A look at the other side of U.S. problems. *Los Angeles Times*, 3 November, B5.

Althusius, J. 1965. *Politics.* London: Eyre.

American Branch of the International Law Association. 1985–1986. *Report of the Committee on Use of Force in Relations among States 1985–1986.* Livingstone: American Branch of the International Law Association.

American Society of International Law. 1926. Conclusion of the Round Table Conference on the Codification of International Law in Respect to Nationality. *American Society International Proceedings*, 20, 136–48.

Amos, S. 1880. *Political and Legal Remedies for War.* London: Cassell, Petter, Galpin & Co.

Anderson, F. 1935. *Peace or War.* Sydney: Angus and Robertson Limited.

Angell, N. 1911. *The Great Illusion.* London: William Heinemann.

Annan, K. 1999a. *Report of the Secretary-General to the Security Council on the Protection of Civilians in Armed Conflict*, S/1999/957, New York: United Nations.

Annan, K. 1999b. Two concepts of sovereignty. *The Economist* [Online] Available at: http://www.un.org/News/ossg/sg/stories/kaecon.html [accessed: 5 June 2007].

Annan, K. 1999c. *Secretary-General's Speech to the 54th Session of the General Assembly*, SG/SM/7136, New York: United Nations.

Annan, K. 2000a. *Report of the Secretary-General on the Work of the Organization*, A/55/1, New York: United Nations.

Annan, K. 2000b. *We the Peoples: The Role of the United Nations in the 21st Century.* New York: United Nations.

Annan, K. 2001a. *Letter dated 21 February 2001 from the Secretary-General to the President of the Security Council, S/2001/160*, New York: United Nations.

Annan, K. 2001b. United Kingdom, 19 June 2001 – Question and Answer session with the Secretary-General, following the Cyril Foster Lecture at Oxford University. *United Nations* [Online, 19 June] Available at: http://www.un.org/apps/sg/offthecuff.asp?nid=196 [accessed: 20 February 2007].

Annan, K. 2002. *Identical Letter dated 1 August 2002 from the Secretary-General Addressed to the President of the General Assembly and the President of the Security Council*, A/57/273, New York: United Nations.

Annan, K. 2003a. *Adoption of Policy of Pre-emption Could Result in Proliferation of Unilateral Lawless Use of Force, Secretary-General Tells General Assembly*, SG/SM/8891, New York: United Nations.

Annan, K. 2003b. The Secretary-General Address to the General Assembly. *United Nations* [Online, 23 September] Available at: http://www0.un.org/webcast/ga/58/statements/sg2eng030923.htm [accessed: 25 October 2006].

Annan, K. 2004. *Rule of Law at Risk around the World, says Secretary-General in Address to General Assembly*, SG/SM/9491, New York: United Nations.

Annan, K. 2005a. *In Larger Freedom: Towards Development, Security and Human Rights For All (Report of the Secretary-General)*, A/59/2005, New York: United Nations.

Annan, K. 2005b. *Secretary-General offers Global Strategy for Fighting Terrorism, in Address to Madrid Summit*, SG/SM/9757, New York: United Nations.

Annan, K. 2005c. We must make the most of the opportunities. *United Nations Chronicle* [Online, 21 March] Available at: http://www.un.org/Pubs/chronicle/2005/issue2/0205p4.html [accessed: 8 August 2007].

Aquinas, T. 1947. *Summa Theologica.* New York: Benziger Bros.

Arend, A.C. 2003a. International law and the preemptive use of military force. *The Washington Quarterly*, 26(2), 89–103.

Arend, A.C. 2003b. International law and rogue states: the failure of the Charter framework. *New England Law Review*, 36(4), 735–53.

Arend, A.C. and Beck, R.J. 1993. *International Law and the Use of Force.* New York: Routledge.

Aristotle. 1992. *The Politics.* London: Penguin.

Arniso, N.D. 1993. International law and non-intervention: when do humanitarian concerns supersede sovereignty? *Fletcher Forum of World Affairs*, 17(2), 199–211.

Aspen Institute. 1996. *Managing Conflict in the Post-Cold War World: The Role of Intervention.* Aspen, Colorado: The Aspen Institute.

Associated Press. 2004. Iraq proves pre-emptive wars fail: Spanish PM. *Associated Press*, 3 May.

Atherton, R. 1928. Further correspondence with Government of the United States respecting the United States proposal for the renunciation of war. *The Avalon Project* [Online] Available at: http://www.yale.edu/lawweb/avalon/kbpact/kbbr.htm [accessed: 7 June 2007].

Auer, P. De 1920. Plebiscites and the League of Nations Covenant. *Transactions of the Grotius Society*, 6, 45–58.

Augustine, St. 1958. *City of God.* New York: Doubleday.

Australian Broadcasting Corporation. 2006. Govt steps up Lebanon evacuation plans. *Australian Broadcasting Corporation* [Online, 17 July] Available at http://www.abc.net.au/news/newsitems/200607/s1687855.htm [accessed: 18 July 2007].

Australian Government AusAID. 2003a. Overseas Aid: Solomon Islands. *Australian Government* [Online] Available at: http://www.ausaid.gov.au/country/country.cfm?CountryId=16 [accessed: 15 June 2007].

Australian Government AusAID. 2003b. Overseas Aid: Pacific. *Australian Government* [Online] Available at: http://www.ausaid.gov.au/country/southpacific.cfm [accessed: 15 June 2007].

Ayoob, M. 2002. Humanitarian intervention and state sovereignty. *The International Journal of Human Rights*, 6(1), 81–102.

Badescu, C.G. 2007. Authorizing humanitarian intervention: hard choices in saving strangers. *Canadian Journal of Political Science*, 40(1), 51–78.

Bakunin, M. 1971. Letters to a Frenchman on the present crisis: September 1870, in *Bakunin on Anarchy*, edited by S. Dolgoff. Montreal: Black Rose Books, 183–211.

Balla, V. De 1932. *The New Balance of Power in Europe.* Baltimore: John Hopkins Press.

Barletta, M. 1998. Chemical weapons in the Sudan: allegations and evidence. *The Non-Proliferation Review*, 6(1), 115–36.

Barnet, R. 1968. *Intervention and Revolution: The United States in the Third World.* New York: World Publishing Co.

Barrett, J. 2007. Court finds 21 guilty of Madrid train bombings. *Reuters [Online*, 31 October] Available at: http://uk.reuters.com/article/idUKL30849132007103I [accessed: 2 January 2008].

Baumann, P. 1991. Limits of the just war: easier said than done. *Commonwealth*, 118(5), 149–50.

Bazyler, M.J. 1987. Reexamining the doctrine of humanitarian intervention in light of the atrocities in Kampuchea and Ethiopia. *Stanford Journal of International Law*, 23(2), 547–619.

Beard, J.M. 2002. America's new war on terror: the case for self-defense under international law. *Harvard Journal of Law and Public Policy*, 25(2), 559–90.

Bellamy, A.J. 2000. Lessons unlearned: why coercive diplomacy failed at Rambouillet. *International Peacekeeping*, 7(2), 95 – 114.

Bellamy, A.J. 2002. *Kosovo and International Society.* Basingstoke: Palgrave Macmillan.

Bellamy, A.J. 2003. International law and the war with Iraq. *Melbourne Journal of International Law*, 4(2), 497–520.

Bellamy, A.J. 2004. Ethics and intervention: the 'humanitarian exception' and the problem of abuse in the case of Iraq. *Journal of Peace Research*, 41(2), 131–47.

Bellamy, A.J. 2005a. Responsibility to protect or Trojan horse? The crisis in Darfur and humanitarian intervention after Iraq. *Ethics and International Affairs*, 19(2), 31–53.

Bellamy, A.J. 2005b. Is the war on terror just? *International Relations*, 19(3), 275–96.

Bellamy, A.J. and Williams, P.D. 2006. The UN Security Council and the question of humanitarian intervention in Darfur. *Journal of Military Ethics*, 5(2), 144–60.

Bellamy, A.J., Williams, P. and Griffith, S. 2004. *Understanding Peacekeeping.* Cambridge: Polity Press.

Bentham, J. 1823. *An Introduction to the Principles of Morals and Legislation.* London: W. Pickering.

Bentwich, N. 1933. The League of Nations and racial persecution in Germany. *Transactions of the Grotius Society*, 19, 75–88.

Berchtold, L. 1914. Die Österreichisch-Ungarische Note an Serbien. *The World War I Document Archive* [Online] Available at: http://wwi.lib.byu.edu/index.php/The_Austro-Hungarian_Ultimatum_to_Serbia_(The_German_original) [accessed: 18 August 2007].

Beres, L.R. 1988. Justice and realpolitik: international law and the prevention of genocide. *American Journal of Jurisprudence*, 33, 123–59.

Berlusconi, S. 2003. President Bush meets with Italian Prime Minister Berlusconi. *The White House* [Online, 30 January] Available at: http://www.whitehouse.gov/news/releases/2003/01/20030130-10.html [accessed: 3 September 2004].

Bernard, M. 1860. *On the Principle of Non-Intervention.* Oxford: J.H. and J.A.S. Parker.

Biersteker, T. and Weber, C. 1996. *State Sovereignty as Social Construct.* Cambridge: Cambridge University Press.

Blair, T. 1999a. Prime Minister's speech: Doctrine of the International Community at the Economic Club, Chicago. *Prime Minister's Office* [Online, 24 April] Available at: http://www.pm.gov.uk/output/Page1297.asp [accessed: 21 September 2005].

Blair, T. 1999b. Prime Minister's speech: the new challenge for Europe. *Prime Minister's Office* [Online, 20 May] Available at: http://www.number-10.gov.uk/output/Page1334.asp [accessed: 1 September 2006].

Blair, T. 2001a. Prime Minister's statement to Parliament on the September 11 attacks. *Prime Minister's Office* [Online, 4 October] Available at: http://www.number10.gov.uk/output/Page1606.asp [accessed: 17 May 2006].

Blair, T. 2001b. Prime Minister's Statement to the House of Commons. *Prime Minister's Office* [Online, 8 October] Available at: http://www.number-10.gov.uk/output/Page1621.asp [accessed: 9 May 2006].

Blair, T. 2003. Address to the Nation. *Prime Minister's Office* [Online, 20 March] Available at: <http://www.number-10.gov.uk/output/Page3327.asp>, [accessed: 22 March 2007].

Blair, T. 2004. Prime Minister warns of continuing global terror threat. *Prime Minister's Office* [Online, 5 March] Available at: http://www.number-10.gov.uk/output/Page5461.asp [accessed: 27 November 2006].

Blockmans, S. 1999. Moving into unchartered waters: an emerging right of unilateral humanitarian intervention? *Leiden Journal of International Law*, 12(4), 759–86.

Bloomfield, S. 2007. Somalia descends into fresh hell. *The Sydney Morning Herald*, 24 November, 19.

Bluntschli, J.C. 1874. *Le Droit International Codifié.* Paris: Guillaumin et cie.

Bodin, J. 1955. *Six Books of the Commonwealth.* Oxford: Basil Blackwell.

Bogen, D.S. 1966. The law of humanitarian intervention: United States policy in Cuba (1898) and in The Dominican Republic (1965). *Harvard International Law Club Journal*, 7(2), 296–315.

Bogue, M. 2004. The legality of war in Iraq: a necessary fiction for the maintenance of international law? *Trinity College Law Review*, 7, 197–214.

Borchard, E.M. 1913. Basic elements of diplomatic protection of citizens abroad. *The American Journal of International Law*, 7(3), 497–520.

Borchard, E.M. 1915. *The Diplomatic Protection of Citizens Abroad.* New York: Banks Law Publishing.

Borchard, E.M. 1928. The Multilateral Pact – 'Renunciation of War': An address delivered at the Williamstown Institute of Politics, August 22, 1928. *The Avalon Project at the Yale Law School* [Online] Available at: http://www.yale.edu/lawweb/avalon/kbpact/kbbor.htm [accessed: 5 April 2007].

Bordelon, C. 2005. The illegality of the US policy of preemptive self-defence under international law. *Chapman Law Review*, 9(1), 111–46.

Bothe, M. 2003. Terrorism and the legality of pre-emptive force. *European Journal of International Law*, 14(2), 227–40.

Boucher, R. 2000. Transcript: State Department Noon Briefing, June 19, 2000. *Embassy of the United States Tel Aviv, Israel* [Online, 19 June] Available at: http://telaviv.usembassy.gov/publish/peace/archives/2000/june/me0619d.html, [accessed: 17 September 2006].

Boutros-Ghali, B. 1992a. *An Agenda for Peace: Preventative Diplomacy, Peacemaking and Peace-keeping. Report of the Secretary General pursuant to the statement adopted by the Summit Meeting of the Security Council on 31 January 1992*, A/47/277-S/24111, New York: United Nations.

Boutros-Ghali, B. 1992b. *Letter Dated 92/11/10 from the Secretary-General Addressed to the President of the Security Council*, S/24794, New York: United Nations.

Boutros-Ghali, B. 1995. *Supplement to an Agenda for Peace: Position Paper of the Secretary-General on the Occasion of the Fiftieth Anniversary of the United Nations*, A/50/60-S/1995/1, New York: United Nations.

Bowett, D.W. 1957. The use of force in the protection of nationals. *Transactions of the Grotius Society*, 43, 111–26.

Bowett, D.W. 1958. *Self-Defence in International Law.* Manchester: Manchester University Press.

Bowett, D.W. 1972. Reprisals involving recourse to armed force. *The American Journal of International Law*, 66(1), 1–36.

Bowett, D.W. 1986. The use of force for the protection of nationals abroad, in *The Current Legal Regulation of the Use of Force*, edited by A. Cassese. Dordrecht: Martinus Nijhoff Publishers, 39–55.

Boyle, F.A. 1987. Military responses to terrorism: remarks by Francis A. Boyle. *American Society of International Law Proceedings*, 81, 287–97.

Branch, A. 2005. American morality over international law: origins in UN military interventions, 1991–1995. *Constellations*, 12(1), 103–27.

Bremer, L.P. 1988. Counterterrorism: strategy and tactics. *US Department of State Bulletin*, 88(2130), 47–8.

Brierly, J.L. 1924. The development of international law after the World War. *The Economic Journal*, 34(133), 125–27.

Brierly, J.L. 1928. *The Law of Nations: An Introduction to the International Law of Peace.* Oxford: Clarendon Press.

Brierly, J.L. 1963. *The Law of Nations: An Introduction to the International Law of Peace*. Oxford: Oxford University Press.

Brierly, J.L. 1995. *The Law of Nations: An Introduction to the International Law of Peace.* Oxford: Clarendon Press.

Britisch Broadcasting Corporation. 2004. Iraq war illegal, says Annan. *British Broadcasting Corporation* [Online, 16 September] Available at: http://news.bbc.co.uk/2/hi/middle_east/3661134.stm [accessed: 28 October 2004].

British Broadcasting Corporation. 2002a. Blair urges action on Africa. *British Broadcasting Corporation* [Online, 6 February) Available at: http://news.bbc.co.uk/1/hi/uk_politics/1803567.stm [accessed: 1 July 2007].

British Broadcasting Corporation. 2002b. Putin ups Georgia strike warnings. *British Broadcasting Corporation* [Online, 12 September] Available at: http://news.bbc.co.uk/2/hi/europe/2253349.stm [accessed: 8 December 2007].

British Broadcasting Corporation. 2003. Japan threatens force against N Korea. *British Broadcasting Corporation* [Online, 14 February] Available at http://news.bbc.co.uk/2/hi/asia-pacific/2757923.stm [accessed: 12 March 2008].

British Foreign and Commonwealth Office. 2002. *Iraq's Weapons of Mass Destruction: The Assessment of the British Government.* London: British Foreign and Commonwealth Office.

Brooks, R.E. 2004. War everywhere: rights, national security law, and the law of armed conflict in the age of terror. *University of Pennsylvania Law Review*, 153(2), 675–761.

Brooks, R.E. 2005. Failed states, or the state as failure? *University of Chicago Law Review*, 72(4), 1159–92.

Brown, P.M. 1918. War and law. *The American Journal of International Law*, 12(1), 162–65.

Brownlie, I. 1958. International law and the activities of armed bands. *International and Comparative Law Quarterly*, 7(4), 712–35.

Brownlie, I. 1963. *International Law and the Use of Force by States.* Oxford: Clarendon Press.

Brownlie, I. 1973. Thoughts on kind-hearted gunmen, in *Humanitarian Intervention and the United Nations*, edited by R.B. Lillich. Charlottesville: University Press of Virginia, 139–48.

Brownlie, I. 2002. International law and the use of force by states 'revisited'. *Chinese Journal of International Law*, 1(1), 1–19.

Brunnée, J. and Toope, S.J. 2004. Slouching towards new 'just' wars: the hegemon after September 11th'. *International Relations*, 18(4), 405–23.

Buchanan, A. 2001. From Nuremburg to Kosovo: the morality of illegal international legal reform. *Ethics*, 111(4), 673–705.

Bunker, E. 1965. Statement by U.S. Representative. *US Department of State Bulletin*, 52(1351), 739–41.

Burkeman, O. and Borger, J. 2003. War critics astonished as US hawk admits invasion was illegal. *The Guardian [Online*, 20 November] Available at: http://www.guardian.co.uk/uk/2003/nov/20/usa.iraq1 [accessed: 17 May 2008].

Burmester, H.C. 1978. The recruitment and use of mercenaries in armed conflicts. *The American Journal of International Law*, 72(1), 37–56.

Burns, J.F. and Myers, S.L. 2000. The warship explosion: the overview; blast kills sailors on U.S. Ship in Yemen. *The New York Times*, 13 October, A1.

Bush, G.H.W. 1989a. President's Statement, May 11, 1989. *US Department of State Bulletin*, 89(2148), 70–71.

Bush, G.H.W. 1989b. Address to the Nation on Panama. *Miller Center of Public Affairs* [Online] Available at: http://millercenter.org/scripps/archive/speeches/detail/3422 [accessed: 8 June 2006].

Bush, G.H.W. 1990. Toward a new world order address. *US Department of State Dispatch*, 1(3), 91–4.

Bush, G.H.W. 1991. Persian Gulf War: supporting a noble cause. *US Department of State Dispatch*, 2(5), 67–8.

Bush, G.H.W. 1992. Humanitarian mission to Somalia: address to the nation. *US Department of State Dispatch*, 3(49), 865–7.

Bush, G.W. 2001a. Remarks by the President upon arrival. *The White House* [Online, 20 May] Available at: http://www.whitehouse.gov/news/releases/2001/09/20010916-2.html [accessed: 16 May 2006].

Bush, G.W. 2001b. Address to a Joint Session of Congress and the American People. *The White House* [Online, 20 September] Available at: http://www.whitehouse.gov/news/releases/2001/09/20010920-8.html [accessed: 15 May 2007].

Bush, G.W. 2001c. President Bush speaks to United Nations. *The White House* [Online, 10 November] Available at: http://www.whitehouse.gov/news/releases/2001/11/20011110-3.html [accessed: 6 May 2007].

Bush, G.W. 2001d. President issues military order: detention, treatment, and trial of certain non-citizens in the war against terrorism. *The White House* [Online, 13 November] Available at: http://www.whitehouse.gov/news/releases/2001/11/20011113-27.html [accessed: 16 September 2006].

Bush, G.W. 2001e. President shares Thanksgiving meal with troops. *The White House* [Online, 21 November] Available at: http://www.whitehouse.gov/news/releases/2001/11/20011121-3.html [accessed: 16 September 2006].

Bush, G.W. 2001f. President welcomes aid workers rescued from Afghanistan. *The White House* [Online, 26 November] Available at: http://www.whitehouse.gov/news/releases/2001/11/20011126-1.html [accessed: 22 February 2003].

Bush, G.W. 2001g. President discusses National Missile Defense. *The White House* [Online, 13 December] Available at: http://www.whitehouse.gov/news/releases/2001/12/20011213-4.html [accessed: 4 May 2006].

Bush, G.W. 2002a. President delivers State of the Union Address. *The White House* [Online, 29 January] Available at: http://www.whitehouse.gov/news/releases/2002/01/20020129-11.html [accessed: 3 February 2006].

Bush, G.W. 2002b. President Bush delivers Graduation Speech at West Point. *The White House* [Online, 1 June] Available at: http://www.whitehouse.gov/news/releases/2002/06/20020601-3.html [accessed: 19 May 2007].

Bush, G.W. 2002c. President's remarks at the United Nations General Assembly. *The White House* [Online, 12 September] Available at: http://www.whitehouse.gov/news/releases/2002/09/20020912-1.html [accessed: 4 May 2006].

Bush, G.W. 2002d. President outlines Iraqi threat. *The White House* [Online, 7 October] Available at: http://www.whitehouse.gov/news/releases/2002/10/20021007-8.html [accessed: 9 March 2007].

Bush, G.W. 2002e. President Bush previews historic NATO Summit in Prague speech. *The White House* [Online, 20 November] Available at: http://www.

whitehouse.gov/news/releases/2002/11/20021120-4.html [accessed: 11 August 2006].
Bush, G.W. 2003a. President delivers 'State of the Union'. *The White House* [Online, 28 January] Available at: http://www.whitehouse.gov/news/releases/2003/01/20030128-19.html [accessed: 18 August 2006].
Bush, G.W. 2003b. President says Saddam Hussein must Leave Iraq within 48 hours. *The White House* [Online, 17 March] Available at: http://www.whitehouse.gov/news/releases/2003/03/20030317-7.html [accessed: 21 March 2006].
Bush, G.W. 2003c. The President addresses the nation. *The White House* [Online, 19 March] Available at: http://www.whitehouse.gov/news/releases/2003/03/20030319-17.html [accessed: 21 March 2006].
Bush, G.W. 2003d. President discusses Operation Iraqi Freedom at Camp Lejeune. *The White House* [Online, 3 April] Available at: http://www.whitehouse.gov/news/releases/2003/04/20030403-3.html [accessed: 15 June 2006].
Bush, G.W. 2003e. President Bush announces major combat operations in Iraq have ended. *The White House* [Online, 1 May] Available at: http://www.whitehouse.gov/news/releases/2003/05/20030501-15.html [accessed: 15 August 2006].
Bush, G.W. 2003f. President addresses the nation. *The White House* [Online, 7 September] Available at: http://www.whitehouse.gov/news/releases/2003/09/20030907-1.html [accessed: 7 September 2006].
Bush, G.W. 2003g. Bush says U.S. considers Thailand 'major non-NATO ally'. *United States Department of State* [Online, 19 October] Available at: http://usinfo.state.gov/eap/Archive/2004/Jun/29-815968.html [accessed: 8 October 2006].
Bush, G.W. 2003h. President honors America's Veterans. *The White House* [Online, 11 November] Available at: http://www.whitehouse.gov/news/releases/2003/11/20031111-8.html [accessed: 4 September 2006].
Bush, G.W. 2005. Memorandum for the Secretary of State: Presidential determination on major drug transit or major illicit drug producing countries for fiscal year 2006. *United States Department of State* [Online, 15 September] Available at: http://www.state.gov/p/inl/rls/prsrl/ps/53327.htm [accessed: 9 November 2006].
Byers, M. 2002a. The shifting foundations of international law: a decade of forceful measures against Iraq. *European Journal of International Law*, 13(1), 21–41.
Byers, M. 2002b. Terrorism, the use of force and international law after 11 September. *The International and Comparative Law Quarterly*, 51(2), 401–14.
Byers, M. 2002c. Präventivkrieg und Selbstverteidigung im Völkerrecht: Der Irak und der Fall Caroline. *Le Monde Diplomatique* [Online 13 September] Available at: http://www.monde-diplomatique.de/pm/2002/09/13/a0040.text.name,askR1jkhU.n,2 [accessed: 20 October 2009]
Byers, M. 2005. *War Law*. London: Atlantic Books.

Byers, M. and Chesterman, S. 2003. Changing the rules about rules? Unilateral humanitarian intervention and the future of international law, in *Humanitarian Intervention: Ethical, Legal, and Political Dilemmas*, edited by J.L. Holzgrefe and R.O. Keohane. Cambridge: Cambridge University Press, 177–203.

Byman, D. 2005. *Deadly Connections: States that Sponsor Terrorism*. Cambridge: Cambridge University Press.

Calhoun, L. 2000. The injustice of 'just war'. *Peace Review*, 12(3), 449–55.

Callender, H. 1933. Revision of Europe's treaties a leading and baffling issue. *The New York Times*, 30 April, XX3.

Camilleri, J.A. and Falk, J. 1992. *The End of Sovereignty? The Politics of a Shrinking and Fragmenting World*. Aldershot: Edward Elgar.

Caprioli, M. and Trumbore, P.F. 2005. Rhetoric versus reality: rogue states in interstate conflict. *Journal of Conflict Resolution*, 49(5), 770–91.

Carment, D. 2003. Assessing state failure: implications for theory and policy. *Third World Quarterly*, 24(3), 407–27.

Carnazza-Amari, G. 1880. *Traite de Droit International en Temps de Paix*. Paris: Montanari-Revest.

Carnegie Endowment for International Peace. 1938. Crisis in Czechoslovakia-April 24–October 13, 1938. *International Conciliation*, 19(344), 297–486.

Carter, J. 1980. US interests and ideals. *US Department of State Bulletin*, 80(2039), 5–8.

Cassese, A. 1989. The international community's 'legal' response to terrorism. *The International and Comparative Law Quarterly*, 38(3), 589–608.

Cassese, A. 2001. Terrorism is also disrupting some crucial legal categories of international law. *European Journal of International Law*, 12(5), 993–1001.

Castro Ruz, F. 2002. Response from Dr. Fidel Castro Ruz to the statement made by the United States Government on Biological Weapons. *Republica de Cuba* [Online, 10 May] Available at: http://www.cubagob.cu/ingles/marquesina/mayo1802response.htm [accessed: 10 June 2003].

Cecil, V. 1929. The Tenth Assembly of the League of Nations. *Journal of the Royal Institute of International Affairs*, 8(6), 541–67.

Cecil, V. 1933. The League as a road to peace, in *The Intelligent Man's Way to Prevent War*, edited by L. Woolf. London: Victor Gollancz Ltd, 256–313.

Chace, J. 2003. Present at the destruction: the death of American internationalism. *World Policy Journal*, 20(1), 1–5.

Chancellor, A. 2002. Friend or foe? *The Guardian* [Online, 23 March] Available at: http://www.guardian.co.uk/lifeandstyle/2002/mar/23/weekend.alexanderchancellor [accessed: 9 November 2007].

Charney, J.I. 1999. Anticipatory humanitarian intervention in Kosovo. *The American Journal of International Law*, 93(4), 834–41.

Charvet, J. 1997. The idea of state sovereignty and the right of humanitarian intervention. *International Political Science Review*, 18(1), 39–48.

Cheney, D. 2004. Remarks by the Vice President. The White House [Online, 22 January] Available at: http://www.whitehouse.gov/news/releases/2004/01/20040122-7.html [accessed: 15 March 2004].

Chesterman, S. 2001a. *Just War or Just Peace? Humanitarian Intervention and International Law.* Oxford Oxford University Press.

Chesterman, S. 2001b. Passing the baton: the delegation of Security Council enforcement powers from Kuwait to Kosovo', in *International Law in the Post-Cold War World*, edited by S. Yee and W. Tieya. London: Routledge, 148–70.

Chesterman, S. 2002. Walking softly in Afghanistan: the future of UN state-building. *Survival*, 44 (3), 37–46.

Chesterman, S. 2004. Bush, the United Nations and nation-building. *Survival*, 46(1), 101–16.

Chesterman, S. and Pouligny, B. 2003. Are sanctions meant to work? The politics of creating and implementing sanctions through the UN. *Global Governance*, 9(4), 503–18.

Cheyes, A. 1962. The legal case for US action in Cuba. *US Department of State Bulletin*, 47(1221), 763–71.

Chilstrom, R.M. 1974. Humanitarian intervention under contemporary international law: a policy-orientated approach. *Yale Studies in World Public Order* 1, 93–147.

Chirac, J. 1999. Visit to Russia press conference given by M. Jacques Chirac, President to the Republic. *Embassy of France in Washington* [Online] Available at: http://www.ambafrance-us.org/news/statmnts/1999/conflict10.asp [accessed: 24 August 2006].

Chol, L.H. 2000. *Letter dated 5 September 2000 from the Permanent Representative of the Democratic People's Republic of Korea to the United Nations addressed to the Secretary-General*, A/55/355, New York: United Nations.

Chol, L.H. 2000. Statement by H.E. Mr. Li Hyong Chol, Ambassador and Permanent Representative of the Democratic People's Republic of Korea to the United Nations to the 55th Session of the UN General Assembly. *United Nations* [Online] Available at: http://www.un.org/ga/webcast/statements/koreaE.htm [accessed: 1 November 2006].

Clapham, C. 1998. Degrees of statehood. *Review of International Studies*, 24(2), 143–57.

Clapham, C. 1999. Sovereignty and the Third World state. *Political Studies*, 47(3), 522–37.

Clark, J. 1912. *Right to Protect Citizens in Foreign Countries by Landing Forces*. Washington, D.C.: Government Print Office.

Claude, I.L. 1959. *Swords into Plowshares: The Problems and Progress of International Organization.* New York: Random House.

Claude, I.L. 1966. Collective legitimation as a political function of the United Nations. *International Organization*, 20(3), 367–79.

Clausewitz, C. von 2007. *On War.* Oxford: Oxford University Press.

Clinton, W.J. 1995. Responding to the security challenges of the 21st Century: Address at the 50th United Nations General Assembly, New York City, 22 October 1995. *United States Department of State Dispatch*, 6(44), 779–81.

Clinton, W.J. 1996. Remarks by the President upon Departure. *Public Broadcasting Service* [Online] Available at: http://www.pbs.org/newshour/bb/middle_east/june96/clinton_departure_6-26.html [accessed: 7 May 2006].

Clinton, W.J. 1998. Letter to Congressional Leaders Reporting on Military Action against Terrorist Sites in Afghanistan and Sudan: August 21, 1998', in *Public Papers of the Presidents*, edited by W.J. Clinton. Washington D.C.: U.S. Government Printing Office, 1464.

Clinton, W.J. 1999. Remarks by the President at United States Air Force Academy commencement ceremony. *The White House* [Online] Available at: http://clinton4.nara.gov/WH/New/html/19990602.html [accessed: 9 June 2006].

Clough, M. 1999. Handling rogue states. *The Moscow Times* [Online, 6 March] Available at: internal.moscowtimes.ru/indexes/1999/06/03/01.html [accessed: 13 May 2008].

Coates, A.J. 1997. *The Ethics of War*. Manchester: Manchester University Press.

Coll, A.R. 1987. The legal and moral adequacy of military responses to terrorism. *American Society of International Law Proceedings*, 81, 297–307.

Columbus, F. 1999. *Kosovo-Serbia: A Just War?* Commack, New York: Nova Science Publishers, Inc.

Commission on Global Governance. 1995. *Our Global Neighborhood: Report of the Commission on Global Governance.* Oxford: Oxford University Press.

Commission on Weak States and US National Security. 2004. *On the Brink, Weak States and US National Security.* Washington DC: Center for Global Development.

Commission to Assess the Ballistic Missile Threat to the United States. 1998. Report of the Commission to Assess the Ballistic Missile Threat to the United States: Executive Summary. *Federation of American Scientists* [Online] Available at: http://www.fas.org/irp/threat/missile/rumsfeld/ [accessed: 3 October 2006].

Committee on Foreign Affairs. 2002. Disarming Iraq: Prospects for disarmament of Iraq: the UN route, and UN weapons inspections. *United Kingdom Parliament* [Online, 17 December] Available at: http://www.publications.parliament.uk/pa/cm200203/cmselect/cmfaff/196/19609.htm#n210 [accessed: 8 May 2007].

Conference Proceedings Part I: The Past. 1973a. in *Humanitarian Intervention and the United Nations*, edited by R.B. Lillich. Charlottesville: University Press of Virginia, 3–41.

Conference Proceedings Part III: The Future. 1973b. in *Humanitarian Intervention and the United Nations*, edited by R.B. Lillich. Charlottesville: University Press of Virginia, 75–138.

Congressional Research Service. 2002. *Export Administration Act of 1979.* Washington DC: Library of Congress.

Connolly, K. 2003. I am not convinced, Fischer tells Rumsfeld. *The Telegraph* [Online, 10 February] Available at: http://www.telegraph.co.uk/news/

worldnews/europe/germany/1421634/I-am-not-convinced-Fischer-tells-Rumsfeld.html [accessed: 19 May 2007].

Conway, D. 2006. Aussies among 70,000 fleeing Lebanon. *AAP General News Wire* [Online, 20 July] Available at: http://www.news.com.au/story/0,10117,19852768-29277,00.html [accessed: 23 July 2007].

Corwin, T. 1861. Mexico: Mr Seward to Mr Corwin, Department of State, April 6, 1861, in *Papers Relating to the Foreign Relations of the United States: Message of the President of the United States to the Two Houses of Congress, at the Commencement of the Second Session of the Thirty-Seventh Congress*, edited by The United States Department of State. Washington D.C.: U.S. Government Printing Office, 65–70.

Council of the League of Nations. 1935. Article 7: Protection-Security of the State. *The American Journal of International Law Supplement: Research in International Law*, 29, 543–61.

Cruce, E. 1909. *The New Cyneas*. Philadelphia: Allen, Lane, and Scott.

Cuellar, J.P. de. 1991. *Report of the Secretary-General on the Work of the Organization*, A/46/1, New York: United Nations.

D'Amato, A. 1985. Nicaragua and international law: the 'academic' and the 'real'. *The American Journal of International Law*, 79(3), 657–64.

D'Angelo, J.R. 1981. Resort to force by states to protect nationals: the U.S. rescue mission to Iran and its legality under international law. *Virginia Journal of International Law*, 21(3), 485–519.

D'Entreves, A.P. 1948. *Aquinas: Selected Political Writings*. Oxford: Oxford University Press.

Daalder, I.H. 2003. The use of force in a changing world-US and European perspectives. *Leiden Journal of International Law*, 16(1), 171–80.

Danish Institute of International Affairs. 1999. *Humanitarian Intervention: Legal and Political Aspects*. Copenhagen: Danish Institute of International Affairs.

Dauth, J. 2003. *Letter dated 20 March 2003 from the Permanent Representative of Australia to the United Nations addressed to the President of the Security Council*, S/2003/352, New York: United Nations.

Dawn, R. 2001. Armed Conflict Prevention, management and resolution, in *Stockholm International Peace Research Institute (SIPRI) Yearbook 2001: World Armaments and Disarmament*, edited by Stockholm International Peace Research Institute (SIPRI). New York: Oxford University Press, 69–127.

Dawn, R. and Holmqvist, C. 2005. Major Armed Conflict, in *Stockholm International Peace Research Institute (SIPRI) Yearbook 2005: World Armaments and Disarmament*, edited by Stockholm International Peace Research Institute (SIPRI). New York: Oxford University Press, 83–137.

De Schutter, B. 1972. Humanitarian intervention: a United Nations task. *California Western International Law Journal*, 3(1), 21–36.

Dee, M. 2001. 'Coalitions of the Willing' and humanitarian intervention: Australia's involvement with INTERFET. *International Peacekeeping*, 8(3), 1–20.

Delcassé, M. 1900. Statements made by Mr. Delcassé in the French Chamber, July 3, in *Papers Relating to the Foreign Relations of the United States, with the Annual Message of the President Transmitted to Congress December 3, 1900*, edited by The United States Department of State. Washington D.C.: U.S. Government Printing Office, 313.

Department for International Development. 2005. *Why We Need to Work More Effectively in Fragile States*. London: British Department for International Development.

Department of Defense. 1987. *Report to the Congress on Security Arrangements in the Persian Gulf*. Washington D.C.: U.S. Government Printing Office.

Department of Foreign Affairs and Trade. 2003. *Advancing the National Interest: Australia's Foreign and Trade Policy White Paper*. Canberra: Department of Foreign Affairs and Trade.

Derrida, J. 2003. Schurkenstaaten, Sorgenstaaten. *Die Tageszeitung* [Online, 17 January] Available at: http://www.monde-diplomatique.de/pm/2003/01/17/a0017.text.name,asksfeNuV.n,0 [accessed: 23 March 2007].

Detter, I. 2000. *The Law of War*. Cambridge: Cambridge University Press.

Deutsch, K.W. 1970. Quincy Wright's contribution to the study of war: a preface to the second edition. *Journal of Conflict Resolution*, 14(4), 473–78.

Deutscher Bundestag. 1998. Plenarprotokoll 13/248. *Deutscher Bundestag Datenbanken* [Online] Available at: http://dip.bundestag.de/cgi-bin/getdokg?s=++bt+p+13/248&b=1207968895-22595&c=/usr7/goldop&d=www.dia.bt/DIA&e=/bt_st3kad&k=1998&m=2002&n=0 [accessed: 14 June 2007].

Devetak, R. 2001. Postmodernism, in *Theories of International Relations*, edited by S. Burchill, et al. New York: Palgrave Macmillan, 161–87.

Dickinson, G.L. 1917. *The Choice Before Us*. London: Allen and Unwin.

Dinstein, Y. 2001. *War, Aggression and Self-Defence*. Cambridge: Cambridge University Press.

Dixon, M. 2005. *Textbook on International Law*. Oxford: Oxford University Press.

Donnelly, J. 1984. Human rights, humanitarian intervention and American foreign policy. *Journal of International Affairs*, 37(2), 311–28.

Downer, A. 2003a. Neighbours cannot be recolonised. *The Australian*, 8 January, 11.

Downer, A. 2003b. Doorstop – Parliament House. *Australian Department of Foreign Affairs and Trade* [Online, 25 June] Available at: http://www.dfat.gov.au/media/transcripts/2003/030625_doorstop.html [accessed: 27 July 2005].

Downes, C. 2004. Targeted killings in an age of terror: the legality of the Yemen strike. *Journal of Conflict and Security Law*, 9(2), 277–94.

Dowty, A. 1978. Nuclear proliferation: the Israeli case. *International Studies Quarterly*, 22(1), 79–120.

Drozdiak, W. 1998. European allies back US strikes: Japan says it 'understands'. *The Washington Post*, 21 August, A20.

Dueck, C. 2006. Strategies for managing rogue states. *Orbis*, 50(2), 223–41.
Duffy, B. 1986. The unmasking of Assad. *U.S. News and World Report*, 101, 26–30
Dugard, C.J.R. 1967. The Organisation of African Unity and colonialism: an inquiry into the plea of self-defence as a justification for the use of force in the eradication of colonialism. *The International and Comparative Law Quarterly*, 16(1), 157–90.
Dugard, J. 1974. International terrorism: problems of definition. *International Affairs*, 50(1), 67–81.
Dunn, F.S. 1932. *The Protection of Nationals*. Baltimore: John Hopkins Press.
Dupuy, P.M. 2004. State sponsors of terrorism: issues of international responsibility, in *Enforcing International Law Norms against Terrorism*, edited by A. Bianchi. Portland, Oregon: Hart Publishing, 3–16.
Durch, W.J. 1993. The UN operation in The Congo: 1960–1964, in *The Evolution of UN Peacekeeping: Case Studies and Comparative Analysis*, edited by W.J. Durch. New York: St. Martin's Press, 315–52.
Duursma, J. 1999. Justifying NATO's use of force in Kosovo? *Leiden Journal of International Law*, 12(2), 287–95.
Eccleston, R. and Wilson, P. 2003. Tyrants beware. *The Australian*, 11 April, 1.
Editorial. 1898. The implied covenant. *The New York Times*, 31 March, 6.
Editorial. 1899. German press war view. *Chicago Tribune*, 30 October, 2.
Editorial. 1918. Quit, says Stowell, to win free speech. *The New York Times*, 3 March, 15.
Editorial. 1926. The next step. *The Los Angeles Times*. 27 April, A4.
Editorial. 1932. Lausanne last hope, declares Bruening. *The New York Times*, 9 May, 5.
Editorial. 1933. Disarmament and revision. *The Times*, 22 December, 11.
Editorial. 2003. Editorial. *The Irish Times*, 30 July.
Einsiedel, S. von 2005. Policy responses to state failure, in *Making States Work: State Failure and the Crisis of Governance*, edited by S. Chesterman, M. Ignatieff, and R. Thakur. New York United Nations University Press, 13–35.
Eisenhower, D.D. 1954. The President's news conference. *The American Presidency Project* [Online] Available at: http://www.presidency.ucsb.edu/ws/index.php?pid=9977 [accessed: 20 October 2007].
Eland, I. and Lee, D. 2001. The rogue state doctrine and national missile defense. *CATO Foreign Policy Briefing*, (65), 1–13.
Elbe, J. von 1939. The evolution of the concept of the just war in international law. *The American Journal of International Law*, 33(4), 665–88.
Eldon, S. 2001. *Letter dated 7 October 2001 from the Charge D'Affaires A.I. of the Permanent Mission of the United Kingdom of Great Britain and Northern Ireland to the United Nations Addressed to the President of the Security Council*, S/2001/947, New York: United Nations.
European Council. 1999. Statement by the European Council concerning Kosovo, Presidency conclusions Berlin European Council. *European Council* [Online]

Available at: http://www.europa.EU.int/council/off/conclu/mar99_en.htm#p3 [accessed: 18 August 2006].

European Parliament. 2002. European Parliament resolution on 'Assessment of and prospects for the EU strategy on terrorism one year after 11 September 2001'. *European Parliament* [Online] Available at: http://europa.eu/bulletin/en/200210/p106008.htm [accessed: 4 August 2007].

Evans, L.H. 1932. The emancipation of Iraq from the mandates system. *The American Political Science Review*, 26(6), 1024–49.

Fairley, H. S. 1980. State actors, humanitarian intervention and international law: reopening Pandora's Box. *Georgia Journal of International and Comparative Law*, 10(1), 29–64.

Falk, R. 1959. The United States and the doctrine of nonintervention in the internal affairs of independent states. *Howard Law Journal*, 5(2), 163–89.

Falk, R. 1966. International law and the United States role in the Viet Nam War. *The Yale Law Journal* 75(7), 1122–60.

Falk, R. 1969a. The Beirut raid and the international law of retaliation. *The American Journal of International Law*, 63(3), 415–43.

Falk, R. 1969b. International law and the United States Role in Viet-Nam: a response to Professor Moore, in *The Vietnam War and International Law*, edited by R. Falk. Princeton: Princeton University Press, 445–508.

Falk, R. 1977. Nuclear weapons proliferation as a world order problem. *International Security*, 1(3), 79–93.

Falk, R. 1981. *Human Rights and State Sovereignty.* New York: Holmes & Meier Publishers, Inc.

Falk, R. 2001. Defining a Just War. *The Nation*. [Online, 11 October] Available at: http://www.thenation.com/doc/20011029/falk [accessed: 20 September 2007].

Falk, R. 2002. Testing patriotism and citizenship in the global terror war, in *Worlds in Collision: Terror and the Future of Global Order*, edited by K. Booth and T. Dunne. New York: Palgrave Macmillan, 325–35.

Falk, R. 2003. Humanitarian intervention: a forum. *The Nation* [Online, 14 July] Available at: http://www.thenation.com/doc/20030714/forum [accessed: 6 September 2007].

Falk, R. 2004. Humanitarian intervention after Kosovo, in *Lessons of Kosovo: The Dangers of Humanitarian Intervention*, edited by A. Jokic. Toronto: Broadview Press, 31–52.

Farer, T.J. 1987. The United Nations and human rights: more than a whimper less than a roar. *Human Rights Quarterly*, 9(4), 550–86.

Farer, T.J. 2002. Beyond the Charter frame: unilateralism or condominium? *The American Journal of International Law*, 96(2), 359–64.

Fawcett, J.E.S 1961. Intervention in international law: a study of some recent cases. *Hague Recueil*, 103, 343–423.

Feil, S.R. 1997. Could 5,000 Peacekeepers have saved 500,000 Rwandans? Early intervention reconsidered. *Report of the Institute for the Study of Diplomacy*, 3 (2). 1–5.

Feinstein, B. 1976. Self-defense and Israel in international law: a reappraisal. *Israel Law Review*, 11(4), 516–62.

Ferencz, B.B. 1972. Defining aggression: where it stands and where it's going. *The American Journal of International Law*, 66(3), 491–508.

Fisk, R. 1985. Assad, the Great Manipulator. *The Times*, 5 July, 12.

Flint, J. 1976. *Cecil Rhodes*. London: Hutchinson.

Fonteyne, J.P.L. 1974. The customary international law doctrine of humanitarian intervention: its current validity under the U.N. Charter. *California Western International Law Journal*, 4(2), 203–70.

Ford, G. 1975. President Ford's Letter to the Congress, May 15. *US Department of State Bulletin*, 72(1875), 721–22.

Forsythe, D.P. 2002. The United States and international criminal justice. *Human Rights Quarterly*, 24(4), 974–91.

Foster, G.D. 2004. Just war doctrine in an age of hyperpower politics. *The Humanist*, 64(2), 23–25.

Franck, T.M. 1962. United Nations law in Africa: the Congo Operation as a case study. *Law and Contemporary Problems*, 27(4), 632–52.

Franck, T.M. 1970. Who killed Article 2(4)? Or: changing norms governing the use of force by states. *The American Journal of International Law*, 64(4), 809–37.

Franck, T.M. 2001. When, if ever, may states deploy military force without prior Security Council authorisation? *Washington University Journal of Law and Policy*, 5, 51–68.

Franck, T.M. 2002. *Recourse to Force: State Action against Threats and Armed Attacks*. Cambridge: Cambridge University Press.

Franck, T.M. and Lockwood, B.B. 1974. Preliminary thoughts towards an international convention on terrorism. *The American Journal of International Law*, 68(1), 69–90.

Franck, T.M. and Rodley, N.S. 1973. After Bangladesh: the law of humanitarian intervention by force. *The American Journal of International Law*, 67(2), 275–305.

Frost, R. 1916. *Mountain Interval*. New York: Henry Holt and Company.

Frowein, J.A. 1989. The present state of research carried out by the English-speaking section of the Centre for Studies and Research', in *The Legal Aspects of International Terrorism*, edited by Centre for Studies and Research in International Law and International Relations. Dordrecht: Martinus Nijhoff Publishers, 56–96.

Fund for Peace and Carnegie Endowment for International Peace. 2005. The Failed States Index 2005. *Foreign Policy*, 149, 56–65.

Fund for Peace and Carnegie Endowment for International Peace. 2006. The Failed States Index 2006. *Foreign Policy*, 154, 50–54.

Fund for Peace and Carnegie Endowment for International Peace. 2007. The Failed States Index 2007. *Foreign Policy*, 161, 54–63.

Ganji, M. 1962. *International Protection of Human Rights*. Geneva: E. Droz.

Garcia-Mora, M.R. 1962. *International Responsibility for Hostile Acts of Private Persons against Foreign States.* The Hague: Martinus Nijhoff.

Garwood-Gowers, A. 2004. Self-defence against terrorism in the post-9/11 world. *Queensland University of Technology Law and Justice Journal*, 4(2), 1–18.

Gathii, J.T. 2005. Assessing claims of a new doctrine of pre-emptive war under the doctrine of sources. *Osgoode Hall Law Journal*, 43(1–2), 68–103.

Gazzini, T. 2005. *The Changing Rules on the Use of Force in International Law.* Manchester: Manchester University Press.

Gibbslondon, P. 1935. Two silent minutes, and then – . *The New York Times*, 10 November, SM1.

Glaser, C.L. and Fetter, S. 2001. National missile defense and the future of U.S. nuclear weapons policy. *International Security*, 26(1), 40–92.

Gleditsch, N.P. et al. 2002. Armed Conflict 1946–2001: A New Dataset. *Journal of Peace Research*, 39(5): 615–63.

Glennon, M.J. 1999. The new interventionism: the search for a just international law. *Foreign Affairs*, 78(2), 2–7.

Goldsmith, J.L. 2002. Iraq: Resolution 1441 (Secret Memo to the Prime Minister. *The Guardian* [Online] Available at: http://image.guardian.co.uk/sys-files/Guardian/documents/2005/04/28/legal.pdf [accessed: 3 August 2007].

Goldstone, J.A., Gurr, T.R. and Harff, B. 2000. *State Failure Task Force Report: Phase III.* Arlington: Political Instability Task Force.

Gordon, R. 1997. Saving failed states: sometimes a neocolonialist notion. *American Society of International Law Proceedings*, 91, 420–22.

Government of the United States of America. 2002. *The National Security Strategy of the United States of America 2002.* Washington: The White House.

Government of the United States of America. 2006. *The National Security Strategy of the United States of America 2006.* Washington: The White House.

Graham, M.W. 1924. Humanitarian intervention in international law as related to the practice of the United States. *Michigan Law Review*, 22(4), 312–28.

Grant, T.D. 2004. Partition of failed states: impediment and impulses. *Indiana Journal of Global Legal Studies*, 11(2), 51–82.

Gray, C. 2002. From unity to polarization: international law and the use of force against Iraq. *European Journal of International Law*, 13(1), 1–19.

Gray, C. 2004. *International Law and the Use of Force.* Oxford: Oxford University Press.

Greenstock, J. 2003. *Letter dated 20 March 2003 from the Permanent Representative of the United Kingdom of Great Britain and Northern Ireland to the United Nations addressed to the President of the Security Council*, S/2003/350, New York: United Nations.

Greenwood, C. 1987. International law and the United States air operation against Libya. *West Virginia Law Review*, 89(4), 933–60.

Greenwood, C. 2002. International law and the 'war against terrorism'. *International Affairs*, 78(2), 301–17.

Greig, D.W. 1970. *International Law.* London: Butterworths.

Greig, D.W. 1976. *International Law*. London: Butterworths.
Grewe, W.G. 1984. *Epochen der Völkerrechtsgeschichte*. Baden-Baden: Nomos Verlagsgesellschaft.
Gros, J.G. 1996. Towards a taxonomy of failed states in the new world order: decaying Somalia, Liberia, Rwanda and Haiti. *Third World Quarterly*, 17(3), 455–71.
Gross, L.M. 1983. The legal implications of Israel's 1982 invasion into Lebanon. *California Western International Law Journal*, 13(3), 458–92.
Grotius, H. 1925. *On the Laws of War and Peace*. New York: Carnegie Endowment for International Peace.
Grotius, H. 2001. *On the Law of War and Peace*. Kitchener: Batoche Books.
Guoliang, G. 2003. Redefine cooperative security, not pre-emption. *The Washington Quarterly*, 26(2), 135–45.
Gwertzman, B. 1986. Shultz supports armed reprisals. *The New York Times*, 16 January, A1.
Haass, R.N. 1999. *Intervention: The Use of American Military Force in the Post-Cold War World.* Washington DC: Brookings Institute Press.
Haass, R.N. 2003. Sovereignty: existing rights, evolving responsibilities – Remarks at the School of Foreign Service and the Mortara Center for International Studies, Georgetown University, 14 January 2003. *United States Department of State* [Online] Available at: http://www.state.gov/s/p/rem/2003/16648.htm [accessed: 2 October 2006].
Habermas, J. 1999. Bestiality and humanity: a war on the border between legality and morality. *Constellations*, 6(3), 263–72.
Haines, C.G. 1936. Book Review: The State in Theory and Practice by Harold J. Laski. *Columbia Law Review*, 36(5), 857–59.
Hales, J.C. 1939. The creation and application of the mandate system: a study in international colonial supervision. *Transactions of the Grotius Society*, 25, 185–284.
Hall, H.D. 1948. *Mandates, Dependencies and Trusteeship*. London: Stevens & Sons Limited.
Hall, W.E. 1884. *A Treatise on International Law.* 2nd Edition. Oxford: Clarendon Press.
Halleck, H.W. 1861. *International Law, or, Rules Regulating the Intercourse of States in Peace and War.* San Francisco: H.H. Bancroft & Company.
Hamdoon, N. 1993. *Letter dated 27 June 1993 from the Permanent Representative of Iraq to the United Nations Addressed to the President of the Security Council*, S/26004, New York: United Nations.
Hamilos, P. 2007. The worst Islamic attack in European history. *The Guardian* [Online, 31 October] Available at: http://www.guardian.co.uk/world/2007/oct/31/spain [accessed: 4 April 2008].
Hannay, D.H.A. 1991. *Letter dated 20 December 1991 from the Permanent Representative of the United Kingdom of Great Britain and Northern Ireland*

to the United Nations Addresses to the Secretary-General, S/23307, New York: United Nations.

Harcourt, W.V. 1863. *On Some Questions of International Law.* London and Cambridge: Macmillan and Co.

Hargrove, J.L. 1987. The Nicaragua Judgement and the future of the law of force and self-defense. *American Journal of International Law*, 81(1), 135–43.

Harkavy, R.E. 1981. Pariah states and nuclear proliferation. *International Organization*, 35(1), 135–63.

Harris, S.E. 1948. Cost of the Marshall Plan to the United States. *The Journal of Finance*, 3(1), 1–15.

Harrison, B. 1891–92. Message, in *The Executive Documents of the House of Representatives for the First Session of the Fifty-second Congress 1891–92*, edited by The United States Department of State. Washington, D.C: U.S. Government Printing Office, iii–xxxix.

Hassan, F. 1981. Realpolitik in international law: after Tanzanian–Ugandan conflict 'humanitarian intervention' reexamined. *Willamette Law Review*, 17(4), 859–912.

Havel, V. 1999. Protecting People from Tyranny of State Sovereignty. *Canadian Speeches*, 13(1), 16–21.

Heatley, D.P. 1921. The plebiscite, nationality and the state in international affairs. *Journal of Comparative Legislation and International Law*, 3(4), 258–72.

Heinze, E.A. 2004. Humanitarian intervention: morality and international law on intolerable violations of human rights. *The International Journal of Human Rights*, 8(4), 471–90.

Heisbourg, F. 2003. A work in progress: the Bush Doctrine and its consequences. *The Washington Quarterly*, 26(2), 75–88.

Helman, G.B. and Ratner, S.R. 1992. Saving failed states. *Foreign Policy*, 89, 3–20.

Henkin, L. 1963a. Force, intervention, and neutrality in contemporary international law. *American Society of International Law Proceedings*, 57, 147–62.

Henkin, L. 1963b. The United Nations and its supporters: self-examination. *Political Science Quarterly*, 78(4), 504–36.

Henkin, L. 1971. The reports of the death of Article 2(4) are greatly exaggerated. *The American Journal of International Law*, 65(3), 544–48.

Henkin, L. 1999. Kosovo and the law of humanitarian intervention. *The American Journal of International Law*, 93(4), 824–28.

Henry, N. 1990. 360 Americans airlifted from Liberia. *The Washington Post*, 11 June, A17.

Herbst, J. 1996. Responding to state failure in Africa. *International Security*, 21(3), 120–44.

Hermann, M.G. and Kegley, C.W. 2001. Democracies and intervention: is there a danger zone in the democratic peace? *Journal of Peace Research*, 38(2), 237–45.

Hershey, A.S. 1898. Intervention and the recognition of Cuban independence. *Annals of the American Academy of Political and Social Science*, 11(3), 52–80.

Hetzer, W. 2007. Terrorist attacks: criminal persecution or national defence. *European Journal on Criminal Policy and Research*, 13(1–2), 33–55.

Higgins, A.P. 1917. *A Treatise on International Law.* London: Oxford at the Clarendon Press.

Higgins, R. 1961. The Legal limits to the use of force by sovereign states United Nations practice. *British Yearbook of International Law*, 37, 269–319.

Higgins, R. 1963. *The Development of International Law through the Political Organs of the United Nations.* Oxford: Oxford University Press.

Higgins, R. 2004. Separate Opinion of Judge Higgins: Legal Consequences of the Construction of a Wall in the Occupied Palestinian Territory. *International Court of Justice* [Online] Available at: http://www.icj-cij.org/docket/files/131/1681.pdf [accessed: 7 March 2007]

Hindmarsh, A.E. 1933. *Force in Peace: Force Short of War in International Relations.* Cambridge: Harvard University Press.

Hobbes, T. 1996. *Leviathan.* Cambridge: Cambridge University Press.

Hobson, J.A. 1915. *Towards International Government.* London: George Allen & Unwin Ltd.

Hodges, H.G. 1915. *The Doctrine of Intervention.* Princeton: The Banner Press.

Hoffman, S. 1981. States and the morality of war. *Political Theory*, 9(2), 149–72.

Holls, F.W. 1900. *The Peace Conference at The Hague and its Bearings on International Law and Policy.* New York: The Macmillan Co.

Holm, H.H. 2002. Failing failed states: who forgets the forgotten? *Security Dialogue*, 33(4), 457–71.

House of Commons. 1956. House of Commons, Wednesday Oct. 31. *The Times*, 1 November, 4.

House of Commons. 1993. Column 657 Iraq. *Hansard* [Online] Available at http://www.publications.parliament.uk/pa/cm199293/cmhansrd/1993-06-28/Debate-1.html [accessed: 7 March 2008].

House of Representatives. Parliamentary Debates. *Official Hansard* [Online] Available at: http://www.aph.gov.au/Hansard/reps/dailys/dr020304.pdf [accessed: 27 March 2008]

Hovell, D. 2004. Chinks in the armour: international law, terrorism and the use of force. *University of New South Wales Law Journal*, 27(2), 398–427.

Howard, J. 2001. ANZUS Treaty-Application of the ANZUS Treaty to terrorist attacks on the United States. *Prime Minister of Australia* [Online, 14 September] Available at: http://www.pm.gov.au/news/media_release1241.htm [accessed: 23 October 2006].

Howard, J. 2002. Press Conference Parliament House. *Prime Minister of Australia* [Online, 20 June] Available at: http://www.pm.gov.au/News/interviews/2002/interview1709.htm [accessed: 2 January 2006].

Howard, J. 2003a. Kerry O'Brien Interview with John Howard, 7.30 Report. *Australian Broadcasting Corporation* [Online, 15 March] Available at: http://www.abc.net.au/7.30/content/2003/s806507.htm accessed: [15 March 2007].

Howard, J. and Blair, T. 2003b. PM and Australian Premier agree on Iraqi reconstruction. *Prime Minister's Office* [Online, 7 May] Available at: http://www.number-10.gov.uk/output/Page3611.asp [accessed: 1 September 2006].

Howe, G. 1990. Sovereignty and interdependence: Britain's place in the world. *International Affairs*, 66(4), 675–95.

Hoyt, P.D. 2000. The 'rogue state' image in American foreign policy. *Global Society*, 14(2), 297–310.

Huddleston, S. 1934. The Wide Horizon: France's Foreign Policy. *Christian Science Monitor*, 16 October, 14.

Hudson, M.O. 1944. The international law of the future. *American Bar Association Journal*, 30(10), 560–63.

Hudson, P. 2003. PM says deaths show regime gone for good. *The Age* [Online, 24 July] Available at http://www.theage.com.au/articles/2003/07/23/1058853136928.html [accessed: 25 February 2007].

Hurrell, A. 2002. There are no rules (George W. Bush): international order after September 11. *International Relations*, 16(2), 185–204.

Hutchings, R.L. 2003. The United Nations and the crisis of multilateralism. *Office of the Director of National Intelligence* [Online, 6 November] Available at: http://www.dni.gov/nic/speeches_un_multilateralism.html accessed: [7 January 2007].

Hyde, C.C. 1945. *International Law: Chiefly as Interpreted and Applied by the United States.* 2nd Edition. Boston: Little, Brown.

Ignatieff, M. 1993. *Blood and Belonging.* Toronto: Viking Press.

Ignatieff, M. 2002. Intervention and state failure. *Dissent*, 49 (1), 115–24.

Independent International Commission on Kosovo. 2000. *The Kosovo Report: Conflict, International Response, Lessons Learned.* Oxford: Oxford University Press.

Inter-American Juridical Committee. 1946. Draft Declaration of the International Rights and Duties of Man and Accompanying Report. *The American Journal of International Law Supplement: Official Documents*, 40(3), 93–116.

International Commission of Jurists. 1972. *The Events in East Pakistan 1971: A Legal Study by the Secretariat of the International Commission of Jurists.* Geneva: International Commission of Jurists.

International Commission on Intervention and State Sovereignty. 2001. *The Responsibility to Protect.* Ottowa: International Development Research Centre.

International Conference on Human Rights. 1968. *Proclamation of Teheran*, ST/HR/1/Rev.5, New York: United Nations.

International Court of Justice. 1949. *Corfu Channel Case, Judgment of April 9th, 1949.* The Hague: ICJ Reports.

International Court of Justice. 1950a. *International Status of South West Africa, Advisory Opinion.* The Hague: ICJ Reports.
International Court of Justice. 1950b. *Request for Interpretation of the Judgement of November 20th, 1950, in the Asylum Case, Judgement of November 27th, 1950.* The Hague: ICJ Reports.
International Court of Justice. 1951. *Reservations to the Convention on Genocide, Advisory Opinion*. The Hague: ICJ Reports.
International Court of Justice. 1969. *North Sea Continental Shelf, Judgement.* The Hague: ICJ Reports.
International Court of Justice. 1971. *Advisory Opinion: Legal Consequences for States of the Continued Presence of South Africa in Namibia (South West Africa) notwithstanding Security Council Resolution 276.* The Hague: ICJ Reports.
International Court of Justice. 1980. *United States Diplomatic and Consular Staff in Teheran, Judgement*. The Hague: ICJ Reports.
International Court of Justice. 1986. *Military and Paramilitary Activities in and against Nicaragua (Nicaragua v. United States of America), Merits, Judgement.* The Hague: ICJ Reports.
International Court of Justice. 1992. *Certain Phosphate Lands in Nauru (Nauru v. Australia): Preliminary Objections, Judgement.* The Hague: ICJ Reports.
International Court of Justice. 1999a. *Public sitting held on Tuesday 11 May 1999, at 4.30 p.m., at the Peace Palace, Vice-President Weeramantry, Acting President, presiding*, CR 1999/24, The Hague: ICJ Documents.
International Court of Justice. 1999b. *Public sitting held on Wednesday 12 May 1999, at 10.00 a.m., at the Peace Palace, Vice-President Weeramantry, Acting President, presiding*, CR 1999/25, The Hague: ICJ Documents.
International Court of Justice. 1999c. *Legality of Use of Force (Yugoslavia v. Belgium), Provisional Measures, Order of 2 June 1999.* The Hague: ICJ Reports.
International Court of Justice. 2003. *Oil Platforms (Islamic Republic of Iran v. United States of America), Judgement*. The Hague: ICJ Reports.
International Court of Justice. 2004. *Legal Consequences of the Construction of a Wall in the Occupied Palestinian Territory, Advisory Opinion.* The Hague: ICJ Reports.
International Court of Justice. 2005. *Armed Activities on the Territory of the Congo (Democratic Republic of the Congo vs Uganda), Judgement*. The Hague: ICJ Reports.
International Criminal Tribunal for Yugoslavia. 1999. *Judgement: The Prosecutor v. Dusko Tadic*, Case No. IT-94-1-A, The Hague: International Criminal Tribunal for Yugoslavia.
International Law Commission. 2001. *Responsibility of States for Internationally Wrongful Acts*, A/56/10(SUPP), New York: United Nations.
International Relations and Post War Planning. London: J. Cape.
Islamic Conference of Foreign Ministers. 2004. Final Communiqué of the Thirty-First Session of the Islamic Conference of Foreign Ministers. *Organisation of*

the Islamic Conference [Online] Available at: http://www.oic-oci.org/english/conf/fm/30/30%20icfm-fc-en.htm [accessed: 15 July 2007]

Israeli Ministry of Foreign Affairs. 2004. Letter dated 29 January 2004 from the Deputy Director General and Legal Advisor of the Ministry of Foreign Affairs, together with the written statement of the Government of Israel. *International Court of Justice* [Online] Available at: http://www.icj-cij.org/docket/files/131/1579.pdf [accessed: 28 April 2007]

Jackson, R.H. 1987. Quasi-states, dual regimes, and neoclassical theory: international jurisprudence and the Third World. *International Organization*, 41(4), 519–49.

Jackson, R.H. and Rosberg, C.G. 1986. Sovereignty and underdevelopment: juridical statehood in the African crisis. *The Journal of Modern African Studies*, 24(1), 1–31.

Jacobsen, H.K. 1964. ONUC's civilian operations: state-preserving and state-building. *World Politics*, 17(1), 75–107.

Janse, R. 2006. The legitimacy of humanitarian intervention. *Leiden Journal of International Law*, 19(3), 669–92.

Jeffrey, A.1981. The American hostages in Tehran: The I.C.J. and the legality of rescue missions. *International and Comparative Law Quarterly*, 30(3), 717–29.

Jenkins, B.M. 1984. New modes of conflict. *Orbis*, 28, 5–16.

Jennings, R. 1986. Dissenting Opinion of Judge Sir Robert Jennings: Military and Paramilitary Activities in and against Nicaragua (*Nicaragua v. United States of America*). *International Court of Justice* [Online] Available at: http://www.icj-cij.org/docket/files/131/1681.pdf [accessed: 17 June 2007]

Jennings, R.Y. 1938. The Caroline and McLeod Cases. *The American Journal of International Law*, 32(1), 82–99.

Jensen, R.B. 1981. The International Anti-Anarchist Conference of 1898 and the origins of Interpol. *Journal of Contemporary History*, 16(2), 323–47.

Jessup, P.C 1959. *A Modern Law of Nations*. New York: Macmillan.

Jessup, P.C. 1946. Force under a modern law of nations. *Foreign Affairs*, 25(1), 90–105.

Johnson, L.B. 1965a. Radio and television report to the American people on the situation in the Dominican Republic, May 2, 1965. *The American Presidency Project* [Online] Available at: http://www.presidency.ucsb.edu/ws/index.php?pid=26932 [accessed: 2 May 2006].

Johnson, L.B. 1965b. Statement by President Johnson, May 2. *US Department of State Bulletin*, 52(1351), 744–48.

Johnson, L.B. 1965c. Statement by President Johnson, April 28. *US Department of State Bulletin*, 52(1351), 738–39.

Johnson, L.B. 1971. *The Vantage Point: Perspectives of the Presidency 1963–1969*. London: Weidenfeld and Nicolson.

Joyce, J.A. 1956. *Revolution on East River: The Twilight of National Sovereignty*. New York: Abelard-Schuman.

Joyner, C.C. 1984. Reflections on the lawfulness of invasion. *The American Journal of International Law*, 78(1), 131–44.
Joyner, C.C. 2005. *International Law in the 21st Century: Rules for Global Governance.* Lanham, MD: Rowman & Littlefield.
Kaldor, M. 2003. American power: from compellance to cosmopolitanism. *International Affairs*, 79(1), 1–22.
Kant, I. 1797. Über ein vermeintliches Recht aus Menschenliebe zu lügen. *Berlinische Blätter*, 1, 301–14.
Kant, I. 1957. *Perpetual Peace.* New York: Bobbs-Merrill Co.
Kant, I. 1983. *Perpetual Peace and Other Essays.* Indianapolis: Hackett Publishing Company.
Keeton, G.W. and Schwarzenberger, G. 1939. *Making International Law Work.* London: Peace Book Company, Ltd.
Keeton, G.W. and Schwarzenberger, G. 1950. *The North Atlantic Treaty, The Brussels Treaty and The Charter of the United Nations.* London: Institute for World Affairs.
Kelly, P. 2003a. Quick victory validates leaders. *The Australian*, 9 April, 11.
Kelly, P. 2003b. Why we fought – really. *The Australian*, 21–22 June, 26.
Kelsen, H. 1920. *Das Problem der Souveranität und die Theorie des Völkerrechts.* Tübingen: J.C.B. Mohr.
Kelsen, H. 1945. The legal status of Germany according to the Declaration of Berlin, *The American Journal of International Law*, 39(3), 518–26.
Kelsen, H. 1952. *Principles of International Law.* New York: Rinehart & Company.
Kelsen, H. 1964. *Law of the United Nations*. New York: Frederick A. Praeger.
Kennedy, J.F. 1962. The Soviet threat to the Americas. *US Department of State Bulletin*, 47 (1220), 715–19.
Kerin, J. 2003. Regional posse goes where UN unable to tread. *The Australian*, 27 June, 6.
Khatami, M. 2002. News Headlines: Iran-US-President. *Presidency of the Islamic Republic of Iran* [Online, 28 August] Available at: http://www.president.ir/cronicnews/1381/8106/810606/810606.htm [accessed: 6 June 2007].
Kirkpatrick, J. 1983. Ambassador Kirkpatrick's Statement, UN General Assembly, Nov. 2, 1983. *US Department of State Bulletin*, 83(2081), 76–7.
Kissinger, H. 2002. Iraq is becoming Bush's most difficult challenge. *Chicago Tribune*, 11 August.
Kissinger, H.A. 1986. Charting a course to the summit. *The Los Angeles Times*, 5 May, F1.
Klare, M. 1998. The rise and fall of the 'rogue doctrine'. *Middle East Report*, 208, 12–15; 47.
Klare, M.T. 1995. The new 'rogue state' doctrine. *The Nation*, 8 May, 625–28.
Klintworth, G. 1989. *Vietnam's Intervention in Cambodia in International Law.* Canberra: Australian Government Publishing Service.

Koizumi, J. 2003. President Bush meets with Japanese Prime Minister Koizumi. *The White House* [Online, 23 May] Available at: http://www.whitehouse.gov/news/releases/2003/05/20030523-4.html [accessed: 12 September 2004].

Kooijmans, P. 2004. Separate Opinion of Judge Kooijmans: Legal Consequences of the Construction of a Wall in the Occupied Palestinian Territory. *International Court of Justice* [Online] Available at: http://www.icj-cij.org/docket/files/131/1683.pdf [accessed: 7 March 2007]

Kopelmanas, L. 1937. The problem of aggression and the prevention of war. *The American Journal of International Law*, 31(2), 244–57.

Krasner, S.D. 2004. Sharing sovereignty: new institutions for collapsed and failing states. *International Security*, 29(2), 85–120.

Krift, T.R. 1977. Self-defense and self-help: the Israeli raid on Entebbe. *Brooklyn Journal of International Law*, 4(1), 43–62.

Krishnaswami, S. 2002. Every country has the right to pre-emption: Jaswant. *The Hindu* [Online, 1 October] Available at: http://www.hinduonnet.com/2002/10/01/stories/2002100103650100.htm [accessed: 8 April 2008]

Kritsiotis, D. 1996. The legality of the 1993 US missile strike on Iraq and the right of self-defence in international law. *The International and Comparative Law Quarterly*, 45(1), 162–77.

Kuhn, A.K. 1935. The complaint of Yugoslavia against Hungary with reference to the assassination of King Alexander. *The American Journal of International Law*, 29(1), 87–92.

Kui, Y.T. 2003. Australia, N. Korea Join 'Preemptive' Bandwagon. *New Straits Times*, 26 October, 4.

Kuperman, A.J. 2001. *The Limits of Humanitarian Intervention: Genocide in Rwanda.* Washington DC: Brookings Institution Press.

Kupperman, R.H. 1982. US is not immune to terrorism, and had better get its act together. *Los Angeles Times*, 4 August, C5.

Kupperman, R.H. and Van Opstal, D. 1983. Here today, gone tomorrow – nuclear deterrence in the 1990s? *Annals of the American Academy of Political and Social Science*, 469, 68–76.

Lacey, M. 2000. Self-defence or self-denial: the proliferation of weapons of mass destruction. *Indiana International and Comparative Law Review*, 10(2), 293–316.

Lake, A. 1994. Confronting backlash states. *Foreign Affairs*, 73 (2), 45–55.

Langford, T. 1999. Things fall apart: state failure and the politics of intervention. *International Studies Review*, 1(1), 59–79.

Lauterpacht, E. 1997. Sovereignty – myth or reality? *International Affairs*, 73(1), 137–50.

Lauterpacht, H. 1927. Revolutionary propaganda by governments. *Transactions of the Grotius Society*, 13, 143–64.

Lauterpacht, H. 1943. The law of nations, the law of nature and the rights of man. *Transactions of the Grotius Society*, 29, 1–33.

Lauterpacht, H. 1948. The subjects of the law of nations. *Law Quarterly Review*, 64, 97–119.

Lauterpacht, H. 1950. *International Law and Human Rights*. New York: Frederick A. Praeger, Inc.

Lauterpacht, H. 1952. *International Law: A Treatise*. London: Longman's, Green and Co.

Lauterpacht, H. 1966. *The Function of Law in the International Community*. Hamden, Connecticut: Archon Books.

Lavrow, S.V. 2004. Statement at the 59th Session of the United Nations General Assembly. *United Nations* [Online, 23 September] Available at: http://www.un.org/webcast/ga/59/statements/russia_eng.pdf [accessed: 12 August 2006].

Lawrence, T.J. 1895. *The Principles of International Law*. 2nd Edition. London: Macmillan.

League of Nations Assembly. 1946. Records of the Twentieth and Twenty-first Ordinary Sessions of the Assembly. *League of Nations Office Journal*, 194, 278–79.

League of Nations Committee of Experts for the Progressive Codification of International Law. 1926. Responsibility of states for damage done in their territories to the person or property of foreigners. *The American Journal of International Law: Supplement Official Documents*, 20(3), 176–203.

League of Nations. 1938. Instruments of the International Conference on the Repression of Terrorism. *Official Journal*, 19(1), 23–65.

Leitel, I. 1970. The United Nations Charter as a restraint upon a nation's right to wage war. *Brooklyn Law Review*, 36(2), 212–39.

Lemkin, R. 1944. *Axis Rule in Occupied Europe*. Washington D.C.: Carnegie Endowment for International Peace.

Lemkin, R. 1947. Genocide as a crime under international law. *The American Journal of International Law*, 41(1), 145–51.

Levitin, M.J. 1986. The law of force and the force of law: Grenada, the Falklands, and humanitarian intervention. *Harvard International Law Journal*, 27(2), 621–57.

Lewis, G.C. 1859. *On Foreign Jurisdiction and the Extradition of Criminals*. London: J.W. Parker and Son.

Lie, T. 1949. *The Charter and Judgement of the Nuremberg Tribunal: History and Analysis – Memorandum by the Secretary-General of the United Nations*, A/CN.4/5, New York: United Nations.

Lillich, R.B. 1967. The forcible self-help by states to protect human rights international procedures to protect human rights: a symposium. *Iowa Law Review*, 53(2), 325–51.

Lillich, R.B. 1969. Intervention to protect human rights. *McGill Law Journal*, 15(2), 205–19.

Lillich, R.B. 1973. *Humanitarian Intervention and the United Nations*. Charlottesville: University Press of Virginia.

Lillich, R.B. 1992. Forcible protection of nationals abroad: the Liberian 'incident' of 1990. *German Yearbook of International Law*, 35, 205–23.

Lillich, R.B., Wingfield, T.C. and Meyen, J.E. 2002. *Lillich on the Forcible Protection of Nationals Abroad.* Newport, R.I.: Naval War College.

Lima, F.X De 1971. *Intervention in International Law.* Den Haag: Uitgeverij Pax Nederland.

Lincoln, A. 1863. President Abraham Lincoln's Address at the dedication of the Soldiers' National Cemetery Gettysburg, Pennsylvania. [Online: Gettysburg Foundation] Available at: http://www.gettysburgfoundation.org/learn/gettysburg_address.html [accessed: 6 March 2006].

Lingelbach, W.E. 1900. The doctrine and practice of intervention in Europe. *Annals of the American Academy of Political and Social Science*, 16(1), 1–32.

Litwak, R.S. 2000a. Rogue states a handy label, but a lousy policy. *The Washington Post*, 20 February, B3.

Litwak, R.S. 2000b. *Rogue States and U.S. Foreign Policy: Containment After the Cold War.* Baltimore: Johns Hopkins University Press.

Litwak, R.S. 2003. The new calculus of pre-emption. *Survival*, 44(4), 53–80.

Livius, T. 1854. *Ab Urbe Condita.* Leipzig: Weidmannsche Buchhandlung.

Llewellyn-Jones, F. 1933. Treaty revision and Art.XIX of the Covenant of the League of Nations. *Transactions of the Grotius Society*, 19, 13–31.

Lobel, J. 1999. The use of force to respond to terrorist attacks: the bombing of Sudan and Afghanistan. *The Yale Journal of International Law*, 24(2), 537–57.

Locke, J. 1988. *Two Treaties of Government.* Cambridge: Cambridge University Press.

Logan, J. and Preble, C. 2006. Failed states and flawed logic: the case against a standing nation-building office. *CATO Institute Policy Analysis*, 560, 1–32.

Longchamp, F. 1994. *Letter dated 9 February 1994 from the Permanent Representative of Haiti to the United Nations addressed to the Secretary-General*, A/48/867-S/1994/150, New York: United Nations.

Lord, E.L. 1892. International arbitration. *Annals of the American Academy of Political and Social Science*, 2(4), 39–55.

Lorimer, J.T. 1872. *The Institutes of Law: A Treatise of the Principles of Jurisprudence as determined by Nature.* Edinburgh: T.&T. Clark, Law Publishers.

Luard, E. 1984. Collective intervention, in *Intervention in World Politics*, edited by H. Bull. Oxford: Clarendon Press, 157–79.

Luttwak, E. 1999. Kofi's rule: humanitarian intervention and neocolonialism. *The National Interest*, 58, 57–62.

Machiavelli, N. 2003. *The Prince.* Oxford: Oxford University Press.

MacQueen, N. 2006. *Peacekeeping and the International System.* London: Routledge.

Maggs, G.E. 2006. The campaign to restrict the right to respond to terrorist attacks in self-defence under Article 51 of the UN Charter and what the United States can do about it. *Regent Journal of International Law*, 4(2), 149–74.

Mahalingam, R. 1996. The compatibility of the principle of non-intervention with the right of humanitarian intervention. *UCLA Journal of International Law and Foreign Affairs*, 1(1), 221–63.

Mahassani, Y. 2003. *Letter dated 3 March 2003 from the Permanent Observer for the League of Arab States to the United Nations Addressed to the President of the Security Council*, S/2003/254, New York: United Nations.

Makinda, S.M. 1998. The United Nations and state sovereignty: mechanism for managing international security. *Australian Journal of Political Science*, 33(1), 101–15.

Maleski, D. 1996. *Letter dated 29 July 1996 from the Permanent Representative of the Former Yugoslav Republic of Macedonia to the United Nations addressed to the Secretary-General*, S/1996/605, New York: United Nations Document.

Malinowski, W.R. 1944. The pattern of underground resistance. *Annals of the American Academy of Political and Social Science*, 232, 126–33.

Mallison, W.T. 1983. Aggression or self-defense in Lebanon in 1982? *The American Society of International Law Proceedings*, 77, 174–82.

Mamvig, H. 2001. The reproduction of sovereignties: between man and state during practices of intervention', *Cooperation and Conflict*, 36(3), 251–72.

Mandelbaum, M. 1999. A perfect failure: NATO's war against Yugoslavia. *Foreign Affairs*, 78(5), 2–8.

Mani, V.S. 2003. International terrorism and the quest for legal controls. *International Studies*, 40(1), 41–67.

Manning, W.O. 1839. *Commentaries on the Law of Nations*. London: S. Sweet.

Maogoto, J.N. 2004. New frontiers, old problems: the war on terror and the notion of anticipating the enemy. *Netherlands International Law Review*, 51(1), 1–39.

Marek, K. 1968. *Identity and Continuity of States in Public International Law.* Geneva: Librairie Droz.

Marshall, G.C. 1947. European initiative essential to economic recovery. *US Department of State Bulletin*, 16(415), 1159–60.

Martens, G.F. de. 1883. *Traité de Droit International.* Paris: Chevalier-Marescq et cie.

Martinez, M.M. 1996. *National Sovereignty and International Organizations.* The Hague: Kluwer Law International.

McCredie, J.A. 1985. The responsibility of states for private acts of international terrorism. *Temple International and Comparative Law Journal*, 1(1), 69–97.

McDougal, M.S. and Bebr, G. 1964. Human rights in the United Nations. *The American Journal of International Law*, 58(3), 603–41.

McFadden, R.D. 1994. Western troops arrive in Rwanda to aid foreigners. *The New York Times*, 10 April, 1.

McKinley, W. 1898a. Message to the Congress of the United States (11 April 1898), in *United States Department of State Papers Relating to the Foreign Relations of the United States*, edited by U.S. Government Printing Office. Washington, D.C: U.S. Government Printing Office, 750–60.

McKinley, W. 1898b. Message to the Congress of the United States, 11th April, in *Papers relating to the foreign relations of the United States, with the annual message of the president transmitted to Congress December 5, 1898*, edited by United States Department of State. Washington D.C.: U.S. Government Printing Office, 750–60.

McNair, A.D. 1961. *The Law of Treaties*. Oxford: Clarendon Press.

Memorial Institute for the Prevention of Terrorism. 2008. *MIPT Terrorism Knowledge Database* [Online] Available at: http://www.tkb.org/RandSummary.jsp?page=method [accessed: 12 February 2008].

Menkhaus, K. 2006. Governance without government in Somalia: spoilers, state building, and the politics of coping. *International Security*, 31(3), 74–106.

Meyer, A. 1908. *Die Erschließung des Luftraums und Ihre Rechtlichen Folgen*. Frankfurt: Druck und Verlag von Gebrüder Knauer.

Middendorf, J. W. 1983. Ambassador Middendorf's statement, OAS, Permanent Council, Oct. 26, 1983. *US Department of State Bulletin*, 83(2081), 72–3.

Middleton, D. 1965. Soviet rebuffed by a vote in U.N. *The New York Times*, 21 December, 1

Millard, T.F. 1925. China would fight any intervention. *The New York Times*, 19 August, 4

Milosevic, S. 1999. Address to the Nation. [Online: Mount Holeyoke College] Available at: http://www.mtholyoke.edu/acad/intrel/speech/milospch.htm [accessed: 22 April 2006].

Mingst, K.A. and Karns, M.P. 2000. *The United Nations in the Post-Cold War Era*. Boulder: Westview Press.

Moir, A. 2003. A Coalition of the Willing 1939. *The Sydney Morning Herald* [Online] Available at: http://www.moir.com.au/sales/image151.htm [accessed: 9 October 2006]

Monroe, J. 1823–1824. President's Annual Message: 2 December 1823, in *Annals of Congress*, edited by United States Congress. Washington D.C.: United

Moore, J.N. 1967. International law and the United States role in Viet Nam: a reply', *The Yale Law Journal*, 76(6), 1051–94.

Moore, J.N. 1969. The control of foreign intervention in internal conflict. *Virginia Journal of International Law*, 9(2), 205–342.

Moore, J.N. 1972. *Law and the Indo-China War*. Princeton: Princeton University Press.

Moore, J.N. 1984. Grenada and the international double standard. *American Journal of International Law*, 78(1), 145–68.

Moore, J.N. 1987. The Nicaragua Case and the deterioration of world order. *The American Journal of International Law*, 81(1), 151–9.

Moore, J.N. 1988. The need for an international convention, in *Legal Responses to International Terrorism: US Procedural Aspects*, edited by M.C. Bassiouni. Dordrecht: Martinus Nijhoff Publishers, 437–44.

Morgan, P.M. 1993. Multilateralism and security: prospects in Europe, in *Multilateralism Matters: The Theory and Praxis of an International Form*, edited by J.G. Ruggie. New York: Columbia University Press, 327–64.

Morgenthau, H. 1948. *Politics among Nations: The Struggle for Power and Peace*. New York: A. A. Knopf.

Mosler, H. 1937. *Die Intervention im Völkerrecht.* Berlin: Junker und Dunnhaupt.

Motshabi, K. 1987. International law and the United States raid on Libya. *The South African Law Journal*, 104(4), 669–83.

Murphy, J.F. 1978. State self-help and problems of public international law, in *Legal Aspects of International Terrorism*, edited by A.E. Evans and J.F. Murphy. Lexington, MA: Lexington Books, 553–73.

Murphy, L.G.B. 1991. A proposal on international legal responses to terrorism. *Touro Journal of Transnational Law*, 2, 67–106.

Murphy, S.D. 2002. Terrorism and the Concept of 'Armed Attack' in Article 51 of the UN Charter. *Harvard International Law Journal.* 43 (1), 41–51.

Murphy, S.D. 2005. The doctrine of preemptive self-defence. *Villanova Law Review*, 50(3), 699–748.

Murray, G. (1914), *How Can War Be Right?* London: Oxford University Press.

Murray, G. 1922. Self-determination of nationalities. *Journal of the British Institute of International Affairs*, 1(1), 6–13.

Murray, G. 1929. *The Ordeal of this Generation: The War, the League and the Future.* London: George Allen & Unwin Ltd.

Murray, J.C. 1960. *Morality and Modern War*. New York: Church Peace Union.

Murswiek, D. 2003. *The American Strategy of Preemptive War and International Law*. [Online, 18 July]. Available at http://ssrn.com/abstract=397601 or doi:10.2139/ssrn.397601 [accessed: 4 September 2004]

Nash, M.L. 1976. Contemporary practice of the United States relating to international law. *American Journal of International Law*, 73(1), 127–37.

Nash, M.L. 1979. Contemporary practice of the United States relating to international law. *American Journal of International Law*, 73(1), 122–37.

National Commission on Terrorist Attacks upon the United States. 2004. *The 9/11 Commission Report.* New York: W.W. Norton & Company.

National Security Council. 1975a. Minutes National Security Council meeting: seizure of american ship by Cambodian authorities. [Online: Gerald R. Ford Presidential Library] Available at: http://www.fordlibrarymuseum.gov/library/document/nscmin/750512a.htm [accessed: 6 June 2007].

National Security Council. 1975b. Minutes National Security Council meeting: seizure of american ship by Cambodian authorities. [Online: Gerald R. Ford Presidential Library] Available at: http://www.fordlibrarymuseum.gov/library/document/nscmin/750513a.htm [accessed: 4 June 2007].

Neff, S.C. 2003. A short history of international law, in *International Law*. 2nd Edition, edited by M.D. Evans. Oxford: Oxford University Press, 31–58.

Negroponte, J.D. 2001. *Letter dated 7 October 2001 from the Permanent Representative of the United States of America to the United Nations addressed to the President of the Security Council*, S/2001/946, New York: United Nations.

Negroponte, J.D. 2003. *Letter dated 20 March 2003 from the Permanent Representative of the United States of America to the United Nations addressed to the President of the Security Council*, S/2003/351, New York: United Nations.

Newland, K., Patrick, E. and Zard, M. 2003. *No Refuge: The Challenge of Internal Displacement*. New York and Geneva: United Nations Office for the Coordination of Humanitarian Assistance.

Ninčić, D. 1970. *The Problem of Sovereignty in the Charter and in the Practice of the United Nations*. The Hague: Martinus Nijhoff.

Nippold, O. 1923. *The Development of International Law after the World War*. Oxford: The Clarendon Press.

Non-Aligned Movement. 2000. Declaration of the Group of 77 South Summit held in Havana from 10 to 14 April 2000. [Online, Non-Aligned Movement] Available at: http://www.nam.gov.za/documentation/southdecl.htm [accessed: 4 April 2007].

North Atlantic Treaty Organization. 2001. International Security Assistance Force [Online, NATO] Available at: http://www.nato.int/issues/isaf/index.html [accessed: 7 March 2007].

Norwegian Nobel Committee. 2009. *Announcement* [Online, 9 October]. Available at http://nobelpeaceprize.org/en_GB/laureates/laureates-2009/announce-2009/ [accessed: 11 September 2009]

Nustad, K.G. and Thune, H. 2002. Norway: political consensus and the problem of accountability, in *Democratic Accountability and the Use of Force in International Law*, edited by C. Ku and H.K. Jacobsen. Cambridge: Cambridge University Press, 154–75.

Nye, J.S. 1982. The US and Soviet stakes in nuclear nonproliferation. *PS*, 15(1), 32–9.

O'Connell, M.E. 2002. Lawful self-defence to terrorism. *University of Pittsburgh Law Review*, 63(4), 889–908.

O'Reilly, K.P 2007. Perceiving rogue states: the use of the 'rogue state' concept by US foreign policy elites. *Foreign Policy Analysis*, 3(4), 295–315.

O'Sullivan, M.L. 2000. Sanctioning 'rogue states': a strategy in decline? *Harvard International Review*, 22(2), 56–60.

Ochoa-Ruiz, N. and Salamanca-Aguado, E. 2005. Exploring the limits of international law relating to the use of force in self-defence. *The European Journal of International Law*, 16(3), 499–524.

Office of Public Information. 1963. *From Dependence to Freedom: The United Nations Role in the Advance of Dependent Peoples towards Self-government or Independence.* New York: United Nations.

Office of the Secretary of Defense. 1997. *Proliferation Threat and Response – 1997.* Washington DC: Office of the Secretary of Defense.

Office of the Secretary of Defense. 2001. *Proliferation Threat and Response – 2001.* Washington DC: Office of the Secretary of Defense.

Offutt, M. 1928. *The Protection of Citizens Abroad by the Forces of the United States*. Baltimore: John Hopkins Press.

Ofri, A. 1984. Intelligence and Counterterrorism. *Orbis*, 28(1), 42–56.

Okun, H.S. 1986. *Letter dated 14 April 1986 from the acting Permanent Representative of the United States of America to the United Nations addressed to the President of the Security Council*, S/17990, New York: United Nations.

Oliver, C. 1963. International law and the quarantine of Cuba: a hopeful prescription for legal writing. *The American Journal of International Law*, 57(2), 373–77.

Oppenheim, L. 1912. *International Law: A Treatise.* London: Longmans, Green and Co.

Oppenheim, L. 1919. *The League of Nations and its Problems.* London: Green and Co.

Oppenheim, L. 1969. *International Law: A Treatise.* London: Longmans, Green and Co Ltd.

Orend, B. 1999. Crisis in Kosovo: a just use of force? *Politics*, 19(3), 125–30.

Orford, A. 2003. *Reading Humanitarian Intervention: Human Rights and the Use of Force in International Law.* Cambridge: Cambridge University Press.

Organization of American States. 2001. *Meeting of Consultation of Ministers of Foreign Affairs: Terrorist Threat to the Americas*, RC.24/RES.1/01, Washington DC: Organization of American States.

Organization of Eastern Caribbean States. 1983. OECS Statement, Oct. 25, 1983. *US Department of State Bulletin*, 83(2081), 67–8.

Orth, S.P. 1916. Law and force in international affairs. *International Journal of Ethics*, 26 (3), 339–46.

Orwin, C. 2006. Humanitarian military intervention: wars for the end of history? in *Justice and Global Politics*, edited by E.F. Paul. New York: Cambridge University Press, 196–217.

Osborn, A. 2001. US has no problem with European force, says Powell. *The Guardian* [Online, 28 February] Available at: http://www.guardian.co.uk/world/2001/feb/28/usa.eu [accessed: 15 February 2007]

Österdahl, I. 2005. The exception as the rule: lawmaking on force and human rights by the UN Security Council. *Journal of Conflict and Security Law*, 10 (1), 1–20.

Paasche, F.W. 1987. The use of force in combating terrorism. *Columbia Journal of Transnational Law*, 25(2), 377–402.

Pallet, A. 2000. Brief remarks on the unilateral use of force. *European Journal of International Law*, 11(2), 385–92.

Pargeter, A. 2005. Libya: from rogue-state to partner. *Journal of Middle Eastern Geopolitics*, 1(2), 5–9.

Patman, R.G. 1999. Security in a post-Cold War context, in *Security in a Post-Cold War World*, edited by R.G. Patman. London: Macmillan Press Ltd, 1–12.

Patrick, S. 2006. Weak states and global threats: fact or fiction? *The Washington Quarterly*, 29(2), 27–53.

Pattison, J. 2007. Humanitarian intervention and international law: the moral importance of an intervener's legal status. *Critical Review of International Social and Political Philosophy*, 10(3), 301–19.

Paust, J.J. 2002. Use of armed force against terrorists in Afghanistan, Iraq and beyond. *Cornell International Law Journal*, 35(3), 533–57.

Pedersen, F.C. 1976. Controlling international terrorism: an analysis of unilateral force and proposals for multilateral cooperation. *University of Toledo Law Review*, 8(1), 209–50.

Pegler, W. 1942. Fair Enough. *Los Angeles Times*, 27 August, A.

Pella, V.V. 1925. *La Criminalité collective des États et le droit penal de l'avenir.* Bucharest: Imprimerie de l'Etat.

Pemberton, G.J. 1989. Australia, the United States, and the Indochina Crisis of 1954. *Diplomatic History*, 6(1), 45–66.

Pemberton, G.J. 2008. The man who saw the future: Vespasian V. Pella – aggression, terrorism and the creation of the International Criminal Court. *The Romanian Journal of International Law*, 6, 203–23.

Pemberton, G.J. forthcoming. *First Fright: Opening Shots in the War on Terror.*

Pennock, J.R. 1958. Reviews: Aggression and World Order: A Critique of United Nations Theories of Aggression. *The Yale Law Journal*, 68 (2), 387–93.

Permanent Court of International Justice. 1923. Judgment: The Case of the S.S. "Wimbledon" (United Kingdom, France, Italy and Japan v. Germany). *International Court of Justice* [Online] Available at: http://www.icj-cij.org/pcij/serie_A/A_01/03_Wimbledon_Arret_08_1923.pdf [accessed: 19 May 2007].

Permanent Court of International Justice. 1927. Judgment: The Case of the S.S. "Lotus" (France and Turkey). *International Court of Justice* [Online] Available at: http://www.icj-cij.org/pcij/serie_A/A_10/30_Lotus_Arret.pdf [accessed: 19 May 2007]

Permanent Mission of Libya to the United Nations. 2001a. Statement of Colonel Muammar Qaddafi, Leader of the First of September Revolution, on the horrific attacks against USA. [Online, 11 September] Available at: http://www.libya-un.org [accessed: 14 June 2007].

Permanent Mission of Libya to the United Nations. 2001b. Statement of Colonel Muammar Qaddafi Regarding the Spread of Anthrax in Parts of the United States. [Online, 19 October] Available at: http://www.libya-un.org [accessed: 14 June 2003].

Pfaff, W. 2001. Die Verselbständigung des Militärischen in der amerikanischen Politik. *Blätter für Deutsche und International Politik*, 45 (2), 177–96.

Phillimore, R. 1854. *Commentaries upon International Law.* Philadelphia: T. & J.W. Johnson, Law Booksellers.

Phillips, R. 1984. *War and Justice*. Norman, OK: University of Oklahoma Press.

Pilgrim, C.M. 1990. Terrorism in national and international law. *Dickinson Journal of International Law*, 8 (2), 147–202.

Pittard, E. 1896. *La Protection des Nationaux á L'Éstranger*. Genéve: Impr. W. Kündig & Fils.

Plato. 1987. *The Republic*. New York: Garland.

Pogany, I. 1986. Humanitarian intervention in international law: the French intervention in Syria re-examined. *The International and Comparative Law Quarterly*, 35 (1), 182–90.

Pomerance, M. 2005. The ICJ's Advisory Jurisdiction and the Crumbling Wall between the Political and Judicial. *The American Journal of International Law*, 99 (1), 26–42.

Popovski, V. and Turner, N. 2008. *Policy Brief: Legality and Legitimacy in International Order, No.5*. Tokyo: United Nations University.

Powell, C.L. 2003, Mugabe's own must aid revolt, *The Age*, 30 June.

Powell, C.L. 2004. The crisis in Darfur: testimony before the Senate Foreign Relations Committee. US Department of State [Online, 9 September] Available at: http://2001-2009.state.gov/secretary/former/powell/remarks/36042.htm [accessed: 7 September 2009].

Pradier-Fodéré, P.L.E. 1885. *Traité de Droit International Public.* Paris: G. Pedone-Lauriel.

Press Wireless. 1933. International Peace moves on as Four-Power Pact is signed. *Christian Science Monitor*, 15 July, 1.

Prime Minister's Strategy Unit. 2005. *Investing in Prevention: An International Strategy to Manage Risks of Instability and Improve Crisis Response*. London: Prime Minister's Strategy Unit.

Progressive Governance Summit. 2003. Communique. *Prime Minister's Office* [Online, 14 July] Available at: http://www.number-10.gov.uk/output/Page4146.asp [accessed: 2 April 2007].

Pryce-Jones, D. 2001. We are waging a just war. *The New Criterion* [Online, 20 November] Available at: http://www.newcriterion.com/articles.cfm/justwar-prycejones-2091 [accessed: 14 February 2008].

Pufendorf, S. von. 1991. *On the Duty of Man and Citizen according to Natural Law*. Cambridge: Cambridge University Press.

Quester, G.H. 1981. Preventing proliferation: the impact on international politics. *International Organization*, 35 (1), 213–40.

Quigley, J. 2003. The Afghanistan war and self-defence. *Valparaiso University Law Review*, 37 (2), 541–62.

Ralston, J.H. 1931. Obervations upon the responsibility of states for damages caused in their territories to the person or property of foreigners. *Virginia Law Review*, 17 (6), 570–78.

Rankin, J. 2003. The US has rogue leaders, but that does not make it a rogue state. *New Statesman*, 132(4468), 51–2.

Rau, J. 1999. Habe keinen Ehrgeiz, nie gehabt. *Die Zeit* [Online] Available at: http://www.zeit.de/1999/15/199915.rau_.xml [accessed: 7 September 2008].

Reagan, R. 1983a. President's remarks, Oct. 25, 1983. *US Department of State Bulletin*, 83(2081), 67.

Reagan, R. 1983b. President's remarks and Question and Answer Session (Excerpts). *US Department of State Bulletin*, 83(2081), 78–9.

Reagan, R. 1985. The New Network of Terrorist States. *US Department of State Bulletin*, 85(2101), 7–10.

Reagan, R. 1986. Address to the Nation on the United States air strike against Libya. *Ronald Reagan Presidential Library* [Online] Available at: http://www.reagan.utexas.edu/archives/speeches/1986/41486g.htm [accessed: 3 March 2007].

Reisman, W.M. and Armstrong, A. 2006. The past and future of the claim of preemptive self-defence. *The American Journal of International Law*, 100 (3), 525–50.

Reisman, W.M. 1984. Article 2(4): The use of force in contemporary international law. *American Society International Proceedings*, 78, 74–86.

Reisman, W.M. 1999. International legal responses to terrorism. *Houston Journal of International Law*, 22 (1), 3–61.

Reisman, W.M. 2000. Unilateral action and the transformations of the world constitutive process: the special problem of humanitarian intervention. *European Journal of International Law*, 11 (1), 3–18.

Reisman, W.M. 2003. Self-defence in an age of terrorism. *American Society of International Law Proceedings*, 97, 141–52.

Reisman, W.M. and McDougal, M.S. 1973. Humanitarian intervention to protect the Ibos', in *Humanitarian Intervention and the United Nations*, edited by R.B. Lillich. Charlottesville: University Press of Virginia, 167–96.

Reuters. 1960. Reds rebuked by Belgium on Congo attack. *Chicago Daily Tribune*, 16 July, S13.

Reuters. 2004. Broad international coalition condemns U.S. torture. *Reuters*, 28 May.

Rice, C. 2000. Promoting the National Interests. *Foreign Affairs*, 79 (1), 45–62.

Rice, C. 2002a. Tracking the defence debate: paper given at Paul H. Nitze School of Advanced International Studies, Johns Hopkins University. *Association of the United States Army* [Online, 29 April] Available at: http://www.ausa.org/RAMPnew/DDriceSAISspeech.htm [accessed: 7 February 2003].

Rice, C. 2002b. Dr. Condoleezza Rice discusses President's National Security Strategy. *The White House* [Online, 1 October] Available at: http://www.whitehouse.gov/news/releases/2002/10/20021001-6.html [accessed: 3 February 2007].

Rice, C. 2003. Dr. Condoleezza Rice discusses the President's trip to Africa. *The White House* [Online, 3 July] Available at: http://www.whitehouse.gov/news/releases/2003/07/20030703-14.html [accessed: 11 August 2005].

Rice, C. 2005. The promise of democratic peace: why promoting freedom is the only realistic path to security. *The Washington Post*, 11 December, B7.

Richardson, B. 1998. *Letter dated 20th August 1998 from the Permanent Representative of the United States of America to the United Nations addressed to the President of the Security Council*, S/1998/780, New York: United Nations.

Rieff, D. 1999. A New Age of Liberal Imperialism? *World Policy Journal*, 16 (2), 1–10.

Roberts, A. 1993. Humanitarian war: military intervention and human rights. *International Affairs*, 69 (3), 429–49.

Roberts, A. 1997. New criteria for intervention in the post-Cold War period, in *International Intervention: New Norms in the Post-Cold War Era*, edited by P. Wallensteen. Uppsala: Department of Peace and Conflict Research, 117–42.

Robertson, G. 2001. Statement by NATO Secretary General, Lord Robertson. *NATO* [Online, 2 October] Available at: http://www.nato.int/docu/speech/2001/s011002a.htm [accessed: 28 March 2007].

Rodley, N.S. 1989. Human rights and humanitarian intervention: the case law of the World Court. *The International and Comparative Law Quarterly*, 38 (2), 321–33.

Rolland, R. 1931. Broaden, Europe, or die! My country is not yesterday, my country is tomorrow. *The Nation*, 22 April, 443–45.

Ronzitti, N. 1985. *Rescuing Nationals Abroad through Military Coercion and Intervention on the Grounds of Humanity*. Dordrecht: Martinus Nijhoff.

Roosevelt, T. 1904. Annual message of the President, 6 December 1904, in *Papers Relating to the Foreign Relations of the United States*, edited by United States Department of State. Washington D.C.: U.S. Government Printing Office, ix–xlviii.

Root, E. 1910. Basis of protection to citizens residing abroad. *American Journal of International Law*, 4 (3), 517–28.

Rosen, S.J. and Frank, R. 1975. Measures against international terrorism, in *International Terrorism and World Security*, edited by D. Carlton and C. Schaer. London: Croom Helm, 60–68.

Rotberg, R.I. 2002a. Failed states in a world of terror. *Foreign Affairs*, 81(4), 127–41.

Rotberg, R.I. 2002b. The new nature of nation-state failure. *The Washington Quarterly*, 25(3), 85–96.

Rotberg, R.I. 2009. Disorder in the ranks. *Foreign Policy* [Online, 22 June] Available at: http://www.foreignpolicy.com/articles/2009/06/22/2009_failed_states_index_disorder_in_the_ranks [accessed: on 31 July 2009]

Rotfeld, A.D. 1994. Introduction: the search for a new security system, in *Stockholm International Peace Research Institute (SIPRI) Yearbook 1994:*

World Armaments and Disarmament, edited by Stockholm International Peace Research Institute (SIPRI). New York: Oxford University Press, 1–10.

Rotfeld, A.D. 1999. Introduction: rethinking the contemporary security system, in *Stockholm International Peace Research Institute (SIPRI) Yearbook 1999: World Armaments and Disarmament*, edited by Stockholm International Peace Research Institute (SIPRI). New York: Oxford University Press, 1–12.

Rotfeld, A.D. 2000. Introduction: in search of a global security system for the 21st Century, in *Stockholm International Peace Research Institute (SIPRI) Yearbook 2000: World Armaments and Disarmament*, edited by Stockholm International Peace Research Institute (SIPRI). New York: Oxford University Press, 1–12.

Roth, K. 2006. Was the Iraq war a humanitarian intervention? *Journal of Military Ethics*, 5 (2), 84–92.

Rougier, A. 1910. La théorie de l'intervention d'humanité. *Revue générale de Droit International Public*, 17(1), 468–526.

Rousseau, J.J. 1997. *The Social Contract.* Cambridge: Cambridge University Press.

Rovere, T.M. della. 1860. *Rights of Nations, or, The New Law of European States, applied to the Affairs of Italy.* London: W. Jeffs.

Rowles, J.P. 1987. Military responses to terrorism: substantive and procedural constraints in international law. *American Society of International Law Proceedings*, 81, 307–18.

Roy, S.N.G. 1961. Is the law of responsibility of states for injuries to aliens a part of universal international law. *American Journal of International Law*, 55 (4), 863–91.

Rubin, B. 1999a. U.S. foreign policy and rogue states. *Middle East Review of International Affairs*, 3(3), 72–7.

Rubin, B. 1999b. Schurkenstaaten: Amerikas Selbstverständnis und seine Beziehungen zur Welt. *Internationale Politik* [Online, June] Available at: http://www.internationalepolitik.de/ip/archiv/jahrgang1999/juni99/download/c19f4cc626dd11dbba2e316fff17e6b2e6b2/original_Rubin_9906.pdf [accessed: 7 August 2009].

Rummel, R.J. 1994. *Death By Government.* New Brunswick, NJ: Transaction Publishers.

Rumsfeld, D. 2004. Secretary Rumsfeld speaks on '21st Century' transformation of U.S. armed forces. *United States Department of Defense* [Online, 17 October] Available at: http://www.defenselink.mil/speeches/2002/s20020131-secdef2.html [accessed: 17 October 2007].

Rumsfeld, Donald. 2002. Annual Report to the President and Congress. *United States Department of Defense* [Online] Available at: http://www.defenselink.mil/execsec/adr2002/index.htm [accessed: 7 July 2007].

Ryan, J.M and Lumley, J.S.P. 2000. And finally...failed states and failing states. *Trauma*, 2 (3), 231–35.

Sabasteanski, A. 2005. *Patterns of Global Terrorism 1985–2005: U.S. Department of State Reports with Supplementary Documents and Statistics.* Great Barrington, MA: Berkshire Publishing Group.

Sabic, Z. 2003. Preventive war or preventive argumentation? discussing international affairs in the 21st Century. *Journal of International Relations and Development*, 6 (4), 399–410.

Said, A.S. 1998. *Letter dated 21 August 1998 from the Charge d'Affaires A.I. of the Permanent Mission of Kuwait to the United Nations Addressed to the President of the Security Council*, S/1998/789, New York: United Nations Document.

Saint Pierre, A. de. 1981. *Projet pour rendre la paix perpetuelle en Europe.* Paris: Garniers Frères.

Sassen, S. 1996. *Losing Control? Sovereignty in an Age of Globalization.* New York: Columbia University Press.

Saul, B. 2005. Definition of 'terrorism' in the UN Security Council 1985–2004. *Chinese Journal of International Law*, 4(1), 141–66.

Saul, B. 2006. *Defining Terrorism in International Law.* Oxford: Oxford University Press.

Sayre, F.B. 1948. Legal problems arising from the United Nations trusteeship system. *The American Journal of International Law*, 42 (2), 263–98.

Scali, J. 1975. U.S. Letter to U.N. Secretary General, May 14. *US Department of State Bulletin*, 72(1875), 720.

Scelle, G. 1936. L'agression et la légitime défense dans les rapports internationaux. *L'esprit international* 10, 372–93.

Schachter, O. 1984. The right of states to use armed force. *Michigan Law Review*, 82(5–6), 1620–46.

Schachter, O. 1991. *International Law in Theory and Practice.* Dordrecht: Martinus Nijhoff.

Schaff, P. 1887. *Augustin: The Writings Against the Manichaeans and Against the Donatists.* New York: Grand Rapids.

Schroeder, T. 1919. Political crimes defined. *Michigan Law Review*, 18 (1), 30–44.

Schwarzenberger, G. 1941. *Power Politics: An Introduction to the Study of International Relations and Post War Planning.* London: Jonathan Cape.

Schwarzenberger, G. 1949. The North Atlantic Pact. *The Western Political Quarterly*, 2(3), 309–16.

Schwarzenberger, G. 1963. *The Misery and Grandeur of International Law.* London: Stevens & Sons.

Schwarzenberger, G. 1976. *The Dynamics of International Law.* Milton: Professional Books Limited.

Schwebel, S.M. 1986. Dissenting Opinion of Judge Schwebel: Military and Paramilitary Activities in and against Nicaragua (*Nicaragua v. United States of America*). *International Court of Justice* [Online] Available at: http://www.icj-cij.org/docket/files/70/6523.pdf [accessed: 17 June 2007]

Schwelb, E. 1965. The United Nations and human rights. *Howard Law Journal*, 11 (2), 356–72.

Scott, J.B. 1928. The Sixth Pan American Conference. *The American Journal of International Law*, 22 (2), 351–62.

Scott, M. 1958. The International Status of South West Africa. *International Affairs*, 34 (3), 318–29.

Secretary-General's High-Level Panel on Threats Challenges and Change. 2004. *A More Secure World: Our Shared Responsibility*. New York: United Nations.

Segell, G. 2003. A reflection on war against rogue states. *The Review of International Affairs*, 3 (3), 479–94.

Senate Subcommittee on Security and Terrorism. 1986. *Libyan-Sponsored Terrorism – A Dilemma for Policymakers Hearing Before the Senate Subcommittee on Security and Terrorism*, NCJ 104846, Washington DC: United States Senate and Congress.

Sestanovich, S. 2002. The world: Putin has his own candidate for pre-emption. *The New York Times*, 6 October, 14.

Seybolt, T.B. 2000. Major armed conflicts, in *Stockholm International Peace Research Institute (SIPRI) Yearbook 2000: World Armaments and Disarmament*, edited Stockholm International Peace Research Institute (SIPRI). New York: Oxford University Press, 15–75.

Seybolt, T.B. 2007. *Humanitarian Military Intervention: The Conditions for Success and Failure.* Oxford: Oxford University Press.

Shah, N.A. 2007. Self-defence, anticipatory self-defence and pre-emption: international law's response to terrorism. *Journal of Conflict and Security Law*, 12(1), 95–126.

Shannon, D. 1976. Uganda, Israel trade bitter charges at U.N. *Los Angeles Times*, 10 July, A1.

Shaw, M.N. 1991. *International Law.* Cambridge: Cambridge University Press.

Shotwell, J.T. 1944. *The Great Decision.* New York: The Macmillan Company.

Shultz, G. 1983. Secretary Shultz's news conference, Oct 25, 1983. *US Department of State Bulletin*, 83(2081), 69–72.

Shultz, G.P. 2002. The work of diplomacy. *Foreign Policy Research Institute* [Online, 11 June] Available at: http://www.fpri.org/enotes/diplomacy.20020611.shultz.workofdiplomacy.html [accessed: 27 April 2007].

Shumilin, A. 2003. The US vs rogue states of the Middle East. *International Affairs*, 49 (5), 32–41.

Simma, B. 1999. NATO, the UN and the use of force: legal aspects. *European Journal of International Law*, 10 (1), 1–22.

Singer, S.F. 1989. Machines won't end air terrorism. *Wall Street Journal*, 20 June.

Singh, N.K. 1986. *Enforcement of Human Rights in Peace and War and the Future of Humanity.* Dordrecht: Martinus Nijhoff.

Slater, J. and Nardin, T. 1986. Nonintervention and human rights. *The Journal of Politics*, 48 (1), 86–96.

Smith, C. 1903. *Perpetual Peace.* London: Swan Sonnenschein & Co.
Smith, W. 1986. A Reporter at large: transition. *The New Yorker*, 3 March, 72.
Smuts, J.C. 1918. *The League of Nations: A Practical Suggestion.* London: Hodder and Stoughton.
Sofaer, A. 1986. Terrorism and the law. *Foreign Affairs*, 64 (5), 901–22.
Solana, J. 1999a. Statement to the press by NATO Secretary General, Dr. Javier Solana. NATO [Online, 28 January] Available at: http://www.nato.int/docu/pr/1999/p99-011e.htm [accessed: 2 February 2007].
Solana, J. 1999b. Press statement by Dr. Javier Solana, NATO Secretary General following the commencement of air operations. *NATO* [Online, 24 March] Available at: http://www.nato.int/docu/pr/1999/p99-041e.htm [accessed: 17 April 2007].
Solana, J. 1999c. Press statement by Dr. Javier Solana, NATO Secretary General. NATO [Online, 25 March] Available at: http://www.nato.int/docu/pr/1999/p99-042e.htm [accessed: 5 May 2007].
Solarz, S.J. and O'Hanlon, M.E. 1997. Humanitarian intervention: when is force justified. *The Washington Quarterly*, 20 (4), 3–14.
Sørensen, G. 2004. *The Transformation of the State: Beyond the Myth of Retreat.* New York: Palgrave Macmillan.
Sørensen, G. 2007. After the security dilemma: the challenge of insecurity in weak states and the dilemma of liberal values. *Security Dialogue*, 38(3), 357–78.
Sornarajah, M. 1981. International colonialism and humanitarian intervention. *Georgia Journal of International and Comparative Law*, 11 (1), 45–78.
Spaight, J.M. 1932. Self-defence and international air power. *Journal of Comparative Legislation and International Law*, 14 (1), 20–29.
Starke, J.G. 1947. *An Introduction to International Law.* London: Butterworth & Co.
Stauffer, J. 2007. The rule of law and its shadow: ambivalence, procedure, and the justice beyond legality. *Law, Culture and the Humanities*, 3 (2), 225–43.
Stedman, S.J. 1993. The new interventionists. *Foreign Affairs*, 72 (1), 1–16.
Steed, W. 1933. The revision of peace treaties. *Transactions of the Grotius Society*, 19, 115–36.
Stein, M.S. 2004. Unauthorized humanitarian intervention. *Social Philosophy and Policy*, 21 (1), 14–38.
Stockholm International Peace Research Institute 2009. *SIPRI Multilateral Peace Operations Database* [Online, July) Available at: http://www.sipri.org/databases/pko [accessed: 14 August 2009].
Stone, J. 1936. Legislation: American neutrality reconsidered. *Columbia Law Review*, 36(1), 105–144.
Stone, J. 1958. *Aggression and World Order.* Berkeley: University of California.
Stone, J. 1959. *Legal Controls of International Conflict: A Treatise on the Dynamics of Disputes and War-Law.* Sydney: Maitland Publications Pty Ltd.
Stowell, E.C. 1914. U.S. should be chief guardian of neutrality. *The New York Times*, 6 August, SM2

Stowell, E.C. 1921. *Intervention in International Law.* Washington D.C.: John Byrne.

Stowell, E.C. 1936. Intercession against the persecution of Jews. *The American Journal of International Law*, 30 (1), 102–06.

Straw, J. 2003. Global Terrorism/Iraq – Statement by the Foreign Secretary, Jack Straw, House of Commons, Tuesday 21 January 2003. *Foreign and Commonwealth Office* [Online, 21 January] Available at: http://www.fco.gov.uk/servlet/Front?pagename=OpenMarket/Xcelerate/ShowPage&c=Page&cid=1007029391629&a=KArticle&aid=1042719056369&year=2003&month=2003-01-01 [accessed: 21 March 2007].

Stuesser, L. 1987. Active defense: state military response to international terrorism. *California Western International Law Journal*, 17 (1), 1–42.

Suarez, F. 1944. *De Legibus: Selections from three works of Francisco Suarez.* Oxford: Clarendon Press.

Sullivan, D. 1986. Legal restrictions on the right to use force against international terrorism. *ASILS International Law Journal*, 10, 169–98.

Sung, K.I. 1991. For a free and peaceful new world. Democratic People's Republic of Korea [Online] Available at: http://www.korea-dpr.com [accessed: 10 June 2003].

Sutherland, T. 2003. Playing diplomacy for very high stakes. *The Australian*, 17 March, 15.

Taft, W.H. 1919. The Paris Covenant for a League of Nations. *The American Political Science Review*, 13 (2), 181–98.

Tago, A. 2007. Why do states join US-led military coalitions?: The Compulsion of the Coalition's Mission and Legitimacy. *International Relations of the Asia-Pacific*, 7 (2), 179–202.

Teson, F.R. 2006. Eight principles for humanitarian intervention. *Journal of Military Ethics*, 5(2), 93–113.

The International Military Tribunal for Germany. 1946b. *Nuremburg Trial Proceedings, Volume 22* [Online] Available at: http://www.yale.edu/lawweb/avalon/imt/proc/09-30-46.htm [accessed: 7 May 2006].

The International Military Tribunal for Germany.1946a. *Nuremburg Trial Proceedings, Volume 19* [Online] Available at: http://www.yale.edu/lawweb/avalon/imt/proc/07-26-46.htm [accessed: 7 May 2006].

The International Military Tribunal for the Far East. 1948. *The International Military Tribunal for the Far East: Judgment* [Online] Available at: http://ibiblio.org/hyperwar/PTO/IMTFE/IMTFE-3.html [accessed: 7 May 2007].

The Knesset: The Israeli Parliament. 2004. Disengagement Plan of Prime Minister Ariel Sharon. *The Knesset* [Online, 28 May] Available at: http://www.knesset.gov.il/process/docs/DisengageSharon_eng_revised.htm [accessed: 6 June 2007].

The White House. 1980. White House Statement, April 23, 1980. *US Department of State Bulletin*, 80(2039), 38.

The White House. 1983. White House Statement, Nov. 3, 1983. *US Department of State Bulletin*, 83(2081), 78.

The White House. 1998. *A National Security Strategy for a New Century*. Washington D.C.: The White House.

Thomas, A.V.W. and Thomas, A.J. 1956. *Non-Intervention: The Law and Its Import in the Americas*. Dallas: Southern Methodist University Press.

Thornberry, P. 1991. *International Law and the Rights of Minorities*. Oxford, Oxford University Press.

Trapp, K.N. 2007. Back to basics: necessity, proportionality, and the right of self-defence against non-state terrorist actors. *International and Comparative Law Quarterly*, 56 (1), 141–56.

Travalio, G.M. 2000. Terrorism, international law, and the use of military force. *Wisconsin International Law Journal*, 18 (1), 145–91.

Tucker, R.W. 1978. *The Just War: A Study in Contemporary American Doctrine*. Westport, Connecticut: Greenwood Press, Publishers.

Tueni, G. 1982. *Letter dated 4 June 1982 from the Permanent Representative of Lebanon to the United Nations addressed to the President of the Security Council*, S/15161, New York: United Nations Document.

Turndorf, D. 1988. The US raid on Libya: a forceful response to terrorism. *Brooklyn Journal of International Law*, 14 (1), 187–221.

Ulfstein, G. 2003. Terrorism and the use of force. *Security Dialogue*, 34 (2), 153–67.

Union of Soviet Socialist Republics. 1968. The Situation in Czechoslovakia, in *United Nations Yearbook 1968*, edited by United Nations. New York: United Nations, 298–304.

Union of Soviet Socialist Republics. 1969. United Nations: Proposals on Defining Aggression. *International Legal Materials*, 8(3), 661–66.

United Kingdom House of Commons. 2000. Select Committee on Foreign Affairs: Fourth Report. *United Kingdom Parliament* [Online] Available at: http://www.publications.parliament.uk/pa/cm199900/cmselect/cmfaff/28/2802.htm [accessed: 19 December 2006].

United Nations General Assembly. 1948a. *139th Meeting, General Assembly Official Records*, A/PV.13-187, New York: United Nations.

United Nations General Assembly. 1948b. *Resolution 217: International Bill of Human Rights*, A/RES/217, New York: United Nations.

United Nations General Assembly. 1950. *Resolution 377: Uniting For Peace*, A/RES/377, New York: United Nations.

United Nations General Assembly. 1960. *Resolution 1514: Declaration on the Granting of Independence to Colonial Countries and Peoples*, A/RES/1514, New York: United Nations.

United Nations General Assembly. 1965. *Resolution 2131: Declaration on the Inadmissibility of Intervention in the Domestic Affairs of States and the Protection of their Independence and Sovereignty*, A/RES/2131, New York: United Nations.

United Nations General Assembly. 1966. *Resolution 2145: Question of South West Africa*, A/RES/2145, New York: United Nations.

United Nations General Assembly. 1970. *Resolution 2625: Declaration on Principles of International Law Concerning Friendly Relations and Cooperation Among States in Accordance with the Charter of the United Nations*, A/RES/2625, New York: United Nations.

United Nations General Assembly. 1971. *Resolution 2793: Question considered by the Security Council at its 1606th, 1607th and 1608th Meetings on 4,5 and 6 December 1971*, A/RES/2793, New York: United Nations.

United Nations General Assembly. 1974. *Resolution 3314: Definition of Aggression*, A/RES/3314, New York: United Nations.

United Nations General Assembly. 1981. *Resolution 36/103: Declaration on the Inadmissibility of Intervention and Interference in the Internal Affairs of States*, A/RES/36/103, New York: United Nations.

United Nations General Assembly. 1983. *Resolution 38/7: The situation in Grenada*, A/RES/38/7, New York: United Nations.

United Nations General Assembly. 1985a. *40th Session, General Assembly Official Records, 40th Year*, A/40/1003, New York: United Nations.

United Nations General Assembly. 1985b. *Resolution 40/61: Measures to prevent international terrorism which endangers or takes innocent human lives or jeopardizes fundamental freedoms and study of the underlying causes of those forms of terrorism and acts of violence which lie in misery, frustration, grievance and despair and which cause some people to sacrifice human lives, including their own, in an attempt to effect radical changes*, A/RES/40/61, New York: United Nations.

United Nations General Assembly. 1986. *Resolution 41/38: Declaration of the Assembly of Heads of State and Government of the Organization of African Unity on the aerial and naval military attack against the Socialist People's Libyan Arab Jamahiriya by the present United States Administration in April 1986*, A/RES/41/38, New York: United Nations.

United Nations General Assembly. 1991a. *Resolution 46/130: Respect for the principles of national sovereignty and non-interference in the internal affairs of States in their electoral processes*, A/RES/46/130, New York: United Nations.

United Nations General Assembly. 1991b. *Resolution 46/137: Enhancing the effectiveness of the principle of periodic and genuine elections*, A/RES/46/137, New York: United Nations.

United Nations General Assembly. 1993. *Resolution 48/83: Review of the implementation of the Declaration on the Strengthening of International Security*, A/RES/48/83, New York: United Nations.

United Nations General Assembly. 2005. *Resolution 60/1: World Summit Outcome*, A/RES/60/1, New York: United Nations.

United Nations News Centre. 1999. *Security Council Debate Said to Help in Creating 'Ethos of Conflict Prevention', Support for Intervention*, SC/6761, New York: United Nations.

United Nations News Centre. 2003. Annan to withdraw UN staff from Iraq. *United Nations News Centre* [Online, 17 March] Available at: http://www.un.org/apps/news/story.asp?NewsID=6479&Cr=iraq&Cr1=inspect [accessed: 18 March 2003].

United Nations News Centre. 2004. Ahead of polls in Afghanistan, President Karzai calls for sustained global aid. *United Nations News Centre* [Online, 21 September] Available at: http://www.un.org/apps/news/story.asp?NewsID=11996&Cr=general&Cr1=assembly [accessed: 1 November 2007|.

United Nations Peacebuilding Commission. 2007. Questions and Answers [Online] Available at: http://www.un.org/peace/peacebuilding/qanda.shtml [accessed: 7 November 2007].

United Nations Security Council. 1961. *Resolution 169: The Congo Question*, S/RES/169, New York: United Nations.

United Nations Security Council. 1966. *Resolution 228: The Palestine Question*, S/RES/228, New York: United Nations.

United Nations Security Council. 1967a. *1347th Meeting, Security Council Official Records, 22nd Year*, S/PV.1347/Rev.1, New York: United Nations.

United Nations Security Council. 1967b. *Resolution 236: The situation in the Middle East*, S/RES/236, New York: United Nations.

United Nations Security Council. 1967c. *1358th Meeting, Security Council Official Records, 22nd Year*, S/PV.1358, New York: United Nations.

United Nations Security Council. 1968. *Resolution 248: The Situation in the Middle East*, S/RES/248, New York: United Nations.

United Nations Security Council. 1969. *Resolution 265: The Situation in the Middle East*, S/RES/265, New York: United Nations.

United Nations Security Council. 1971a. *1606th Meeting, Security Council Official Records, 26th Year*, S/PV.1606, New York: United Nations.

United Nations Security Council. 1971b. *Resolution 303: The Situation in the India/Pakistan Subcontinent*, S/RES/303, New York: United Nations.

United Nations Security Council. 1971c. *1611th Meeting, Security Council Official Records, 26th Year*, S/PV.1611, New York: United Nations.

United Nations Security Council. 1971d. *Resolution 307: The situation in the India/Pakistan Subcontinent*, S/RES/307, New York: United Nations.

United Nations Security Council. 1972. *Resolution 316: The situation in the Middle East*, S/RES/316, New York: United Nations.

United Nations Security Council. 1979a. *Telegram dated 79/01/03 from the Deputy Prime Minister in Charge of Foreign Affairs of Democratic Addressed to the President of the Security Council*, S/13003, New York: United Nations.

United Nations Security Council. 1979b. *2110th Meeting, Security Council Official Records, 34th Year*, S/PV.2110, New York: United Nations.

United Nations Security Council. 1981a. *2109th Meeting, Security Council Official Records, 34th Year*, S/PV.2109, New York: United Nations.

United Nations Security Council. 1981b. *2288th Meeting, Security Council, Official Records, 36th Year*, S/PV.2288, New York: United Nations.

United Nations Security Council. 1981c. *Resolution 487: Iraq-Israel*, S/RES/487, New York: United Nations.

United Nations Security Council. 1982a. *2374th Meeting, United Nations Security Council Official Records, 37th Year*, S/PV.2374, New York: United Nations.

United Nations Security Council. 1982b. *Resolution 509: Israel-Lebanon*, S/RES/509, New York: United Nations.

United Nations Security Council. 1985. *Resolution 573: Israel-Tunisia*, S/RES/573, New York: United Nations.

United Nations Security Council. 1986a. *Provisional Verbatim Record of the 2655th Meeting*, S/PV.2655/Corr.1, New York: United Nations.

United Nations Security Council. 1986b. *Provisional Verbatim Record of the Two Thousand Six Hundred and Eighty-Second Meeting*, S/PV.2682, New York: United Nations.

United Nations Security Council. 1990a. *Provisional Verbatim Record of the 2933rd Meeting*, S/PV.2933, New York: United Nations.

United Nations Security Council. 1990b. *Resolution 678: Iraq-Kuwait*, S/RES/678, New York: United Nations.

United Nations Security Council. 1991a. *Resolution 687: Iraq-Kuwait*, S/RES/687, New York: United Nations.

United Nations Security Council. 1991b. *Resolution 688: Iraq*, S/RES/688, New York: United Nations.

United Nations Security Council. 1992a. *Note on the Summit Meeting of the Security Council to be held on 31 January 1992*, S/23500, New York: United Nations.

United Nations Security Council. 1992b. *United Nations Security Council Summit Declaration*, S/3046, New York: United Nations.

United Nations Security Council. 1992c. *Resolution 748: Libyan Arab Jamahiriya*, S/RES/748, New York: United Nations.

United Nations Security Council. 1992d. *Resolution 794: Somalia*, S/RES/794, New York: United Nations.

United Nations Security Council. 1993. *Resolution 841: Haiti*, S/RES/841, New York: United Nations.

United Nations Security Council. 1994a. *Resolution 940: on authorization to form a multinational force under unified command and control to restore the legitimately elected President and authorities of the Government of Haiti and extension of the mandate of the UN Mission in Haiti*, S/RES/940, New York: United Nations.

United Nations Security Council. 1994b. *Resolution 956: on termination of the status of Palau as a Trust Territory*, S/RES/956, New York: United Nations.

United Nations Security Council. 1996a. Resolution 1054: *Letter dated 9 January 1996 from the Permanent Representative of Ethiopia to the United Nations addressed to the President of the Security Council concerning the extradition of the suspects wanted in the assassination attempt on the life of the President of the Arab Republic of Egypt in Addis Ababa, Ethiopia, on 26 June 1995*, S/RES/1054, New York: United Nations.

United Nations Security Council. 1996b. *Resolution 1070: Letter dated 9 January 1996 from the Permanent Representative of Ethiopia to the United Nations addressed to the President of the Security Council concerning the extradition of the suspects wanted in the assassination attempt on the life of the President of the Arab Republic of Egypt in Addis Ababa, Ethiopia, on 26 June 1995*, S/RES/1070, New York: United Nations.

United Nations Security Council. 1996c. *Resolution 1078: The situation in the Great Lakes region*, S/RES/1078, New York: United Nations.

United Nations Security Council. 1996d. *Resolution 1080: The situation in the Great Lakes region*, S/RES/1080, New York: United Nations.

United Nations Security Council. 1997a. *Resolution 1101: The situation in Albania*, S/RES/1101, New York: United Nations.

United Nations Security Council. 1997b. *Resolution 1127: The situation in Angola*, S/RES/1127, New York: United Nations.

United Nations Security Council. 1998a. *Resolution 1160: on the letters from the United Kingdom (S/1998/223) and the United States (S/1998/272)*, S/RES/1160, New York: United Nations.

United Nations Security Council. 1998b. *Resolution 1192: on Lockerbie case*, S/RES/1192, New York: United Nations.

United Nations Security Council. 1998c. *Resolution 1199: on the situation in Kosovo (FRY)*, S/RES/1199, New York: United Nations.

United Nations Security Council. 1998d. *Resolution 1203: on the situation in Kosovo*, S/RES/1203, New York: United Nations.

United Nations Security Council. 1998e. *3937th Meeting, Security Council Official Records, 53rd Year*, S/PV.3937, New York: United Nations.

United Nations Security Council. 1998f. *Resolution 1214: on the situation in Afghanistan*, S/RES/1214, New York: United Nations.

United Nations Security Council. 1999a. *3988th Meeting, Security Council Official Records, 54th Year*, S/PV.3988, New York: United Nations.

United Nations Security Council. 1999b. *Resolution 1264: on the situation in East Timor*, S/RES/1264, New York: United Nations.

United Nations Security Council. 1999c. *Resolution 1267: on the situation in Afghanistan*, S/RES/1267, New York: United Nations.

United Nations Security Council. 1999d. *Resolution 1269: on the responsibility of the Security Council in the maintenance of international peace and security*, S/RES/1269, New York: United Nations.

United Nations Security Council. 1999e. *Resolution 1272: on the situation in East Timor*, S/RES/1272, New York: United Nations.

United Nations Security Council. 2000. *Resolution 1333: on the situation in Afghanistan*, S/RES/1333, New York: United Nations.

United Nations Security Council. 2001a. *Resolution 1368: Threats to international peace and security caused by terrorist acts*, S/RES/1368, New York: United Nations.

United Nations Security Council. 2001b. *4370th Meeting, Security Council Official Records, 56th Year*, S/PV.4370, New York: United Nations.

United Nations Security Council. 2001c. *Resolution 1373: Threats to international peace and security caused by terrorist acts*, S/RES/1373, New York: United Nations.

United Nations Security Council. 2001d. *4414th Meeting, Security Council Official Records, 56th Year*, S/PV.4414, New York: United Nations.

United Nations Security Council. 2001e. *Resolution 1378: on the situation in Afghanistan*, S/RES/1378, New York: United Nations.

United Nations Security Council. 2002a. *Resolution 1390: The situation in Afghanistan*, S/RES/1390, New York: United Nations.

United Nations Security Council. 2002b. *Resolution 1441: The situation between Iraq and Kuwait*, S/RES/1441, New York: United Nations.

United Nations Security Council. 2003a. *Resolution 1456: High-level meeting of the Security Council: combating terrorism*, S/RES/1456, New York: United Nations.

United Nations Security Council. 2003b. *4701th Meeting, Security Council Official Records, 58th Year*, S/PV.4701, New York: United Nations.

United Nations Security Council. 2003c. *4709th Meeting, Security Council Official Records, 58th Year*, S/PV.4709, New York: United Nations.

United Nations Security Council. 2003d. 4836th Meeting, Security Council Official Records, 58th Year, S/PV.4836, New York: United Nations.

United Nations Security Council. 2003d. *Resolution 1506: Letters dated 20 and 23 December 1991, from France, the United Kingdom of Great Britain and Northern Ireland and the United States of America (S/23306, S/23307, S/23308, S/23309 and S/23317); Letter dated 15 August 2003 from the Chargé d'affaires a.i. of the Permanent Mission of the Libyan Arab Jamahiriya to the United Nations addressed to the President of the Security Council (S/2003/818); Letter dated 15 August 2003 from the Permanent Representatives of the United Kingdom of Great Britain and Northern Ireland and the United States of America to the United Nations addressed to the President of the Security Council (S/2003/819); Voting on draft resolution S/2003/824*, S/RES/1506, New York: United Nations.

United Nations Security Council. 2004a. *Resolution 1540: Non-proliferation of weapons of mass destruction*, S/RES/1540, New York: United Nations.

United Nations Security Council. 2004b. *Resolution 1566: Threats to international peace and security caused by terrorist acts*, S/RES/1566, New York: United Nations.

United Nations Security Council. 2006. *Resolution 1701: The situation in the Middle East*, S/RES/1701, New York: United Nations.

United Nations. 1980. Questions concerning Asia', in *Yearbook of the United Nations 1980*, edited by Department of Public Information. New York: United Nations, 296–342.

United States Agency for International Development. 2005. *Fragile States Strategy*. Washington DC: U.S. Agency for International Development.

United States Department of State. 2002. *A Decade of Deception and Defiance: Saddam Hussein's Defiance of the United Nations.* Washington: United States Department of State.

Urquhart, B. 1991. Sovereignty vs. Suffering. *The New York Times*, 4 April, A23.

Varè, D. 1936. British Foreign Policy Through Italian Eyes. *International Affairs*, 15 (1), 80–102.

Vattel, E. de. 1805. *The Law of Nations, or, Principles of the Law of Nature: applied to the conduct and affairs of nations and sovereigns.* Northampton, MA: S. & E. Butler.

Vattel, E. de. 1964. *The Law of Nations, or, Principles of the Law of Nature: applied to the conduct and affairs of nations and sovereigns.* Dobbs Ferry NY: Oceana Publications.

Verdirame, G. 2004. International law and the use of force against Iraq, in *The Conflict in Iraq 2003*, edited by P. Cornish. New York: Palgrave Macmillan, 92–106.

Visscher, C. de. 1968. *Theory and Reality in Public International Law* Princeton: Princeton University Press.

Vitoria, F. de. 1917. *De Indis De Jure Belli.* Washington: The Carnegie Institution of Washington.

Voeten, E. 2005. The political origins of the UN Security Council's ability to legitimize the use of force. *International Organization*, 59 (3), 527–57.

Wade, M. 2003. Danger begins when weapons amnesty runs out. *The Sydney Morning Herald* [Online, 4 August] Available at: http://www.smh.com.au/articles/2003/08/03/1059849282300.html [accessed: on 17 July 2008]

Waldheim, K. 1984. The United Nations: the tarnished image. *Foreign Affairs*, 63 (1), 93–107.

Waldock, H. 1952. The regulation of the use of force by individual states in international law. *Hague Recueil*, 81, 451–67.

Walker, G.K. 2002. The lawfulness of operation enduring freedom's self-defence responses. *Valparaiso University Law Review*, 37 (2), 489–540.

Wallace-Bruce, N.L. 1996. Taiwan and Somalia: international legal curiosities. *Queen's Law Journal*, 22, 453–85.

Wallensteen, P. 1997. New actors, new issues, new action, in *International Intervention: New Norms in the Post-Cold War Era*, edited by P. Wallensteen. Uppsala: Department of Peace and Conflict Research, 5–16.

Walsh, N.P. 2004. Putin puts £6m price on rebels' heads. *The Guardian* [Online, 9 September] Available at: http://www.guardian.co.uk/world/2004/sep/09/chechnya.russia2 [accessed: 7 August 2008].

Walzer, M. 2000. *Just War and Unjust War*. 3rd Edition. New York: Basic Books.

Walzer, M. 2002. Über den gerechten Krieg. *Die Welt [Online* 12 March] Available at: http://www.welt.de/print-welt/article378685/Ueber_den_gerechten_Krieg.html [accessed: 24 November 2007]

Ware, G. 1965. Somalia: from trust territory to nations, 1950–1960. *Phylon*, 26(2), 173–85.

Weber, M. 1926. *Politik als Beruf.* 2nd Edition. München: Duncker und Humblot.

Weber, M. 1966. *Staatssoziologie*. 2nd Edition. Berlin: Duncker und Humblot.

Webster, D. 1857. Correspondence between Great Britain and the United States, Respecting the Arrest and Imprisonment of Mr. McLeod for the Destruction of the Steamboat Caroline – April 24, 1841. *British and Foreign State Papers*, 29, 1129–38.

Wedgewood, R. 1998. The enforcement of Security Council Resolution 687: the threat of force against iraq's weapons of mass destruction. *The American Journal of International Law*, 92 (4), 724–28.

Wedgewood, R. 2005. The ICJ Advisory Opinion on the Israeli Security Fence and the limits of self-defence. *The American Journal of International Law*, 99 (1), 52–61.

Weisman, S. R. 2002. US and France near compromise on action on Iraq. *The New York Times*, 30 October, A1.

Weiss, T.G. 2004. The sunset of humanitarian intervention? The responsibility to protect in a unipolar era. *Security Dialogue*, 35 (2), 135–53.

Westlake, J. 1858. *A Treatise on Private International Law, or, The Conflict of Laws.* London: W. Maxwell.

Westlake, J. 1904. *International Law.* Cambridge: The University Press.

Wheaton, H. 1836. *Elements of International Law: With a Sketch of the History of the Science*. Philadelphia: Carey, Lea & Blanchard.

Wheeler, N.J. and Dunne, T. 2001. East Timor and the new humanitarian interventionism. *International Affairs*, 77 (4), 805–27.

Whitman, J. 2005. Humanitarian intervention in an era of pre-emptive self-defence. *Security Dialogue*, 36 (3), 259–74.

Whitney, C.R. 1997. France snips at the old ties that bind it to Africa. *The New York Times*, 25 July, 10.

Wilk, K. 1951. International law and global ideological conflict: reflections on the universality of international law. *American Journal of International Law*, 45 (4), 648–70.

Wilkinson, P. 1978. Terrorism: the biggest human rights violation of all. *The Times*, 29 August, 12.

Wilks, I. 1955. A note on sovereignty. *The Philosophical Quarterly*, 5(21), 342–47.

Williams, Paul D. and Bellamy, Alex J. 2005a. Who's keeping the peace? Regionalization and contemporary peace operations. *International Security*, 29(4), 157–95.

Williams, Paul D. and Bellamy, Alex J. 2005b. The Responsibility to Protect and the crisis in Darfur. *Security Dialogue*, 36(1), 27–47.

Wilson, W. 1918. President's Address to Congress a Reply To Hertling's and Czernin's Peace Terms. *The Washington Post*, 12 February, 5.

Wilton Park Conference. 2004. Intervention: Why? When? How can it succeed? Conference Report No.733. [Online, 18 March] Available at: http://www.wiltonpark.org/documents/ conferences/WP733/pdfs/WP733.pdf [accessed: 6 October 2007].

Winfield, P.H. 1924. The grounds of intervention in international law. *British Yearbook of International Law*, 5 (149–62).

Wingfield, T.C. 2000. Forcible protection of nationals abroad. *Dickinson Law Review*, 104 (3), 439–69.

Wiseberg, L.S. 1975. An international perspective on the African famines. *Canadian Journal of African Studies*, 9 (2), 293–313.

Wolf, D. 1988. Humanitarian intervention. *Michigan Yearbook of International Legal Studies*, 9, 333–66.

Wolfowitz, P.D. 2002. Building coalitions of common values. *International Institute for Strategic Studies* [Online, 2 December] Available at: http://www.iiss.org/recent-key-addresses/wolfowitz-address/ [accessed: 16 March 2007].

Woodward, S.L. 1999. Failed states: warlordism and 'tribal' warfare. *Naval War College Review*, 52 (2), 55–68.

Woolf, L. 1933. *The Intelligent Man's Way to Prevent War*. London: Victor Gollancz.

Woolsey, T.D. 1872. *Introduction to the Study of International Law.* New York: Scribner, Armstrong.

World Bank. 2002. *World Bank Group Work on Low-Income Countries Under Stress: A Task Force.* Washington D.C.: World Bank.

World Bank. 2003. *Low-Income Countries Under Stress: Implementation Overview.* Washington DC: World Bank.

Wright, Q. 1924. Changes in the conception of war. *The American Journal of International Law*, 18(4), 755–67.

Wright, Q. 1925. The outlawry of war. *The American Journal of International Law*, 19(1), 76–103.

Wright, Q. 1935. The concept of aggression in international law. *The American Journal of International Law*, 29(3), 373–95.

Wright, Q. 1936. National sovereignty and collective security. *Annals of the American Academy of Political and Social Science*, 186, 94–104.

Wright, Q. 1938. The denunciation of treaty violators. *The American Journal of International Law*, 32(3), 526–35.

Wright, Q. 1954. Human rights and Charter revision. *Annals of the American Academy of Political and Social Science*, 296, 46–55.

Wright, Q. 1957. The legality of intervention under the United Nations Charter, the intervention under the Charter of the United Nations and under the Charter of the Organization of American States. *American Society of International Law Proceedings*, 51, 79–88.

Wright, Q. 1963. The Cuban quarantine. *The American Journal of International Law*, 57(3), 546–65.

Wright, Q. 1976. *International Law and the United Nations.* Westport, CT: Greenwood Press.

Wright, R.G. 1989. A contemporary theory of humanitarian intervention. *Florida International Law Journal*, 4 (3), 435–63.

Wu, S. 2003. Taiwan military doesn't rule out pre-emptive attack on mainland. *China News Agency*, 8 October.

Xego, M.K. and Olivier, M.E. 2003. The permissibility of unilateral intervention under international law. *Strategic Review for Southern Africa*, 25 (2), 78–105

Yoo, J.C. 2004. Using Force. *The University of Chicago Law Review*, 71 (3), 729–97.

Zartman, I.W. 1995. Introduction: posing the problem of state collapse, in *Collapsed States: The Disintegration and Restoration of Legitimate Authority*, edited by I.W. Zartman. London: Lynne Rienner Publishers, 1–14.

Zedalis, R.J. 1987. Preliminary thoughts on some unresolved questions involving the law of anticipatory self-defense. *Case Western Reserve Journal of International Law*, 19 (2), 129–75.

Zedalis, R.J. 1990. Protection of nationals abroad: is consent the basis of legal obligation? *Texas International Law Journal*, 25 (2), 209–70.

Index

9/11 *see* September 11

Abu Ghraib ix
Abyssinia 32, 34–5, 38, 101
Accumulation of attacks 175, 179–80, 190
Act of aggression 32–3, 48, 79, 86–7, 108, 113, 119, 152, 154, 187, 190, 221
Ad hoc coalitions
- Iraq 67–8, 197, 218
- use of force by 2, 10, 47, 51, 55, 63, 64–8, 70–71, 73, 115–18, 123, 140, 142, 162, 182, 189 *see also* hierarchy of authority
- Vietnam 50

Ad hoc committee on terrorism 47, 177, 185
Afghanistan
- intervention in x, 64, 70, 73, 112, 120–22, 140–41, 144–45, 157, 182–83, 189–90, 193–94, 218–19, 222
- missile strikes against 187, 192–93, 195
- sanctions against 184, 188
- Soviet intervention in 52, 54, 67, 175, 179, 203

African Union
- humanitarian intervention 112, 115, 122
- non-interference 59, 64

Agenda for Peace 64, 144
Aggression
- definition of 52–4, 87
- failed states 128
- humanitarian intervention 105–106, 108, 113, 118–19
- pre-emption 150–54, 158, 164–66
- prohibition of vii, viii, ix, 20, 31–6, 38–9, 42, 44–5, 48, 216, 221
- protection of nationals 78–9, 86–7
- rogue states 200–201, 208, 223
- terrorism 174–75, 177–78, 180–81, 187, 190, 192

Al-Qaeda ix, 157, 159, 168, 183–84, 186–88, 190–92 *see also* Osama bin Laden, terrorism
Albania 117
Albright, Madeleine 190, 205
Algeria 151, 174
Alliances 37, 44, 49, 79, 202
Allied forces 39, 130, 134
Altruism 71–2, 120
American Society of International Law 23, 101
Anarchy 14, 57, 135, 140, 168–71
Annan, Kofi *see also* UN
- civil war 5, 8
- failed states 142–43
- humanitarian intervention 59, 111, 113
- international law 57, 63, 67–8, 112, 116–17, 121, 162–63, 165, 187, 215

Annexation of territory viii, 26, 32, 126–27, 134
Anticipatory self-defence *see* pre-emption
ANZUS Pact 49
Arbitration 14, 20–21, 23–4, 27, 29, 31, 41, 201, 216
Arend, Anthony C. 88, 151, 165, 213
Aristotle 18, 78
Attack
- armed
  - definition of 53–5
  - terrorism 174, 181, 182, 186–93
  - protection of nationals 82–3, 86
  - humanitarian intervention 123
  - pre-emption 151–52, 154–59, 163, 165
  - terrorism 163, 168, 173, 175
  - self-defense 1, 4, 42, 44, 46, 48, 66, 221–22

imminency of 82, 85, 151, 155–56, 158–60, 163, 202
severity of 54, 180, 190–91
Armed bands 34, 52, 54, 151, 159, 167, 177–78, 192 *see also* non-state actors
Assassination 29, 126, 169, 170–72, 178, 184, 188, 190
Asylum 97, 104, 170, 172
Australia *see also* ANZUS
Fiji 89
global warming 206
human rights 104
Indonesia 47
intervention in East Timor 117
intervention in Solomon Islands 61, 141, 142
Iraq War 46, 58, 70, 160–61, 198, 210
Lebanon 90
mandate system 127, 130–31
SEATO 50
terrorism 184 *see also* Bali Bombings
Austria
Anschluss with Germany 34
Boxer Rebellion 79
First World War 29, 171–73, 193, 199 *see also* Franz Ferdinand
Holy Alliance 21, 25
plebiscites 126, 128
protection of Christian subjects 98
Second World War 130, 134
Axis of evil 122, 157, 205, 211 *see also* rogue states

Balance of power 25, 41, 152, 154, 214 *see also* superpower rivalry
Bandit nation 197–201, 213 *see also* rogue states, outlaw states, pariah states
Biafra 106 *see also* Nigeria
Bazyler, Michael J. 107–109, 123
Belgium *see also* ICJ
anarchism 170–71
colonialism 78, 126
extradition treaty 170
independence 98
intervention in Congo 85, 106, 132
plebiscites 127–28
protection of Christian subjects 21
protection of nationals 81, 85, 88–90, 92
revision 200
terrorism 171
Treaty of Locarno 32
violation of neutrality 33, 100
Bellamy, Alex J. 112, 114–15, 118, 120–22, 132, 164–65, 167
Bentham, Jeremy 17–18
Bernard, Montague 22, 100
Bin Laden, Osama 157, 183–84 *see also* Al-Qaeda, terrorism, Afghanistan
Bipolarity 8, 152, 203 *see also* balance of power, superpower rivalry
Blair, Tony *see also* liberal interventionism, United Kingdom
Afghanistan 192
collective security 62
Doctrine of the International Community 2
failed states 139
humanitarian intervention 2, 39, 95, 123
Iraq 69–70, 210
just war 2, 69
pre-emption 160, 223
Bluntschli, Johann K. 23, 33, 79
Bolivia 34
Borchard, Edwin M. 26, 37, 80, 85, 99, 151
Boutros-Ghali, Boutros 64, 115
Bosnia 5, 97, 110, 113, 171
Bowett, Derek W. 49, 53, 87–8, 105, 155, 179, 190
Brezhnev Doctrine 51
Briand, Aristide 200
Brierly, J.L. 31, 36–7, 82, 215
Brownlie, Ian 53–4, 63, 81, 105, 107, 155, 175
Bryan Treaties 24, 31
Bulgaria 25, 33, 97–8, 199
Bush, G.H.W. viii, 1, 69, 115, 215
Bush, G.W. *see also* United States, Iraq, Afghanistan
failed states 61, 141
international law 1–2, 11, 69, 223, 224
Iraq 27, 194, 210–12
just war 2, 69, 71

pre-emption 2, 157, 165, 221
rogue states 197, 205–206, 210 *see also* Iraq, Axis of Evil
terrorism ix, 120, 157, 184, 187, 190–92 *see also* terrorism, Afghanistan
Boxer rebellion 79 *see also* China
Burundi 61, 114, 142, 145
Byers, Michael 111, 121, 150, 189, 191, 223

Cambodia
UN transitional administration 140
US intervention in 54, 83, 104
Vietnam's intervention in 46, 60, 108
Canada 27, 90, 116, 151
Capitalism viii, 202
Caprioli, Mary 207–208, 214
Caroline case 27, 150–51, 158, 169
Carter, Jimmy 204
Ceasefire 107, 115, 132
Cecil, Robert 34, 36–7
Central African Republic 89, 113–14, 141–42
Central Treaty Organization 49, 66, 73, 175
Chad 51, 88–9, 114, 142
Chamberlain, Austen 201–202
Cheney, Dick 72
Chesterman, Simon xiii, 1, 63, 110–11, 113, 115, 118, 209, 223
China *see also* Manchuria, Boxer rebellion
human rights 112
indirect aggression 174–75
Kosovo 118
rogue states 199
Sudan 122
Taiwan 161
territorial concessions 46
Chirac, Jacques 137
Christianity
just war 2, 14, 18–19, 68–9, 96
forceful protection of Christians 21, 25, 38–9, 79, 95, 97, 122
Civil war *see also* internal unrest, failed states, humanitarian intervention
American 22–3
Dominican Republic 83
intervention in instances of 5, 6, 66, 99, 138, 143
Lebanon 179
Rwanda 116
Spanish 34–5
state failure 91
Sudan 122
The Congo 132
Clausewitz, Carl von 13, 72, 169
Clinton, Bill 2, 62, 157–58, 183, 187, 197, 205
Coalition of the Willing 65, 164, 210 *see also* Iraq
Collapsed states 125, 132, 133–36, 139 *see also* failed states, weak states
Collective security *see also* UN
efficiency 149, 217
humanitarian intervention 59, 66
Iraq 1, 62
Korea 11
prior to World War I 21, 26, 27, 28
regional 73
under League 32, 36–8, 42, 217
under UN 42, 44–5, 47–9, 53, 55, 57, 69, 70, 83, 132, 158, 178, 182, 187, 194, 209
Colombia 21
Colonialism *see also* decolonization, self-determination
humanitarian intervention 104, 109
Latin America 35
Monroe Doctrine 25
protection of nationals 77–9, 81–2, 85, 89, 91–2, 218
self-determination x, 43, 46–8, 50–51
state failure 125–28, 130–32, 134, 139–40, 144
terrorism 168, 173–76, 185
Commission of Global Governance 14
Common law 87, 99
Commonwealth 84
Communism *see also* superpower rivalry
containment of 52, 60, 83, 133
Soviet Union 179, 202
terrorism 174, 181
Concert of Europe 21, 23, 28
Concessions 46, 78–9, 199

Congo 81, 85, 87, 98, 106, 132–33, 135
see also peacekeeping
Congo, Democratic Republic of 63, 112, 117, 144–45 *see also* ICJ
Conservatism 29, 31, 35–6, 126 *see also* neo-conservatism
Constitutional law 17, 81
Costa Rica 54, 174
Côte d'Ivoire 89, 114
Coup d'état 83, 116, 167
Covert action 52, 60, 110, 186, 203, 212 *see also* ICJ
Crete 5
Crimes against humanity x, 33, 36, 102–103, 112, 114, 185
Crusades 2, 19, 96 *see also* just war
Cuba
failed state 137
relationship with Soviet Union 84
relationship with US 91, 152–53
rogue state 203, 206–207, 212
terrorism 174, 179
US intervention in 25–6, 52, 78, 98–9
Customary international law *see also* Caroline case
collective use of force 105
establishment of new rules ix, 216
humanitarian intervention 105, 111
pre-emption 154–55
protection of nationals 77, 80, 87–8, 92
self-defense 36, 44, 48
state practice 3, 4, 17, 215–16, 218–19, 221
terrorism 186–87, 193
Cyprus viii, 97
Czechoslovakia
German intervention in 79–80, 101
revision 33, 200
Soviet intervention in 44, 50, 52–3, 64, 104, 108, 143

Darfur 115, 122
Declaration of Paris 22, 24, 97
Declaration of St. Petersburg 22, 27–8
Decolonization *see also* colonialism, self-determination
protection of nationals 77
self-determination 125
sovereignty 46, 105, 122
UN 104, 130, 131, 133
violent conflicts related to viii, 7, 43, 47, 81, 130, 134, 138
Democracy
establishment of 71, 97, 106, 134, 139
human rights 60, 102
just war 69
suppression of 25, 113
UN 135
use of force 24, 37, 52, 119, 143, 181, 213
Denmark 128, 151
Detente 202–203
Deterrence viii, 60, 104, 122, 153, 157, 161, 167, 210
Detter, Ingrid 5, 157
Dickinson, G. Lowes 28–9, 32, 39
Dinstein, Yoram 88, 91, 157, 159, 190
Diplomacy
humanitarian intervention 97, 99, 118–19
rogue states 210, 212
terrorism ix, 193, 204
UN 44, 209, 224
use of force 24, 37, 71, 85
Diplomatic immunity 17, 85
Disarmament 21, 160, 199, 200, 208, 211
Dixon, Martin 17, 63, 67
Djibouti 89
Doctrine of containment 60, 157, 209, 211 *see also* communism
Domestic jurisdiction 20, 43, 46, 58, 103, 111, 171–72, 194, 219
Dominican Republic
Indirect aggression against Haiti 175
US intervention in 44, 54, 83, 106, 176
Droit de gens 16, 18
Drug trafficking 61, 62, 84, 135, 141, 211
Dueck, Colin 209–211, 213
Dugard, John R. 47, 102, 105–106, 170, 177–78
Dynamiter 169 *see also* terrorism

East Timor
Indonesian attack on viii, 51

UN intervention in 63–5, 110–11, 113, 115, 118, 129, 136, 140
Economic Community of West African States (ECOWAS) 118, 142, 178
Ecuador 21
Eisenhower, Dwight 152
Egypt *see also* Suez Crisis, Six Day War
international law 18
intervention against 21, 79
terrorism 184
use of force against Yemen 51
Yom Kippur War 203
El Salvador 54
Enlightenment 13, 96, 97
Eritrea 141
Ethiopia 61, 141, 199
Ethnic cleansing 59, 61, 70, 114, 118, 219 *see also* genocide, Holocaust
European Union
intervention in Democratic Republic of the Congo 112, 117
Kosovo 119
pre-emption 161, 162
Security Strategy 162
sovereignty 16
Evacuation of nationals 77, 83, 88–92 *see also* protection of nationals
Extradition 86, 103, 170, 173, 182–86 *see also* terrorism

Failed states viii, 2, 5, 6, 8–9, 59, 61, 69, 75, 91, 125–45, 162, 192–93, 198, 220, *see also* weak and collapsed states
Falk, Richard vii–xi, xiii, 1, 51, 53–4, 70, 105–106, 109–110, 114, 121, 158, 178, 182, 189, 203, 224
Falklands 47
Feeble states 73, 125, 169, 192, 217 *see also* weak and collapsed states
Fiji 89, 142
Fischer, Joschka 215
Fonteyne, Jean-Pierre 25, 82, 87, 95, 97–8, 100, 106–107
Foreign aid 115, 117, 133, 137, 139, 141
France *see also* Suez crisis, Manchuria, Central African Republic
arbitration 24
attack by UK on 151
colonialism 131
financial aid to 134
intervention in Congo 85, 98, 112
intervention in Syria 97
plebiscites 127–28
pre-emption 161
protection of nationals 78–9, 81, 88–92
protection of Christian subjects 21, 97
Republic 13, 20, 97
revision 33, 200
Revolution 20, 26, 128, 168–69
Rwanda 89, 90, 115–16
SEATO 66
terrorism 168–71, 173, 176–77
Treaty of Locarno 32
Vietnam 46, 50, 133, 174
Franck, Thomas M. 107–108, 133, 155, 163, 177
Franz Ferdinand, Archduke of Austria 29, 126, 171

Gabon 89, 142
Gandhi ix, 173
Gaza Strip 161 *see also* Palestine
Geneva Conventions ix, 22–4, 27–8, 199
Genocide *see also* ethnic cleansing, Holocaust
criminalization of vii, 44–5, 60, 103–104, 107
Darfur 122
intervention 59–61, 70, 90, 95, 111–12, 114, 120, 162, 166, 219
Rwanda 62, 66, 116
state failure 19–20
Georgia 136, 194, 213
German Democratic Republic 108
Germany *see also* Adolf Hitler, Manchuria, Marshall Plan, national socialism, Treaty of Versailles, World War II
Allied occupation 37, 39, 130, 134
annexation of Austria 34, 38
annexation of Czechoslovakia 34, 38, 79
annexation of Sudentenland 34–5, 38, 79–80, 101
anticipatory self-defense 151–52, 161

colonialism 78, 102, 126–27
intervention in Rhineland 34
invasion of Poland 11
Iraq 215
plebiscites 128
revision 34
rogue state 198–201 *see also* Treaty of Versailles, revision
Rwanda 90
suppression of democracy 25
terrorism 85, 169–73, 176–77 *see also* Berlin bombing
Treaty of Locarno 32
war crimes vii, 33, 52, 100, 134, 151, 171 *see also* Nürnberg trials
withdrawal from League 38
Gibraltar 47
Globalization viii, xi, 8, 14, 20, 28, 50, 61–3, 78, 89, 221
Gran-Colombia 21
Gray, Christine 63, 88, 187
Great Lakes Region 63
Greece 21, 25, 90, 97–8, 176,
Grenada 54, 83–4, 106, 143
Grewe, Wilhelm G. 17, 37–8, 40–41, 55
Grotius, Hugo 13, 18–20, 77–8, 96, 149–50
Group 77 112, 118, 144 *see also* non-aligned movement
Guantanamo ix
Guatemala 52

Haass, Richard N. 16, 159
Hague Conventions 22, 24, 28, 33, 199
Haiti
conflict with Dominican Republic 175
failed state 136, 142–43, 145
intervention in 63, 110, 113–14, 116, 144
Hall, William Edward 22, 26, 28–9, 37–8, 43, 45, 79, 98, 99
Hamas 211
Harcourt, W.V. 2, 22
Henkin, Louis 62, 118–20, 152, 154–55
Herzegovina 25, 97, 110, 113
Hezbollah 90
Hierarchy of authority 51, 71, 115
Higgins, Rosalyn 82, 175, 186
High Level Panel on Threats, Challenges and Change 59, 61, 111–12, 163, 185
Hitler, Adolf 79, 200–201, 210 *see also* national socialism, World War II, Germany
Hobson, J.A. 28–9, 32
Holocaust vii, 39, 101
Holy Alliance 21, 24–5, 28
Honduras 54, 79
Hostage 85–6, 161, 185, 193, 203–204
Howard, John
international law 11, 141, 160, 190, 206, 210, 223
Iraq War 69
just war 2, 70
Human rights *see also* humanitarian intervention
as threat to international peace and security 113, 119, 135
development of viii, 26, 96–8
failed states 135, 138–39, 142
legislation on 45, 101–104
protection of 46, 58, 70, 75, 84, 95, 105, 110–12, 114, 116, 122, 219 *see also* humanitarian intervention
severity of abuse 96, 106, 108–110, 121, 123, 220
UN 41, 45, 102, 223
Human trafficking 61, 141
Humanitarian intervention viii, 2, 4, 6, 8–9, 15, 25–6, 35, 38–9, 41, 45–6, 95–123, 95–123, 144, 162, 217, 219–20
humanitarian law 20, 27, 38, 95
humanity, crimes against x, 33, 36, 102–103, 112, 114, 185
Hungary *see also* Austria
Cambodia 108
First World War 172, 175, 199
intervention by Soviet Union 44, 50, 104
Hussein, Saddam 72, 120, 206, 211

ICISS 59, 60, 70–73, 95, 111–12, 114–15, 117, 119–20, 123, 143, 162, 219
Imperialism 53, 81, 92, 97, 105, 109–110, 126, 144, 202

India
Indonesia 47
intervention in East Pakistan (Bangladesh) 46, 106–107
pre-emption 161–62, 221
rogue state 206–208
terrorism 174, 217
Indirect aggression 174–75, 181
Indonesia
East Timor viii, 117, 174
independence from the Netherlands 46, 47, 81, 174
Dutch New Guinea 51
terrorism 184 *see also* Bali bombings
Internal conflict *see also* civil war, failed states, humanitarian intervention
intervention in instances of 9, 53, 62, 77, 216
international law relating to ix, 69, 143
failed states 75, 125, 135, 141
International Court of Justice (ICJ)
Statue 3, 4, 17, 185
Advisory Opinion
Concerning the international status of South West Africa 102–103
Legal consequences for states of the continued presence of South Africa in Namibia (South West Africa) 121
Legal consequences of the construction of a wall in the Occupied Palestinian Territory 163, 186
Cases
Case concerning armed activities on the territory of the Congo (*Congo v. Uganda* 163, 191–92
Case concerning certain phosphate lands in Nauru (*Nauru v. Australia*) 131
Case concerning Corfu Channel (*UK v. Albania*) 173
Case concerning legality of use of force (*Yugoslavia v. Belgium*) 118, 119
Case concerning military and paramilitary activities in and against Nicaragua (*Nicaragua v. US*) 3, 36, 42–3, 54–5, 110, 154, 164, 181, 188
Case concerning oil platforms (*Iran v. US*) 163, 190, 192
Case concerning United States diplomatic and consular staff in Teheran (*US v. Iran*) 86
Colombian–Peruvian asylum case 3
North Sea Continental Shelf Cases (*Germany v. Denmark and Netherlands*) 3
International Criminal Tribunal for the former Yugoslavia 109, 185, 191
International peace and security
humanitarian intervention 113, 116
failed states 125, 133, 137
threat to vii, 8, 66, 68, 217
protection of under UN x, 17, 21, 32, 36, 44, 45, 47–8, 51–3, 63–4, 113, 147, 153, 163
protection of under League 37
regional organizations 83, 104
terrorism 175, 180, 183, 188–89
rogue states 209
Instability of states 61, 138, 141–43, 145, 179 *see also* failed states
Intelligence 151, 154, 159, 164–65, 183, 185, 188, 192, 212
International Community 2, 3, 27, 34, 42, 44, 58–9, 62, 66, 68, 77, 88, 100, 104, 109–112, 115–17, 125, 134, 137, 139–41, 143, 152, 172, 181, 187, 194, 198, 200, 202, 208–209, 213, 216, 219, 224
Interstate conflict 8, 9, 16–17, 24, 38, 69, 167, 215
International Union of American Republics 23–4
International Union of American Republics 23–4, 44
International Red Cross 23, 27, 36
International Criminal Court 23, 28, 103, 122, 173, 183–84, 206
Institut de Droit International Penal 23, 28
Intervention

by invitation viii, 5, 50, 67, 84–5, 91–2, 106, 109, 114–15, 122, 132–34, 140, 142–43, 218, 220 *see also* peacekeeping
in domestic affairs vii, 2, 26, 57, 86, 103, 108 *see also* humanitarian intervention, Security Council authorization
disinterestedness of action 71, 91–2, 96, 99, 106–107, 121
duration of 59, 72, 80, 86, 106, 134
duty to intervene 63, 85, 95–6, 105, 110, 112–13, 119 *see also* humanitarian intervention
right to intervene vii, 20, 26, 87, 111, 170 *see also* humanitarian intervention
Iraq *see also* Saddam Hussein
Israel's attack against 67, 154–55
mandate system 127–29
Persian Gulf War viii, 48, 62–4, 110, 113, 217
portrayal as rogue state 204–207, 209–214
Turkish intervention in 186–87
US military strikes 187–88, 190
War ix, 1, 2, 4, 27, 38, 46, 64, 65, 67–72, 112, 114, 120–22, 157–62, 164–65, 181, 185, 192, 194, 197–98, 215, 218–19, 221–22
Iran *see also* Case concerning oil platforms, Axis of Evil
Afghanistan 190
rogue state 164–65, 179, 204–206, 208–209, 211–12
sanctions against 85
US intervention in 86–7
Irish Republican Army 167
Islam
Crusades 96
intervention by Christian countries 21, 38, 79, 95, 97
just war 19 *see also* jihad
terrorism 168, 179 *see also* Al-Qaeda, Jemaah Islamiyah, Osama bin Laden
Israel *see also* Six Day War
Iraq 67, 154–55
Lebanon 90, 178, 189, 222
pariah state 202–203, 207
pre-emption 158, 161–62
Suez crisis viii, 132
terrorism 47, 85, 86, 177–80, 190, 193–95
Uganda 85, 106, 217
Italy *see also* Abyssinia
Albania 117
financial aid 133
mandate system 128
pre-emption 161
protection of nationals 90
revision 199, 200, 214
suppression of democracy 25
terrorism 176, 180
Ius gentium 18, 185

Jacobins 168
Japan *see also* Manchuria, Boxer rebellion, Tokyo International Military Tribunal
financial aid 130–33
Hiroshima vii
mandate system 127–28
pre-emption 161
terrorism 171, 174, 176–77
Tripartite Pact 210
withdrawal from League 38
Jemaah Islamiyah 184
Jessup, Philip C. 41, 48, 62, 73, 87, 106, 155
Jihad 2, 19
Johnson, Lyndon B. 83, 214
Joyner, Christopher, C. 63, 66, 155
Jus ad bellum 68, 70, 71, 72,
Jus cogens 43–4, 111, 121, 219
Jus in bello 68
Just War
contemporary use ix, x, 2, 10–12, 57, 68–74, 182, 218, 224
criteria
just cause 19, 36, 68–71
last resort 68, 70–72
legitimate authority 19, 68, 70–71
proportionality of ends 68, 70, 82
reasonable chance of success 68, 70, 72

right intention 19, 68, 70–71
development of doctrine 14, 18–19, 29, 32, 216
humanitarian intervention 9, 38, 95–6, 119, 123

Kaiser Wilhelm I 33 *see also* World War I, war crimes
Kant, Immanuel 13, 15–16, 18, 20, 24, 26, 35, 37, 97 *see also* perpetual peace
Kellogg-Briand Pact 1, 15, 32, 36, 41, 48, 52, 149, 151, 199, 216
Kelsen, Hans 44, 134, 155, 175
Kennedy, John 152–53
Kenya 136, 141, 157, 160, 166, 183
Kissinger, Henry 82, 84, 157, 204
Korea
Korean War 11, 48, 62, 64, 174
North Korea viii, 48, 61, 157, 164–65, 179, 203, 205–209, 211
South Korea viii, 50, 202
terrorism 171, 174
Kosovo *see also* humanitarian intervention
impact on humanitarian intervention 95, 110–12, 114, 117–22
NATO intervention 2, 4, 63, 64, 67, 70, 219
transitional administration 140
Kuwait 62, 108, 177

Laos 54, 175
Lauterpacht, Hersch 27, 35, 40, 48, 96, 102–103, 105
Lawrence, T.J. 23–4, 39
League of Arab states 81, 178 *see also* Middle East
League of Nations 1, 15, 21, 23, 32–6, 38, 42, 44, 47–8, 69, 80, 100–101, 151, 168, 171–72, 175, 200, 216–17
Covenant 15, 31, 34, 35, 37, 39, 45, 73, 149, 199, 201
Plebiscites 102, 126–30, 140
Lebanon
conflict with United Arab Republic 175
independence 129
Israel's use of force against 67, 90, 175, 178–79, 189, 195, 222
rogue state 198, 202
terrorism 184, 203
Legitimacy of use of force viii, 4, 10, 26, 33, 37, 60, 63–5, 67–8, 71, 73–4, 85, 110, 115, 117–18, 120, 143, 165, 194, 218, 221
Leigh, Monroe 81–2, 86
Liberal interventionism 2, 21 *see also* Tony Blair, humanitarian intervention
Liberalism 29, 31, 35–7, 43, 48, 51, 97, 106, 109, 169
Liberia
civil war 113, 142–43, 145
humanitarian intervention 110, 114
protection of nationals 89, 91
Libya
failed states 137
intervention in Chad 51
sanctions 184, 188
terrorism 179–80, 183, 203–208, 212
US strikes against 67, 156
Lieber Code 22
Lillich, Richard B. 45, 85, 86, 88, 90–91, 105, 107
Lingelbach, William E. 25–6, 100
Locke, John 15, 19
Lorimer, James 22, 73, 126, 198

Macedonia 25, 38, 97, 172
McDougal, Myres 51, 54, 102, 105, 107, 154–55
Machiavelli, Niccolo 14, 149
McKinley, William 78, 98, 171
Malaysia 46, 51, 174, 190
Manchuria 26, 32, 34–5, 38, 79, 101
Mandate system 39, 78, 100, 126–31, 134, 140 *see also* plebiscites, trusteeship
Marshall Plan 133
Marshall, George C. 104, 133
Martens, Georg Friedrich de 22, 25, 97
Marx, Karl 169–70
Massacres 25, 97, 99, 112 *see also* humanitarian intervention, genocide
Mercenaries 22, 52, 54, 159, 177, 192

Mexico 21, 78, 154
Middle East 65–6, 79, 174, 178 *see also* League of Arab States
Migration 78, 89, 104 *see also* refugees
Monarchies 13–15, 25, 97, 168–69
Money laundering 61–2, 135, 141
Monopoly over the use of force 67, 136, 142 *see also* hierarchy of authority, Security Council authorization
Monroe Doctrine 25
Montenegro 97–8, 118
Montevideo Convention 16, 80, 129, 136, 220
Moore, John Norton 50, 51, 54, 85, 87, 106, 179, 181
Morality xi, 1, 4, 12–13, 18, 26, 37, 39, 45, 69–70, 72–3, 103, 107, 109, 116, 118–20, 123, 184, 216, 218–19
Mosler, Herman 35, 37–8
Mozambique 61
Multilateralism viii, 10–11, 26, 48, 53–4, 63, 66–8, 70–71, 73, 101, 107, 115–17, 120–21, 142, 167, 170, 182, 188–89, 192, 217, 224
Munich agreement 201 *see also* Germany, Adolf Hitler, national socialism, World War II
Municipal law 16, 29, 99, 183
Murray, Gilbert 29, 32, 74, 127
Mussolini, Benito 200, 210

Napoleon III 169–70
National Intelligence Council 68, 138
National security 62, 138, 150, 179, 187, 205–206
National Security Council 83–4
National Security Strategy 2, 137, 156–58, 160, 162, 164, 189, 192, 197–98, 207, 212
National socialism vii, ix, 37, 39, 101, 152, 174–75, 201 *see also* Hitler; Germany, World War I
Natural law 14, 18–19
Nauru 127, 130–31 *see also* Case concerning certain phosphate lands in Nauru
Nicaragua
  rogue state 203
  terrorism 174, 179
  US intervention in 52, 54, 110 *see also* ICJ
Neo-conservatism ix, 164 *see also* George W. Bush
Neo-liberalism viii
Neutrality 33, 85, 100, 131, 169, 183, 189
New Zealand 49, 89, 127, 130–31, 142
Nigeria 106, 142
Nobel Peace Prize ix, 28, 200, 224 *see also* Barack Obama
Non-aligned movement 47, 177, 187, 190 *see also* Group 77
Non-governmental organizations 22–3
Non-interference, right to 10–11, 15–16, 20–21 *see also* non-intervention doctrine
Non-intervention doctrine
  early notions 14–16, 20, 25, 29
  failed states 59, 134–35, 142–44, 220
  humanitarian intervention 11, 60–61, 95, 103, 106, 111–12, 116, 217, 219, 220
  pre-emption 162, 223
  protection of nationals 218
  rogue states 210–211
  under League 31, 35–7, 216
  under UN 41, 43, 46, 49, 51, 58, 60, 73, 217
Non-state actor viii, ix, x, 21–2, 33, 52, 163, 167–68, 170, 173, 176–77, 186–88, 195, 209, 222 *see also* terrorism
Non-violence ix, 173
North Atlantic Treaty Organization
  Afghanistan 189–90, 192
  Democratic Republic of the Congo 112–13
  establishment of 49
  interventions, Cold War 50, 66, 175
  Kosovo 2, 63–4, 66, 67, 73, 95, 117–21, 218 *see also* humanitarian intervention
Norway 128, 151
Nuclear weapons vii, viii, 152–55, 161, 174–75, 184, 194, 202–206,

211 *see also* weapons of mass destruction, deterrence
Nürnberg Trials vii, 41, 52, 102–103, 151–52 *see also* Germany, World War II

O'Reilly, K.P.O 207–209
Obama, Barack ix, xi, 224
Opinio juris 3–4, 219, 221
Oppenheim, Lassa 5, 19, 23, 25–6, 28, 80, 93, 100, 103, 128, 155
Order
legal vii, ix, 13, 52, 193
new world order viii, 1, 45, 57, 215
world viii, x, xi, 4, 7, 13–15, 17, 44, 87, 121, 137, 162, 214, 216, 220
Organizations
international viii, 9, 11, 13, 25, 28, 31, 37–8, 62–3, 65, 106, 111–12, 130, 154–55, 162–63, 165
regional x, 20, 23, 42, 47, 49, 50, 51, 54, 55, 63–7, 70, 71, 73, 91–3, 107, 109, 115, 117, 118, 123, 140, 142, 161, 177, 193, 203, 216–18, 221
Organization of African Unity 43
Organization of American States 21, 43–4, 49, 64, 73, 83, 116, 153, 177, 190, 217
Organization of Eastern Caribbean States 64, 73, 84, 217
Organization of the Islamic Conference 161, 178, 184–85
Ottoman Empire 21, 25, 33, 38, 97, 127, 199
Outlaw states viii, 198–99, 201–205, 208, 213 *see also* rogue, pariah and bandit states

Pakistan 46, 106–107, 141, 161–62, 187, 202, 206–209
Palau 131, 140
Palestine 1, 85, 127, 176, 189, 202–204
Palestine Liberation Organization 176–79
Pan-American conference 34–5
Panama 21, 49, 83–4, 106
Papua New Guinea 51, 104, 127, 130, 142
Paraguay 34
Paramilitary activities 54, 178, 181 *see also* Case concerning military and paramilitary activities in and against Nicaragua
Pariah state 202–203, 209, 213, 219 *see also* rogue states, bandit nation, outlaw states
Peacekeeping
Regional organizations 83, 112, 115, 118, 122, 189, 220
UN Operations x, 5–6, 48, 113–17, 129–30, 132–35, 140, 142, 144, 220
Peace enforcement 5, 6, 42–4, 49, 55, 60, 62–3, 106, 114–15, 117, 122, 132–33, 188, 217
Peace of Westphalia 15, 20, 73 *see also* Thirty Years War
Peace Research Institute Oslo 7, 8
Pella, Vespasian V. 31, 33–4, 36, 103, 172
Pemberton, Gregory J. 23, 28, 33–4, 50, 103, 167, 168, 169, 174
Permanent Court of Arbitration 24
Permanent Court of International Justice 16, 38, 216, 218
Case of the S.S. Lotus 216
Perpetual peace 13, 18, 20, 23, 97
Persian Gulf War *see* Iraq
Peru 21, 25, 98
Philippines 66, 90, 174
Phillimore, Robert 22, 39, 99, 125, 151, 169, 191
Piracy viii, 83, 172, 185
Plebiscites 126–29 *see also* mandate system, trusteeship
Poland
German invasion of 11, 201
Iraq War 210
plebiscites 128
revision 33–4, 200
Police action 25, 46, 105
Political independence
protection of 35, 43, 53, 132,
road towards 126 *see also* plebiscites, mandate system, colonialism
violation of 4, 52, 84, 86–8, 91, 107–108, 118, 179, 193, 218–19

Political instability 61, 75, 138, 141–43, 145, 179 *see also* civil war, internal unrest
Portugal 35, 47, 78–9, 98, 126, 177
Poverty vii, 8, 120
Powell, Colin 122, 143, 206
Power politics xi, 39
Pre-emption 1, 2, 10, 25, 27, 149–66, 181, 194, 221–23
Privateering 22
Proliferation of weapons vii, 62, 159, 197, 203, 207–209, 211 *see also* nuclear weapons, weapons of mass destruction
Protection of nationals 2, 9, 53, 75, 77–93, 98, 101–102, 106, 154, 218–19
Protection of Property 15, 77–8, 80, 90, 92, 98
Protestant reformation 96, 170
Prussia 13, 21–3, 25, 97, 169

Qadhafi, Muammar 156, 180, 183, 204, 210 *see also* Libya, terrorism, rogue state
Quagmire 210, 212
Quasi-legality 12, 73, 95, 108, 110

Reagan, Ronald 51–2, 84, 156–57, 180, 201, 203–205
Realism 40, 42
Reconstruction 134, 140, 144 *see also* Marshall Plan
Red Army Faction 176 *see also* terrorism
Refugees 45, 61, 101, 116–18, 120, 138, 141, 169, 172
Regime change 71, 138–39
Reisman, Michael 51, 102, 105, 107, 115, 149, 155, 161, 164, 192
Renunciation of war 15, 31–3, 41–2, 44, 53, 151, 216
Reparation payments 200 *see also* Treaty of Versailles
Reprisal 178, 180, 187, 191
Republic 13, 15, 21, 25–6, 78, 97, 168–69
Rescue missions 77, 83–6, 88–92, 204, 218 *see also* protection of nationals
Resistance movements x, 173, 176
Responsibility to protect x, 112, 123, 162
Retaliation 153, 174–75, 178–79
Retribution 81
Revision 33–4, 127, 197–201, 207, 213–14
Revolution
  American 26
  French 20–21, 26, 97, 128, 168
  Industrial 20, 78
  Iran 179, 203
  Russia 29, 34, 169, 170
Rhodesia 104, 106, 126
Rice, Condoleezza 61, 113, 115, 162, 214
Rights and duties of states 16, 39, 44, 49, 129
Rockefeller, Nelson 83–4
Rodley, Nigel 102, 107–108, 110
Rogue states viii, 1, 2, 10, 57, 60–61, 69, 125–26, 147, 157, 164–65, 197–214, 221–23 *see also* pariah, bandit, outlaw states
Rollback 209–210 *see also* communism
Romania 33, 98
Rougier, Antoine 26, 96, 99
Rubin, Barry 208, 210, 212–13
Rule of law vii, ix, xi, 1, 3, 39, 68, 181, 223
Rumsfeld, Donald 65, 149, 191, 205, 215
Rwanda 62, 66, 89–90, 113–16, 122, 142, 185

St. Augustine of Hippo 14, 19, 96
St. Thomas Aquinas 14, 19, 96
Samoa 27, 130, 142
Sanctions viii, 5, 32, 37, 86, 103, 106, 116, 141, 183–84, 188, 201, 209, 211–12, 222–23
Schachter, Oscar 109–110, 119
Schwarzenberger, Georg 38–40, 43, 45, 49, 204, 213
Secession 107, 129, 132, 177
secularization of law 14, 18–19, 25, 29, 69, 96, 98, 100, 122, 170, 216
Self-defense *see also* UN Charter, armed attack, territorial integrity, political independence
  Cold War era vii, x, 42, 44, 46–9, 53–5
  collective self-defense 2, 11, 15, 27, 42, 44, 47, 49, 53–5, 57, 75, 82,

106, 147, 152, 174–75, 188, 190, 217, 221
contemporary notions 1, 4, 5, 6, 10, 57, 61, 64, 66, 69–70, 74
early notions 2, 11, 12, 15, 20–21, 26–7
humanitarian intervention 99, 105, 106, 108, 121–22
interwar years 32, 36, 39
pre-emption 149–66
protection of nationals 77, 81–3, 86–8, 90, 92
rogue states 197–214
terrorism 167–95
Self-determination 21, 39, 47, 51, 105, 125–32, 135, 139, 143, 177, 185
Self-help 27, 31, 36, 38, 47, 53, 57, 189, 217
self-interest 33, 66, 71, 111, 120, 165
Serbia 97–8, 118, 126, 171
Seybolt, Taylor B. 5, 113
Shotwell, James T. 14, 42
Shultz, George 84, 156, 157
Sierra Leone 63, 89, 110, 113, 118, 120, 138–39, 145
Six Day War 153, 176
Slavery 39, 101, 104, 109
Solomon Islands 61, 89, 141–43
Somalia 60, 63, 66, 110–11, 113–16, 122, 135–39, 141, 145
South Africa
Apartheid 104, 106
mandate Southwest Africa 102, 131
pariah states 202
terrorism 47, 177
South East Asia Treaty Organization 49, 50, 64, 66, 73, 107, 175
Sovereignty *see also* non-interference, non-intervention, territorial integrity, political independence, Treaty of Westphalia, *see* UN Charter
absolute viii, x, 15, 26, 36, 58, 99, 103
contemporary notions vii, x, 10, 57–62, 63, 65, 71, 73, 217–20
early notions of 14–16, 20, 23, 25–6, 29, 216
failed states 136–37, 140, 143–45
humanitarian intervention 95–6, 100, 102–193, 105, 111–15, 119–20, 122–23
interwar years 35–6, 38, 43, 45
pre-emption 151
protection of national 86
rogue states 210
suspension of 58–9, 61, 217, 219–20
terrorism 172, 179, 189
UN Charter vii, 46
Soviet Union *see also* superpower rivalry, Holy Alliance, Manchuria, Boxer rebellion
Afghanistan 52, 54
aggression 174–76
Czar 22, 29
Czechoslovakia 50, 52, 64, 67
Disintegration of viii, 7, 138
human rights 104
humanitarian intervention 112
Hungary 50
intervention 37, 46, 55, 217
intervention for protection of Christians 97, 98
Korea 48
Kosovo 118–19
occupation of Germany 134
pre-emption 161, 194, 221
relations to Cuba 84, 152–53
Revision 33
Revolution 33
rogue states 200, 212
Sudan 122
terrorism 170, 179, 187, 193, 195, 204
war of aggression 29, 32
Spain
Civil war 34–5, 103
colonialism 35, 78, 126
Iraq War 161, 164
protection of Christian subjects 98
suppression of democratic movements 25
terrorism 176 *see also* Madrid bombings
War with US 23
States, descriptions of
barbarous 73, 98, 100, 126, 198–99, 214 *see also* rogue states

civilized states 3, 18, 22, 25, 37, 74, 79, 95, 97–9, 121, 126–27, 198–99
feeble 73, 125, 192, 217 *see also* failed states
non-civilized 73, 95, 217
savage 73, 126, 198
State terrorism 177–78, 182, 186–88, 190
Stimson Doctrine 32
Stockholm International Peace Research Institute (SIPRI) 61–2, 115, 207
Stone, Julius 36, 38, 48, 52
Stowell, Ellery C. 26, 36, 39, 45, 48, 80, 99–101
Stresemann, Gustav 200
Suarez, Francisco 18–19
Sudan
peacekeeping in 114, 142, 144
state failure 136, 145
strikes against 67, 157, 187, 192
terrorism 122, 177, 184
Sudetenland 34–5, 79–80, 101, 201 *see also* Germany, World War II
Suez crisis viii, 53, 82
Superpowers, rivalry between viii, 7, 43, 47, 50, 52, 57, 104, 132, 157, 202, 217 *see also* bipolarity, balance of power, Soviet Union, United States
Syria *see also* Six Day War
intervention in 25, 97
mandate system 127, 129
relations with Israel 162
rogue state 202–204, 207
terrorism 179, 184, 189, 195, 198, 211

Taiwan 161, 202
Taliban 120, 183–84, 187–88, 190, 192–93 *see also* Afghanistan, Al-Qaeda
Tamil Tigers 167
Tanzania
intervention in Uganda 46, 60, 108, 217
terror attacks in 157, 183
Territorial integrity
protection of vii, ix, 35, 43, 52–3, 59, 86, 132–33
Violation of 4, 87–8, 91, 107–108, 118, 179, 186, 193, 218–19
Terrorism
Attacks *see also* Kenya
Bali bombings 157, 184, 186
Berlin bombings 180, 183, 204
Lockerbie bombings 183, 186, 204, 205, 208
Madrid train bombings 157, 184, 186
September 11 attacks viii, ix, 156–57, 160, 184–91, 193, 195, 208 *see also* Al-Qaeda, Osama bin Laden
USS Cole 183, 187
World Trade Centre bombing 157
Tokyo subway station attack 157
financing 184
state-sponsorship of 34, 47, 60, 69, 156, 158–60, 165, 197, 202–204, 207–208, 210–13
threat of 1, 33, 109, 121–22, 206
training camps 184, 187, 189
use of force against 2, 8, 10, 57, 147, 156–58, 161, 163–64, 167–95, 221, 222
use of territory by vii, 61, 120, 125, 140–41, 220
Thailand 46, 54, 66, 130, 175
Thatcher, Margaret 84
Third World vii, 59, 81, 105, 109, 112, 176
Thirty Years War 15 *see also* Peace of Westphalia
Tokyo International Military Tribunal vii, 103, 155
Torture ix, 45, 104, 109
Transnational crime 31, 33–4, 103, 140–41 *see also* money laundering, drug trafficking, human trafficking
Treaty of Berlin 23, 98
Treaty of Locarno 32, 200
Treaty of London 97–8, 100
Treaty of Sèvres 33, 39, 100, 127
Treaty of Versailles 32–3, 36–7, 127–28, 138, 199–200
Truman 49, 174
Trusteeship 102, 125, 129, 131, 140, 144 *see also* mandate system, plebiscites
Turkey *see also* Cyprus, Armenia
First World War 126
French Intervention in 79

intervention in Iraq 186–87
terrorism 176
treatment of Christian subjects 97–8
Tyranny 26, 96, 99

Ukraine 39
Unilateralism ix, xi, 2, 10, 20, 45–6, 48, 50–51, 55, 62, 63, 66–8, 70, 73, 97, 101, 106–108, 116, 118, 121, 147, 162, 164, 178, 182, 185, 187–90, 192, 209, 215, 217–18, 221, 223–24
United Arab Republic 153, 175, 193
United Kingdom *see also* Falklands, Caroline case, Tony Blair, Suez crisis
arbitration 24
foreign aid World War II 133
humanitarian intervention 95, 97–100, 102, 105, 108
India 173, 217
intervention and law 21, 46, 69, 79, 200, 223
Iraq War 46, 58, 70, 159–61, 198, 210, 223
just war 70
Kosovo 2, 119
mandates 126–28, 131
occupation of Germany 134
protection of nationals 78–9, 81, 88, 90, 92
revision 202
rogue states 198
self-determination 130
terrorism 170, 172, 174, 183–84, 189, 190, 192
Vietnam 50
United States 22, 36, 46 *see also* George W. Bush, Iraq, Afghanistan, superpower rivalry, Vietnam, Barack Obama
arbitration 24
civil war 22–3, 26, 43
failed states 130–31, 133–34, 137–38, 142–43 *see also* Somalia
humanitarian intervention 72, 115–16, 120–22 *see also* NATO, Kosovo
international law 2, 24, 44, 58, 64, 67, 216, 223, 224 *see also* Kellogg-Briand Pact; Case concerning military and paramilitary activities in and against Nicaragua
pre-emption 149–50, 152–53, 156–60, 162, 164–65, 180–82 *see also* Cuba
protection of nationals 78, 82–6, 89–90 *see also* Iran
rogue states 198, 203–212, 214
terrorism 174–75, 179, 180–84, 187–91, 193–94 *see also* September 11, Al-Qaeda, Berlin bombings
United Nations *see also* Security Council, General Assembly, UN Charter, collective security, peacekeeping
establishment of vii, 43–9
failed states 130–32, 135, 140, 142
General Assembly
definition of aggression 52
failed states 130–31
humanitarian intervention 109, 115–16, 118
pre-emption 156, 160
protection of nationals 84
resolutions 43, 47–8
terrorism 177, 180
humanitarian intervention 95, 102–103, 105, 107–109, 112–14, 119, 121–22
pre-emption 152–55, 157, 163, 165–66
protection of nationals 81, 84, 87–8
regulation of the use of force ix, 1, 5, 27, 36, 44, 49, 51, 55, 61, 67, 69, 73, 84, 87, 133, 185 *see also* self-defense, armed attack, Security Council
rogue states 197, 202, 209, 212
Security Council
authorization vii, 10, 15, 38, 42, 49, 51, 55, 60, 66, 71, 81, 95, 111, 114, 117–18, 121–22, 140, 152, 162–63, 178–79, 193, 217, 221
bypassing of 67, 106, 115, 119, 120

humanitarian intervention 108, 110, 117, 121
maintenance of international peace and security 44, 47, 53, 113, 116, 143, 154, 175, 183, 209
membership vii, 47, 112, 131, 159
paralysis of viii, 45, 47–8, 50, 107, 132, 217
protection of nationals 86, 91
resolutions 67, 87, 118, 121, 132, 143, 160–61, 184–85, 211
subcontracting of duties 62–4 *see also* regional organizations, *Ad hoc* coalitions
terrorism 185, 187–89, 192
terrorism 173–75, 178, 180, 182, 186–90
UN Charter
Article 1(3) 121
Article 2(1) 58
Article 2(4) vii, 15, 41, 42, 43, 53, 86–7, 90, 107, 118, 218–21
Article 2(7) vii, 43, 46, 49, 58, 60, 103, 219
Article 39 vii, 113, 115, 143, 221
Article 41 44
Article 42 44
Article 44 44
Article 50 44
Article 51 vii, 15, 42, 49, 54, 82, 83, 86–8, 92, 142–55, 157, 163, 168, 178, 186, 190, 193, 195, 221–22
Article 52 153
Article 53 49, 83
Article 55 45, 121
Article 76 130
Article 77 140
Article 78 140
Article 80(1) 103
Article 86 131
Article 88 131
Chapter VI 132
Chapter VII 15, 43, 44, 46, 60, 113, 117, 132
Chapter VIII 64

Vattel, Emerich de 14, 19, 78, 79, 96, 150, 169
Venezuela 21, 79
Vietnam
independence 46–7, 50, 81, 168
intervention in Cambodia 46, 60, 108, 217
US intervention in 44, 50–51, 53–4, 64, 104, 175–76, 214
Vitoria, Francisco de 18–19

Waldock, Humphrey 85, 154–55
Walzer, Michael 18, 106
War crimes 21, 23, 33–4, 100, 103, 109, 112, 114
War on terror 122, 163, 168
Warsaw Pact 50, 52, 64, 73, 143, 217
Weak states 8, 17, 61, 81, 125, 129–30, 135–36, 138–39, 220 *see also* failed states
Webster, Daniel 27, 151
Westlake, John 22, 100, 151
Wheaton, Henry 22, 98, 185
White House 84, 158
Wilson, Woodrow 126–27, 130
Woolsey, Theodore Dwight 22, 99, 151
World War I 24, 26–9, 31, 37–8, 41, 100, 122, 126, 128, 167, 171, 194, 199, 201, 207, 216, 221–22
World War II 2, 7, 9, 31, 38, 41, 48, 60, 77, 95, 103, 117, 128–30, 133–34, 140, 152, 173, 198, 210, 217
Wright, Quincy 32, 34, 36, 38, 42, 44, 48, 82, 101, 105, 155

Yemen 51, 183, 187
Yugoslavia
disintegration of 7, 128, 136, 143
NATO intervention in 66, 118–19 *see also* Kosovo, International Criminal Tribunal
revision 33, 200
terrorism 172–73

Zedalis, Rex 90, 92, 155
Zaire 89, 116–17
Zimbabwe 126, 136, 138, 143